D1135504

ALL THE MADMEN

Also by Clinton Heylin

So Long As Men Can Breathe: The Untold Story of Shakespeare's Sonnets

Still on the Road: The Songs of Bob Dylan vol. 2 (1974–2008)

Revolution In The Air: The Songs of Bob Dylan vol. 1 (1957–73)

The Act You've Known For All These Years:

A Year In The Life of Sgt. Pepper and Friends

Babylon's Burning: From Punk to Grunge

From The Velvets To The Voidoids: The Birth of American Punk

All Yesterdays' Parties: The Velvet Underground in Print 1966–71 [editor]

Despite The System: Orson Welles versus The Hollywood Studios

Bootleg – The Rise & Fall of the Secret Recording Industry

Can You Feel The Silence? – Van Morrison: A New Biography

No More Sad Refrains: The Life & Times of Sandy Denny

Bob Dylan: Behind The Shades – Take Two

Dylan's Daemon Lover: The Tangled Tale of a 450-Year-Old Pop Ballad

Dylan Day By Day: A Life In Stolen Moments

Never Mind The Bollocks, Here's The Sex Pistols

Bob Dylan: The Recording Sessions 1960–94

The Great White Wonders: A History of Rock Bootlegs

The Penguin Book of Rock & Roll Writing [editor]

Gypsy Love Songs & Sad Refrains:

The Recordings of Sandy Denny & Richard Thompson

Rise/Fall: The Story of Public Image Limited

Joy Division: Form & Substance [with Craig Wood]

ALL THE MADMEN

Barrett, Bowie, Drake, Pink Floyd, The Kinks, The Who & A Journey To The Dark Side of English Rock

CLINTON HEYLIN

Constable • London

For Scott, a true custodian of the vocal era.

Constable & Robinson Ltd
55–56 Russell Square
London WC1B 4HP
www.constablerobinson.com

First published in the UK by Constable,
an imprint of Constable & Robinson Ltd, 2012

A copy of the British Library Cataloguing in
Publication data is available from the British Library

ISBN: 978-1-84901-880-7

Printed and bound in the UK

1 3 5 7 9 10 8 6 4 2

Contents

Preface: 'Whom The Gods Destroy . . .'

The frequency in the modern world of works of art that explode out of madness no doubt proves nothing about the reason of that world, about the meaning of such works, or even about the relations formed and broken between the real world and the artists who produced such work. And yet this frequency must be taken seriously . . .

– Michel Foucault, *Madness and Civilization*, 1967

The acid brought out his latent madness. I'm sure it was the latent madness which gave him his creativity. The acid brought out the creativity, but more important it brought out the madness.

– Peter Jenner, talking about Syd Barrett, *A Day in the Life*, 1988

The Sixties has been defined by any number of those 'so-and-so met whatsisname' moments: the day John met Paul; the night Dylan turned The Beatles on; the evening Kennedy purportedly trounced Nixon on the presidential TV debate. But perhaps the strangest of strange meetings was the day in late 1967 when (anti-)psychiatrist R.D. Laing encountered Pink Floyd frontman

Syd Barrett, an event so unlikely that no one can agree on what or whether it happened.

Dave Gilmour has claimed it never did, but then he wasn't even in Pink Floyd at the time[1]. Drummer Nick Mason, in his own memoir, wrote that Barrett refused to go in to see Laing, sitting in the car instead. But manager Peter Jenner, whose idea it was and who perhaps has less of an axe to grind, insists that Syd and Laing did talk. Jenner had become convinced that Syd was showing worrying signs of schizophrenia, and Laing was someone he personally knew (he had played a minor role in the establishment of the London Free School in the summer of 1966, where Floyd first developed their psychedelic show at a weekly residency Jenner organized). It was both a collision of pop culture with academia and the summation of a particular 1960s sensibility, as the ley lines of psychiatry and psychedelia crossed for the first and last time.

Syd's slip into said mental state had been as sudden as it was unexpected. In the summer of 1967, the season of Love, sitting high in the charts with the Floyd's otherworldly second single, 'See Emily Play' (hard on the heels of the knicker-nicking 'Arnold Layne'), and awaiting the imminent release of their inspirational debut LP, *Piper at the Gates of Dawn* – fittingly named after a chapter in *The Wind in the Willows* – Barrett had the whole wide world at his feet. But his own inner world was closing in. In a single weekend at the end of July, so the story goes, he went from been the pied piper of English pop to Mr Madcap.

Earlier in the week he had turned up to mime along to 'See Emily Play' on *Top of the Pops*, and for the first time he appeared both dishevelled and distracted to the rest of the band, if not of another world. Then on the Friday, scheduled to record an all-important *Saturday Club* radio session, again for the BBC, he turned up in body but not in mind and, as the studio manager complained to Jenner, 'left the studio without [even] completing the recording of the first number'. This simply wasn't done. Later the same day, he arrived at a jam-packed UFO (pronounced 'U-Fo') for the closing night of the original underground club, where a harassed Joe Boyd, the club founder, looked into his friend's eyes and saw 'black holes' (an image Roger Waters would later appropriate for his own eulogy to Barrett, 'Shine On You Crazy Diamond'). As Boyd recently noted, he was not wholly surprised, having realized for some time 'that if you did [LSD] every day, you were jeopardizing the wires that held everything together in your mind'.

Throughout that night's performance, according to drummer Nick Mason, Syd stood with 'his arms hung by his side . . . occasional[ly] strumming'. Keyboardist Rick Wright recalled things slightly differently, but with the same outcome: 'He went missing for the whole weekend and when he reappeared again . . . he was a totally different person.' A week later, the whole band assembled at Abbey Road to record a third single to consolidate the success of 'See Emily Play', and they were relying on Syd to deliver the goods again. The song he arrived with, a little burnt-out but ready to record, was the prophetic 'Scream Thy Last Scream': 'Fling your arms madly, old lady with a daughter / . . . Flitting and hitting and fitting, quack quack.' Gone for good were the adult fairy stories and space-age explorations of yore, replaced by such cerebral ministrations.

At a session in September, Barrett delivered his next song, which was stranger still. 'Vegetable Man' seemed almost like a celebration of catatonia ('It's what I wear it's what you see / It must be me, it's what I am / Vegetable man'). As Jenner recalls: 'He sat there and just described himself.' The band were now really starting to worry. Had they given up lucrative careers as

3

architects for *this*?! Or was the ever-playful Syd just messing with their minds? It certainly seemed that way when he proceeded to teach them his most dissociated song to date, 'Jugband Blues', which he wanted to record with a bridge that incorporated a brass section playing completely at random, before everything was washed away, leaving just a single guitar strumming and the following sung queries: 'What exactly is a dream? / And what exactly is a joke . . . ?'

No wonder the band wanted someone to give Syd the once over, wave his magic wand and restore their friend to his former productive, radio-friendly self. And as Peter Sedgwick points out in *Laing and Anti-Psychiatry* (1971), Laing was the *trendmeister* when it came to treating this particular strain of madness 'not as a psychiatric disability, but as one stage in a natural psychic healing process, containing the possibility of entry into a realm of "hyper-sanity"'.

Laing had come to public prominence – amid the predictable opprobrium from psychiatric circles for breaking ranks – with the Pelican mass-market paperback edition of his 1960 tome, *The Divided Self: An Existential Study in Sanity and Madness*, published in this form in 1965. It was a copy of the Pelican paperback that a young art-school student called Roger 'Syd' Barrett symbolically cut up into quotes, which he pasted into a twelve-page art-collage he was preparing called *Fart Enjoy*.

The Divided Self was a serious-minded study, designed (or so Laing claimed) 'to make madness and the process of going mad comprehensible'. It was followed by two further speculative shots across the bows of Freudians and Jungians alike, *The Self and Others* (1961) and *Sanity, Madness and the Family* (1964). But by 1965 there had been a dramatic shift in Laing's thinking. Ironically, it was while reviewing interviews conducted with so-called normal families for the follow-up volume to *Sanity,*

Madness and the Family that he began to formulate a view that they were at least as disturbed as the dysfunctional families depicted in his 1964 tome. He recalled the moment in a conversation shortly before his death:

> These families of normals were like gas chambers: the reciprocal effect of deadening. Every member of the families totally fitted – getting up and going to work and going to school and coming back and watching television and doing nothing and going to bed. Nothing to say really. To get them to say anything about anything was almost impossible. They thought about nothing, they said nothing very much, they were just fucking dead and there was no edge or no sharpness or no challenge . . . Just fuck all, an endless drone, about nothing . . . and these were the people we were going to study, who were *not* in despair.

This epiphany would have profound consequences for Laing's worldview, leading inextricably to a key shift in his theoretical position. The sea-change was signalled in a new preface he added to the Pelican *Divided Self*, the publication of which was a notable step on the road to 'anti-psychiatry', and which reflected Laing's cultural position at the time he met Barrett: 'In the context of our present pervasive madness that we call normality, sanity, freedom, all our frames of references are ambiguous and equivocal . . . Our "normal", "adjusted" state is too often the abdication of ecstasy, the betrayal of our true potentialities, [for] many of us are only too successful in acquiring a false self to adapt to false realities.'

It was a position he had been edging towards ever since he wrote in *The Divided Self*: 'The man who is said to be deluded may be in his delusion telling me the truth, and this in no equivocal or metaphorical sense, but quite literally . . . The cracked mind of the schizophrenic may let in light which does not enter the intact minds of many sane people whose minds are closed.'

Laing's fiercest critics were quick to point out that he was creating a dangerous precedent by treating some very disturbed persons not as medical patients but as 'individuals who due to the strength of their inner perceptions and experiences, are exceptionally eloquent critics of society'. In fact, such an idea was at least fifty years old. Arch-cynic and professional curmudgeon Ambrose Bierce had defined the adjective 'mad' in his infamous 1911 *Devil's Dictionary* thus: 'Affected with a high degree of intellectual independence; not conforming to standards of thought, speech and action derived by the conformants from study of themselves; at odds with the majority; in short, unusual.' And it had been further developed in the 1940s by French critic Antonin Artaud, fresh from the asylum himself, who laid the groundwork for the next generation of psychiatric iconoclasts with his own vivid portrait of 'modern medicine, in collusion with the most sinister and debauched magic, subject[ing] its [inmates] to electric shock or insulin therapy so that every day it may drain its stud farms of men of their selves, and may present them thus empty'. Laing, taking his lead from a later French thinker, Foucault, unequivocally sided with Artaud.

A larger problem, at least as far as the wider psychiatric community was concerned, was the language with which Laing – and that other attention-seeking anti-psychiatric advocate, David Cooper – were polemicizing the grand experiment. They seemed to be suggesting that introducing the psychedelic experience of LSD under scientific conditions might actually benefit some already very disturbed people. How else could one explain a passage like the one in Laing's *The Politics of Experience* (1967), which argued: 'Madness need not be all breakdown . . . It may also be breakthrough. It is potentially liberation and renewal as well as enslavement and existential death . . . [What is needed is] an initiation ceremonial, through which the person will be guided with full social encouragement and sanction into inner space and time, by people who have been there and back.'

In 1965, Laing set up Kingsley Hall – a 'therapeutic community' he hoped would 'provide a sympathetic setting for the completion of the schizophrenic's cyclical voyage'. Although hallucinogenic drugs were never part of the Kingsley therapy, Laing did subsequently admit: 'We were trying to find out what are the chemical things that change mental functions, like perception and memory, and . . . which drugs induce something comparable to a psychosis, produced hallucinations and different other shifts . . . There was a lot to think about . . . [regarding] the altered states of mind that acid put you into, and the way that people got confused and lost and shipwrecked in psychotic states of misery.'

Two years later the already notorious Laing would be introduced to Syd Barrett, perhaps the most famous pop figure to be 'shipwrecked in [this] psychotic state of misery'. According to the attending Jenner, though, the meeting wholly failed to stem the tide in Syd's own sea of madness. There was no great meeting of minds, as he explained to Jonathon Green: 'We took him to R.D. Laing. Laing didn't say much. We tried to take what he said literally, we tried to use the inner meaning of what he was saying, we tried to change the objective situations. We moved him out of [his flat in] Cromwell Road but . . . it was too late.'

Nick Mason, however, paints a far more bizarre picture in *Inside Out* (2004), suggesting that Barrett steadfastly refused to cross Laing's threshold, 'so Laing didn't have much to go on. But he did make one challenging observation: yes, Syd might be disturbed, or even mad. But maybe it was the rest of us who were causing the problem, by pursuing our desire to succeed, and forcing Syd to go along with our ambitions. Maybe Syd was actually surrounded by mad people'. If Laing gleaned all this from a conversation with bassist Roger Walters, who according to Mason, drove Syd up to North London for the consultation then he really did have a gift for reading people.

One thing is certain: by the end of 1967 Barrett was hardly alone, inside or outside 'his band', in his struggle to retain both his creativity and his sanity. A whole generation of English singer-songwriters were wrestling with their inner demons, usually – though not necessarily – let out of the bottle by the LSD genie. For now, the catch-all phrase for the happening scene was psychedelia, and great things were expected of this incipient movement. Even three of Laing's fiercest critics – Drs Siegler, Osmond and Mann – considered the worlds of psychedelia and psychosis to be contradistinct. The trio wrote in a 1969 article for the *British Journal of Psychiatry* of how 'the psychedelic world has provided new music, new fashions in clothing and the decorative arts, new vocabulary, new life-styles, and a new inter-generational dialogue. But not a single new art form has come out of the mental hospital.'

The next five years would prove the trio to be wrong on both counts. Awaiting the emergence of an 'inter-generational dialogue' they missed an art-form emerging from the nuthouse. Between 1967 and 1973, at an unprecedented height of international influence for English song, its songwriters addressed (usually from direct personal experience) the subject of madness in their disordered droves. What began as the occasional B-side or album filler as young would-be bards scrambled around for any subject matter that seemed slightly psychedelic, by the end of 1971 became a central theme in English rock, dominating writers' song-ideas and forming the thematic core of a series of important albums released in a steady drip-feed from this eclectic Eden.

Yet it seems no one has yet attempted to draw an indelible line connecting the drugs and madness of the era to the music that emerged out of it. Not even the ever-readable Mikal Gilmore, whose collected 'writings on the 1960s and its discontents', published in 2008 as *Stories Done*, he prefaced with the following observation: 'The commonality of the role of drugs and alcohol in these stories could hardly be coincidental, and though that trait . . . wasn't what attracted me to those stories . . . what drew me was something else. Almost every person . . . suffered from depression at various times and in varying degrees.' Despite this common concern, however, Mikal's book and mine only cross paths when discussing Syd Barrett, though his accounts of the troubles that plagued ex-Beatles George Harrison and John Lennon might have convinced me to find room for them if the subject matter of (in)sanity had spilled over into their songs more overtly. But then, Lennon never seems to have doubted his sanity as much as his genius.

Likewise, Jenny Diski's highly personal 140-page contribution to Profile Books' Big Ideas series, *The Sixties* (2009), devotes two of its six sections to drugs ('Altering Realities') and madness ('Changing Our Minds') respectively, while namechecking the music enjoyed by that era's willing outcasts at every opportunity. Diski also contrasts her generation's experience with those of today's 'kids [who] take Es and party . . . they even call it "loved up", but it doesn't seem to have any other cultural aspect attached to it. No books or art, and the music is [just] too mechanical.' But Diski never connects the dots that, joined together, illustrate how the most cogent of populist 'art-forms' turned her generation's inner confusion and rampant experimentation into Art.

And that is surely a key difference. For in the years 1971–73, a period when English rock dominated the airwaves, band after band, songwriter after songwriter produced fully conceived works from either side of what was almost a communal nervous breakdown, a psychic aftershock in the collective unconscious of this sceptred isle. In this period, the finest songwriters from this fervent scene produced their defining works. And among these notable notches would be Ray Davies' *Muswell Hillbillies*, Nick Drake's *Pink Moon*, David Bowie's twin-set *Ziggy Stardust* and *Aladdin Sane*, Pink Floyd's *Dark Side of the Moon* (an album made in the shadow cast by erstwhile leader Syd Barrett's collapse into secret songs of silence) and Pete Townshend's *Quadrophenia* – every one of which, directly or indirectly, took as its central theme 'the subject of madness'. How they got there – and, in most cases, got out alive (just about) – is the nub of our story.

(ii)

Outside a lunatic asylum one day
a gunner was picking up stones;
Up popped a lunatic and said to him,
Good morning Gunner Jones,
How much a week do you get for doing that?
Fifteen bob, I cried.
He looked at me with a look of glee, and this is what he cried:
Come inside, you silly bugger, come inside — World War II
marching song.

What is an authentic madman?

It is a man who preferred to become mad, in the socially accepted sense of the word, rather than forfeit a certain superior idea of human honour.

So society has strangled in its asylums all those it wanted to get rid of or protect itself from, because they refused to become its accomplices in certain great nastinesses.
– Antonin Artaud: *Van Gogh, The Man Suicided by Society*, 1947

I saw the best minds of my generation destroyed by madness, starving hysterical naked . . .
– Allen Ginsberg, *Howl*, August 1955

R.D. Laing's other major contribution to countercultural confusion in 1967 was co-organizing the Dialectics of Liberation 'conference' that summer at London's Roundhouse. The seeds of this particular confluence of movers and shakers had been sown in the aftermath of the Second World War, as the English asylums seemed less keen on locking up high-strung poets – especially if female – letting the likes of Virginia Woolf and Sylvia Plath take their own lives instead. Meanwhile, the French saw fit to release their self-proclaimed 'authentic madman', essayist Antonin Artaud, in 1946, after nine years of being shuttled from asylum to asylum. The American asylums, though, quickly took up the slack, starting the same year with the internment of Ezra Pound, who had been found to be of unsound mind when facing charges of treason for broadcasting pro-fascist views on Italian radio.[2] Once again, the question of who was mad and who was sane was back on the front-burner of pop culture.

It took until 1955 for Archibald MacLeish and Ernest Hemingway – confident that the danger had passed, and in tandem with T.S. Eliot and Robert Frost – to begin pushing the

US attorney general to quash Pound's indictment for treason. In the same year, an excerpt from a first novel by ex-fighter-pilot Joseph Heller in *New World Writing #7* – included in the same issue as a similar-length extract from another unpublished novel, Jack Kerouac's *On the Road* – reinvigorated the whole debate as to who might be sane, and who mad. It even gave a name to this mental bind, the (short-lived) 'Catch-18'. Six years (and four digits) later, the world of *Catch-22* held a mirror upside down to the whole crazy idea of war, becoming a catchword and a publishing phenomenon, inspiring a series of rave reviews with titles such as 'The Logic of Survival in a Lunatic World', 'A Deadly Serious Lunacy' and 'Under Mad Gods', as it became the must-read novel of the early 1960s.

In addition to *Catch-22*'s first appearance (of sorts), 1955 saw the birth of the madness they christened rock & roll; and from the initial hysterical press coverage one would be inclined to think an entire generation had lost its collective marbles. It also saw the composition of a poem written for the committed, what the poet himself called 'a gesture of wild solidarity, a message into the asylum'. The poem signalled another turning of history's page, and an entirely new conception of the madman in postwar pop culture.

The poem, Allen Ginsberg's *Howl* – part of which was written after a peyote-fuelled trek through downtown San Francisco in the company of Peter Orlovsky – took much of its form from the poem of an eighteenth-century inmate of the English asylums, Kit Smart's 'Jubilate Agno'. Making its first public appearance in print in 1956, *Howl* was addressed by former asylum inmate Ginsberg to current inmate Carl Solomon, committed to a Californian institution for his 'protest against the verbal, the rational and the acceptable [by a form of] neo-dada clowning', for which he was 'deposited in a nut factory where I was shocked into a renunciation of all my reading'.

All the Madmen

One of the first people Ginsberg sent the finished poem to was Ezra Pound, who responded by writing to Ginsberg's mentor, William Carlos Williams, suggesting he learn 'the value of time to those who want to read something that will tell 'em wot they don't know'. There were subtexts going on here that the cantankerous Pound wholly failed to recognise.

As Ginsberg himself admitted in the thirtieth-anniversary facsimile edition of his landmark poem, 'I'd used Mr Solomon's return to the asylum as occasion of a masque on my feelings towards my mother, in itself an ambiguous situation since I had signed the papers giving permission for her lobotomy a few years before.' Three years later, he directly addressed his mother Naomi's madness and the resultant cross-generational misery in the second of his epic 'hymns to the mad', the unsparing *Kaddish*:

> On what wards – I walked there later, oft – old catatonic ladies, grey as cloud or ash or walls – sit crooning over floorspace – Chairs – and the wrinkled hags acreep, accusing – begging my 13-year-old mercy –
>
> 'Take me home' – I went alone sometimes looking for the lost Naomi, taking Shock – and I'd say, 'No, you're crazy Mama – Trust the Drs.' – . . .

Eleven years after *Howl*'s now-hallowed appearance, Ginsberg would be a key guest at the fortnight-long Dialectics of Liberation 'conference' in London. In the intervening years he had become, along with Dr Timothy Leary, the perceived spokesman of the pro-hallucinogenic movement – such as it was – even penning a series of poems that embraced LSD's inspirational attributes, notably 'Lysergic Acid': 'It is a multiple million eyed monster / it is hidden in all its elephants and selves

/ it hummeth in the electric typewriter / it is electrically connected to itself, [as] if it hath wires.'

The Dialectics of Liberation – perhaps the defining moment in the counterculture's decade-long flirtation with 'outsider' status as a *raison d'être* – had been arranged by R.D. Laing and his fellow 'anti-psychiatrists' to air common concerns. In the decade since *Howl*, an entire intellectual caucus of sorts had sprung up from the root belief that societal notions of madness remained a moveable feast, and that the relationship between art and madness was such that it was hard to know where one ended and the other began. And such views were fast infecting the body artistic.

Although everyone associated with the nascent 'anti-psychiatry' movement was at the Roundhouse – along with the usual ragbag of counter-revolutionaries from that season's Judean People's Front – one thinker not in attendance was French social historian Michel Foucault, though his ideas certainly informed this much-hyped event. Foucault's *Histoire de la folie à l'âge classique* (1961) – better known by the snappier title given its 1964 English translation, *Madness and Civilization* – was, in that fine Marxist tradition, a philosophical work passing itself off as social history.

In his preface, Foucault postulated the idea that madness and reason had once enjoyed a far closer co-relationship than in the modern world, and decided something important had been lost: 'We must try to return, in history, to that zero point in the course of madness at which madness is an undifferentiated experience, a not yet divided experience of division itself . . . Modern man no longer communicates with the madman, thereby authorizing a relation only through the abstract universality of [mental] disease.' After a further 300 pages concerning France's institutional response to its own ship of fools, he reached the conclusion: 'Where there is a work of art, there is no madness.'

Such a view was taken very seriously by those who followed in Foucault's footsteps. It was the artist-madman who validated, or was seen to validate, a lot of the work being conducted in Britain by R.D. Laing and David Cooper. In fact, it was Laing who was directly responsible for the English-language publication of Foucault's work in his extra-curricular role as reader for the Tavistock Press. ('I put out feelers . . . and got the manuscript of *Madness and Civilization* . . . It was one of the books that I would consider to be a really major book, [but] his name was totally unknown in English.') Published in an abridged form in 1967, the translated appearance of Foucault's work coincided with an outpouring of essays and articles from Laing, Cooper and co. In fact, it was Cooper – the lesser light, but the greater proselytizer – who was given the opportunity to connect Foucault's work to his own, writing an introduction to the Tavistock edition of *Madness and Civilization*:

> Foucault makes it quite clear that the invention of madness as a disease is in fact nothing less than a peculiar disease of our civilization. We choose to conjure up this disease in order to evade a certain moment of our own existence – the moment of disturbance, of penetrating vision into the depths of ourselves, that we prefer to externalize into others. Others are elected to live out the chaos that we refuse to confront in ourselves . . . People do not in fact go mad, but are driven mad by others who are driven into the position of driving them mad by . . . social pressures.

Cooper, who had cemented his association with Laing as early as 1964, co-authoring *Reason and Violence: A Decade of Sartre's*

Philosophy (1964), was keen to codify their joint cause and ride the greater notoriety of Laing. For now, Laing was happy to go along with him. But Cooper went further than Laing ever would – tainting him by association – making outlandish claims such as: 'Madness . . . is not "in" a person, but in a system of relationships in which the labelled "patient" participates: schizophrenia, if it means anything, is a more or less characteristic mode of disturbed group behaviour. There are no schizophrenics.'

If Laing went to some pains to bring elements of the psychiatric establishment along on this journey – albeit largely without result – David Cooper was fully prepared to mount the barricades. In 1967 he published his provocative handbook for (what he hoped was) this new movement, *Psychiatry and Anti-Psychiatry*. From his 'private psychiatric practice in Harley Street', he was already claiming his principal concern was 'to develop an existential psychiatry in Britain and to elaborate principles to overcome . . . [the] compartmentalization of the human sciences'. Calling schizophrenics 'the strangled poets of our age', Cooper thought it was 'about time that we, who would be healers, took our hands off their throats'.

Like Laing, Cooper had come to believe that normality was 'at an opposite pole not only to madness but also to sanity', and that 'very few manage to slip through the state of inertia or arrest represented by alienated, statistical normality and progress to some extent on the way to sanity'. And so, in July 1967, he helped Laing co-organize the Dialectics of Liberation, two-week conflab between pot-smokers, psychiatrists, poets, potential terrorists and peaceniks; or, as Cooper characterized them in the introduction to his book of the conference, 'this curious pastiche of eminent scholars and political activists'. The whole event was, as 1960s chronicler Barry Miles has commented, 'a very sixties idea – the concept was to get together all of the different factions involved in the liberation struggle and have a good talk about it'. There was even a musical component, Mick Farren's Social Deviants.

Cooper, there in all his pomp, took the opportunity to reiterate a now-familiar mantra: 'Schizophrenia is a half-compelled, half-chosen retreat from the precariously and artificially stabilized level of highly differentiated experience that passes as sane in our culture.' Carried away by what he saw as the event's import, he announced at the end of proceedings, in a talk entitled 'Beyond Words', that: 'This was really the founding event of the Antiuniversity of London which now functions full-time, carrying over the spirit of the Congress in what may be a permanent form.'

It didn't, and it wasn't. As with many a hare-brained activity conceived during the Summer of Love, the conference was not a new beginning, but the beginning of the end for the 'anti-psychiatry movement'. For Laing, at least, the Dialectics of Liberation proved a turning point, but not in a good way. Rather, as he quickly realized: 'From the point of view of . . . something gelling, it was, in fact, a total fiasco. I was about the only one who could stand all the different sorts of people that were there . . . I mean, most people came along entirely in their own shell to propagate their own propaganda of their particular point of view.' He had even come face to face with some people who thought that putting acid into the general water supply was a good idea – and perhaps the solitary achievement of the conference was convincing said folk that it wasn't.

It took another invited speaker, anthropologist Gregory Bateson, to cast a necessary caveat at Blake's philosophical dictum that the road of excess may lead to the palace of wisdom, already appropriated as an endorsement for copious consumption of mind-altering substances. Bateson alone told the assembled few: 'It is characteristic of the 1960s that a large number of people are looking to the psychedelic drugs for some sort of wisdom or some sort of enlargement of consciousness, and I think this symptom of our epoch probably arises as an attempt to compensate for our excessive purposiveness. But I am not sure that wisdom can be got that way.' In the end, he decided he'd rather study dolphins, retreating to Hawaii's Oceanic Institute.

Meanwhile, to Laing's eternal chagrin, he had now become perceived in populist terms as an advocate of psychedelic drugs, when all he really wanted was for people to expand their horizons *intellectually*. As the TV director Jo Durden-Smith, who attended the conference in the company of Miles, later said, 'Laing was misinterpreted and misused [so much that] he became, or his attitude towards madness became, a sort of hooray attitude, with not very much thought put into it at all.' By 1969, even the *British Journal of Psychiatry* willingly ran a lengthy attack by three distinguished psychiatrists on 'Laing's models of madness', who all but accused him of advocating LSD as a treatment for schizophrenia: 'Although Laing does not use the term [psychedelic] in this book . . . it is obvious that he thinks that schizophrenics may have, sometimes have, and ought to have the same kind of experiences that normal individuals seek when they take mind-expanding drugs.'

It was a vantage for which the psychiatric community had very little time. In the big wide world, though, Laing's handbook for 'bright young schizophrenics' – as the *BJoP* article sarcastically portrayed his 1967 volume, *The Politics of Experience* – was certainly making its influence felt. Syd Barrett's friend David Gale – who also claims he tried to get the songwriter to visit Laing – delineated Laing's readers thus: '[He] – inadvertently, I think – heroised the idea of madness. And hippies made of it what they wanted. The ones that read books made Laing's . . . into what they wanted to hear.'

All the Madmen

While the Floyd turned to Laing in the hour of their leader's weakness, the counterculture continued to paint any 'straights' as the ones needing psychiatric 'evaluation'. Any generational awareness that there might be an underlying proclivity among English poets and lyricists for 'despondency and madness', which could be triggered by powerful medicines, would have to await the end of the Sixties' all-night fancy-dress party.

It would be April 1970 before English singer-songwriter David Bowie encapsulated the Laing position perfectly in a song written for and about his half-brother Terry, a recently diagnosed schizophrenic. Destined to provide the thematic hub to his first hard-rock album, *The Man Who Sold the World*, the song was called 'All the Madmen'. It signalled the start of an era when songs directly addressed the damage (being) done to eccentrics, and the end to a time when poking fun at them was a bloodless sport for English songwriters:

> Day after day they send my friends away
> To mansions cold and grey
> To the far side of town
> Where the Thin Men stalk the streets[3]
> While the sane stay underground . . .

1. 1965–68: Here Comes That Nineteenth Nervous Breakdown

I felt a Cleaving in my Mind –
As if my Brain had split –
I tried to match it – Seam by Seam –
But could not make them fit.
– Emily Dickinson, *c.*1864

Making love with his ego, Ziggy sucked up into his mind
Like a leper messiah . . .
– David Bowie, 1971

Each [LSD] trip is just a side street, and before you know it, you're back where you were. Each trip is more disturbing than the one that follows, till eventually the side street becomes a dead end.
– Pete Townshend, 1969

The spring of 1965 was a dangerous time for the more delicate English psyches, especially if they were inclined to treat their mind as just another Petri dish. The increasingly wide availability of the still-legal high LSD and a propensity for 'free spirits' to dispense it freely – and even secretly, by 'dosing' drinks with dissolvable tabs of the stuff – made every hip London party that season a potential minefield for the right-minded.

Two parties, in particular, seem to have had lasting consequences for those in the upper echelons of the new rock aristocracy. The first of these was held on 8 April at a society dentist's home in Hampstead, where two Beatles and their wives were attendees and unwitting guinea pigs. For George Harrison, the effects were cataclysmic: 'I didn't know about acid . . . There was no way back after that. It showed you backwards and forwards and time stood still . . . It cuts right through the physical body, the mind, the ego. It's shattering, [it's] as though someone suddenly wipes away all you were taught or brought up to believe as a child.' The experience affected Lennon just as deeply. Although in terms of his songwriting it would not become manifest for a few months yet, within eighteen months he would travel all the way from 'Help!' via 'She Said, She Said' to the full-blown psychedelia of 'Strawberry Fields Forever'.

The other party, held in folk-rocker Dylan's suite at the Savoy Hotel on 21 May, was to welcome Bob back after a brief European break prior to his first-ever TV concert, to be broadcast by the BBC in two parts over the coming weeks. Dylan himself was no stranger to LSD, having taken his first trip on a New England concert tour in April 1964, but he had wisely limited his consumption and there is no evidence he had yet experienced *le dérèglement de tous les sens* – the kind of Rimbaudian trip that really did leave one 'demented . . . destroyed in his ecstatic flight through things unheard of, unnameable'.

Well, something happened that night, because the following day the BBC broadcasts were postponed and Dylan was being rushed to St Mary's Hospital in Paddington suffering from 'food poisoning'. Whatever his true ailment, and food poisoning seems most unlikely, he was soon back at the Savoy, attended full-time by a private nurse, laid up in bed for a week. During this time he occupied his shattered mind by penning what he later euphemistically described as 'this long piece of vomit about twenty pages long, and out of it I took "Like a Rolling Stone"'. This particular stone turned out to be solid rock.

Dylan was not the only one at the party that May night who emerged from it changed for all time. Also in attendance was someone who, pre-Beatles, had been considered the great white hope for British rock. Vince Taylor, one of those swept away by the British Invasion tide, is now largely remembered for a single song, his classic 1959 single 'Brand New Cadillac', and as the inspiration for two others, David Bowie's 'Ziggy Stardust' and Van Morrison's 'Going Down Geneva'. At this time he still had an audience on the continent, where old rockers had not fully faded into obscurity, and he still had a record deal with French label Barclay. And so it was that he appeared backstage at the Locomotiv in Paris the following night, looking more like a tramp than a rock & roll star. For his then-drummer, the night was etched on his memory even three decades later:

Bobbie Woodman: Six o'clock in the evening on Saturday, we're all sitting there and in walks Vince – shoes filthy, he's got this big roll of crimson material under his arm, his hair he hasn't washed. He's got this bottle of Mateus wine in his hand. He'd been to this Bob Dylan party in London and someone told him, 'This is LSD, try one Vince.' He tried one, thought it was so good [that] at the same party two hours later he said, 'Could I have some of that before you guys go back to the States?' . . . [Backstage in Paris,] Vince [now] said, 'You all think I'm Vince

Taylor, don't you? Well, I'm not. My name is Mateus, I'm the new Jesus, the son of God.'

When questioned by the band about their fee, Taylor threw some banknotes on the floor and set light to them, proclaiming, 'Money is the root of all evil.' What happened next is shrouded in myth, but either that night or the next he apparently took to the stage in a white robe and preached to the audience, informing them that he was Mateus the Messiah. The rest of the residency was cancelled and Taylor returned to England, where he was persuaded to enter a psychiatric clinic. It didn't do the trick and, according to music journalist Kieron Tyler, he 'spent the next four years drifting from café to café in London, subsisting on a diet of wine, acid, speed, eggs and religious visions'.

By now, few of the new wave of would-be pop stars knew or cared who this dissolute figure might be, save for a young David Bowie, who met him in the La Giaconda café some time around 1966–67, and later recalled, 'He said he was [either] an alien or the Son of God – but he might have been both' – a most telling aside. Bowie would eventually claim that this sighting of Taylor provided the first building block for his very own 'leper messiah', the equally ill-starred Ziggy Stardust:

David Bowie: He always stayed in my mind as an example of what can happen in rock & roll. I'm not sure if I held him up as an idol or as something not to become. Bit of both, probably. There was something very tempting about him going completely off the edge. Especially at my age then, it seemed very appealing: 'Oh, I'd love to end up like that, totally nuts.' Ha ha! And so he re-emerged in this Ziggy character. [1990]

One can't help wondering what would have happened if it had been Dylan, not Taylor, who in late May 1965 announced he was in fact the Messiah. As it is, Taylor proved to be just the first in a long line of LSD casualties in English pop echelons that by the end of 1967 would resemble the queue for the Marquee toilets on a busy night. By then, even the music papers were prepared to print the news. The Kinks' Pete Quaife told *Melody Maker* readers in November of that year about how LSD had 'changed a lot of good blokes, who everybody rated, into creeps. Instead of expanding minds, LSD seemed to close minds into little boxes and made a lot of people very unhappy. [But] you still can't beat going to the pictures, a couple of pints and a fag. The Kinks all agree that Sunday dinner is the greatest realization of heaven.'

What Quaife omitted to mention was that The Kinks' own singer-songwriter, Ray Davies, had already proved conclusively that one did not need a tab of acid to set the English creative mind on auto-destruct. He had managed his very own nervous breakdown in March 1966 without the slightest help from mind-expanding stimulants. Unlike Taylor's, this was a breakdown everyone had seen coming though, when it happened, he went to some lengths to play it down in the music media.

Ray had been wondering 'When?' all his life, admitting in his 1994 autobiography, *X-Ray*, 'I spent [all of] my early childhood waiting for signs of abnormality to show.' He had even briefly attended a school for disturbed children at the age of eleven. By the time he joined his brother Dave in The Kinks (in time to write and sing their first three hit singles – released between August 1964 and January 1965, and charting at number one, two and one respectively) his manager, Larry Page, was 'aware that Ray had a history of mental problems. I wasn't aware of it right away, but I soon was . . . [because] Ray would always come up with some reason not to turn up at shows.'

In *X-Ray*, Davies would reveal he had first 'freaked out' after a May 1964 show in Redcar when, walking with his then-girl-friend 'along the beach in the moonlight, I suddenly started screaming . . . I blamed it on the moon, the drink and my sister emigrating to Australia. Anita blamed it on . . . my overwhelming fear of failure . . . my complete and utter insecurity and lack of confidence in myself.'

At that time he *was* a failure – the band's first two singles, including the self-penned A-side, 'You Still Want Me', had both tanked. But by March 1966, with eight Top Ten singles to his name, he had no reason to feel this way. Yet he still felt a profound 'lack of confidence' and it all came to a head on return from a six-date tour of Switzerland and Austria. Although he made light of the significance of his first serious crack-up at the time – even doing a light-hearted interview with *NME*'s Keith Altham the very day he was diagnosed by a doctor with 'nervous exhaustion' – he later admitted the break-down was no joke:

Ray Davies: I had to come off the road. I was ill. I cracked up . . . I was a zombie . . . I was completely out of my mind. I went to sleep and I woke up a week later with a beard. I don't know what happened to me. I'd run into the West End with my money stuffed into my socks, I'd tried to punch my press agent, I was chased down Denmark Street by the police, hustled into a taxi by a psychiatrist, and driven off somewhere. And I didn't know. I woke up and I said, 'What's happening? When do we leave for Belgium?' And they said, 'Ray, it's all right. You've had a collapse. Don't worry, you'll get better.' And I just sat in a room in darkness at the middle of the day, and I would eat salads and go to bed early. The first music I heard was a Frank Sinatra album. I couldn't listen to anything to do with rock 'n' roll, it made me go funny. [1977]

Aside from Sinatra, Glen Miller and Bach, Davies also spent his time listening to Dylan's first (semi-)electric album, *Bringing It All Back Home*, non-stop, and in particular, 'Maggie's Farm'. He later asserted, 'I just liked its whole presence.' One suspects it was Maggie's message, not the medium, that really got through to Davies, particularly the couplet, 'She says, "Sing while you slave," and I just get bored / I ain't gonna work on Maggie's farm no more.'

He would have been entirely unaware that Dylan had written 'Maggie's Farm' just four months before he also briefly decided to quit making music, having found it to be 'very tiring having other people tell you how much they dig you, if you yourself don't dig *you*'; or that it was the six-minute song Dylan began penning during his May 1965 recuperation that made him change his mind. Or, indeed, that it was with these two songs Dylan announced a new, electric self at the 1965 Newport festival, thus turning pop on its formerly empty head, and giving Davies and all fellow singer-songwriters a licence to write about whatever they damn well pleased.

By June 1966 Davies had penned his own declaration of independence with which he announced a return to the public arena, only to hide it away on the B-side of the next Kinks single (and their third number one). Caught up in the rearside grooves of the crumbling stately home that is 'Sunny Afternoon', he put 'I'm Not Like Everybody Else'. Here, at last, Davies finally allowed his dissatisfaction with his unhappy lot full rein. Indeed, for a while it seemed like the real Ray was only on offer to actual owners of Kinks records, as they alone had the opportunity to flip them over. Thus, the November 1965 classic 'Till the End of the Day' kept itself sunny-side-up to garner radio play, reserving the recondite 'Where Have All the Good Times Gone?' purely for purchasers of Pye product.

And when 'Sunny Afternoon' was succeeded by the equally magnificent 'Dead End Street', it was B-side 'Big Black Smoke' that really showed Ray laying waste to any allure the big city held ('She took all her pretty coloured clothes and ran away from home . . . for a boy named Joe / And he took her money for the rent / And tried to drag her down in the big black smoke'). Relentlessly driving his songwriting muse, Davies refused to admit that a sustained break was in order. Only belatedly did he admit, 'I thought that I had recovered sufficiently to continue work, but I discovered that I was forgetting people's names and walking into walls.' For the first time he took to self-medication, with predictably disastrous results, 'I stayed at home and started drinking heavily, until I couldn't walk at all.'

'Sunny Afternoon', which took an altogether different approach to songwriting that would make him feel alive again, was his way of turning things around. As he commented in 1977, this remarkable A-side, '[all] about a man who [had] made it . . . wasn't a factual thing. It was the idea, the picture . . . I was getting away from making statements that were natural to me. I started to have characters. I had to invent a character to sing, . . . "Save me".'

The change in worldview was also flagged on a couple of cuts on the album Pye released in October 1966 on the back of the success of 'Sunny Afternoon', even if *Face to Face* continued to mix songs of personal disintegration like 'Too Much On My Mind' and 'Rosie Won't You Please Come Home' with pre-breakdown ephemera ('Dandy' and 'You're Looking Fine').

And rather than include heavily sarcastic attacks on his fellow man, such as 'Mr Pleasant' ('about a man who's kind to every-body on the exterior but doesn't realize the pitfalls and traps involved in being superficially happy') and 'Mr Reporter', Davies held them back, afraid that they would come across as 'totally hate-orientated'.

In fact, condescension towards working stiffs was fast becoming another necessary subtext to mid-Sixties English pop. Even The Beatles had started putting songs such as 'Taxman' and 'Dr Robert' on their latest long-player, but Davies had yet to make an album that was an entity unto itself. And he duly acknowledged as much. By February 1967, he was already calling *Face to Face* 'more of a collection of songs than an LP'. The next album would, for sure, be more than a 'mere' collection of fine songs.

After the failure of *Face to Face*, Ray spent a whole year putting together the magnificent *Something Else*, which was eventually released in September 1967 on the back of a run of singles that were frightening in the perfection of their conception. But although 'Sunny Afternoon', 'Dead End Street' and 'Waterloo Sunset' had all proven huge commercial (and critical) hits – as had brother Dave's first foray into singledom, 'Death of a Clown' – the album containing the last two of these, along with twelve more gems from Davies' endlessly plentiful locker, was another resounding commercial flop.

As such, despite ongoing singles successes, by the start of 1968 The Kinks were in crisis. No matter how many carefully crafted three-minute masterpieces Davies could construct out of his personal insecurities, the British popscape had changed for good. In post-*Pepper* Albion, it was album acts who got treated seriously, and, more importantly, got off the ballroom/package-tour merry-go-round that had already brought Davies to the brink of mental collapse twice. Pye, wholly unaware of the shift, issued the embarrassingly anachronistic 'in concert' album, *Live at Kelvin Hall*, in January 1968, complete with fake audience screams, as if it was still the era of Beatlemania.

Davies, still fearful of another nervous breakdown, decided to get back to his English roots – and away from the big black smoke. Returning to a song he had recorded in the aftermath of his 1966 mental collapse, 'Village Green', he began to conceive of a Village Green Preservation Society whose house-band would be The Kinks. According to brother Dave, discussing the project before its appearance, 'It was originally Ray's idea to do it as a stage musical . . . It's about a town and the people that have lived there, and the village green is the focal point of the whole thing.' For Ray, there was a therapeutic purpose underlying the whole exercise:

> **Ray Davies:** *Village Green* was in some way an album of repentance, if you like; we'd been a bunch of incredibly big-time young guys, and it suddenly occurred to me when I got home after some tour or another. I thought about how I'd been interested in getting whatever I could, and that I'd been turning my back on the things I grew up from . . . It was sorta like the prodigal son suddenly discovering the world he'd been ignoring for so long; these things that were really valuable. [1972]

As a prelude to the album's appearance, in late June 1968, Pye issued Davies' most original single to date, his first fully fledged valedictory to days of yore, 'Days'. But it was a year too late – an accusation levelled at it the very week it was released, by none other than Keith Moon, who, in *Melody Maker*'s Blind Date column, dismissed the song as 'pretty dated, like one of the songs Pete [Townshend] keeps under his sink'. The plaintive

'Days' was actually a rather desperate song, with Ray describing it to official Kinks biographer Jon Savage as 'like saying goodbye to somebody, then afterwards feeling [this] fear: you actually *are* alone'.

As such, it would have been the more natural follow-up to 'Dead End Street' than 'Autumn Almanac'. But Davies was no longer in sync with the times. And *The Kinks are the Village Green Preservation Society* (*VGPS*) would prove another step back, when the world was expecting him to take two steps forward. Talking to *The Onion* in 2002, Davies fully owned up to the charge, 'I withdrew into my little community-spirited . . . my trivial world of little corner shops and English black-and-white movies. Maybe that's my form of psychedelia.'

Almost anticipating the imminent collapse of the psychedelic brotherhood, he beat his own retreat. As he told *Melody Maker*, in a song-by-song breakdown of *VGPS*, which briefly centred on the catchy 'Animal Farm': 'That was just me thinking everybody else is mad . . . which is really the idea of the whole album.' Already he felt chastened by the chart failure of The Kinks' first two singles of the year, 'Wonder Boy' and 'Days'. The former troubled the chart compilers not a jot, while the latter barely tiptoed into the Top Twenty. And Davies never entirely relinquished his belief that he had done the wrong thing foisting his new persona on the public (and the band), like it or not:

Ray Davies: 'Village Green' . . . was my ideal place, a protected place. It's a fantasy world that I can retreat to, and the worst thing I did was inflict it on the public. I should have left it in my diary. [1984]

In truth, the released album was a fudge. What had begun life as two distinct albums – 'an LP about manners and things' solely for the US market, to be called *Four More Respected Gentlemen*, plus a twelve-track *Village Green Preservation Society* – became a single, jam-packed fifteen-track long-player instead. Despite sacrificing songs of the quality of 'Days', 'Did You See His Name' (Davies' first song to address the subject of suicide directly), 'Rosemary Rose' and 'Mr Songbird' at the last minute, it was too much of a good thing.

The trio of songs he added to the album in October – each one a choice cut – helped kill the album conceptually, while suggesting he could not entirely suppress a more autobiographical view of the world. 'Last of the Steam Powered Trains', 'Big Sky' and 'All of My Friends Were There' were all major statements on Davies' part, directly anticipating the next two concept albums but – big but – they sent the album some place that was more Muswell Hill than village green. The result was an album that 'confused the record-buying public'.

All three of these songs continued the vein of songwriting he'd first established with 'I'm Not Like Everybody Else'. 'Big Sky' was inspired by an evening at a pop junket in Cannes 'with all these people doing deals . . . I watched the sun come up and I looked at them all down there, all going out to do their deals'. 'Last of the Steam Powered Trains', as he openly admitted, was 'about not having anything in common with people . . . It's about me being the last of the renegades. All my friends are middle class now . . . They've all made money and have happy faces.' 'All of My Friends Were There', meanwhile, specifically addressed his 1966 breakdown, told as if the crack-up happened on stage, surrounded by bewildered friends – a disturbing presentiment of the next nervous breakdown he would suffer in 1973. Just months before that crack-up, he talked about 'All of My Friends Were There' in a way that suggested he remembered the feeling all too well: 'I was feeling bad . . . I'd just been very ill, and I went over the edge as they say. It does happen. I was working very hard, I'd just finished a lot of work. I was very disturbed, and very unhappy because I had a lot of friends in the audience. I wanted to make them happy.'

The reconfigured *VGPS* was again mistimed. The original twelve-track version, reviewed by Keith Altham in a September 1968 *NME*, when it was scheduled for release, was cancelled when Davies decided he wanted to record the above songs – just as he had done with *Something Else*, delaying that LP's appearance. The revised record came out the same day (22 November 1968) as The Beatles' eagerly awaited, whiter-than-white double album. And though Davies would later claim, '[*VGPS*] was not heavy, and everything was heavy at the time, so it just got lost', his brother's take on the album's fate was the more astute:

> **Dave Davies:** There was a really good atmosphere on [*Village Green*] *Preservation Society*, through the whole summer . . . There was a great aura around everything at that time. [But] when it came out it was a big flop. I think it was because . . . at that time when everyone was buzzing about change and revolution, and we were about keeping things and respecting things . . . It was a bit out of time. [1978]

Ray felt the failure of *VGPS* keenly, though he was soon wistfully looking back on what he liked to call 'the first genuinely constructed musical play by a rock band'; even if he preferred to 'remember it for what it might have been, rather than what was eventually realized'. For the first time he was embracing his own past and its all-too-real ghosts across an entire LP. As he later told *Uncut*, 'Village Green . . . is the youth that I thought I missed. The record's about childhood really; lost childhood.' At least some fellow English songwriters recognized its worth, Pete Townshend calling the album, 'Ray's masterwork . . . his *Sgt. Pepper*'. But its resounding commercial failure affirmed the fact that the 'rock album' audience had now tuned out The Kinks.

★

In this, The Kinks were hardly alone. This was a predicament facing a number of bands that had emerged in the wake of The Beatles, as the tricky transition from single– to album–band took its toll on many of the pre-psychedelic vanguard. It was a concern Pete Townshend himself voiced to *Beat Instrumental* as early as February 1969, while putting the finishing touches to his own gambit, the 'concept album' *Tommy*:

> **Pete Townshend:** For a long time, we had a position somewhere behind The Beatles and The Stones and above all the rest of the English groups. It was a strange situation. We had a spell when all records made about number four without fail . . . We changed our attitude about the time The Kinks suddenly started to have flops; we were like them in a lot of ways, and it brought home the fact that we couldn't afford to take it easy any more. You get in a ridiculous state when the hits come automatically. [1969]

Like Davies, Townshend had had his own epiphany in the middle of relentless touring; like Taylor, it was the result of a bad acid trip as opposed to the hectic pace of performing. Ironically, it came as he was savouring one of The Who's greatest triumphs, their explosive set at the 1967 Monterey Pop Festival. The effects would prove just as profound. Townshend was boarding a plane leaving California when he was given what he thought was a tab of acid. He had, by his own admission, been experimenting with mind-expanding hallucinogenics for almost a year (and even now has a vivid memory of 'being in the UFO club with my girlfriend, dancing under the effect of acid . . . I was just totally lost: she's there going off into the world of Roger Waters and his impenetrable leer'). However, this post-Monterey trip was something completely different:

> **Pete Townshend:** I took what I thought was acid, but turned out to be STP . . . It was after the Monterey Pop Festival, and I spent more time outside of my body looking inside myself than I've ever spent . . . I [had] to learn to listen to music all over again, and . . . how to write all over again. [1972]

Contrary to what Townshend had been led to believe by LSD evangelists, his consumption of acid coincided with major-writer's block. As he later revealed in *The Story of Tommy*, 'During the year I was taking acid I wrote hardly anything, probably the most revealing testimony to its uselessness I ever experienced.' He had been faking it through most of 1967, and it was starting to show. First, a stop-gap single in support of the recently busted Stones saw The Who cover two Jagger-Richards classics. Then they were about to put out a studio version of their show-stop-ping cover of Eddie Cochran's 'Summertime Blues' when West Coast proto-punks Blue Cheer beat them to it, causing Townshend to ruefully note, 'We needed a chart hit at that point, but they came out with it [first].' Even the song he had been holding back for such an eventuality, the expertly bombastic 'I Can See for Miles', which he had demoed as early as 1966, barely bothered the Top Ten. It was 'Days' all over again.

Such was Townshend's dearth of inspiration that at the beginning of 1968 The Who announced the intended follow-up to 'I Can See for Miles' would be their very own get-back-to-the-country track, the risible 'Now I'm a Farmer'. Thankfully, it was shelved. Townshend came up with 'Dogs' instead; inspired, as it were, by a joint Who/Small Faces tour of Australia in January 1968, which ended with both bands being arrested for asking for a drink on an internal flight from Sydney to Melbourne. The song was, by Townshend's own admission, 'my response to The Small Faces' 'Lazy Sunday' from *Ogdens*'. [Because] I wanted to be in their band, really.'

'Lazy Sunday', though, had been a number two single; while 'Dogs' did not even dent the Top Twenty. In desperation, Pete dusted off another old song, set to the diddley daddy of all Bo Diddley rip-off riffs, 'Magic Bus', and offered it up to the gods of chart success. Although it failed to do the trick in The Who's homeland, stalling one place lower than 'Dogs' (#26), it proved their biggest hit in the US since 'My Generation'. On the back of Monterey, and a relentless attempt to break the States by bringing auto-destruction to the clubs and theatres of America, The Who slowly began to carve out the niche they would make their own with Townshend's next grandiloquent statement. But that was almost a year away. As he told *NME* at the end of 1968, as the UK pop world wondered where The 'Oo went:

> **Pete Townshend:** I can no longer sit down with a straight face and write things like ['My Generation' and 'Magic Bus'], although I was quite serious about them at the time . . . It's very difficult to know just what is going to be a hit for us now, especially in America where we were not able to do those discs like 'Happy Jack', 'Pictures of Lily' and 'I'm a Boy', which were a novelty in England because they had the strange attraction of being 'sweet songs' by a violent group. In America we have to find instant hits, and that's really what 'Magic Bus' is. [1968]

His solution was, on the face of it, simple: turn The Who into an album band. Townshend, though, was just as much at sea as Ray Davies when it came to the means of manufacturing such a transition. Even as the godfather of rock operas, as the man who as far back as 1966 gave the pop world the ten-minute 'A Quick One, While He's Away', he had been slightly nonplussed by *Sgt. Pepper*, expressing amazement that The Beatles got away with such a 'very loose concept'.

In *Pepper*'s wake, his own band promptly set about producing an album with an even more tenuous thread, *The Who Sell Out*. By May 1968, though, Townshend was openly admitting the radio-station format on that set had been something 'we thought we needed . . . throughout the album to make it stand up within the terms of other albums coming out today . . . Having a form for an album seems to be what is happening.' Try as he might he could not turn 'concept' songs such as 'Rael', an edited version of which appeared on *Sell Out*, and 'Glow Girl' (a song about reincarnation after a plane crash, probably inspired by his post-Monterey experience) into a grander conceit. In fact, at one stage in 1967 it seemed that The Who's underused 'other' songwriter, bassist John Entwistle, might produce his own concept album before Townshend came up with one of his own:

John Entwistle: 'Silas Stingy' and 'Dr Jekyll and Mr Hyde' were meant to go on a kids' rock album. Young kids love[d] 'Boris the Spider'. So we were gonna release a children's album with all these snakes and spiders and creepy things, a project Kit Lambert dreamed up. But they all ended up being used as B-sides. [And] I ended up with this black image. [1995]

Entwistle tapping into childhood themes was not, however, the same as Townshend tapping into them. Deliciously macabre as the above songs are, they still inhabited a more conventional world than the likes of 'Happy Jack' (about an adult with a child's IQ), 'I'm a Boy' (enforced transvestism) and 'Pictures of Lily' (teenage masturbation), the three 45s Townshend issued in 1966 to show how the world could be a cruel place. It was to this place he now needed to return, preferably with a few post-LSD insights, if he was going to turn an idea he had for an album about a deaf, dumb and blind boy subjected to repeated, systematic abuse into a worldwide chart-topper.

*

Meanwhile, if Entwistle's fledgling 'children's collection' was being wasted on B-sides and the odd album cut, another English eccentric was using leftover ideas from a set of 'adult fairy stories' to mount a serious assault on the UK single charts. Through 1967 and into 1968, Roy Wood – via his band of fellow Brummies, The Move – dispensed a series of singles detailing some very damaged individuals: in toto, 'Disturbance' (the B-side to debut 45, 'Night of Fear', and actually Wood's preferred choice for the A-side); 'I Can Hear the Grass Grow' ('I didn't particularly write it with psychedelia in mind – I thought more of some sorta mad person'); 'Cherry Blossom Clinic' (scheduled to be The Move's third single, until their label decided Wood was poking fun at mental patients); 'Flowers in the Rain' and its even loopier B-side, '(Here We Go Round) The Lemon Tree'; and finally, 'Fire Brigade', about a particularly determined female pyromaniac. According to Wood, all these songs had a common inspiration:

Roy Wood: 'Cherry Blossom Clinic' was about a nuthouse, basically, but a nice one. That was one of my early songs. When I left art-school it was one of my ambitions to write a children's book for adults – fairy stories with strange twists to them. I had a lot of ideas written down and I used them in my songs. [1978]

It was with this lexicon of lunacy that The Move now challenged The Who's vaunted position in Popdom. All the things that had marked out The Who's territory in the pre-psychedelic era – 'Pop-art music, Union Jack jackets, all my kind of auto-destruction, post-art college ideas', to quote Townshend – were appropriated and refined by the Brummies. In the case of auto-destruction, The Move took Townshend literally, and started destroying cars on stage. And through 1967 and well into 1968, the strategy seemed to be paying dividends. While The Who's current bagatelle of hits – 'Pictures of Lily' through 'Magic Bus' – went to #4, #44, #10, #25 and #26 respectively, The Move's first five 45s – 'Night of Fear' through 'Blackberry Way' – charted at #2, #5, #2, #3 and #1. Townshend was rightly worried. (He subsequently suggested, 'I don't think I moved away from pop. I think it moved away from me. Maybe psychedelia did it'.)

The Move, however, had their own problems, including at least one increasingly unstable band-member. Not Wood, but their bassist Ace Kefford, who by the end of 1967 was, by his own admission (to Alan Clayson), 'having a mental breakdown [from] dropping acid every day . . . I was cracking up, just like Syd Barrett was'. The departure of Kefford in the New Year would effectively stop The Move dead in their tracks. It would take Wood eight months to come up with his first non-adult fairy-story single, 'Blackberry Way', and even that seemed to be a return-to-childhood song. Another irresistible hook took it to number one, but it would be April 1970 before they enjoyed another Top Ten single.

By the time The Move took to the stage of the Kensington Olympia on 22 December 1967, for what was billed as a Christmas pop extravaganza, they were – at least temporarily – a spent creative force. In fact, the bill that night – and one could make a pretty good case for it being the greatest package bill ever, even without The Who, replaced by Traffic after Townshend injured his hand – was full to the rafters of bands who had transformed British pop in the past year. But several bands that night were now imploding from within as band-members surrendered their minds to a lysergic night of the soul.

If Kefford was the main Move casualty, Olympia headliner Jimi Hendrix was doing a good job hiding behind wah-wah pedals and pyrotechnics, hoping to disguise the toll drugs were taking on his creative juices even as he completed his second album of 1967, the trenchantly trippy *Axis: Bold as Love*. But amongst these Olympians it was the UK's leading psychedelic combo, Syd Barrett's Pink Floyd, that were the first to reach the end of the line – less than a year after they startled the pop world with their astonishing debut 45, the gender-bending 'Arnold Layne'. Psychedelic Psyd had been taking his, and everyone else's, medicine. Now, six months after 'See Emily Play' and the equally challenging *Piper at the Gates of Dawn* suggested a new heavyweight had entered the pop arena, frontman Barrett was by all reports unravelling before unknowing eyes. And some contemporaries were not greatly surprised:

Pete Townshend: Syd was someone with psychotic tendencies who by using too much LSD pushed himself over the edge. Remember that LSD was developed for use in psychiatry in clinical circumstances. I only used acid a few times . . . [but] I [also] have certain psychotic tendencies and found it extremely dangerous. [1991]

There have been no shortage of eyewitnesses who have characterized Barrett's behaviour in his last couple of months in the Floyd as out to lunch, tea and dinner. Kefford, while admitting he was 'cracking up' himself, depicted Barrett on tour as someone who 'never spoke to anyone. He could hardly move sometimes. He was on another planet.' Floyd bassist Roger Waters remembers the autumn 1967 Syd as someone 'way out there . . . he'd get into the car in drag' (in Waters' ultra-straight world, a sure sign of insanity). A week before the Olympia Extravaganza, Floyd's co-manager Peter Jenner was obligingly penning a letter to *Melody Maker* explaining that 'the Pink Floyd [in concert] are largely unpredictable both to the audience and to themselves. They can be sublime. They can be awful' – a brave attempt to counteract negative reports coming from the month-long tour they had just completed with Hendrix and The Move.

Yet Barrett's own memory of the tour, expressed during his last-ever interview in December 1971, was that it was Hendrix who was 'very self-conscious about his consciousness. He'd lock himself in the dressing-room with a TV and wouldn't let anyone in.' And *objective* evidence for the mental collapse that precipitated Syd's removal from the Floyd (rather than vice-versa) is thin on the ground. His 'catatonic' performance on *American Bandstand* the first week in November – according to co-manager Andrew King, 'Syd wasn't into moving his lips that day' – subsequently surfaced, and is nothing of the sort. Indeed, Syd seemed to be making a better job of miming 'Apples and Oranges' than the other members of the band. Another appearance on BBC's *Tomorrow's World*, recorded just days before Syd's departure – jamming on a blues instrumental while Mike Leonard showed off some of his light designs – again presented a perfectly together Barrett.

Meanwhile, there was plentiful evidence that any inner disturbance was still offset by the man's continued brilliance as a songwriter and frontman. Much of it can be found on the *Top Gear* radio session the Floyd recorded just two days before the Olympia extravaganza. In a single afternoon, they recorded three remarkable new Barrett originals – 'Vegetable Man', 'Scream Thy Last Scream' and 'Jugband Blues' – plus a dramatically rearranged 'Pow R Toch H', from *Piper at the Gates of Dawn*.

These new originals, indicative of a new direction – and, perhaps, the incipient disintegration of a fragile psyche – seem to have disturbed the other members of the Floyd far more than any of the man's legendary onstage antics (detuning his guitar; rubbing Mandrax in his hair, &c.). Such was their distaste that they decided against including the first two on their next album, even though Barrett had effectively disowned them[4] and the post-Barrett quartet was chronically short of strong original material. Roger Waters, someone ultimately unconvinced that one had to be nuts to have insights as profound as Barrett's, was the first to push for Syd's removal from the band:

Roger Waters: There were a whole team of [writers] who all believed it was rather good to be mad, and it was the rest of us who were making less sense . . . In Syd's case, you could say that it was his potential for decline into schizophrenia that gave him the talent to express mildly untouchable things. But I . . . feel that a lot less now than I may have done then. [2005]

All the Madmen

When 1968 dawned, two weeks after Olympia, Barrett was on borrowed time. The rest of Pink Floyd didn't mind performing songs about closet transvestites and sexually liberated free spirits, but given a choice between the kind of improvisational 'space age' songs that now constituted the majority of their live set and a version of psychedelic pop that was not so much 'head' music as 'in your head' music, they were always likely to go with the former. Anyway, they weren't sure they liked the looks Barrett kept giving them; as if he'd just heard a private joke at their expense. As co-manager Andrew King subsequently recalled, 'Syd could be very cruel, making fun of how strait-laced they all were.'

The others decided to cast him adrift, though not before test-running replacement guitarist Dave Gilmour for half a dozen gigs in a five-piece Floyd. Gilmour himself would later insist, 'If [Syd] had stayed, the Floyd would have died an ignominious death . . . we had no choice' – quite a snap judgement from someone who had enjoyed membership status for less than a fortnight when the others jettisoned Barrett. If they hoped that firing Syd might bring him to his senses, it appeared to have the opposite effect. In conversation with *Melody Maker*'s Michael Watts three years later, Barrett hinted that their decision actually precipitated a(nother) mental collapse: 'We did split up, and there was a lot of trouble. I don't think The Pink Floyd had any trouble, but I had an awful scene, probably self-inflicted, having a Mini and going all over England and things.' His fragile self-confidence, already teetering, was shattered.

Part of Barrett's understandable bemusement seems to have resulted from the rest of the band not having the balls to tell him to his face that he was ousted. And so for a six-week period, from the end of January to the beginning of March, Barrett was genuinely perturbed to discover that they were recording and performing without him. In 1974 Andrew King remembered how Syd would sit, 'with guitar in tow . . . in the reception area of Abbey Road studios for days on end while *Saucerful of Secrets* was being recorded, waiting to be asked to contribute'. And try as the others might to keep details of their gig schedule from him, Barrett would turn up unexpectedly (which is presumably what he meant when referring to 'having a Mini and going all over England'). And when he did, he would stand a hair's breadth away from Gilmour:

Jerry Shirley [drummer]: Dave went through some real heavy stuff for the first few months [in Floyd]. Syd would turn up at [some] gigs and stand in front of the stage looking up at Dave, 'That's my band.'

Emo [Floyd roadie]: You could tell Syd didn't understand what was happening. He was standing so close to Dave he was almost an inch from his face . . . then [he] started walking around him, almost checking that Dave was a three-dimensional object.

Matters finally came to a head during a meeting on 2 March at the management offices in Edbrooke Road. According to one account Waters gave in 1973, '[It] came down to me and Syd sitting in a room talking together, and I'd worked out what I thought was the only way we could carry on together, which was for him to . . . become a sort of Brian Wilson figure, if you like, write songs and come to recording sessions. And by the end of the afternoon I thought I'd convinced him that it was a good idea, and he'd agreed.' But as Nick Mason asserts, Barrett then allowed himself to 'be influenced by some people, who kept repeating he was the only talent in the band and should pursue a solo career'. This was a clear reference to Jenner and King, neither of whom could see how a Barrett-less Floyd would have a shelf-life not measured in months.

And on the evidence of what Jenner and King heard coming out of EMI's Abbey Road studios in the winter of 1968, it would be hard to challenge their assessment. Determined to use just two of the songs cut with Barrett the previous autumn – 'Jugband Blues' and Waters' own 'Set the Controls for the Heart of the Sun' – the reconstituted Floyd set out to make an album that 'has nothing to do with what Syd believed in or liked' (Gilmour's own 1975 description of the released artefact). The five additional songs that eked the album out to thirty-nine minutes included at least one faux-Barrett pastiche, 'Corporal Clegg', that was, in the words of Julian Palacios, 'so crude an approximation of the Barrettian songwriting style as to constitute [mere] parody' (Waters' other contemporary stab at Barrettian whimsy, 'Julia's Dream', was wisely placed as a single B-side). Even then, they had to resort to the twelve-minute title track – an indulgent recasting of the pre-*Piper* psychedelic jam, 'Nick's Boogie' – to fill out the album. Unimpressed producer Norman Smith, still at the helm, told them, 'I think it's rubbish, but go ahead and do it if you want.'

Meanwhile, Jenner and King put their faith in the erstwhile Floyd frontman, feeling that Barrett probably still had enough good days in him to complete a solo album. Jenner says that he 'knew he had the songs . . . [and] I kept thinking if he did the right things he'd come back to join us'. And crucially, as far as he was concerned, 'There was no indication that [Syd] didn't want to do it any more.' As such, in early May 1968 they began work – or so they thought – on the first Syd Barrett solo album, Jenner taking on the role of producer that *Piper*-producer Norman

Smith, who had never been entirely at ease in Syd's company, happily relinquished.

Sadly, Jenner's conviction that Syd 'had the songs' was not borne out by the eight or so recording sessions conducted at EMI over the next two-and-a-half months, only three of which produced any genuinely usable new music. In the end, the results comprised just four worthwhile songs – 'Silas Lang', 'Late Nights', 'Golden Hair' (a James Joyce poem set to music) and 'Clowns and Jugglers' (which, according to Jenner, began life as a piece of pre-Floyd whimsy). The last of these was only pulled out of Barrett's irregular hat at the final session on 20 July, when they were supposed to be getting final mixes of the few usable songs. Jenner was already thinking of combining what little they had got with three usable Floyd leftovers: 'Vegetable Man', 'Scream Thy Last Scream' and 'In the Beechwoods'; Floyd having knowingly overlooked all three for the wafer-thin *Saucerful of Secrets*.

But the material simply wasn't there, and time out was called on Syd's solo LP, even as the eight 1968 sessions set the pattern for future Barrett sessions. Some days had proven a total waste of time – such as the 14 May session, which was given over to two tedious jams, the eighteen-minute 'Rhamadam' and the five-minute 'Lanky'. Other days Barrett was focused and brimming with ideas. The first proper session, on 6 May, produced two fine songs; one, 'Silas Lang', in a single take. But Barrett was already struggling to master his demons. As what he later called 'an awful scene' consumed him for most of 1968 and into the following winter, Jenner and EMI began to wonder if he would ever make music again.

And yet Jenner's experience with Barrett failed to persuade either him or the record label to steer a wide berth around any future madcap mavericks. Barely had Jenner abandoned the

Barrett sessions than he began working on an album with the almost equally eccentric Roy Harper, whose pedigree to date included a spell in Lancaster Moor Mental Institute that inspired his notorious 1966 song 'Committed', and a period in jail for trying to climb the clock tower of London's St Pancras station. As Harper himself said of the songs from this period: 'The area of discovery I've got going is inside my own head, and there are a lot of places I've not been yet . . . I'm into it as a conscious trip . . . [though] it's probably got to stop soon – I've come to the realization that . . . I've really got to give my head a chance, not only to do something else, but to have a rest from that trip.'

Harper was another songwriter who, to adopt Jenner's own choice phrase, was 'a bit crazy – like all the best people'. He was also the perfect artist for the new 'prog' label EMI had set up to house their weirder coves, Harvest Records. The resultant album, the appositely named *Flat Baroque and Beserk* (1969)[5], would appear just behind Barrett's debut LP and establish what would be a decade-long association with the new label. Harper used the album to exorcize some demons of his own, resulting from a childhood being raised by a Jehovah's Witness step-mother and a combative Dad (as he wrote in the notes to the 1970 reissue of his 1966 debut LP, 'My forebears . . . are actually just as mad as I am'). In 'Feeling All the Saturday', in particular, he embraced the madness, partly feigned, that allowed him to escape his more pious parent:

> and mum's just bought herself a leaning-post
> made of words and pages
> it says god gives us all our daily toast
> but dad still earns the wages
> and i've just bought a jigsaw puzz

it's made of cotton wool
and when i've undone every piece
the truth will fit my skull.

*

The maverick clientele of Peter Jenner were not alone in scrabbling around for some way forward in the aftermath of the inevitable post-psychedelic implosion, casting its patented pall over the English pop scene through 1968. Nor was Syd Barrett the only one disposed to take a year off. The young David Bowie had also temporarily opted out of the pop world, not in homage to his idol, but because he had nowhere to run.

Bowie himself never quite got over the impact of seeing the Floydian Syd onstage. In 1990 he described Barrett's 'huge influence' thus: 'He had this strange mystical look to him . . . He was like some figure out of an Indonesian play or something, and wasn't altogether of this world.' That last phrase, akin to his description of Vince Taylor, suggested Bowie had thus acquired another building-block for future use. In Bowie's case, though, no one except his parents and his gay manager, Ken Pitt, was eagerly awaiting the imminent reinvention of David Jones of Brixton.

Through 1966–67 Bowie had been experimenting – at his record label Deram's expense – with a style of pop lyric that shared a kinship with the weirder ministrations of Ray Davies, Pete Townshend and New York's own demi-monde degenerate, Lou Reed. Even on Bowie's first eponymous album, recorded in the second half of 1966 and issued the same day as *Sgt. Pepper* – though destined to have a more negligible effect on pop culture – he was already writing about some seriously dysfunctional characters. 'Uncle Arthur' was about a thirty-something man who still 'likes his mummy, still reads comics, [and] follows Batman'. 'Little Bombadier' was about a demobbed soldier who spoils children with 'treats', only to be warned off by a policeman. As Nicholas Pegg has observed in his all-encompassing Bowie encyclopaedia, the Deram 'album's motif of wartime nostalgia, its Blakean evocations of childhood innocence, and above all its rogues' gallery of lonely misfits and social inadequates, are all very much of a piece with contemporary work by the likes of Syd Barrett's Pink Floyd, The Bonzo Dog Doo-Dah Band and . . . The Beatles.'

However, the tunes Bowie then applied to these eccentric vignettes had more in common with music hall, French chanson and stage songs than anything from contemporary pop. At the time he claimed he started out 'by changing the words of nursery rhymes and then graduated to a more serious form of song writing', an assertion that the best-known song from this particular learning curve, 'The Laughing Gnome'[6], would seem to affirm.

Nor did the songs become any less peculiar through 1967, as Bowie continued his overwrought attempt to make these modern Grimm tales fit the zeitgeist, all the while (mis)reading the tea leaves of pop culture. Even he remained unsure that the world was ready for the full-on ministrations of his darkling point of view, on the evidence of one song he demoed with The Riot Squad on 5 April 1967, 'Little Toy Soldier' (and perhaps it still isn't – the oft-bootlegged track was omitted from the 2010 'Deluxe' two-CD reissue of the 'complete' Decca recordings). 'Little Toy Soldier' shows that he had already embraced the test-pressing of the first Velvet Underground album his manager had presented to him the previous January on returning from a trip to New York. Bowie actually nabs a couplet from 'Venus in Furs' ('taste the whip in love not given lightly . . .'), as he tells the story of a girl, Sadie, who winds up a clockwork toy soldier, which then comes to life and whips her. One day she overwinds it, and the toy beats her to death. As a songwriter, already more than weird enough for Gilly.

Although Bowie continued releasing antiseptic fare such as 'The Laughing Gnome' and 'Love You Till Tuesday' through Decca's hipper Deram subsidiary, 'Little Toy Soldier' was the first sign of him recording more sexually ambiguous material. 'Let Me Sleep Beside You', recorded in September, was offered to Decca as a potential follow-up to 'Love You Till Tuesday' but was passed on, probably because they had noticed a certain metrosexual undertone in couplets such as, 'Wear the dress your mother wore / Let me sleep beside you.' His mother certainly expressed her disquiet, as Bowie carelessly admitted at a 1969 BBC radio session.

In fact, Decca now began to develop something of a habit of passing on Bowie's increasingly challenging would-be singles, turning down two more in 1968, 'London Bye Ta-Ta' b/w 'In the Heat of the Morning', and 'Ching a Ling' b/w 'Back to Where You've Never Been'. The last of these tracks, recorded in October 1968 under the watchful eye of producer Tony Visconti, was a Tony Hill composition, and as such omitted from the 2010 'Deluxe' edition of Bowie's Deram recordings. However, one does wonder if the song has some relationship to another of Bowie's fabled lost recordings, the song 'Tired of My Life', which includes the line, 'I'm leading you away, home where you've never been.'

Possible corroboration for such a thesis comes from a seemingly innocuous aside by Visconti, the producer of that 1968 session, who has stated that Bowie wrote the song 'It's No Game' – the 1980s incarnation of 'Tired of My Life' – 'when he was sixteen'. 'Tired of My Life' – which has been bootlegged extensively from an undated solo demo acetate, repeatedly credited to the *Man Who Sold The World* era, but without any clear basis or concrete accreditation – also includes the prescient line, 'Put a bullet in my brain and I make the papers', reused in 'It's No Game', throughout demonstrating a world-weariness that very much anticipates the next phrase in Bowie's work, best represented by the *Space Oddity* outtake, 'Conversation Piece', a song he (also) composed at the end of 1968.

We do know that mortality was much on Bowie's mind in that 'lost' year. One project that did not even make it to the Decca studio was a rock musical called *Ernie Johnson*, about a character who throws a party to mark his own intended suicide, the first time an act of suicide was the culmination of a Bowie project. A demo tape recorded in February 1968 (and subsequently sold at a pop memorabilia auction in London) featured some nine already-penned songs, although this was the last that was ever heard of ol' Ernie.

*

Meanwhile, a quite similar idea was the centrepiece of one of the more eccentric albums released that year. 'The Birthday' was a Jeff Lynne song featured on Idle Race's much-delayed *The Birthday Party* that October, it being told from the viewpoint of a woman who invites all her friends to a birthday party, but they 'are too busy doing other things' and so no one comes. The song ends with the narrator killing herself. Another song on the same quirky LP, 'I Like My Toys', about an adult refusing to grow up, could almost qualify as a rewrite of Bowie's 'Uncle Arthur', though Lynne's song is far funnier ('My mum says sixteen years is a long enough rest' being my favourite line).

In reality, Lynne's mentor was friend and fellow Brummie, Roy Wood, whose '(Here We Go Round) The Lemon Tree' he had hoped to issue as Idle Race's first single before The Move pre-empted them. Idle Race songs such as 'The Lady Who Said

She Could Fly' and 'Sitting in My Tree' could have been ripped clean from Roy Wood's private volume of 'adult fairy stories'. Sadly for Lynne and his band, their own unique overview of English eccentricity failed to register with the very audience who had already flocked to snap up the equally eccentric album the Small Faces had issued four months earlier, the ostentatiously packaged *Ogdens' Nut Gone Flake*.

This chart-topping album devoted an entire side to its very own adult fairy story, which told of Happiness Stan's journey to discover who was stealing the moon, until finally he found himself deposited at the home of Mad John, who would 'find . . . not only the moon itself, [for] which you looked, but the philosophy of life . . . itself'. 'Mad John', the song tells us, 'had it sussed . . . yes, his bed was the cold and the damp, but the sun was his friend / he was free'. (According to Steve Marriott, the initial idea was to write a song about 'these characters . . . that people were scared of through ignorance'.) The fact that the English pop audience embraced the Small Faces' ersatz psychedelia but rejected other, more left-field contemporaries, was already causing concern to some fellow popsters. Townshend, talking to *Rolling Stone* at year's end, offered his own explanation:

Pete Townshend: People just felt that pop was getting out of their hands; groups like the Pink Floyd were appearing, scary groups, psychedelic . . . What were they all about? With their flashing lights and all taking trips and one of them's a psycho. So they all turn over to good old Englebert Humperdink . . . It's a sign of the fact that the music got out of step with the people. [1968]

All the Madmen

The Kinks' Dave Davies told *Beat Instrumental* he felt equally baffled: 'Just looking at the charts makes [me] feel a bit . . . insecure. More insecure now than a couple of years ago. The Scaffold getting to number one with "Lily the Pink", for instance. I mean, it's hardly a predictable number one, is it? . . . I find it strange – you look ahead at what might happen during 1969 and find out that it could be anything at all. No distinct pattern anywhere.'

As summations of the 1968 charts go, 'no distinct pattern' is as good as any. If bands were uncertain of the way ahead, a number of them concluded that it was better to disband than stay together and figure things out. And almost the first to abandon ship was the very band that seemed to have bucked the trend and kept its pre-psychedelic audience, Small Faces. At year's end, they announced that they were going their separate ways, as if the job was done. Townshend, for one, was not surprised: 'I think it was natural in a way that the Small Faces broke up after *Ogdens' Nut Gone [Flake]* . . . You do your classic album and then you really have to use every ounce of stamina and guts to stick together, because it's so tempting to relax.'

The Kinks, too, were wondering whether or not they should soldier on – in their case, issuing their defining album had done nothing to reverse their fortunes. And at least one member had made it clear he'd had enough. Pete Quaife made his decision during Christmas 1968, and though briefly talked out of it, by the following March he was officially 'out'. For some time he had been of the opinion that 'we were pandering to what Ray wanted to be, how he wanted to be perceived', but he kept his counsel, only expressing such thoughts to the Kinks chronicler Andy Miller in 2002.

Year's end brought no shortage of bands following their lead. These included three English bands whose contribution to the psychedelic pop scene had already been significant: Cream, Traffic and the appositely named The Crazy World of Arthur Brown. If The Move had survived the loss of live wire Ace Kefford, and the Floyd were soldiering on regardless, it was increasingly hard to see where the future of English rock lay. As of 10 January 1969, when George Harrison walked out on The Beatles (although he returned to complete the ill-fated *Let It Be* and, ultimately, *Abbey Road*), the writing was on the wall even for England's greatest pop export. Pete Townshend again had his own take on what was causing this sense of doubt that was eating away at more progressive pop outfits at this time:

Pete Townshend: At that time the Moody Blues and [other] people were doing ambitious works ... and they were instantly getting labelled as pretentious, and at the same time garbage was being pushed out into the charts ... Anybody that was any good ... was more or less becoming insignificant again. They weren't new anymore, they weren't fresh, and a lot of the new stuff that was coming out was really trash. There was a lot of psychedelic bullshit going about. [1974]

Ray Davies and David Bowie were two such figures determined to fight against the tide of 'psychedelic bullshit'. In both cases, it was the same concern that kept them on the straight and narrow – fear that the rattling skeletons of a troubled childhood might be unleashed. Bowie would tell a sceptical *Playboy* in 1976: 'Acid only gives people a link with their own imagery. I already had it ... I never needed acid to make music.' But his landlady and lover at that time, Mary Finnegan, offered a more prosaic explanation: 'David was terrified of mind-warping drugs like LSD, and he used to lecture his fans on the dangers of tripping.' The last thing he wanted was for some drug to 'wipe away' all he was 'brought up to believe as a child'.

At the same time, the failure of *VGPS* had not done a great deal for Davies' precarious hold on his mental equilibrium; and his response was to withdraw still further from the kind of pop productions DJs tended to play. As 1969 dawned, he had become a songwriter for hire, writing a song a week for a TV series called *Where Was Spring?* Typically, he personalized the sense of loss implicit in the title, writing the great lost Kink classic 'Where Did My Spring Go?', further proof that he intended to retreat more into the past. Unfortunately, his private little war against 'psychedelic bullshit', at Pye's expense, was yielding only the most pyrrhic of victories.

Perhaps the only sane solution was to send up all the 'psychedelic bullshit'. Roy Wood's pseudonymous 1969 Acid Gallery single, 'Dance 'Round the Maypole', recorded while the post-Kefford The Move found its feet, was one oft-overlooked, gloriously silly riposte. Another was Fleetwood Mac's 'Intergalactic Magicians Walking Through Pools of Velvet Darkness', recorded in May 1968. Containing lines such as, 'I am here and you are there / And we are all going nowhere', it was a largely improvised, one-day-at-the-Beeb send-up of those still pushing a psychedelic agenda. The powerhouse blues combo, who had yet to sight their bird of ill omen, or associate with the kind of people that liked to dose their 'friends', would soon be taking their own stroll through pools of velvet darkness leading nowhere.

The only contribution Syd Barrett had made to the output of the mighty EMI Records in 1968 was the last cut placed by 'his band' on the Floyd's first post-Barrett outing, 'Jugband Blues', recorded back in October 1967. For anyone paying attention, it seemed like a not-so-fond farewell to psychedelia from a man looking to strip away the insane instruments that once played in his head, in this instance manifested as a Salvation Army band who had been instructed by Barrett to play whatever they liked in the coda. After previewing the song in session, BBC DJ John Peel confessed that he, for one, was baffled by the meaning behind the title. Well, if, as I have suggested elsewhere, the title is a self-conscious reference to The Lovin' Spoonful's 1966 paean to 'Jugband Music', then Barrett was finally ready to take the doctor's advice: 'The doctor said, give him jugband music / It seems to make him feel just fine.'

If Barrett had barely started on the road to recovery from his own acid explorations, by the start of 1968 Pete Townshend had finally unblocked the creative dam that had resulted from kowtowing to the counterculture's 'explore thyself' mantra. Providing a remarkable parallel to Dylan's own experience after his bad acid trip in May 1965, Townshend's poetic way of coming to terms with his post-Monterey burn-out was his own 'piece of vomit about twenty pages long'. And it included passages of scourging self-analysis such as:

> I am alone. More alone in my ignorance now than ever before.
> At least before I thought I knew what life was about . . .
> The darkness of this place is unbelievable.
> It's so dark it clouds my mind. As though this
> Is where nothing only exists. But fear . . .
> Trapped in womb-like darkness, my mind is
> Creating its own lying illusion to save its sanity.
> Here, my mother, here my father, here other
> Reasons to cling to prejudged life as I know it.

Aside from its fair share of similar poetic couplets, it had one persistent refrain:

All the Madmen

Sickness will surely take the mind
Where minds can't usually go
Come on the amazing journey
And learn all you should know.

Dylan, stripping away the verbal vomit, chanced upon 'Like a Rolling Stone'. In Townshend's case, he had come upon his own 'Amazing Journey'. Which would prove to be 'the very first composition for *Tommy*. [Indeed,] *Tommy* was originally going to be called *Amazing Journey*, and this song really summarizes the "plot" of the [original] story.' It would be a largely drug-free voyage of discovery, one designed to realign his own divided self.

2. 1969: Something In the Water

Madness (contrary to most interpretations of 'schizophrenia') is a movement out of familialism *towards autonomy*. This is the real 'danger' of madness and the reason for its violent repression. Society should be one big happy family with hordes of obedient children. One must be mad not to want such an enviable state of affairs.'
– David Cooper, *The Language of Madness*, 1978

I'm only a person with Eskimo chain
I tattooed my brain all the way.
Won't you miss me?
– Syd Barrett, 'Dark Globe', 1969

Pop is a light medium. A pop song about the horrors of war is out of place ... This means that the sick things [on our new album] have a pre-emphasis. We hope that people's preconceptions will get screwed around by this.
– Pete Townshend, May 1969

Hippy ideals had initially precipitated a headlong rush back to childhood, triggered by Lennon's expressed desire to go back there (on the back of another quick flip through the collected works of Lewis Carroll, Edward Lear and Kenneth Grahame). Yet it had apparently not occurred to those bent on regression – Lennon included – that what awaited them there was far more terrifying than anything they'd experienced to date. Or that, to quote another European son, in dreams begin responsibilities. Those English songwriters born to the baby boom generation, the spectre of war, the decline of Empire, protracted postwar rationing and a national struggle to make ends meet, were hoping all such concerns had been washed away by the lysergic tide. But when the tide went out, the racial memories came back.

Such was the subject matter for a series of albums that would define rock music in the year 1969, heralded by perhaps the last album to make it into the shops in 1968, The Pretty Things' *S.F. Sorrow*. One of the bands who ran for cover just as psychedelia's arch collapsed at the end of 1967, The Pretty Things had close ties to Pink Floyd, sharing a record label, producer, booking agent and post-acid transition from r&b combo to psychedelia incarnate (Dave Gilmour even sat in when they performed *S.F. Sorrow* for the first time in thirty years in 1998).

And just like the Floyd, it was in November 1967 that they found out the hard way psychedelia no longer tickled the tastes of a wider audience, in their case by issuing the masterful 'Defecting Grey'. As frontman Phil May explained, 'The character in the song was a defecting grey, i.e. he had found something in his life, which took him out of what was perceived as normal . . . We used to call everybody who did a normal job "greys".' Pieced together from three or four separate song ideas, 'Defecting Grey' was a wildly ambitious ragbag of musical notions. In its original acetate form, it ran to five-and-a-quarter minutes. Much influenced by *musique concrete*, the one thing it was not was commercial. It prompted Chris Welch, an early

Pretties advocate at *Melody Maker*, to lament the very fact that 'groups [like The Pretties] ever discovered that word "progress"'.

Dispirited by this turn of events, The Pretty Things held back from issuing the catchier 'Turn My Head'. Instead, they rush-released 'Talking About the Good Times' as a further stop-gap – to a similarly negligible response from the record-buying public – whilst commencing work on an ambitious year-long project, *S.F. Sorrow*, that would hopefully reinvent the 12" wheel. As singer Phil May informed the *New York Times* just before the album's 1998 reprise: 'I could never understand why an album had to be five A-sides and five B-sides with no connection.'

Based on a short story by May, *S.F. Sorrow* was another work from this heady period to address a troubled childhood in code. It is at the mid-point of the album, as the hero walks the streets trying to come to terms with the death of his fiancée, that he encounters Baron Saturday, who invites Sorrow on a journey, and then, without waiting for his response, 'borrows his eyes', which promptly initiates a trip through the Underworld. The trip – and we are left in no doubt that this is the appropriate term – begins with Sorrow convinced he is flying towards the moon, but it is in fact his own face. The Baron pushes him through the mouth and down the throat, where they come upon a set of doors. Saturday throws them open, showing a room full of mirrors. Each of them displays a memory from Sorrow's childhood, which the Baron suggests he studies. Leaving the hall of mirrors, they come upon a long winding staircase that leads to two opaque mirrors that show Sorrow further ghastly truths from his own life. Sorrow is psychologically decimated by this trip and becomes the loneliest man in the world; a curious conclusion coming from a band that was still popping tabs like they were Smarties.

Unbeknownst to The Pretties, Pete Townshend had also started to construct his own album around a single central character traumatized by experiences from his childhood. But as *S.F. Sorrow* took on a life of its own, The Pretties became increasingly aware that The Who were hard at work on their own ambitious concept album. The difference was that The Pretties were well advanced with theirs, at a time when Townshend was still trying out the storyline on a number of accommodating rock journalists (he later came to feel he'd said 'so much of what I had wanted to say in *Tommy* in print . . . [it actually] made it harder to say musically and get off on it').

The genesis of *S.F. Sorrow* goes back to before the release of *Sgt. Pepper* – i.e. the spring of 1967 – when the media seemed to be suggesting the forthcoming Beatles LP would have more conceptual unity than would prove to be the case, much to the surprise of The Pretties' bassist, Wally Waller, when he finally gave it a spin: 'I heard people tell me about *Sgt. Pepper* before I heard it, [and] it sounded like they had done a story. I mean the words rock opera never occurred to me but I thought they did a story with music. I thought what a brilliant idea, why on earth didn't somebody else think of that? Trust The Beatles to do that. When I got *Sgt. Pepper*, it wasn't that . . . [so] I thought, Why don't *we* do it?'

However, a number of contagions were eating away at The Pretties at a time when they needed all hands to the volume-pump. Their record label, EMI, had lost faith in the band's potential to deliver the goods, and it took producer Norman Smith's wholehearted support to even complete what was in truth a piecemeal project, constructed over some nine months, using other bands' downtime at Abbey Road studios.

Equally unfortunately for The Pretties, they had already used up some of their best melodies on the five songs recorded for singles the previous autumn; while drummer Skip Alan had, by his own admission, 'OD'd on the scene', and wanted out. Just as problematic was Phil May's industrial drug use. His own apposite description of the *S.F. Sorrow* sessions – 'fourteen [sic] months on acid' – says it all. Guitarist Dick Taylor also had his fractured mind on other things and he, too, would quit on its completion. The result was an album no tighter in the way the songs linked together than *Sgt. Pepper*. In fact, though the record purported to relate the life story of a disturbed lad from the cradle to the grave, it required a brief chapter between each song to elucidate the actual storyline. And these were only printed on the sleeve, not recited à la *Ogdens' Nut Gone Flake*.

S.F. Sorrow had another major disadvantage over the album The Who were close to finishing – it couldn't be played live. The only two performances they gave of the finished work, at the Roundhouse in January 1969, billed as 'The Pretty Things in Mime – A new production: *S.F. Sorrow* is Born', were of necessity performed to backing tapes. Nonetheless, when *Tommy* finally appeared in May 1969, there were assorted folk happily pointing out that the first 'rock opera' had been released five months earlier, and it was by The Pretty Things. Initially, even Pete Townshend seemed prepared to own up to certain similarities, telling *Beat Instrumental* three months before his own album's appearance, 'It's fairly similar in format to the Pretty Things' *S.F. Sorrow*, but a little tighter.'

What the author of 'A Quick One, While He's Away' didn't expect was that people would extrapolate from this open admission some kind of thematic debt to its predecessor that simply wasn't there. Although Townshend was some months behind The Pretties in terms of studio time, he was years ahead when it came to stockpiling songs that could work in a 'rock opera' context. And *he* was in no doubt in whose tradition he was really treading:

> **Pete Townshend:** I felt a series of three-minute songs, vignettes, cameos, each one very different, none of them musically related to each other, none of them having shared themes or anything, would be able to tell a story. It was as simple as that . . . There was [also] a sense that what we were thinking of had already happened on *Sgt. Pepper* or *Pet Sounds* or *Ogdens' Nut Gone Flake*. [2004]

The one part of the *Tommy* storyline that could, at a pinch, be said to resemble *S.F. Sorrow* – its 'from the cradle to the grave' arc (or in *Tommy*'s case, from birth to rebirth) – originated with producer Kit Lambert. In fact, it was only introduced after Townshend had already started telling journalists he was 'working on an opera . . . I am thinking of calling it "The Amazing Journey". I've completed some of it . . . The theme is about a deaf, dumb and blind boy who has dreams and sees himself as the ruler of the cosmos.' Townshend, who had a great deal of faith in Lambert's ideas, decided to make *Tommy* an amalgamation of the two conceits:

> **Pete Townshend:** Actually, the overall concept of the new album does come from two ideas that we originally had. The idea I had was of a deaf, dumb and blind boy and his path through life and the simplicity of his thoughts. They were interpreted musically, and all kinds of things happened . . . Then Kit Lambert came up with an equally unreal idea . . . He said he'd like to see us do a new stage show which would be . . . like, The Ages of Man . . . Each one of us would write a song about a certain period of

our life . . . and then we would link them all together . . .
Suddenly, I thought about combining the two ideas. [1969]

Roger Daltrey has himself claimed in a 1994 interview, that 'it
was Kit Lambert's idea to do the full rock opera; and basically
the storyline of *Tommy* – the [whole] holiday camp [thing] – was
more Kit Lambert than Pete Townshend'. If so, it was Lambert
who imposed a lot of *Tommy*'s grandiosity. Reflecting on their
early discussions, Townshend recalls how Kit's 'whole thing
was, "This is opera, y'know?" I used to argue . . . but he'd be,
"No, no, no! This is fucking OPERA!"'

Lambert had actually been pushing Townshend in this direction for some time. As Townshend readily admitted, the original
rock opera, 'A Quick One', had been Kit's idea: 'The whole
concept came from the manager . . . He said . . . "Let's have a
whole track – say, six different numbers – run into each other,
all turning on the same idea."' It was Townshend's idea, though,
to make *Tommy* the story of an abused, disabled kid. And
initially that is all it was:

> **Pete Townshend:** My original conception was that there
> would be a boy, born deaf, dumb and blind, whose parents
> don't really know what to do . . . He gets to the age of
> about seventeen before he's actually cured, but during this
> period they have several operations on him . . . His father
> gets angry one night because the boy won't respond to
> him, and he beats him up . . . Then you get a song written
> by me about what is happening inside the boy. [1969]

'Sparks' and 'Underture' – both musical ideas that predated
the project, in the former's case being demoed as far back as
1966 – were commandeered to the cause even before

Townshend excitedly informed *Rolling Stone* editor Jann Wenner in July 1968: 'The deaf, dumb and blind boy is played by The Who, the musical entity. He's represented musically . . . [first] by a theme which we play, which starts off the opera itself and then [by] a song describing the deaf, dumb and blind boy.' Representing the (still unnamed) boy musically was a key part of Townshend's original concept. 'Sparks' seems to have been the song he intended to convey 'what is happening inside the boy' when his father beats him up, while a (lost) song from Entwistle was supposed to depict things from the father's point of view:

Pete Townshend: His father gets pretty upset that his kid is deaf, dumb and blind. He wants a kid that will play football and God knows what. One night he comes in and he's drunk and he sits over the kid's bed and he . . . starts to talk to him, and the kid just smiles up, and his father is trying to get through to him . . . and he starts to say, 'Can you hear me?' The kid, of course, can't hear him. He's groovin' in this musical thing . . . out of his mind. Then there's his father outside of his body, and this song is going to be written by John . . . this song about the father who is really uptight. The kid won't respond, he just smiles. The father starts to hit him and at this moment the whole thing becomes incredibly realistic. On one side you have the dreamy music of the boy wasting through his nothing life. And on the other you have the reality of the father outside, uptight . . . The father is hitting the kid; musically then I want the thing to break out . . . And the kid doesn't catch the violence. He just knows that some sensation is happening. He doesn't feel the pain . . . He just accepts it. [1968]

At this stage Townshend had yet to formulate an ending more cogent than the very Sixties idea of the boy figuring out a way to 'get over his hangups', thus achieving Laing's 'hyper-sanity'. But by the time Townshend talked to *Beat Instrumental* at the turn of the year he had integrated Lambert's holiday-camp idea, elements of messianism and even that bizarre cipher for rock stardom, becoming a pinball champion[7]. For now, though, the protracted attempts at a cure would come *after* his success as a pinball champion:

> **Pete Townshend:** The central character is a boy who is blind, deaf and dumb . . . People start to notice him when he becomes the first ever pinball champion of the world, and the kids gradually turn him into a sorta superhero. He doesn't give a toss and keeps on playing his pinballs while a religion grows up around him. His family realizes that he's big business and the nastiness moves in – his followers start wearing fascist uniforms and the organization develops. In the meantime they've done all manner of strange things to the boy – like giving him LSD and finding that it has no effect – in an effort to bring him out. The central moment comes when they force him to look in the mirror – the doctor breaks it. That's the moment of revelation. The time-scale of the opera covers the life of the boy from his birth in 1914 . . . The point is that the breaking of the mirror is *now*. [1969]

Townshend, unlike The Pretties, had no shortage of songs already stockpiled, some of which he commandeered to the narrative cause. The ever-changing story was necessarily modified by these songs, and vice-versa. Some of them slipped into the new narrative with relative ease. 'It's a Girl', the reincarnation coda from 'Glow Girl', required only a sex-change. 'Sensation' didn't even need that. However, it was not alone in needing some new words. 'We're Not Gonna Take It', another song 'originally about fascism and phoney leaders' ('You lost us at Sunday school, and the Lord gained us today / We're not gonna take it, nothing will be said'), slipped surprisingly easily into its preordained slot as album-closer once it focused on a false messiah, not a phoney leader:

> **Pete Townshend:** ['We're Not Gonna Take It'] was originally a song about something else entirely, with similar words. It didn't have the 'Listening [to You]' chorus then and . . . was written before *Tommy* was started. The interesting thing is how a person's mind, (my mind), becomes very one-track at certain times. When I decided to put *Tommy* together as an 'opera', I simply amassed all the songs I had, and remarkably about eighty per cent of them fit somewhere. I seemed to have been unconsciously writing on a theme for almost a year without realizing it. [1974]

The songs took over in a way that Townshend soon grasped was more than mere happenstance. He told *Zigzag* in 1971, when writing songs solely to fit a preordained concept, '*Tommy* was long and in the end we were digging about a bit, and so we pulled from all sorts of sources . . . "Joker James" [was] a little thing I'd done years before and never got used. I had a little demo of it, redid the words and there it was, "Sally Simpson" . . . "I'm Free" was written long before *Tommy* was ever thought of . . . It definitely seemed to be something that was happening outside of me. Something was putting it together.'

Townshend still hit a snag, however, in his depiction of child abuse, which remained a central part of the narrative. A paedo-phile uncle was one character he had discussed with Jann Wenner before he had even demoed the album, though he tried to make light of the intended episode: 'The uncle is a bit of a perv, you know. He plays with the kid's body . . . and the boy experiences sexual vibrations, you know, sexual experience, and again it's just basic music, it's interpreted as music and it is nothing more than music. It's got no association with sleazi-ness.' But then he let slip: 'Most of those [kind of] things just come from me.' It was quite a telling remark, though it would take him two more decades to realize just how telling:

> **Pete Townshend:** I think [using the child abuse] was unconscious . . . It's quite possible that when I was with my grandmother, she had a boyfriend who came into my bedroom. I don't know quite what happened, but I've got that far in my mind. I've tried to bring it out through therapy and I've failed. She used to make me call all her boyfriends – and there were several – 'Uncle'. I think that's where it came from. I actually said to John Entwistle, 'I've got this song about a pederastic old uncle and I can't write it. Can you?' [1996]

Entwistle remembered Townshend telling him he had this 'kid called Tommy who was gonna go through all these traumatic experiences with some chick who slips him acid, a homosexual uncle and a bully. He then asked me if I could write songs for the last two because he felt that he couldn't write nearly as nasty as me.' Rather than wondering why the guitarist baulked at his own subject matter, Entwistle simply penned 'Fiddle About' and 'Cousin Kevin' to Townshend's exacting specifica-tions. Townshend was delighted with Entwistle's 'ruthlessly brilliant songs, because they are just as cruel as people can be. [And] I wanted to show that the boy was being dealt with very cruelly . . . he was being dismissed as a freak.'

However, when it came to a song about 'some chick who slips him acid', Townshend didn't need any of the Ox's help. The resultant track, 'The Acid Queen', a highlight of *Tommy*, finally allowed him to address 'the whole drug thing, the drink thing, the sex thing wrapped into one big ball. It's about how you get it laid on you that you haven't lived if you haven't fucked forty birds, taken sixty trips, drunk fourteen pints of beer' – a clear rejection of the mantra that the road of excess ultimately leads to the palace of wisdom even if it involves a protracted truck-stop at a town called Dissipation. For now, Townshend refused to over-analyse where such stuff was coming from. It would be 1991 before he felt compelled to draw some requisite dots:

Pete Townshend: When I wrote it, I saw all this weird shit in there, and I couldn't really explain it. Every time I go back to it I find much more unconscious cohesion in it than I'd imagined . . . when I wrote it . . . I was a very, very clear-cut postwar victim of two people who were married in the war too young, had problems because of the war, so I went to stay with my grandmother, who happened to be off her fucking head . . . [It was only] when I sat down . . . to work on the Broadway [production of] *Tommy*, [that] I finally knew that there was a strong literal autobiographical component. Particularly in the opening scenes, which I hadn't really quite gotten before. Y'know, my father coming back and saying to my mother, 'We have to get back together for the sake of the boy.' So there was this almost metaphorical killing of the lover. It was the first time I'd realized where all this weird shit comes from. Sexual abuse, forcing drugs down children's throats, bullying, power struggles, family lies, family denials, secrets . . . *Tommy* was where I started to see evidence of a troubled childhood. [2004]

Back in 1969, the critics were not in denial, some targeting this very subtext at the time of the album's release. The banner headline to Richard Green's *NME* review condemned The 'Who's Sick Opera', while his actual review suggested that the word 'sick' 'certainly applies' to the material. Not surprisingly, Townshend leapt immediately to his songs' defence, insisting, 'I'm very pleased with the way the album has turned out . . . Sure, the boy is raped and suffers, but we show that instead of being repulsed and sickened, he has the means to turn all these experiences to his own good.' Only with time did he come to accept that a premise in which 'suffering, whether it's self-inflicted or it comes from outside, leads to spiritual growth . . . is actually quite dangerous, because what you're actually . . . saying [is], "Oh, it's okay to abuse children, 'cause they spiritually grow".'

But if Townshend feared that this critical flak might put the kibbosh on the album's commercial chances, he need not have worried. *Tommy* was a smash, especially in America, where the deluxe packaging, complete with twelve-page libretto, seemed to vindicate everything Lambert had argued for so vehemently. Townshend had his 'fucking OPERA' – even if the songwriter still insisted: 'It certainly isn't the same as an accepted opera. It was just a name I used to give some indication of the scope and continuity of *Tommy*. When we perform it, we like to keep the sort of end-of-the-pier feeling.'

Whatever its category, the band now had the very vehicle needed to ignite their powerhouse performances and set

America alight. Trekking across the continent with this rather English tale of redemption, they stopped off at the Woodstock mud-fest, before heading back to Blighty where, during 1969's August Bank Holiday, they performed the entire work to 200,000 hardy Brits who had trekked to the Isle of Wight to see, mostly, Bob Dylan's first full post-accident performance. It had been a long, hard climb but, for now at least, The Who were top of the heap:

> **Pete Townshend:** By the time we got round to that Isle of Wight [Festival] we knew what worked and what you skipped over quickly. It was a great concert for us because we felt so in control of the situation. We were able to just come in, do it and not need to know anything about what was going on . . . We knew we were on to a good thing. [1982]

★

The combination of high-falutin' ideas, cod-mysticism, psychological scars, rasping riffs and maximum r&b may have broken The Who's commercial dam but, as the 1960s wound down, Ray Davies continued swimming against the tide of commercial conformity. Taking precious little heed of any lesson he might have learnt from the muted reception that greeted the generally well-conceived *VGPS*, he was bent on another thematic album, and this one would directly address past hurts.

When *VGPS*'s successor, *Arthur, or The Decline and Fall of the British Empire*, sent The Kinks down what, in commercial terms, was another dead-end street, Davies asserted it was not really his idea. In a 1977 *NME* career overview, he said it came about because 'Granada Television took me out to lunch and said, "We want you to write an opera." I said I would write a musical. They said, "We want it to be The Decline and Fall of

71

the British Empire." I said "I can't do it, but I'll write an album about somebody who lives in a place where everything is crumbling around him."' And in his own 'unauthorized auto-biography' Davies went to some pains to proclaim that *Arthur* originally met with near universal acceptance in The Kinks, camp: 'I knew that *The Village Green* was about the decline of a certain innocence in England, and when I suggested that I go the whole way and write about the decline and fall of the British empire everyone . . . thought that it was the perfect subject matter.' Of course, it had really been *him* pitching the idea to the TV execs. And although they initially gave him the green light, they were never fully convinced – as events were to show.

Perhaps he thought social realism set atop the *fin de siècle* feel of *VGPS* made for a winning formula – *S.F. Sorrow* notwith-standing – and that he could finally get the band back to the position they enjoyed at the time of 'Waterloo Sunset', a perfect storm of critical and commercial acclaim. In fact, he had started thinking again about that song, and 'how the imaginary Julie, who suddenly symbolized England, met my nephew, Terry, on Waterloo Bridge. A reunion of past and future . . . [Then] I thought about Terry's father Arthur, and how his bitterness and sense of betrayal by Britain had forced him to emigrate to Australia to a new life.'

The resultant album would pit family against country, a suburban 'Shangri-La' contrasted with the promise of an Antipodean paradise. Like Sebastian F. Sorrow, Arthur's work-ing life was spent at the Misery Factory, looking for a way out (or, as it says in the album notes, 'Arthur has spent most of his life on his knees, laying carpets'). But it was not Arthur's frustra-tions that would suffuse The Kinks' next album, it was Ray's. As he told biographer Jon Savage, when questioned as to the reasoning behind another 'concept album', '*Arthur* was a labour of love. I was angry with a society that had built me to be factory fodder; I wasn't angry about older people because I could see that they'd been victims of it.'

The new songs certainly teemed with caustic comments on a class system that demanded the compliant attitude of 'Yes Sir, No Sir'. Questioning for the first time why any mother's son needed to fight and die just because 'Mr Churchill Says', Davies poured scorn on that national aspiration for some mock-tudor suburban idyll (and anyone who doubts the sincerity of this Arthurian point of view should remember this man also once said, 'I've got nothing against suburbia other than it destroys people'). In Davies' mind's eye, Arthur's generation had been 'Brainwashed' into believing English society constituted 'one big happy family'. Having previously avoided the 'My Generation' school of social commentary, Davies had become an angry older man. The burning question was, how to address all these issues and still retain a narrative thread strong enough to keep Granada TV firmly engaged?

At least he had a name for the new genre, telling *Record Mirror*, 'I'm writing a pop opera at the moment – I suppose that's the best way of describing it – we're doing it for television, and . . . as our next album.' He was more expansive to *Beat Instrumental*, informing them that the next album would be about 'this chap Arthur [who] hasn't done anything in his life. He's not really lived at all. And the opera concerns a weekend in his life when his son and daughter-in-law stay at his home and the total worthlessness of his life is exposed.' The problem, as Julian Mitchell's perceptive sleevenotes noted, was that 'nothing happens very much – everyone has Sunday dinner together, then Ronnie turns up and the men go to the pub where Ronnie gets all worked up about The System, while Liz and Rose talk about the past'.

Amazingly, Ray was left to get on with the project by the Quaife-less Kinks, the band's management and their increasingly bemused record label. At least his brother was wholly supportive, later calling *Arthur* his 'favourite Kinks album . . . Ray was writing fantastic, sensitive words that were so relevant to what was going on . . . I was really surprised at the response we got to [the] 'Shangri-La' [single]. I thought it was going to be a massive hit.'

But what Davies had devised was never very visual. Even he expressed concerns about its viability as a filmable narrative at the time: '*Arthur* has a story – but the points are made by songs rather than direct actions or dialogue. I suppose it's really more an opera than a musical play. I'm not sure when it'll be screened.' Sure enough, by the time another elegiac Kinks 45 appeared, in September 1969, the TV musical had been 'delayed' permanently. Ray was mortified. All his grand plans had hinged on getting Granada to finance the TV version.

Arthur's abandonment by Granada hit Davies hard. Ever willing to invoke his fine-tuned persecution complex, he subsequently claimed he 'got shafted. [And] our careers hinged on that. I spent a year on that – a year-and-a-half nearly – and [then] it fell through.' Meanwhile, the critical reception for the album, released in October, was coloured by the remarkable success of Townshend's prior conceit. With *Tommy* widely lauded as a significant breakthrough in rock, The Who had beaten The Kinks to the punch. Even Davies begrudgingly admitted: 'We came in for a lot of criticism from people who said we were imitating *Tommy*.' His brother Dave once again feared for his younger sibling's sanity: 'Ray was driving himself into breakdown after breakdown trying to come up with ideas for songs. And . . . I felt that we were doing something original, developing our art. [But] it did absolutely nothing!'

The hasty release of another 45 from the album *Victoria*, merely meant three consecutive single stiffs went with another chartless album. It was time to start rebuilding the brand name; and, perhaps surprisingly, The Kinks decided the place to do that was America, where a three-year live ban by the American Federation of Musicians had finally been lifted. At the same time, *VGPS* and *Arthur* were being championed by the hip young rock critics who were writing for the likes of *Rolling Stone*, *Crawdaddy*, *Fusion* and *Creem*. Following the lead of his brother-in-law, Arthur, Ray had decided 'he loved the old country so much he didn't want to stay around to watch it disintegrate'. And it seemed like only a really big hit would bring them back home, which in autumn 1969 looked a long way off.

*

Davies' disillusionment with the pop process was directly related to the English public's rejection of the two rather fine albums with which he had tried to resume that compact with the charts The Kinks effortlessly enjoyed through 1967.

Meanwhile, another overtly English songwriter, David Bowie, had spent the past five years trying to emulate Davies' initial chart success, and was just finding out that fame was not all it was cracked up to be. As 1969 dawned, he was hard at work on a series of demos with which he hoped to secure a record deal with Mercury. The year ended with the release of his second album, again unhelpfully called *David Bowie*; it singularly failed to capitalize on the Top Five success of the single that both preceded and introduced it, the unearthly 'Space Oddity'.

After five years of trying every which way to connect with some kind of audience on an emotional level, Bowie had written a song about alienation – in the immediate aftermath of his break-up with long-term girlfriend, Hermione Farthingale

– and discovered emotional resonance had been there all along. Of course, as soon as the song charted he began a career-long attempt to suggest otherwise, though not before telling part-time rebound-girlfriend Mary Finnegan, then freelancing for the *International Times*, 'Major Tom, the hero, anti-hero if you like, is a loser . . . At the end of the song Major Tom is completely emotionless and expresses no view at all about where's he at . . . He gives up thinking completely . . . He's fragmenting . . . At the end of the song his mind is completely blown.'

By making the lyrics to 'Space Oddity' an increasingly fraught dialogue between the astronaut and 'ground control' Bowie personalized Major Tom's sense of separation from the world. And while on the original January 1969 demo it is fellow Feather, John 'Hutch' Hutchinson, who intones the parts of the lyrics that are 'ground control' talking, on the single Bowie sings both parts, suggesting a more interior type of conversation, heightening the sense of someone whose 'mind is completely blown'.

Although Bowie had spent the past two-and-a-half years celebrating eccentrics in song, this was the first time he had dared to make the narrator's mental breakdown the crux of one. Yet he already knew all about the subject, having been born into a family where on one side schizophrenia was, not to put too fine a point on it, endemic. Aunt Una had died in her late thirties after electric shock treatment and periods in a mental institution. Aunt Vivienne had also been diagnosed with schizophrenia, while Aunt Nora had been lobotomized to 'treat' her 'nervous disposition'. And now Bowie's half-brother Terry was showing enough worrying signs to suggest insanity did not so much run in his mother's family as positively gallop. By the end of 1969, Terry would be committed to the Cane Hill asylum, where he would see out most of his days.

The alienation expressed in 'Space Oddity' was further

compounded by its apocalyptic B-side, the equally dissociative 'Wild-Eyed Boy from Freecloud'. In the notes to the songs on *David Bowie* – printed by *Disc* at the time of its release – Bowie summarizes this, his first 'prophet figure' as someone who 'lives on a mountain and has developed a beautiful way of life . . . [but] the villagers disapprove of the things he has to say and they decide to hang him. He gives [himself] up to his fate, but the mountain tries to help him by killing the village.' In other words, it not only addressed messianism but also a very personal sense of separation from the wider world, which in a 1993 BBC radio interview Bowie finally admitted was something that could be traced all the way back to his childhood: 'This feeling of isolation I've had ever since I was a kid, [but] was really starting to manifest itself through songs like ['Wild-Eyed Boy . . .'].'

Slowly but surely the young man was learning to put a truer, deeper self into his songs, something not lost on his latest love, Angie Barnett, whom he had chanced to meet through a mutual bisexual liaison. As she says in her most recent memoir: 'When I met David, the paranoid vision and the language of life's darkness were second nature to him. "Space Oddity", "Wild-Eyed Boy from Freecloud" – that's how he really thought about the world.'

'Conversation Piece', his next exposition on isolation ('And the world is full of life / Full of people who don't know me . . .'), was another song he demoed along with 'Space Oddity'. He also made it the first song recorded for the album that he hoped would reinforce the reputation he'd recently gained. For now, though, he preferred to lament the loss of ex-girlfriend Hermione, and in passing the ideals of the Summer of Love, thus producing an album that sat uneasily between two stools of (singer-)songwriting – the confessional and the character-driven.

As a result, this superb song was sidelined to B-side status on the throwaway 'Prettiest Star' (an oversight Bowie almost corrected in 2000, when he re-recorded the song for the aborted *Toy* album[8]). Meanwhile, he artfully constructed a partly fictional potted biography for the press release to accompany the November 1969 release of *David Bowie* (a.k.a. *Man of Words, Man of Music*), hoping to explain away a two-and-a-half-year hiatus between albums and the attendant change in him. It would be the first of many fabricated pasts bestowed by Bowie on credulous critics:

[Age] 20 – Dropped out of music completely and devoted most of my time to the Tibet Society

– Helped get the Scottish monastery underway

21 – Acted, wrote and produced with mime company

21 1/2 – Formed own mime, music, mixed media trio

21 3/4 – Fell in love

22 – Solo again and making an L.P., for Phillips

– Started Arts Lab in Beckenham, Kent, to try and promote the ideals and creative processes of the underground.

At least he was being upfront about the Arts Lab, which was a genuine attempt to 'promote the ideals and creative processes of the underground', though by the time of the album's appearance it had pretty much run its course, as the only other real talents to emerge from its weekly sessions at the Three Tuns pub – the enigmatic Keith Christmas and acid-folk combo Comus – had gone in search of their own record deals. As record producer Tony Visconti told one Bowie biographer: 'His Arts Lab . . . was his way of buying time and sharpening a few skills when important people weren't looking.' But when the new *David Bowie* appeared in the shops he was forced to decide (with a little help from Angie) what mattered most – his own career or aiding perennial underachievers.

By November 1969, young David knew he had an album he needed to promote – even if his new record label, Phillips, seemed to think *David Bowie* would promote itself, as evidenced by their unpersuasive press ad: 'Now Try His Album . . . You'll Want It!' However, the space cadet simply wasn't ready. An important gig at the Purcell Room went badly, leading Bowie to recall: 'As soon as I appeared, looking a bit like Bob Dylan with his curly hair and denims, I was whistled at and booed . . . It turned me off the business. I was totally paranoid and I cut out.' In fact, according to the manager of Comus, Bowie's chosen support-act that night, the singer-songwriter was blown off the stage by his fellow lab-rats from Beckenham:

Chris Youle: Bowie was . . . the folkie, doing Jacques Brel ballads. We were the underground oddballs writing songs about necrophilia, crucifixion, madness – there wasn't anything like that in Bowie's repertoire at the time. So we went down really well at the Purcell Room. He didn't.

Actually, the audience at the Purcell Room proved remarkably forgiving of the solo Bowie, even after he apologized upfront that his repertoire was mostly his own songs, which he disarmingly admitted, 'sound all very much the same'. The one national reviewer to cover the show – the influential Tony Palmer, writing in the *Observer* – offered some astute advice for the pretty young thing: 'His love reveries are dreary, self-pitying and monotonous. But when he turns his eyes to the absurdities of technological society, he is razor-sharp in his observations.'

It was advice Bowie eventually did take on board (along with Comus's whole *schtick*). But at this stage, still consumed by fear of failure, and with his greatest supporter, his father, recently deceased, he was looking for an excuse to drop out again. And the Purcell show provided it. When he asked his ever-supportive manager, Kenneth Pitt, 'Which papers were here tonight?' and was erroneously informed that not one single journalist had turned up, he said in a loud voice, there on stage, 'Fuck it.'

And fuck it, he did. Over the next six months he did everything he could to sabotage the hard-won success he'd finally achieved with 'Space Oddity'. Even before Phillips issued the follow-up to that major hit, he was telling teen-mag *Jackie*, 'I hate the chart system. I think whether anyone has talent as a performer should be more important than whether or not they have a hit disc.' As for the prospect of further singles, he informed *Mirabelle* that he hoped the two albums due for release – the second of which was a *World of* . . . compilation of earlier Decca tracks, including three songs rejected back in 1968 – 'go well because I really don't want to have to do another single. They're really not worth the bother and time.' At one point, he was even considering putting out a re-recording of one of the previously rejected 45s from 1968, 'London Bye Ta-Ta', as his next single, before he was persuaded to plump for 'The Prettiest Star'.

Not yet surrounded by figures for whom success was measured in units alone, Bowie elected to turn his back on the charts before they turned their back on him. He would talk about the choice he made back then – similar to the one Dylan took in May 1965 – during a 1974 interview with *NME*'s Charles Shaar Murray. Speaking from a position of real (and enduring) stardom, he suggested: 'When "Space Oddity" became a hit, that was when I really started . . . [to] see how needs are achieved

– all the human needs and wants, and trying to be this and that. [And I found] there's no gratification in it.'

★

Perhaps in the interim Bowie had acquired an understanding of why his great inspiration, Syd Barrett, had opted out at the end of 1967. By 1974, each of them had certainly learnt that when one wanted back in – which Barrett did by spring 1969, and Bowie did by autumn 1971 – it usually proved easier said than done. By 7 June 1969, when a letter appeared in *Melody Maker* asking why the Barrett solo LP 'promised over a year ago, [hasn't] been released yet', it had been eighteen months since Syd had been hoofed out of 'his band'. Remarkably, this letter provoked a reply from the man himself, who claimed: 'There have been complications regarding the LP, but it is now almost finished and should be issued by EMI in a few months. I now spend most of my time writing.'

These new songs, though, were no longer the cosmic fairy tales of a pie-eyed piper. Rather, they tried to make sense of a world that lost its sense of purpose even before he had scrambled it some more with his own form of self-medication. As for those 'complications' he hinted at in *Melody Maker*, according to the EMI producer who had just spent two months working with him, it all dated back to the 1968 sessions and involved 'broken microphones in the studios and [mutterings of] general disorder . . . This had resulted in a period when, if not actually banned, Syd's presence at Abbey Road wasn't particularly encouraged.'

This unexpected response to a fan's open letter seemed like the first public clue that Syd was emerging from his own 'awful scene'. But the real return dated back to a night at the end of March, when he turned up at the 100 Club to see his old pals Soft Machine play. And afterwards, he even said hi. As bassist

Hugh Hopper recalls it: 'Syd was muttering away in his usual way and said, "Would you like to come along and do some recording?"' They assumed, not unreasonably, that he had some specific idea in mind.

What Barrett actually had planned was to take up where he had left off nine months earlier. In fact, it was almost as if there had been no break at all. When he turned up at Abbey Road on 10 April for his first session of the year, with in-house producer Malcolm Jones at the helm, the two songs he recorded were the very ones he had been working on the previous July when the sessions had ground to an abrupt halt – now he duly overdubbed new vocals and guitar onto the Jenner-produced basic tracks for 'Swan Lee' and 'Clowns and Jugglers'. If Jones was worried whether this suggested Syd had nothing new to bring to the party, the following day's session shook any such thoughts from his mind. As he wrote in his privately published diary of the sessions: 'Syd was in a great mood and in fine form, a stark contrast to the rumours and stories I'd been fed with. In little over five hours we laid down vocal and guitar tracks for four new songs and two old. At Syd's request, the first thing we did was "Opel". We both felt at the time it was one of his best new songs . . . It had a stark attraction to it.'

Perhaps Jenner hadn't been quite so crazy in hoping that if one 'did the right things [Syd] would come back to join us'. On the evidence of the 11 April 1969 session – which resulted in pukka takes of 'Opel', 'Love You', 'It's No Good Trying' and 'Terrapin' (in a single take); as well as usable vocal takes for 'Late Night' and 'Golden Hair' – it did seem as if Syd had indeed been spending time writing songs. And what he had was worth hearing. Both 'Terrapin' and 'Opel' were old-school Barrettian exemplars of elliptical wordplay, set to melodies one could not hope to hum. 'Terrapin', with its startling image, 'We're the fishes and . . . the move about is all we do', suggested he continued to see things in a way few others did, even as he pleaded for understanding from this woman who set his hair on end. Meanwhile, 'Opel' begins by almost parodying a *Piper*-era Floyd lyric, 'On a distant shore, miles from land / Stands the ebony totem in ebony sand', but quickly dissolves into a painful interior quest where you is I, is another – defining itself with its own, increasingly desperate coda, 'I'm living, I'm giving, to find you.'

A further session, six days later, added two lesser songs to the mix – 'No Man's Land' and 'Here I Go'. Barrett now had enough for an album without resorting to Floyd leftovers (though 'Here I Go' was technically another pre-*Piper* song recast). He also seemed to have formulated a sound that allowed for a mixture of band performances (the two 17 April songs being cut with Jerry Shirley and John Wilson as rhythm section) and starker solo pieces, i.e. elements of 'Jugband Blues', now separate and distinct.

On 25 April, he compiled an eight-track 'master' (from original four-track tapes) of the eight songs he was looking to overdub and/or mix. Excluded from this 'master' were the two songs he'd cut on 17 April, presumably because they were already in the requisite form. Three of these tracks Barrett dubbed to a reference reel for himself – 'Terrapin', 'Clowns and Jugglers' and 'Love You' – which he took with him at the end of the session. He had supervised the transfers himself as Jones was ill; and when he returned to the studio on 3 May, it was to supervise laying some backing over certain tracks, specifically the ones he had taken home with him. None of this conforms to the common portrait of a man at odds with the requirements of making an album. In fact, it rather suggests someone on a mission to finally complete a solo album 'promised over a year ago'.

Nor had Barrett forgotten about his old friends from Soft

Machine. On 3 May they were finally summoned to Abbey Road for one of the stranger episodes from the Softs' own rollercoaster career – their one session with Madcap Syd. Because of the erratic tempos of the solo recordings to which they were expected to play along, some of the Softs had a hard time of it. Mike Ratledge complained to Barrett's most recent biographer: 'Nothing was ever written down. Nothing was ever the same. I wouldn't have minded if it was uniformly irregular, but it changed from take to take' – quite an achievement when one considers he was overdubbing to an existing basic track.

Barrett's own suggestions hardly helped, being no more transparent than the songs' nebulous structures. After one take, he apparently opined, 'Perhaps we could make the middle darker and maybe the end a bit more middle-afternoonish. At the moment, it's too windy and icy.' Ever an artist who relied on first impressions, it seems Barrett wanted the Softs' first impressions, too. Which, as long as one went along with his rationale, could make for the kind of rewarding experience drummer Robert Wyatt remembered it being: 'Working with Syd Barrett's a piece of cake. I found him courteous and friendly . . . Almost too easy . . . So easy going that you didn't necessarily know what he wanted, or whether he was pleased with it or not, because he seemed quite pleased with what[ever] you did.'

Among the songs the Softs worked on that May day was *The Madcap Laughs*' centrepiece, 'Clowns and Jugglers' (a.k.a. 'Octopus') – one line of which, 'The madcap laughed at the man on the border', would give the album its title. It was a song Barrett had been working on since at least the previous July, striving to say what he wanted with a minimum of verbiage. The song even recast a line from John Clare's 'Fairy Things' ('Wineglasses . . . to the very rim / Are filled with little mystic shining seed' he transmuted into, 'Clover, honey pots and mystic shining feed'), suggesting he had been reading one first-rate poet who continued to produce poetry from the madhouse. 'Clowns and Jugglers', originally demoed with Jenner, was now recast as the syllogical extension of that 'Jugband Blues' mind-set, its dissonant discords mirroring the thirst for life's purpose in those madrigal lyrics:

> The winds they blew and the leaves did wag
> They'll never put me in their bag
> The raging seas will always seep
> So high you go, so low you creep
> The wind it blows in tropical heat
> The drones they throng on mossy seats
> The squeaking door will always squeak
> Two up, two down, we'll never meet
> Please leave us here
> Close our eyes to the octopus ride!

Barrett had probably hoped to record a hefty chunk of the album with his old friends from the U-Fo. He would hint as much during an interview with Michael Watts in the spring of 1971, during which his disjointed conversation occasionally strayed from and returned to the same internal illogics as the *Madcap* songs. Thinking back to halcyon days, he responded, 'All that time . . . you've just reminded me of it. I thought it was good fun. I thought the Soft Machine were good fun. They were playing on *Madcap*.'

However, the *Madcap* EMI eventually released overlooked Syd and the Softs' *pièce de résistance*, 'Clowns and Jugglers', for a less Barrettian recrafting. And the session that was supposed to follow the one with Soft Machine, which was scheduled for further overdubs, at the last minute became a solo session as Barrett himself decided he would put the finishing touches to three more songs – 'Terrapin' included. Still with a good balance of solo and band performances, he could now begin compiling the album 'promised over a year ago'. But for some reason he didn't do this. A rough mix tape of some eight tracks *was* made on 6 May, but it was clearly not an intended sequence.

In fact, what happened next is still mired in controversy forty years later. It would appear that Syd still felt there was something missing. As he told Giovanni Dadomo on the album's release, 'I wanted [*Madcap*] to be a whole thing that people would listen to all the way through, with everything related and balanced, the tempos and moods offsetting each other.' And though he was reluctant to use anything he'd recorded with his former band, it seems he *did* want some reference point that connected to those 'tempos and moods'. As such, he decided to go see how Floyd were getting on without him, and to ask ex-Jokers Wild guitarist Dave Gilmour if he might lend a hand.

On 30 May, Barrett thus trundled down to Croydon's Fairfield Hall to see the 1969 Floyd. The previous month they had debuted their first post-Barrett performance-piece, the portentous *The Massed Gadgets of Auximines – More Furious Madness from Pink Floyd*, which was performed a couple more times over the next six months. But the show that Syd saw was a standard 1969 set, featuring just two songs from his tenure, 'Astronomy Domine' and 'Interstellar Overdrive'.

After the show he asked Gilmour (and possibly Waters) to help him complete his own, overdue album. Malcolm Jones, who had worked so hard to make Syd's album a realization, insists there was no conflict of interest: 'I never felt any sense of being ousted from my role as producer . . . When Dave came to me and said that Syd wanted him and Roger to do the remaining parts of the album, I acquiesced . . . [But] I still feel that there was enough already made to complete an album.'

Over the years, Gilmour has repeatedly given the impression that a lot more work was required to complete *The Madcap Laughs* than was ever the case. The eight tracks transferred on 25 April were all but an album in the can. Barrett was looking for the icing on his individual nutcake, which his May 1969 comment to *Melody Maker*'s correspondent that 'it is now almost finished' affirms. At some point, though, Gilmour decided to assume a grander role. Perhaps he simply failed to appreciate how much worthy material was already in EMI's London tape-vault.

Gilmour, it seems, made only the most cursory perusal of this previous body of tapes, which is perhaps why he came to the conclusion that a whole second side was needed to bulk up the album. He later typified the result as one side that 'was six months' work, [while] the other tracks we did in two-and-a-half days. [But] some of those songs . . . could have really been fantastic.' Some already were. By the 1980s, he seemed to be conflating his experience of working on *both* Barrett albums. Ostensibly describing *The Madcap Laughs*, he claimed he was 'trying to make sense of it with varying degrees of success. At least we got the album out – EMI had spent a lot of money on something it thought wasn't going to happen.'

In truth, as in-house producer Malcolm Jones has confirmed, 'There was enough already made to complete an album.' Gilmour and Waters hijacked Barrett's album, not just taking it away from Jones, but from Syd himself. How complicit Barrett was in this decision it is impossible to say at this distance. He did record a lot of new material at the two sessions Gilmour supervised, as well as reworking songs he already had in a releasable state (as confirmed by the ultimate inclusion of 'Clowns and

Jugglers', 'Swan Lee', and the original 'Golden Hair' on the 1988 archival release *Opel*).

In fairness to Gilmour, his first session with Barrett on 12 June, witnessed by The Pretty Things' Phil May, can be termed a success. May, who accompanied Gilmour to the session, found it 'exciting because Syd still had enough of the plot to be musically exciting . . . [even if] it was absolutely pointless trying to regiment him into any rehearsals or such like'. With just Gilmour there interpreting the worth of the material, Barrett spent the first part of the session reprising two songs already captured alive and kicking: 'Clowns and Jugglers', now trimmed of a verse and retitled 'Octopus', and the Joycean 'Golden Hair'.

Barrett then produced two new songs, both ideal additions to the album, 'Long Gone' and the luminous 'Dark Globe', the latter a perfect coda to the Jones and Jenner material. However, even after this genuinely productive session, Gilmour was still not inclined to build the album around the wealth of material already recorded, most of which he had had no hand in. Instead, he and Barrett returned to Abbey Road six weeks later for one final session. And this time Roger Waters 'and his impenetrable leer' were *in situ*, too. According to Gilmour, the co-producers' technique that day involved 'Roger and I [sitting] down with him, after listening to all his songs at home, and say[ing], "Syd, play this one, Syd, play that one."'

But on this inauspicious day Barrett was in one of his strange moods. It could well be that the presence of Waters – supposedly at his request – genuinely freaked him out. Or the well had simply run dry again. But what is sure is that Roger Waters, by turning up for a single day's work, gained a co-production credit on an album into which his creative input verged on the non-existent; and on which his one definable contribution was to ensure that, although the 26 July session was essentially a bust, of the five songs cut that day, four made it on to the album – even though Barrett self-evidently had nothing left in the tank.

A retake of 'Dark Globe' with a double-tracked vocal that heightened Syd's dissociative approach to vocalizing didn't work, and was quickly scrapped in favour of the version cut at the previous session. 'Long Gone', a marginal improvement on the earlier version, got the nod. But the next three songs – 'She Took a Long Cold Look', 'Feel' and 'If It's in You' – all recorded in quick succession, came dangerously close to sending up the whole Mr Madcap myth that was already starting to take hold. Astonishingly, Gilmour and Waters decided to use all three takes, including a painfully off-key false start to 'Feel' as part of some *audio vérité* thing they had going on in their heads – and bugger any perception of an artist careening out of control it would engender, or reinforce. Even more than three decades on, they continue to defend their original decision-making:

Roger Waters: We wanted something real, like when Joe Cocker's voice cracks at the end of 'You're So Beautiful'. It's *so* full of feeling. [2002]

Dave Gilmour: Perhaps we were trying to show what Syd was really like . . . perhaps we were trying to punish him . . . [But] I wanted him to come across as a jester, not as stark, raving mad. [2002]

Pressed to explain himself at another juncture, Gilmour would claim that the intention all along was 'to inject some honesty into it, to try and explain what was going on. We didn't want to appear cruel, but . . . we were digging around for stuff to put on the album.' Actually, we know full well that this last statement is patently untrue. The fact that neither 'Swan Lee' nor

'Opel' were shortlisted for *The Madcap Laughs*, yet 'Feel' and 'If It's in You' made the cut, still beggars belief.

Purportedly pressed for time, with EMI supposedly breathing down their necks, Gilmour and Waters proceeded to spend two-and-a-half months tinkering with songs already fit for use, ensuring the album missed its pre-Christmas slot. The result was an album that for all its intermittent brilliance lacked balance; one where 'tempos and moods' did not always offset each other. Neither of the other producers who had relinquished the chair thought much of the choices Gilmour and Waters made on Barrett's behalf:

> **Malcolm Jones:** The false starts to the tracks that I had personally supervised were far more interesting than those left in the final album. They certainly would have been more of a candid insight to the atmosphere of the sessions and less detrimental to Syd's abilities than the ones left in. Those left in show Syd, at best, out of tune, which he rarely was, and at worst as out of control (which, again, he never was).

> **Peter Jenner:** No disrespect to Dave and Roger, who were trying to do something good, but it wasn't what I heard in the studio, and it was a shadow of the Syd I knew.

Barrett himself simply seems to have relinquished any control over the finished product, letting his erstwhile co-workers do their worst. Malcolm Jones thinks Barrett convened with Gilmour on 6 October to approve the final running order, but even if he did – and I find it hard to believe that a *compos mentis* Barrett would have approved the artefact as is – the album he okayed put the 26 July three-song verité segue on side one. Only at the last minute were the sides swapped around, so that the abiding memory at record's end, for this listener at least, became the caterwauling false start before 'Feel'.

It is hard not to conclude that Barrett's one-time friends ended up amplifying his mood swings at the sessions, while placing the blame for the album's failure squarely at Syd's door. Even now Gilmour feels that 'it was important that some of Syd's state of mind should be present in the record – to be a document of Syd at that moment'. Malcolm Jones vehemently disagrees: 'When I first heard the finished product it came as a shock. This wasn't the Syd of two or three months ago. I felt angry. It's like dirty linen in public and very unnecessary and unkind . . . I fail to see how the sound of pages being turned can do anything for Syd, I fail to see the point.'

With the album's release now delayed until the new year, November saw the release of the recast 'Octopus' on 45. Having hoped for an album in which 'everything [was] related and balanced', Barrett in interview merely expressed a 'hope [that] that is what it sounds like'. When pushed, though, he admitted, 'I don't listen to it much.' An album which had required four producers and almost a year-and-a-half of sessions, and had been recorded between the bouts of inertia that could at any time consume Barrett, was reheated in this lukewarm guise by the very folks who had driven him from 'his band' in the first place. And Gilmour seems to have been as compliant as Syd when it came to allowing Waters to release 'proof' that he had been right all along to push for Barrett's removal from the band; while in the end the public got the *Madcap* it had been prepped to expect. In that sense, at least, Waters warranted his co-producer credit.

*

But then the era when producers pushed the record button, and told a band when another take was required, were long gone. The new breed of producers were determined to impose themselves on the process at almost any cost. And the producer least like a wallflower on the London scene of the late 1960s was a figure who some moons ago had made his name producing the first Pink Floyd single, 'Arnold Layne', and could, in December 1969, still lay claim to being the most sympathetic producer with whom Syd Barrett ever worked. Joe Boyd had abandoned psychedelia after his experience with the Floyd and the club he ran largely for their benefit, U-Fo. By the summer of 1967 he was busy assembling the finest roster of English singer-songwriters ever contained under a single management/production roof, Witchseason. Sole proprietor, J. Boyd.

By the time Gilmour and Waters were making a right royal mess of Syd's solo debut, Boyd was preparing for imminent release the debut LP of another quintessentially damaged English artist, the maudlin Nick Drake. Unlike Barrett, whom Boyd knew before he started 'jeopardizing the wires that held everything together in [his] mind', Drake was already monosyllabic by the time the pair first met in May 1968. The statuesque Anthea Joseph, who kept the whole Witchseason operation running, remembers him arriving at the office, 'this tall, thin, very beautiful man . . . who didn't speak'.

The album in question, *Five Leaves Left*, had taken almost as long to complete as *The Madcap Laughs*. Despite work starting in June 1968, the album only finally appeared in September 1969, largely because of a somewhat ad hoc approach to recording. As Boyd said in 1986, 'I just kept throwing ideas at him or throwing him in the studio with various different people, and sometimes he would respond and sometimes he wouldn't.' Throughout it all, Boyd remained convinced that the Cambridge undergraduate could do for the English singer-songwriter what Leonard Cohen had recently done for the North American, creating a series of albums that would find a home in every student bedsit room in the land. His assistant at Witchseason, on the other hand, was not entirely sure album #1 would ever appear:

Anthea Joseph: The first album took ages. Ages. It went on for months . . . What I always felt was that Nick would sort of pack up mentally, so you had to stop. There was no point in trying to push it, because you weren't going to get any further.

Drake, neither the most gifted songwriter (that would be Richard Thompson) nor the most gifted singer (Sandy Denny) on Boyd's exclusive roster, certainly had a style all his own and, like Cohen, it was rolled out ready to be captured the first time he appeared at Boyd's office with a crude reel of demos in his long-fingered, tobacco-stained hands. If it seemed as if he had come out of nowhere, in a sense he had. Drake had led a cocooned existence for almost all of his privileged life, which seemed to be heading down its preordained path – from prep school to Marlborough, and then to Cambridge – when he and a friend took time out, pre-college, to spend a heady season (or two) not so much *en Enfer*, but rather the France memorialized by Rimbaud, Verlaine and Baudelaire.

It was the spring of 1967, and Drake was learning all about the young Rimbaud, who had come to Paris a century earlier an ingénue degenerate and began almost immediately drinking absinthe and writing illuminated script. And just as the youthful Drake began an intense course of reading these French poets, he immersed himself in the blues of Robert Johnson, the great shaman of the Mississippi Delta who, legend says, sold his soul to the devil at the crossroads in exchange for unearthly powers suddenly and mysteriously acquired. At the time, Drake could only dream of such things – and smoke copious amounts of 'weed' in the hope that it would somehow invoke some dormant Rimbaudian and/or Johnsonian self. The young female song-writer Robin Frederick, whom he met on that trip, would subsequently write about the Drake she encountered there:

> 'When I knew him, Nick had not written a single song; he played blues guitar with exceptional fluidity, but there was nothing to indicate that he had unusually great ability or talent . . . Nick would appear at odd hours of the night at the door of my flat. I'd let him in and we'd pass the time playing songs for each other. He stared at the wall or the floor or into the fire. So did I.'

For now, Drake was just another lovelorn soldier from the army of would-be bedsit poets for whom Leonard Cohen sang his songs. But his influences were already more eclectic than most of his cannabis-toking contemporaries, and along with the French symbolists, he was digesting Dostoevsky, Blake and the war poets, while musical influences were just as likely to be favourites of his parents (such as Bach) as those folk-rock lynch-pins Dylan, Donovan and Phil Ochs. While in Aix-en-Provence, Drake would play Bach Brandenburg concertos repeatedly on the cheap gramophone he and his friend Jeremy invested in. The same set would be on the more expensive turntable at his bedside the night he died, seven short years later.

But the album that really drew Drake tightly to its solipsistic self through 1967 was an obscure offering recorded in London in the summer of 1965 by an American singer-songwriter friend of Paul Simon's, Jackson Frank. Recorded in two afternoons, the self-titled ten-song set was the only record Frank would release in his lifetime (a start was made on a second album in 1975, only for Frank to confront solid walls of disinterest and another writer's block).

Chronically self-conscious, Frank remembered 'hiding behind a screen while I was singing and playing, because . . . I didn't want anyone to see me'. But before Frank's album was even in the shops, its producer, Paul Simon, was already planning a return to the States. Frank, meanwhile, began a serious relationship with another fledgling folkie, then training to be a nurse, the nubile Sandy Denny (who briefly became pregnant by him). At the same time, he started booking acts for the music club Les Cousins, known as singer-songwriter central for any West End folkie looking for a gig. While there, he befriended the likes of John and Beverley Martyn, John Renbourn and Bert Jansch.

However, Frank was already in the grip of psychological problems dating back to when he was eleven and a furnace at school blew up and nearly killed him, scarring him for life both mentally and physically. By the time Drake began to learn the songs of Jackson Frank, the American had returned to New York, hoping to find and renew his friendship with Simon. He never did, and soon he was wandering the streets homeless, suffering from what was clearly undiagnosed schizophrenia, until he was finally institutionalized[9]. Meanwhile, the likes of Denny, Jansch and Martyn continued to talk about Frank and sing his songs, making that soon-deleted eponymous debut a reverently whispered soundtrack to the English singer-songwriter boom.

None of this was known to Drake at the time. And yet he was playing no less than four songs from that singular longplayer: 'Milk and Honey' and 'Blues Run the Game', both popularized by Denny and others in the Cousins crowd; the almost Johnsonesque 'Here Comes the Blues', which Aussie folkie Ross Grainger recalled being still part of Drake's repertoire in autumn 1969; and the traditional 'Kimbie', Drake's home-demo that unmistakeably mimics Frank's one-off interpretation. All of these he faithfully transposed on to his trusty reel-to-reel in the months after returning from France.

Something of Frank's tortured personality had evidently possessed Drake. And such was Frank's baleful influence that, when Drake wrote his first documented original song, 'Princess of the Sand', in the summer of 1967, it was a barely disguised musical adaptation of 'Milk and Honey'. And assuming that Robin Frederick was the princess who 'moved her mouth but there came no sound', as seems likely, the song was also the first in a series of chaste idealizations of women he just couldn't bring himself to know biblically. Drake's family, unconversant with Frank or Frederick, were greatly impressed by the new-born songwriter who returned from his summer sojourn ready, or so they thought, to prepare for a university education amid Cambridge's lofty spires. His actress sister, Gabrielle, remembers how 'he came home from Aix-en-Provence, [and] in the drawing room he played mum and dad and me "Princess of the Sand", and a couple of other songs. I thought, "Gosh, he's become a fully fledged writer."'

In fact, such was that initial outpouring of original songs that at least an album's worth of titles fell by the wayside before Drake even began recording his debut platter, a year hence. 'Blue Season', 'Joey in Mind', 'Mickey's Tune', 'Outside', 'Leaving Me Behind', 'Blossom', 'Bird Flew By', 'My Love Left with the Rain', 'Princess of the Sand (Strange Meeting II)' and 'To the Garden' were all songs he reserved for the family-home tapes and/or exercise-book of lyrics, which he began filling in the first flush of enthusiasm for his own songs and maintained to the bitter end.

The nature of these songs only serves to bolster Anthea Joseph's contention that 'when he started seriously writing songs, and Joe acquired him, it was too late, the damage was [already] done. The growth wasn't there – the intellectual growth in songwriting terms.' There were already disturbing undertones to many of the songs that now poured forth. 'Bird Flew By', one of the songs he committed to reel, took the traditional image of 'the wind and the rain', and made them complicit in a world-weary compact: 'The wind and the rain shook hands again / Untouched by the world, they managed to stay sane . . .', while the song's chorus regularly repeated an imponderable query, 'What's the point of a year / Or a season?'

Elsewhere, too, the changing of the seasons would often as not permeate these songs, invariably imbued with a self-conscious, almost Keatsian melancholy. In 'My Love Left With the Rain', the burden repeats the message: 'This was our season, but sorrow waited round the bend.' 'Blue Season' goes further still, the 'you' chastized in the lyric being another 'I' in disguise: 'Everything's wrong and you know you're to blame / Nothing will change while you're still the same.'

Such defeatism remains a consistent motif in these early lyrics, which is somewhat surprising coming from someone so young and privileged. In 'Outside', which survives only as a lyric, he already envisages the likelihood that he will end up defeated by the world, even as he celebrates his new-found poetic sensibility: 'Going to find a word / Make myself be heard / But if the world is too loud / I'll be home from the crowd / Keep it soft inside, if it's strange outside.' Perhaps the strongest premonition of failure, though, can be found in a 'lost' verse from 'River Man', one of the finer songs with which he announced himself on *Five Leaves Left*. In its fuller, original guise, it caught the sound of beating wings of mortality:

> Betty fell behind awhile,
> Said she hadn't time to smile,
> Or die in style.

But still she tries.

Said her time was growing short,

Hadn't done the things she ought . . .

Arriving at Cambridge in September 1967, the collegiate Drake proved just as hard to pin down as the man who wrote such lyrics. Fellow student Brian Wells, who got closer than most, remembers how, in the middle of a convivial evening with 'friends', 'he would get up and go; because you got the impression that he thought it was uncool to stay there and get pissed, or whatever'. To many there, he remained throughout his short tenure a slightly spectral figure. His college tutor described him as 'pleasant but beyond reach – beyond my reach anyway', while his college supervisor prophetically wrote in a March 1968 supervision report of 'a Mona Lisa smile [that] seems to be the main stock-in-trade; what's going on behind it I have little means of knowing'.

Cambridge dons like these were used to bringing out the hidden gifts of introspective, bright young things, but Drake was already, in the words of another contemporary tutor's report, 'find[ing] difficulty in expressing [himself] orally . . . [while] his written work . . . is vague, rather scrappy and invariably inconclusive'. Being 'vague . . . and invariably inconclusive' when writing an essay could be a real problem, but as a songwriter it would prove to be Drake's great strength. He always seems on the brink of revealing some poetic profundity; and all one need do to discern that true meaning, is listen again. And again.

From the very first, Drake was not at all sure he wanted to be surrounded by the flat fells of Cambridgeshire. The previous summer he had told a travelling companion, 'I'm doomed to Cambridge', a point of view that prompted his friend to ask what he meant. He explained, 'It's all organized from the moment you're born.' Once there he did work, but not at his English course. It was his guitar-playing that consumed him, until he could play circles around any of his Cambridge contemporaries. As Wells recalls: 'He was more than averagely lazy – he didn't do any [course] work at all . . . [But] he would find a tuning and a riff and play it to death. He would muck about with tunings, put a capo on, get an interesting sound, then put a vocal melody on top.'

And somehow, serendipitously, the phrasing, the picking, the lyrical flights all came together in a cohesive whole with precocious alacrity. One night in late January 1968 at the Chalk Farm Roundhouse, somewhere in the nether regions of another all-night bill (this one for students from Brunel), Drake wove his magic long enough to catch the attention of the ever-attentive Ashley 'Tyger' Hutchings[10], Fairport Convention's bassist. Hutchings gave Joe Boyd the diffident Drake's number and suggested he call him up, which he did, expressing an interest in hearing something. It took Drake a few weeks to find his way to the office, but when he did, he had a tape for the already-prepped Boyd. The demo tape Drake gave to Boyd showed he hadn't been entirely wasting his time in Cambridge.

Still consumed by the torrent of songs spitting forth from his flighty muse, he was writing up a storm, and playing the results to those few friends at Cambridge who shared his obsession with music, among them Paul Wheeler, who had already struck up a friendship with another remarkable guitarist on Boyd's radar, John Martyn. Drake permed the five strongest songs he felt he had at this point, the same ones he had just performed at his first 'official' Cambridge concert in the Bateman Room, and recorded them specifically for Boyd's benefit. However, just two of these songs – 'The Day is Done' and 'The Thoughts of Mary Jane' – would feature on his debut album[11]. One of the songs ultimately overlooked was actually his signature piece at the time, 'Time of No Reply', the first time he directly addressed his own 'difficulty in expressing [himself] orally', blaming it all on the seasons:

> Summer was gone and the heat died down,
> And autumn reached for her golden crown,
> I looked behind as I heard a sigh,
> But this was the time of no reply.

The recording Boyd heard came with no extraneous embellishment – a kind of preview for the Drake who would be defined by *Pink Moon* and his final 1974 recordings – but this was not just some home tape the undergrad had slung together. He had persuaded Peter Rice, a fellow student with a 15 i.p.s. reel-to-reel, who knew something about how to mike up a room, to record this handful of originals. According to Rice: 'It took several goes to get him to be in a suitable state to do any recording.' After all, a lot hinged on the results – even if Drake never revealed the purpose of these recordings to an out-of-pocket Rice.

As well as finding 'the clarity and strength' of the performances 'striking', Boyd immediately thought he could hear a space for strings, and began to talk to Drake in terms of Leonard Cohen's 1967 debut, *Songs of . . .* , a record that, surprisingly, Drake said he hadn't heard. However, as Boyd relates in his own memoir: 'He liked the idea of strings. He described performing with a string quartet at a Cambridge May Ball [sic], the first moment of our meeting when he became animated.' So Drake and Boyd were agreed; the songs would be embellished with strings, to sweeten them for public consumption.

But the strings in Drake's head sounded nothing like those

on Cohen's album, or the ones that London arrangers gratuitously dolloped across other contemporary pop records. Boyd's initial suggestion for an arranger, Richard Hewson – who had just worked on James Taylor's Apple LP – proved 'too mainstream' for this young artist, who seemed unable to articulate what he wanted, but knew right away what he *didn't* want. The Sound Techniques engineer John Wood, Boyd's right-hand man at all those miraculous late-Sixties Sound Techniques sessions, was not the only one surprised to catch first sight of the intransigent side to this polite and well-spoken man:

> **John Wood:** Some people in a recording studio will do what you tell them. But he was getting quietly more and more aggravated. In the end he dug his heels in and dismissed the [original] arrangements . . . He knew what he wanted and if he didn't get it, he would do it again, which is why [that first album] took such a long time.

Boyd thought of himself as something of a perfectionist – that is, until he met Drake, who would introduce a song, then go away and work on it until he thought he'd got it, before eating up yet more tape working on the song, only to change his mind. But this was hardly the only reason why that all-important first album became such a drawn-out affair. Even if, for the moment, we discount Joseph's view that 'Nick would sort of pack up mentally' (and we should not), another problem was that Drake's idea of the album kept changing. This was not only as a result of the songs he was now writing, most of which were superior to those flights of fancy with which he'd wowed Boyd initially, but also due to some of the music he was being exposed to by other Cambridge conspirators.

The songs and songwriters he had been covering on his

home reels, with the exception of Frank, were standard folk revivalist fare. On these oft-bootlegged reels a couple of Dylan's early acoustic paeans to an absent Suze trade places with love-lorn trad. stalwarts such as 'The Water is Wide' and 'Man of Constant Sorrow'. But in Cambridge he was exposed to Tim Buckley, Randy NewmanThe 5th Dimension and mid-period Donovan – all great models for someone still in the formative stages of establishing an independent identity as a songwriter.

Then, probably early in 1969, he chanced upon the second solo album of a blustering but surprisingly sensitive Ulster cowboy by the name of George Ivan 'Call Me Van' Morrison. Although Nick Kent has claimed, '*Astral Weeks* was another Drake Cambridge listening innovation', it is more likely that the folk-oriented Drake was introduced to this devastating work by fellow students Brian Wells or Paul Wheeler. But whoever heard it first, the effect of the album was profound on all concerned. And once again, Drake latched on to an artefact made by a damaged soul, this one with a profoundly British sensibility.

Morrison, an undiagnosed Asperger case, (still) prone to irra-tional outbursts and deep melancholia, which he self-medicated with hard booze, had been trying to make this album for the past two years. A singular suite of songs about his own East Belfast childhood, Morrison said in 1970 that he 'wrote it as an opera'. The themes were as big as they come. As the late great Lester Bangs wrote for his definitive piece on the album (in Greil Marcus's *Stranded* anthology): 'It sounded like the man who made *Astral Weeks* was in terrible pain, pain most of Van Morrison's previous work had only suggested; but . . . there was a redemptive element in the blackness, ultimate compassion for the suffering of others, and a swath of pure beauty and mystical awe that cut right through the heart of the work. I really don't know . . . [if] there's anything guiding it to people enduring dark periods. [But] it did come out at a time when a lot of things that a lot of people cared about passionately were beginning to disintegrate.'

Drake's Cambridge friend Robert Kirby later recalled the shared experience of listening to that album with Nick: 'We were certainly listening to *Astral Weeks* heavily at that time . . . the string-bass playing, the violinist.' But Drake did not just latch on to Morrison's blues-infused, damaged-by-life sensibility, he seized on the subtle combination of flute, acoustic bass and guitar that producer Lewis Merenstein had skilfully applied as aural brushstrokes; and although he was a long way along with his own album, modelled on Cohen, Drake began to almost imperceptibly change the focus of his own album so that it sounded not so much like that, and more like *this*!

Kirby, though, now had his own personal investment in the album. He had, after all, been brought in at Drake's behest as someone who could arrange strings sympathetically, and had quickly inveigled himself into the process – much to a despairing Boyd's relief. But now Drake seemed keen to get Pentangle acoustic bassist Danny Thompson – as close to a Richard Davis-type figure as he or Boyd could find – to dub his jazzier inflections on to parts of the album as a counterbalance to the more Cohenesque conceit initially imposed by Boyd.

'River Man' – the final song Drake recorded – was one song he cut with Thompson, though only after Kirby had admitted that scoring the song effectively was beyond him. But Boyd, still convinced it needed strings, drafted in another arranger, the eminent Harry Robinson, to whom Drake 'played the song through, then strummed chords as the tape played, showing Harry the textures he wanted for the string parts'. By now, Drake wasn't about to let an 'outside' arranger ruin such a key song, and cut the song live while an impressed Robinson conducted the fully prepped string-section to play along, as the unexpressed battle with Boyd for the album's sound continued to the last.

Like Barrett's *The Madcap Laughs*, Drake's *Five Leaves Left* suffered its own series of delays, not all down to the artist's increasingly demanding vision. As such, despite being advertised as early as May, it did not appear until September 1969. And when it did appear, it was to the sound of one hand clapping. Boyd's confidence in the capacity of the songs to communicate on the artist's behalf proved unfounded. As he openly admits, 'I was probably over-confident with Nick, thinking since everything had gone to plan with The Incredible String Band and Fairport Convention . . . Nick proved the exception. I didn't have a Plan B.'

As far as Drake himself was concerned, he seemed to think the album would find its audience in much the same way he himself had stumbled on Jackson Frank's album and Morrison's *Astral Weeks*, by word of mouth, maybe after enjoying a period of critical recognition. But the former album was already a second-hand rarity while the latter, pre-*Moondance*, was still known only to a nominal cognoscenti of discerning folk (one of whom was a certain David Bowie, who again showed his magpie instincts were second to none by introducing 'Madame George' into his winter 1970 set).

Like Barrett, Drake mustered every ounce of creative energy to make his statement, even though he suspected he was destined to be a prophet without honour (hence 'Fruit Tree', which argued that 'fame . . . can never flourish / till its stalk is in the ground'). At least he *had* achieved this precious goal, and when a box of the pink-label ILPS 9105 arrived at his flat, he immediately headed over to his sister Gabrielle's already a notable actress was slightly taken aback by this unexpected appearance: 'By this time, he had become much more introverted. [But] he suddenly came into my room one day, said, "Here you are", and threw down this record.'

She would be one of the fortunate few who got to hear *Five Leaves Left* in the moment. Like *The Madcap Laughs*, *Arthur* and *David Bowie* – all of which appeared in, and disappeared from, the shops in the closing months of that tumultuous decade – *Five Leaves Left* was destined to be viewed initially as something of a commercial curio, and only in the fullness of time as a prescient way of announcing darker days. So, which way to blue?

3. 1970–71: There's More Out Than In

The madman is not the man who has lost his reason. The madman is the man who has lost everything except his reason.
– G.K. Chesterton, 1908

I'd rather stay here with all the madmen,
Than perish with the sad men roaming free . . .
'Cause I'm quite content they're all as sane as me.
– David Bowie, 1970

The performance that really makes it, that makes it all the way, is the one that reaches into the realms of insanity.
– Mick Jagger as 'Turner', *Performance*, 1970

By the summer of 1969, London had no shortage of casualties returned from the unknown regions with their minds destroyed. Vince Taylor, whose attempted 1967 'comeback' had proven not so much messianic as plain messy, was back in London. According to the latterday Bowie, he was here befriended by the boy from Brixton, a case of the has-been meets the wannabe:

David Bowie: [He had] these strange plans showing where there was money buried, that he was going to get together; he was going to create this new Atlantis at one time. And he dragged out this map of the world, just outside Tottenham Court Road tube station . . . and he laid it on the pavement . . . [] . . . in rush hour traffic, and us kneeling and looking, and he was showing me where all the space ships were going to land . . . [with] all these commuters going backwards and forwards over our map! [1990/2000]

Although I'm not fully convinced Bowie ever enjoyed such an experience with his very own 'leper messiah', in 1969–70 he hardly needed to look hard to find a role model for a megalomaniacal rock star whose mind had turned to mush with all that adulation and imbibing of ill-advised substances. In the post-Altamont soundscape, figures who had previously been basking in the iridescent light of a warm sun were melting visibly as their own starlight turned up the heat inside their heads. Fleetwood Mac's Peter Green and former Floyd frontman Syd Barrett were two actual models for Ziggy who were about to find that fame was a dish that quickly grew cold. And another well-respected, contemporary English rock artist, surely known to Bowie, spent almost as much time behind four enclosed walls at this time as Bowie's half-brother, Terry.

As one loco Vince was fast disappearing into the hinterland, culturally and psychologically, another Vince was returning from a spell in the local asylum with a half-share of all the royalties accrued from the classic 1968 number-one single 'Fire'. Classically trained organist Vincent Crane – prophetically named after Van Gogh by his arty parents – had just returned from a four-month spell in the Banstead mental institution, after a cataclysmic breakdown on the first Crazy World of Arthur Brown US tour; only to find himself heading back to the States for another make-or-break tour in the winter of 1969 on the back of the band's chart-bound debut album.

The Crazy World was literally teeming with borderline basket cases – Brown had himself taken the psychedelic tag of the band a tad literally, while the band's original drummer, Drachen Theaker, found a unique way of handing in his resignation: walking out to sea with a guitar above his head. And while the band was in the States for a second time, replacement drummer Carl Palmer discovered: 'Arthur had gone off with his wife to live in some commune in New Jersey. We did manage to locate him but he just wouldn't pick up the phone . . . Arthur at that stage had really lost the plot.' Stuck in a New York hotel on salary, Palmer and Crane began cooking up ideas for a band of their own, a powerhouse trio that would comprise just organ, bass and drums (an idea Palmer would take to Emerson Lake & Palmer). The name of the band came courtesy of a lady to whom Palmer had brought Crane, hoping to get him off LSD:

Carl Palmer: One evening in New York we went out together, with Vincent's girlfriend at the time, to this girl's apartment. Now, Vincent's problems . . . stemmed from him taking too much acid and the reason we took him down to this apartment was to see this girl . . . She was going to explain how bad it was and that he should stop taking it, basically. The person she chose to talk about was the bass player in this group called Rhinoceros [who had] taken a lot of chemical substances and started calling himself 'the atomic rooster' . . . When we got back to England I said to Vincent, 'Why don't we call our band the Atomic Rooster?'

Not that Palmer ever thought Crane's problems ended with acid. Even he realized that, 'It wasn't entirely to do with drugs with Vincent – he *was* mentally ill.' Before they could pursue their common musical goals, Crane again returned to Banstead for a short stay, while Palmer lined up a manager (the mighty Robert Stigwood) and a record deal (with the not so mighty B&C Records). By 29 August 1968 the new power-trio and a recuperated Crane were ready to take over the recently disbanded Cream's mantle, headlining a triple Lyceum bill on the back of the Arthur Brown association, above the Mk. 2 version of Deep Purple, themselves just nine gigs old and destined for greater things. (Purple's latest composition, 'Child in Time', a breakthrough in every sense, could almost have been penned with Crane in mind: 'Sweet child in time, you'll see the line / The line that's drawn between good and bad . . .')

Atomic Rooster's set that night and in the months preceding the February 1970 release of their meticulously assembled first LP largely comprised Crane's meditations on his still-intermittent madness, penned while the experience of another confinement remained freshly raw. Of the seven originals that constituted that doom-laden debut, the overbearingly powerful 'Banstead', a coruscating plea to 'take me out of this place / I'll swear you'll never see me here again / . . . though I know this life is driving me insane', was the least ambiguous. Not that there was a lot of shade elsewhere. Just darker shades of black. 'Friday the 13th', the album-opener and single, was a voyeuristic voyage into the interior of a split personality ('Someone please, please save me / No one will save you, they won't try / Someone please, please help me / Everyone's lonely when they die'). Then there was 'Winter', which made Nick Drake's musings on the passing of the seasons seem positively bucolic:

Summer's dead – winter's coming on.
All of my hopes for the future now are gone.
All of my battles are lost, for Time has won . . .
What is the point of going on, and on, and on, and on?

The album had another, attendant theme – the unreality of fame. In the orchestrated hard-rock number, 'Decline and Fall', Crane describes seeing 'the crowd as they pack the hall', then the same crowd 'as they turn away', all the while wondering aloud, 'Who will catch me as I fall?' Elsewhere he chides one particular face in the crowd who craves some sexual connection with the rock God. The sarcastic 'And So to Bed' – one of a number of 'groupie' songs penned at this time by English rock bands (following The Rolling Stones' expansive lead) – seeks to make her change her view, if not her ways: 'You think that up here I'm so special / But put in a crowd I would be just like you / You think to be with me would make a change in you . . .'

But this was just a tangent to the overarching theme underlying Crane's compositions now and forever: the loneliness of the long-suffering head case. Even in the period August 1969 through May 1970, as an audience rapidly grew for this unique trio, Crane felt that the band really needed a different point of view. The recruitment of guitarist John McCann gave Rooster a much-needed second songwriter. But despite the chart success brought by McCann's more pop-oriented songs ('Tomorrow Night' and 'Devil's Answer'), Crane sensed a dilution of purpose and changed his mind again, unable to stomach a subsidiary role in his own band.

In the summer of 1971, after Rooster's second album, *Death Walks Behind You* (with its memorable cover, replicating William Blake's stark image of the mad king Nebuchadnezzar), had consolidated their initial success, Crane disbanded the second incarnation of Atomic Rooster; and though there would be three more Rooster albums in name, he would never again recapture the unity of purpose that the original band enjoyed in the brief time when he and Carl Palmer – ELP bound by May 1970 – adhered to their original brief: heavy soul music used as a form of exorcism for all-too-real inner demons.

If a combination of the bright lights of fame and LSD's flashing lights triggered something deeply disturbing inside Crane, another impressionable musical virtuoso was finding it equally hard to reconcile his public persona with his inner self. Peter Green, the baby-faced blues guitarist who had taken the Bluesbreakers template into the mainstream with Fleetwood Mac, was struggling to keep his own deep-rooted demons at bay. Mac had been formed in the summer of 1967 as a straight blues cover-band. At the time, Green actually poured scorn on Cream's Eric Clapton, the man he replaced in John Mayall's Bluesbreakers, because 'he's lost the feeling. He could get it back but he's so easily influenced. He sees Hendrix and thinks, "I can do that." . . . But I'll always play the blues.'

Despite professing these purist intentions, though, Fleetwood Mac soon morphed into a vehicle for Green's own musical meditations, a chord change first signalled in a June 1968 *Melody Maker* interview where Green announced, 'In the past I've sung other people's songs. But now I sing all my own songs on stage and the next album will be all our own songs.' Four months earlier, he had recorded the song that shifted the band's sensibility in this new direction, propelling them towards a Clapton-like superstardom for which Green himself was psychologically ill-prepared. The tom-tom voodoo of 'Black Magic Woman' was initially only a minor UK hit, but it showed that a talent as great as Green's was never going to be content to let *his* band remain the Elmore James 'cover' combo that second guitarist Jeremy Spencer wanted them to be. Instead, the addition of Danny Kirwan in August 1968 gave Mac a three-guitar sound and a more playful foil for Green, sidelining Spencer and his James obsession.

Like so many others in these interesting times, Green's burgeoning creativity as a songwriter was the direct result of a great deal of soul-searching and copious drug-taking. The results to begin with were a steady stream of wrenchingly powerful blues songs fully the equal of anything to come out of sweet home Chicago – although his was the blues of the wondering Jew, not the put-upon black man. During the first of his regular columns for *Beat Instrumental*, inserted in its September 1968 issue, he bared some of these personal concerns, singling out the song 'Trying So Hard to Forget', first recorded at a February session with Duster Bennett, as 'probably the most meaningful of my own blues . . . [it] sums up my past life and present feelings in one very blue song'. He was already writing in terms that suggested the painful past was something that remained ever-present:

> People, I've tried so hard to forget,
> But I can't stop my mind wandering,
> Back to the days I was just a downtrodden kid . . .

This was clearly not someone who should have received any psychedelic substance, let alone LSD, but introduced he was by the dean of dosers himself, Augustus Owsley Stanley III. It was Owsley, a year on from dosing several thousand 'free' sandwiches at the Human Be-In in Golden Gate Park, who spiked the soft drinks of the whole band backstage at San Francisco's Fillmore West in January 1969. In fact, any immediate effect was more pronounced on Jeremy Spencer than it was on Green.

As L.A. scenester Judy Wong has said of her then-house-guest: 'Jeremy was literally two people. I didn't expect some lunatic Englishman [who would] open my windows at four in the morning [to] shout obscenities . . . [at] the neighbours.' (Owsley finally got his comeuppance when he spiked the water-fountain at a later Mac gig in New Orleans and a concert-goer returned home announcing he was Jesus. His parents called the cops, who went looking for Owsley, but found his house band, the Grateful Dead, instead.)

According to Green, for whom the star-trip had already palled anyway, Owlsey's rarefied acid initially had a cleansing effect: 'Once I took LSD, that got rid of all that vanity.' The cleansed Green was inspired to write a barrage of songs about loneliness and despair. Just as 'Albatross' was hitting the number one spot in the UK, Green and Mac were in a studio in New York cutting his most plaintive work to date, 'Man of the World', a song of unbearable sadness, which contrasted that public persona with the tortured soul inside ('I guess I've got everything I need . . . but I just wish that I'd never been born').

Green soon began to worry whether he had laid too much of himself on the line. By April 1969, he was insisting, 'On the record it was a story of me . . . [but] it's not true of me now.' Meanwhile, 'Man of the World', rush-released by Fleetwood Mac to capitalize on 'Albatross' (and subsequently re-recorded by their manager Clifford Davis[12]), was storming the charts, peaking at number two. Two more companions pieces in both sentiment and chronology, 'Before the Beginning' and 'Do You Give a Damn for Me', were also recorded for the first time in January 1969. They showed any claim on Green's part that he had passed beyond such feelings to be a scented smokescreen. The former, in particular, suggested someone determined to get back to some place that was there before the pain: 'And how many times must I be the fool / Before I can make it, make it on home?'

Despite the band originally being conceived as an electric blues outfit, pure and uncut, Green was becoming increasingly ambitious with his musical ideas. 'Albatross' had been the first time he had used the spatial potential of stereo (Mick Fleetwood's tom-toms being panned left and right), overdubbed guitar and cymbals accentuating the positives his original idea contained. It was also the first Mac single made without Spencer on hand. Even as he continued democratically dividing up the songs on each Fleetwood Mac album, allowing Spencer and Kirwan to flex their more limited musical muscle, every time a new single was needed it was Green who decided what it would be. And with good cause. In the space of two years, each of five Green-composed A-sides – 'Black Magic Woman', 'Albatross', 'Man of the World', 'Oh Well' and 'Green Manalishi' – not only represented a clear advance on its predecessor but, after the minor hiccup that was 'Black Magic Woman', all would go Top Ten in the UK.

The follow-up to 'Man of the World' was Green's most ambitious musical excursion to date. 'Oh Well', according to Green, was an attempt to 'represent my two extremes – as wild as I can be and [also] my first sort of semi-classical attempt'. It was too ambitious to be contained by a single side of seven-inch vinyl, and was spread across both sides of the disc, the B-side being a five-minute-forty departure from the basic musical idea that saw Green play acoustic and electric guitars, timpani and cello, while Spencer – the only other band-member on hand – tiptoed around on the piano.

More worryingly, the terse lyrics appeared to include a partial transcription of Green's first conversation with God: 'Now, when I talked to God I knew he'd understand / He said, "Stick by my side and I'll be your guiding hand.'" And this was no metaphysical discourse, à la 'Highway 61 Revisited'; Green really had started to believe he had a direct line to the Man Upstairs, a source of real concern to his then-girlfriend, Sandra:

'That summer Peter was really excited by all the possibilities that were presenting themselves. This correlated with . . . [us] both for quite some time [being] very spiritually connected and searching . . . [It was] then I made the robes – one white and one red velvet. For Peter, they were nothing to do with any Christian faith. I think psychologically it was definitely a move into psychosis, or perhaps a precursor to it – he was getting stuck into identification with God! Because of all the adoration people were giving him, he was finding it very hard to differentiate between that exalted state and mere mortality – albeit with a God-given talent.'

The rest of the band were now just as nonplussed by Green's state of mind as by their new musical direction. Mick Fleetwood and John McVie had both bet Green that 'Oh Well' would not chart – a bet they roundly lost; and with that loss, they perhaps lost their old friend for good. Their openly agnostic attitude to his new interest in Jesus certainly did not sit well with him. The song 'Closing My Eyes', on Green's last album with Mac, *Then Play On*, was one lyrical diatribe he admitted the following year had been 'written around the time I had such a great faith in Jesus that I felt I was walking and talking with God. I wanted to tell people about it, but they turned it round and tried to shatter my dreams. This was written after they had broken my faith.' The 'they' go unnamed, but it is clear that as far as Green was concerned, the Us that was once Fleetwood Mac was fast becoming Them.

At least the critical and commercial reception accorded

'Oh Well' convinced the remainder of Mac that Green still knew where they should be heading musically; and they gamely went along with him, even as the songs became elongated explorations of space, time and rhyme. 'Rattlesnake Shake' – provisionally ear-marked as the follow-up to 'Oh Well' until somebody realized what would happen if the Beeb ever found out the song was about jerking off – became in concert a prelude to twenty-five-minute jams that tended to wander the gamut of Green's imagination in search of the lost chord.

Sometimes, as in one magnificent version captured at Boston's Tea Party the first week of February 1970, he found it. By then, though, he had already succumbed to the belief that he was being held back by the band, and that once he was free of them – just as his mind had been 'freed' by LSD – he would be at one with God. A series of sessions in the fall of 1969 with Clifford Davis, ex-Mac member Bob Brunning's new band, and Peter Bardens, demonstrated how much he felt constrained by a band he had cast in his own image.

This conviction took full possession of Green during another US tour in January 1970 that included a three-day residency at the Fillmore West and a two-day stint in New Orleans with Grateful Dead; and another shattering experience, courtesy of Owsley's acidic assistance (during the Louisiana jaunt, Green told Patti Boyd's sister Jenny, 'Stay away from me. I don't want to get caught in *your world'*). Playing with real fire, he was about to get burned. Yet in the lysergic present the outcome was the gloriously grandiloquent 'Green Manalishi', a song beyond anything dreamed of in Elmore James' philosophy. If the long-term result was a mind prone to shutting down, in the here and now this outlandish epic became the centrepiece of some of the most experimental rock sets since Barrett took Floyd into overdrive. Green later sought to explain how his true masterpiece came about; the result of what he says was a dream, but was in all probability an acid trip:

> **Peter Green:** This little dog jumped up and barked at me while I was lying in bed dreaming. It scared me because I knew the dog had been dead a long time. It was a stray and I was looking after it. But I was dead and had to fight to get back into my body, which I eventually did . . . [] . . . I woke up and looked around. It was very dark and I found myself writing a song . . . The reason this happened was this fear I got that I earned too much money, and I was separate from all the people . . . [The song] wasn't about LSD, it was [about] money, which can also send you somewhere that's not good. [In this] dream I saw a picture of a female shop assistant and a wad of pound notes, and there was this other message saying, 'You're not what you used to be. You think you're better than them.' I had too much money . . . The Green Manalishi is the wad of notes. The devil is green, and he was after me. [1994/1996]

By now, the dog wasn't the only thing barking: Green was giving some of the wackiest interviews to ever appear in the UK music press. One dating from the previous December contains a description by himself of 'someone who does try to do the will of God in an earthly way . . . I want to do something and it's difficult to know what. I don't want to just waste my life . . . Sometimes I think music is everything, other times I don't think it's anything . . . I want to put something in my head because there's nothing there.' This now oft-voiced concern soon led to the infamous front-page headline in the 28 February 1970 *NME*, 'Why Peter Green Wants to Give His Money Away'.

It seems he felt increasingly 'guilty about squandering my money on myself'. If bemused band-members were wondering where this was all heading, Green had confided his state of mind to Mick Fleetwood during that ill-fated US tour: 'I want to find out about God. I want to believe that a person's role in life is to do good for other people, and [that] what we're doing now just isn't shit.'

Two months after he bared his soul to his closest confidant in the band, Green found himself at an all-night party in Munich. He had decided to disregard the concerns of the rest of the band and escape to a hippy commune in the company of roadie Dennis Keane, where he could be free to do drugs and make music, in that order. For an unprepared Keane, imbibing the wine laced with LSD resulted in 'all hell [breaking] loose in my head'. If Keane somehow made his way back to the band, Green stayed on through the whole dark night of his soul. This would be the trip that finally tripped Green's mind. Two decades on, with Green finally returned to a halting lucidity after many painful years in and out of mental wards, he offered a surprisingly metaphorical explanation of the events that evening: 'I just sat around and thought about everything. I was thinking so fast! I couldn't believe how fast I was thinking! And I kinda run out of thoughts.'

Shortly before Keane stumbled away from the weird scene at the Munich all0nighter, he had ventured into the basement, where he found Green jamming with his equally high German hosts. To Keane's ears: 'The sound they were making was awful, this kind of freaky electronic droning noise. It wasn't music as I knew it.' Jeremy Spencer, who had made his own way to the party and briefly sat in on the jam session, was equally critical of the results: 'It was pretty weird. I didn't like what [Peter] was playing. He was just jamming.'

Green, though, was convinced that he had found what he had been looking for, even telling *Beat Instrumental* in May: '[When] I played on the commune [in Munich] . . . it was then that I found out how much I've changed, through playing personally for them. When the pressure is off, it all comes out naturally.' He even took a tape of the session with him when he finally emerged from the twenty-four-hour party, and on occasions played 'this LSD tape' (as he called it) for friends. One of them, percussionist Nigel Watson, 'found the playing weird, even scary at times, but it was still there, free-form in one sense but spot-on in another. He was obviously really pleased with it.' Even after Green mislaid the tape in Los Angeles at the end of his lost decade, he recalled the experience with surprising fondness: 'When we jammed, I couldn't believe what I was coming out with. I was playing things that I didn't know I could play and the notes seemed to be going all round the room.'

He now tried to take this sense of freedom into the studio when, after a six-month hiatus from recording, he returned there in April to cut 'Green Manalishi'. Although it would be his last recording with Fleetwood Mac before he quit – the band had already been apprised of his decision – there was precious little required of the others. As John McVie recalls: '"Manalishi" . . . was very much Peter sitting at home with his Revox . . . He came in with a demo and said, "Here's the parts".'

Green himself was delighted with the outcome: 'Making "Green Manalishi" was one of the best memories [from that time]. The mixing down of it in the studio . . . I thought it would make number one. Lots of drums. Bass guitars. All kinds of things . . . Danny Kirwan and me playing those shrieking guitars together.' In fact, the single stalled at number ten; probably because the whole thing was just too widescreen to be contained on the seven-inch format. Certainly compared with the stunning fifteen-minute version Mac recorded for the BBC in the last few weeks of Green's tenure in the band (available on Receiver's second archival trawl, *Showbiz Blues*), the single barely qualified as a prototype.

In the months after his departure from Mac, Green cut two singles and an experimental album of instrumentals (*End of The Game*), hoping to get back to that Munich vibe – 'trying to reach things that I couldn't before, but I had experienced through LSD and mescaline' – only to find when he came to edit the tracks that 'there wasn't enough to make up a record; it was *only* freeform'. The first of two solo singles – 'Heavy Heart' b/w 'No Way Out' – continued in a similar vein. The second single, 'Beast of Burden' – not issued until the beginning of 1972, when it sank without trace – was more like the Green of old, castigating the world for its ill-treatment of 'beasts of burden who worked for the right to live', to a crescendo of congas and wailing guitars.

But Green the guitar-god was done; it was time to go home. Sometime in 1971, back with his parents, the diffident East End boy went down the pub with original Mac bassist Bob Brunning. While there he confessed 'he'd given away all his guitars, didn't want to play music and didn't want to talk about it'. The damage had been done in double-quick time. The repair work would proceed at an altogether more painstaking pace. Meanwhile, for some years his former band continued trying to bring him back into the fold, before chancing on an FM-friendly sound a million miles and ten million sales removed from 'Green Manalishi'.

*

Green's journey from 'Black Magic Woman' to 'Green Manalishi' almost exactly replicates the travails of Syd Barrett, another figure who back in the spring of 1966 was playing

Slim Harpo with his own r&b combo, The Pink Floyd Sound, but had by the close of 1970 reached the end of his creative tether. A key difference, though, was that Green's relationship with the band he formed and fronted for the first three years of its existence was generally a supportive one, even when the others were plagued by doubts as to Green's creative direction, or Green himself was experiencing acid flashbacks or demonic visions.

Unlike Green, Barrett had conflicting emotions about his former band – its ongoing status had been eating away at him ever since he left them to their own game plan. The experience of working with two of his erstwhile colleagues on *The Madcap Laughs* had produced decidedly mixed results. And he seemed profoundly unimpressed by what Pink Floyd had achieved on their own, telling one journalist in the stint of promotional interviews arranged around his debut solo offering: 'When I went I felt the progress the group could have made [without me]. But it made none, none at all, except in the sense it was continuing . . . [So] I didn't have anything to follow.'

He had a point. The latest in a series of stop-gap Floyd long-players was the double album *Ummagumma*, released on 1 November, which comprised a series of individually composed song-suites, resulting in four different shades of 'Saucerful of Secrets', bumped up by a 'bonus' live album of old tracks. The latter had been due to include their concert tour de force 'Interstellar Overdrive' before the track was removed at the last minute, perhaps because it was too much of a reminder of the Barrett-era. A tepid 'Astronomy Domine' had to suffice instead. From the other side of *Dark Side . . .* , Barrett's replacement, Dave Gilmour, duly admitted: 'At the time we felt . . . *Ummagumma* was a step towards something or other. Now I think [we] were . . . just blundering about in the dark.'

When Barrett himself heard what they had done to the brand, he was underwhelmed, telling one journo who summoned the nerve to ask: 'They've probably done very well. The singing's very good, and the drumming is good as well' – the muso equivalent of the kindly teacher typing a school report on some backward kids left in his charge, looking for positives, but failing to hide the condescension (and the clue is: the studio album contains exactly one vocal track).

And yet, despite everything, when Barrett began work (with surprising haste) on a second solo album, with *Madcap* barely in the racks, it was to Dave Gilmour he again turned to make it happen – barely a month after he had told one rock critic: 'There [will be] no set musicians [on the next album], just people helping out . . . which gives me far more freedom in what I want to do.' Waters, though, would not be required; either because Barrett had had enough of that kingly leer, or because Waters didn't need no more education.

For now, Barrett seemed full of enthusiasm and ideas, insisting that he was keen to discover whether 'it's possible to continue some of the ideas that came from a couple of tracks on the first album', while dismissing his debut offering as 'only a beginning – I've written a lot more stuff'. And on the evidence of a BBC session and a couple of EMI sessions at the end of February 1970, he really did seem to have developed some ideas first explored on 'Octopus' and 'Dark Globe', the two most successful tracks on *The Madcap Laughs*.

On 24 February 1970, Barrett turned up at the BBC's Maida Vale studios for the first time since his Christmas 1967 farewell to the Floyd. There ostensibly to plug a new LP, he decided instead to again use a *Top Gear* session as an opportunity to work up new songs. And, just as in 1967, this chronically unreliable artist breezed through the session, recording five tunes in an afternoon, only one of which – 'Terrapin' – came from *The Madcap Laughs*. Of the other four, one was a Richard Wright song he had always liked, but never returned to ('Two of a Kind'). The remaining three were new Barrett originals, 'Baby Lemonade', 'Effervescing Elephant' and 'Gigolo Aunt', though the last of these for now only consisted of a single verse, which Barrett sang three different ways. As Gilmour later told journo Tim Willis: 'Syd was great that day. Listen to those perfect double-tracked vocals. [And] he only had three hours for mixing.' The experience seems to have convinced Gilmour to give producing his friend another try. And this time he would hold the fort the whole night through.

The nice pair thus convened at Abbey Road studios two days later to begin work on a second Syd LP, with drummer Jerry Shirley requisitioned to play whenever the song demanded it, and engineer Peter Bown there to press record (and hold Barrett's dick, if we are to believe one particular Bown tall-tale[13]). On day one they worked quickly and efficiently, cutting 'Baby Lemonade' in a single take and two vocal takes of another new song, 'Maisie', which would be cross-cut on the released take. All very professional.

The following day Barrett began proceedings by demoing to two-track (i.e. stereo) no less than four 'new' songs, none of which he'd recorded at the BBC session: 'Wolfpack', 'Waving My Arms in the Air', 'Living Alone' and 'Dylan Blues'. The last of these actually pre-dates Floyd. Perhaps it was recalled here because Barrett thought it was time he recast himself as a singer-songwriter by doffing his satirical hat to the daddy of them all. He then moved on to 'Gigolo Aunt', one of his funniest, finest songs, now with three distinct verses. It was a good start – in fact, the following month Barrett happily boasted to *Sounds'* Giovanni Dadomo that he already had 'four tracks in the can' (it was actually three). At the same time, Gilmour was telling a *Disc* reporter he was the only man for the job: 'No one else can do [a Syd album]. It has to be someone who knows Syd, someone who can get him together.'

It was a fateful comment. As Gilmour knew all too well, only Syd could get himself together, and between the end of February and the start of April he once again lost his way in the woods. The relatively lucid interviewee of January became in just two months someone who, to evoke Andrew King's depiction of the latterday Barrett, 'was trying to battle his way through the most enormous barrier to say two coherent words'. When sessions resumed the first three days in April, they proved exponentially less productive, the musical equivalent of pulling teeth.

Barrett's flatmate, artist Duggie Fields, who went with him to the final session on 3 April, remembers: 'He was so dysfunctional [he] literally sat there, not knowing what he was doing. Forgot what he was supposed to be singing, was certainly not focused at all.' It was a shock to Fields, who recalls that 'he didn't have those problems when . . . we first got the flat[14]. They developed. Maybe he had symptoms of them which one didn't really register, but . . . he wasn't like that at first – he functioned.' Meanwhile, though Gilmour continued to be remarkably patient, gently prodding and prompting, ever prepared to play the waiting game, EMI engineer Pete Bown was about as unsympathetic as a collaborator can be:

Peter Bown: I made sure they were closed sessions. Because if anyone had seen Syd, that would have been it. He used to wander around, couldn't stay still in the studio; his legs were jittery and nervous all the time. I had to follow him around the studio with a microphone in my hand – wearing a pair of carpet slippers so I didn't make any noise – just to get a take. He was wandering all over the place musically too. His pitch was out and his timing completely shot. They took down everything on tape in those days, so it's all there somewhere, with David trying to keep him calm and relaxed. It was like a teacher trying to help a forlorn child.

At some point during these April sessions, Gilmour (and Bown) decided they would have to work with what they could get – or abandon the album altogether. Barrett's performances in the studio had always sat somewhere between erratic and idiosyncratic, but it now seemed he could no longer control his vocal cords. As the *Barrett* album sessions progressed, the inclusion on *Madcap* of those three songs from the Gilmour/Waters session began to seem positively prescient. As drummer Jerry Shirley told Kris DiLorenzo: 'Sometimes he'd sing a melody absolutely fine, and the next time around he'd sing a totally different melody, or just go off key . . . You never knew from one day to the next exactly how it would go.' In the end, Gilmour realized that this time around he would *have* to intervene:

Dave Gilmour: We had basically three alternatives at that point . . . One, we could actually work with him in the studio, playing along as he put down the tracks – which was almost impossible . . . The second was laying down some kind of track before and then having him play over it. The third was him putting the basic ideas down with just guitar and vocals and then we'd try and make something out of it all. It was mostly a case of me saying, 'Well, what have you got there, Syd?' and he'd search around and eventually work something out. [1974]

By now, Barrett could slip from one mode of synaptic discourse to another with nary a nod. When the authors of the *British Journal of Psychiatry* article 'Laing's Models of Madness' challenged the validity of Laing's worldview, they went to some pains to describe how someone sliding into madness would be unable to 'distinguish two very different kinds of experience, [the] psychedelic and [the] psychotic': when it came to the former, the person would be 'seeing more possibilities that can be acted upon, which makes life exciting', whereas with the latter, s/he would be 'seeing so many possibilities that action [became] impossible'. This was now Barrett. The April 1970 sessions demonstrated that his capacity to see things through was fast evaporating, replaced by an often overwhelming feeling of inertia. He had passed through the fire too many times, and each time it was becoming harder to wend his way back.

And yet he still had the odd song, or four, lying around. When two sessions in a single day (7 June) were squeezed between Floyd tours of the USA and Germany and work on their own album, *Atom Heart Mother*, the result was another quartet of demos: 'Milky Way', 'Rats', 'Wined and Dined' and 'Birdie Hop'. The demos were further evidence that Gilmour was now committed to getting Barrett to put 'basic ideas down with just guitar and vocals and then we'd try and make something out of it all'. But just as with the February demos, Gilmour did nothing with these particular tracks, 'Milky Way' becoming yet another mystifying discard. Only 'Rats' and 'Wined and Dined' were revived at the pukka album sessions, which finally resumed on 14 July as Gilmour succeeded in squeezing three solid days of work out of Syd (14, 15 and 17 July).

The first July session demonstrated that Barrett, knowingly or unknowingly, had fallen in line with Gilmour's plan, as he ran down solo takes of 'Effervescing Elephant', 'Dolly Rocker', 'Love Song', 'Let's Split' and 'Dominoes'. The whole of the following day was then spent overdubbing 'Dominoes', the one first-rate new original he had brought to these sessions; contributing his legendary backward guitar solo, achieved by turning the tape over and letting it play in reverse. At the third and last session, he returned to 'Effervescing Elephant', a ninety-second-long piece of Lear-like nonsense he'd been carrying around for the last six months, to provide a fitting end to the recording career of a man who had made the nursery rhyme such an integral part of the late-Sixties pop sensibility.

Yet even at the end of this 17 July session, it is doubtful whether anyone in attendance thought they had an album in the can. Certainly EMI engineer Alan Parsons, who presided over tape operations at the February and June sessions, carried no such conviction: 'If it hadn't been for dropping in and out and cutting up tapes and doing things it would have just been laughable. There would just have been nothing releasable there at all . . . just a series of "madcap laughs".'

It now devolved to Dave Gilmour to salvage the album by applying a palette of overdubs to the twelve songs he had picked out as *Madcap*'s successor. Over nine sessions in just four days he had available before leaving for France with Floyd – 21–24 July – Gilmour bounced from tape to tape, sculpting something that was more than a set of demos, but less than a strong second LP. Barrett turned up for the first couple of sessions, after which, according to Parsons, 'he was discreetly told, "Thank you very much Syd, we don't need you."'

The result was another album that fell short of what Barrett continued to believe he had in him. He confessed to Michael Watts the very week *Barrett* was released that the songs 'are very pure, you know; the words . . . [but sometimes] I feel I'm jabbering'. That was pretty much what the music press thought, too, and Barrett now decided to leave them to it. But some months later, in conversation with *Beat Instrumental*'s Steve Turner, he revealed just how disappointed he had been with the released artefact: '[The songs] have got to reach a certain standard, and that's probably reached in *Madcap* once or twice . . . On the other one only a little – just an echo of that.'

Nonetheless, whatever Syd thought of the failings inherent in his own effort, it was as nothing to what he thought of the Floyd's continued attempts to supersede their psychedelic past. Floyd's first 1970s album, *Atom Heart Mother*, had been released a fortnight before his, so the subject inevitably came up in conversation with Watts. Barrett again proved unsparing in his assessment of their work to date: 'Their choice of material was always very much to do with what they were thinking as architecture students. Rather unexciting people . . .'

And he did not confine his investigations on their 'progress' to the just-released platter. Syd was still keeping tabs on them, at some point visiting the sessions themselves, probably in early June, when Ron Geesin was wrestling with arranging *Atom Heart Mother*'s side-long title track (still at that juncture called 'The Amazing Pudding'). Geesin, on the verge of a nervous breakdown from the strain, says he 'just thought he [Syd] was a nutter. He didn't know what was going on.' But Geoff Mott, who accompanied Barrett to the session in question, insists: 'There was nothing sad about Syd's behaviour. I can still see him keeping an eye on proceedings, sitting on his hands with that quizzical smile on his face.'

Actually, try as Syd might to continue dismissing Floyd's current work as simply their way of 'working their entry into an art school', the quartet were finally on the right track, producing music that was not only architectural, but instantly identifiable. Over the next year they would become one of the more interesting live acts in the world, building their set around two side-long songs – 'Atom Heart Mother' and 'Echoes' – that would start to cement their post-Barrett reputation as one of the more adventurous exponents of English 'prog-rock'.

At the same time, Barrett's own influence would diminish in almost exact proportion to his dissipating presence from the public arena. And it wasn't all down to the failure of his commercial output. In part, he simply lacked that necessary work ethic – inspiration came quick or not at all, and when it slid away, he let it slide (hence the perfunctory technique in much of his 'art'). It was one thing that set him apart from the others in the Floyd family. The Floyd, month on month, year on year, remorselessly worked on building their reputation as a live act, refusing to be collectively dissuaded even when individually convinced that they were 'blundering about in the dark'. Barrett preferred to mention in passing how awfully nice it would be to get up and do something, then leaving it at that.

He had hinted as much at the beginning of 1970, in conversation with Journo Chris Welch, suggesting: 'I'd like to play sometime on the scene. Got to do something. It would be a splendid thing to get a band together.' It would take him a further six months to arrange *anything*, but eventually he agreed to play a short set at Extravaganza '70, a four-day 'music and fashion festival' at Kensington's cavernous Olympia exhibition hall, the first week in June. When he did take the stage, for the first time in thirty months, the set was shorter than the February 1970 John Peel Session, comprising three of those songs, plus the strongest track from *Madcap*. As for getting a band together, basic backing was provided by Gilmour and Shirley, the only musicians he trusted to bring to the Extravaganza.

Yet that final song at Olympia, a fiery five-minute 'Octopus', suggested Syd was still capable of some musical pyrotechnics. Containing more than a whiff of its original 'Clowns and Jugglers' self, its skidding guitar runs were a flickering reminder of the U-Fo Barrett. But just as Syd started to feel the glow again, he cut short the performance, and with it his London performing career. Without a performing self prepared to promote the product, and increasingly circular in conversation, he was never going to turn *Barrett* into a viable commercial release. It was destined to remain 'just an echo' of former triumphs. Released the first week in November 1970, the album engendered less of the natural curiosity Syd's solo debut received, and EMI expressed minimal interest in perpetuating this maddening maverick's recording career.

*

Across town at Island HQ they were having a similar problem with *Bryter Layter*, the second album of their own introspective singer-songwriter Nick Drake, also released that first week in November 1970. Like Barrett, Drake had abandoned playing live before he had even completed the follow-up to his solo debut. The only promotional avenue now open was press interviews, and that avenue was all but bricked up for good the day Drake met Island press officer, David Sandison:

> **David Sandison:** The first time I ever met Nick Drake was the week . . . *Bryter Layter* was released. He arrived an hour late, wasn't very interested in a cup of coffee or tea or anything to eat. During the next half hour he said maybe two words. Eventually I ran out of voice, paid the bill and walked him back to Witchseason.

If Barrett had never been part of the singer-songwriter scene, and knew little of the circuit of ex-folk clubs and college gigs that provided an ideal arena in which to forge a golden era of English singer-songwriters, for an artist like Drake – who never enjoyed even one 45 in his lifetime, recorded just two early radio sessions (only one of which appears to have survived[15]), and was chronically self-conscious in person – there was one route and one route alone to recognition. But by June 1970 he had already abandoned performing.

The one journalist who persisted in trying to get a Drake interview, *Sounds*' Jerry Gilbert, got almost the same treatment as Sandison at a prearranged meeting in February 1971, when he tried to push the songwriter to explain the lack of live performances. But Drake finally offered up an explanation of sorts: 'There were only two or three concerts that felt right, and there was something wrong with the others. I did play [Les] Cousins, and one or two folk clubs in the North, but the gigs just sort of petered out.'

In fact, Drake was cocooned from the very start, offered only to audiences who would 'understand' where he was coming from and might forgive the more protracted tune-ups between songs. In an era when promoters thought nothing of putting Jimi Hendrix on the same bill as The Monkees, or an acoustic David Bowie with the stodgy boogie of Humble Pie, he was consistently mollycoddled by the Witchseason family.

And if his introduction to the core Witchseason audience was certainly daunting – third on the bill to Fairport Convention at the Royal Festival Hall on 24 September 1969, the night they debuted their English folk-rock masterpiece, *Liege & Lief* – anyone else would have seen it as an extraordinary break. No slogging around 'folk clubs in the North' for this privileged youth. Even the other act on that night's landmark bill, John and Beverley Martyn, were in perfect tandem with Drake's musical direction. The pair soon took Drake to their collective bosom; and when in May 1970 they moved to a 'traditional house' surrounded by Hampshire countryside, they provided Drake with an escape from the city (directly inspiring his most idiomatic song, 'Northern Sky').

The Martyns also had an album to promote; and from a similar commercial base point. Although John Martyn already had two Island albums to his own name (*London Conversation* and *The Tumbler*), the duo's debut, the warmly received *Stormbringer*, had just appeared in the shops. Only now did the new husband's perceptible talent in those earlier offerings begin to deliver on Chris Blackwell's faith. Not surprisingly, Joe Boyd was quick to suggest the pair share a further bill with Drake at the altogether more intimate Queen Elizabeth Hall, another potentially prestigious South Bank affair that would hopefully bring further press attention, along with another sympathetic, patient audience.

The February 1970 showcase, though, only proved that Nick Drake was fast losing what little performing craft he had mustered from months of unbilled performances at Les Cousins. John Martyn, internally fuelled by liberal amounts of alcohol before every performance, was pained to see such a self-conscious performer: 'When he played live it was just soul-destroying to watch him. It was like watching a man being stripped naked.' Reports of the show reached an old friend from Marlborough, Simon Coker, who recalled the teenage Drake as 'a confident performer. And [then] I heard about this particular performance . . . from people . . . who said he mumbled. And I remember saying at the time, "That doesn't sound like Nick at all."' Not the Nick he had known, anyway.

It had never occurred to Joe Boyd – and why would it? – that he wasn't doing Drake a huge favour by foisting him on the very folk who bought Witchseason's assorted Island output. And now, following the QEH showcase, he assigned the fledgling songster the support slot on two short but important tours. The first of these announced the fifth Fairport Convention incarnation in two-and-a-half years (Sandy Denny and Ashley Hutchings having quit on *Liege & Lief*'s completion, to pursue their own individual visions of English folk-rock); the second slot was on a five-date foray for Fotheringay, Denny's eagerly awaited post-Fairport combo. Drake didn't even last the five dates. As Boyd relates in his own memoir, 'When he called me from the road after the third date, his voice had the crushed quality of defeat, "I, uh, I don't think I can do any more shows, uh, I'm sorry." He just wanted to come home.' And that appears to have been that.[16]

If Boyd was nonplussed by this impasse, Island boss Blackwell adopted the stoical view: 'It was hard to put pressure on someone who wouldn't tour when their record only cost five hundred quid.' Both remained convinced that the terrible beauty of Drake's songs would eventually register with record buyers, and continued to fund further sessions. Displaying remarkable faith (and foresight), the pair coerced the increasingly withdrawn ex-student into turning up at the studio with whatever songs he was still writing, while Boyd persevered in his search for the perfect sonic backdrop to this songwriter's uniquely English vision.

The discernible deterioration in Drake's daily demeanour concerned Boyd, and his Sound Techniques compadre John Wood, less than this indeterminate quest; perhaps because, to them, introspection was now the chosen response of many to the Sixties' more overt excesses. As Drake's friend and arranger, Robert Kirby, points out: 'Walking around Cambridge in those days, there were fifty people worse than Nick that you would pass on the pavement every hour.' And it wasn't like Boyd and Wood weren't surrounded by such types. Two equally extraordinary guitarists on the Witchseason roster – John Martyn and Richard Thompson – could be just as withdrawn:

> **John Martyn:** I was actually very shy and retiring and ever so sweet and gentle until I was twenty, and then I just got the heave with . . . all that terribly nice, rolling-up-joints-and-sitting-on-toadstools-watching-the-sunlight-dapple-its-way-through-the-dingly-dell-of-life's-rich-pattern stuff. Back then, everybody expected you to be like that . . . I very consciously turned away from that. [1990]

Thompson, already something of an enigma (where did that *darkness* in those early songs come from?), inspired a sense of awe in fellow musicians that kept most prying eyes at bay. Linda Peters, who before marrying Thompson got to know Drake as well as any lady friend, believes that 'there was a point when . . . Richard could [have] go[ne] Nick's way . . . It was very hard for him to pull himself out of that, but he . . . latched onto people who were outgoing enough to pull him out of it . . . He made a definite effort to do that, and Nick didn't.' Anthea Joseph, too, found Thompson and Martyn 'in their individual ways . . . equally difficult to deal with. But you could talk to them . . . I don't remember any "ordinary" conversations with Nick . . . not one.'

The naturally taciturn Thompson was in a particularly traumatized state of mind in the early months of 1970. His songs of the period remain the darkest ever penned by someone who once okayed the release of a compilation of archival recordings entitled *Doom and Gloom from the Tomb*. 'Crazy Man Michael' and 'Farewell, Farewell', his two original contributions to the *Liege & Lief* LP, were songs from the brink – as was 'Never Again', another song penned at the time that he did not record until 1974. In 'Crazy Man Michael', the darkest from a pitch-black lot, the narrator is driven mad when he stabs a talking raven in a rage (as you do), only to discover that he has killed his true love and is now 'cursed be', an outcome previously fore-told by the garrulous bird. The depiction of mad Michael fully reflected the way Thompson now appeared to some:

> Crazy Man Michael, he wanders and walks
> And talks to the night and the day-o
> But his eyes they are sane and his speech it is clear
> And he longs to be far away-o.

In reality, Thompson was channelling some very real grief and guilt; for back in May 1969 he and his girlfriend Jeannie 'the Taylor' Franklin had been travelling in the back of the Fairport van on the way home from a gig in Birmingham when the roadie fell asleep at the wheel, and the van crashed into the central reservation. Thompson survived, but Jeannie (and origi-nal Fairport drummer Martin Lamble) did not.

Although in a recent interview with *Mojo*, Thompson claimed he 'was never in the studio at the same time' as Joe's private project, quarter of a century earlier he described his experience at a 1970 Drake session to *Zigzag* magazine's Connor McKnight, who wrote the only profile of Drake published in his lifetime: 'It was at Trident[!] I think, and I asked him what he wanted; but he didn't say much, so I just did it and he seemed fairly happy. People say that I'm quiet, but Nick's ridiculous.' Thompson's first experi-ence of dubbing guitar to a Drake song live, which resulted in *Bryter Layter*'s 'Hazy Jane II', might actually have provided him with the kind of jolt *he* needed; and, as wife Linda Thompson suggests, would continue to need.

Hoping to make that 'breakthrough' album, which might

chase away all of Witchseason's financial problems, Joe Boyd's concerns remained primarily musical. But even he had to work away at Drake in order to get a clear indication of what he thought about a particular performance, or performer: 'I had to cross-examine him to make sure he liked the arrangements. He definitely was a big fan of [Richard] Thompson . . . [but] most people, myself included, were too careful, wary of disturbing his silences.'

In fact, Thompson seems to have recognized Drake as some-one who drained people of their bonhomie even when, as in his case, it was in short supply. When Boyd dispatched Nick Drake to Fairport's rural retreat in Little Hadham, to work on some songs for his second album with the new Fairport rhythm-section, Dave Pegg and Dave Mattacks, he seems to have stayed largely out of their way. The larger-than-life Danny Thompson, whose acoustic bass played such a part in defining *Five Leaves Left*'s unique feel, was not being invited back for Drake's second album, perhaps because, as Boyd says, 'Danny would slap [Drake] on the back, tease him in rhyming slang, make fun of his self-effacement and generally give him a hard time.' And so it would be left to Dave Pegg to interpret Drake's non-verbal signs, playing along to the songs he was shown at Little Hadham for 'three or four days'.

Even Pegg, though, had to admit the poor boy was now 'so introverted, you could never tell if he liked stuff or not . . . It was just running through arrangements . . . He had all the songs, and [some] fairly positive ideas about how he wanted them done.' Thrown in at the deep end of Drake's dark sea, Pegg got on with it. As did Mattacks. Even if Drake never really explicated what he wanted done with the music he made up, he was presumably okay with Fairport's contribu-tion because Pegg's plangent bass would burble away on nine of the ten songs on *Bryter Layter*, while Dave Mattacks gently taps his way through half the album. But there were still strings a-plenty to pull.

In the end, the new sonic smorgasbord again failed to thrill Drake, who mumbled the most veiled of criticisms to his one public interrogator, Jerry Gilbert: 'We started doing [*Bryter Layter*] almost a year ago. But I'm not altogether clear about this album – I haven't got to terms with the whole presentation.' He made much the same ill-expressed point to David Sandison who, as an Island insider, knew something of the circumstances involved in making the album: 'At the time . . . I got the impression from Nick that he didn't like the strings, or the way the album was presented . . . [Yet] *Bryter Layter* took a year to make *because* Nick Drake spent that long making damn sure it was precisely the way he wanted it.'

Like Barrett, Drake was the kind of artist who, even when unconvinced by what a musical overseer-cum-producer was doing to his songs, kept his thoughts largely to himself. It left Boyd to interpret the most intangible of clues. Because whatever Drake thought of Joe as a producer, he was still to a large extent in awe of the person himself. (Anthea Joseph again called it right when observing: 'He was emotionally tied to Joe, it was a mental thing.') Only when the album was done did he finally 'confront' Boyd.

So what *was* his problem? According to Boyd: 'He felt that it was too arranged, too produced, too many other personalities.' This, though, was precisely Boyd's forte. As arranger Kirby pointed out shortly before his death, the man 'was more of a facilitator [than a] producer. He would put the deals together and then get various inspired combinations of musicians to make up the terrific range on the [Witchseason] albums.'

One 'inspired combination' Boyd brought about during the

Bryter Layter sessions did provide Drake with the musical context he'd always craved. Welsh-born Velvet Underground founder John Cale – who was back in Britain formulating the sound for his own baroque rock symphony, *Paris 1919* – was both an arranger and a fine songwriter in his own right, classically trained (under Aaron Copeland, no less), and demonstrably capable of bringing out strange fruit in artists as diverse as Nico, The Modern Lovers and The Stooges. The two songs Cale now arranged for Drake – 'Northern Sky' and 'Fly' – were the product of a single brainstorming session; Boyd's description of the pair arriving at the studio the next morning, 'John with a wild look in his eyes and Nick trailing behind', perfectly capturing the nature of these contradistinct personalities.

The ever-eclectic Cale proceeded to play viola, harpsichord, celeste, piano and organ, while the ever-dependable Pegg plucked away on his bass. And, for once, Drake rose to the challenge of a great arranger, delivering in 'Northern Sky' perhaps his finest vocal performance; as Cale's uplifting arrangement vies for dominion over the atypically downbeat Drake lyric: 'Would you love me through the winter? / Would you love me till I'm dead? / Oh, if you would and you could / Come blow your horn on high.'[17] But Cale found his experience of working with 'the genius musician' (as he later described him) no more edifying than previous nominees, telling Nick Kent in 1975, 'You couldn't talk to him. He was like a zombie, like he just had no personality left.'

The exquisite high of 'Northern Sky' was an impossible act to follow, and Drake didn't really try. The low-key instrumental 'Sunday' would be its solitary successor and album coda – one of three instrumentals with which Drake bookended his latest ten-song collection (the other two, 'Introduction' and the title track, would open each side). Boyd told American collector

Frank Kornelussen, when co-compiling the posthumous *Time of No Reply* LP, 'Nick was reluctant to introduce other songs to the *Bryter Layter* sessions for fear [I] might choose a vocal performance in place of any of the three instrumentals, of which Nick was very proud.' But that may well not be the whole truth and nothing but. Given the problem Drake was having summoning up single sentences in conversation – and as Linda Thompson says, by now he 'made monosyllabic seem quite chatty' – it seems highly likely he was experiencing similar difficulties with the lyrics he once pored over.

Whether Drake sensed it or not, the songs were starting to dry up – just three years after he first found his muse. Because he had made the fateful decision not to return to any of the songs he had accumulated in the long lead-up to *Five Leaves Left* – even 'Things Behind the Sun', which Boyd pushed him continually to record – Drake placed an unnecessary burden across his own back. As engineer John Wood recalls, 'He [simply] didn't have the [*Bryter Layter*] material ready, for unlike *Five Leaves Left* he was actually still writing for this album.' 'Northern Sky' may be where it is on the album, the penultimate spot, because it was the last song he penned. Certainly if it was written in Hampshire while staying with the Martyns, as Beverley has indicated, then the song dates from the summer of 1970, by which time he was fast disappearing into an interior world. And for one of the Martyns it was quite a shock:

John Martyn: When I first met [Nick] he was rather more urbane than he became. He was always charming, delicately witty. But he just became more and more withdrawn . . . He just slipped and slipped further and further away into himself and divorced himself from the mundane. It [was] very sad, really.

It was only now that those who had always been closest to Drake began to sense that their boy was not so much introspective as almost cataleptic. For his parents, far removed from the hurly burly of London in pastoral Henley-in-Arden, their physical distance was as nothing to the growing chasm between their son and the world at large. According to his mother, Molly, it had been – at least in the beginning – a conscious choice: 'He took this room [in Hampstead], all alone, and he decided to cut off from all his friends and that he was just going to concentrate on music.' His father was left nonplussed: '[Once] he shut himself off in this room . . . it was rather difficult to get at him.' Those who could still get to London easily, such as college friend Brian Wells, 'would go and see him, [but] by then he'd become odd'. Drake could have been one of Laing's case studies, as Barrett almost was. He was shutting down from within, a paradigm for the divided self that Laing previously identified in that controversial work:

> The [divided] individual in the ordinary circumstances of living may feel more unreal than real; in a literal sense, more dead than alive; precariously differentiated from the rest of the world, so that his identity and autonomy are always in question . . . He may feel more insubstantial than substantial, and unable to assume that the stuff he is made of is genuine, good, valuable. And he may feel his self as partially divorced from his body . . . Such an individual, for whom the elements of the world . . . have a different hierarchy of significance from that of the ordinary person, is beginning, as we say, to 'live in a world of his own' . . . It is not true to say, however . . . that he is losing 'contact with' reality, and withdrawing into himself. External events no longer affect him in the same way as they do others: it is not that they affect him less; on the contrary,

frequently they affect him more . . . It may, however, be that the world of his experience comes to be one he can no longer share with other people . . . It is lonely and painful to be always misunderstood, but there is at least from this point of view a measure of safety in isolation . . . He maintain[s] himself in isolated detachment from the world for months, living alone in a single room . . . But in doing this, he [begins] to feel he [is] dying inside . . . [so] he emerge[s] into social life for a brief foray in order to get a 'dose' of other people, but 'not an overdose' . . . [before] withdraw[ing] again into his own isolation in a confusion of frightened hopelessness.

If by the end of 1970 Drake was cutting himself off from the world that lay outside his music, he was evidently intent on reflecting this shift in the music itself. He told Jerry Gilbert that he planned to make his third album a solo album in the true sense: 'For the next one I [like] the idea of just doing something with John Wood, the engineer at Sound Techniques.' He had already told Joe Boyd as much as the producer was preparing to pack his bags and take off for a job with Warners in L.A.: 'The next record is just going to be me and guitar.' Until now he had gone along with Boyd's way of making him a household name. It was increasingly clear it wasn't working. And though he failed to articulate his feelings to Boyd at this crucial juncture, when it might have made a difference, Drake felt let down.

He did, however, voice his disenchantment to three friends: Robert Kirby, Paul Wheeler and Brian Wells. Wheeler was surprised to find his friend even thought in terms of commercial success ('I didn't think he was in it for that'); while Wells, having sat and listened to the whole of *Bryter Layter* in Drake's presence, felt constrained to comment: 'Well, if I'd made a record like that and it hadn't sold I'd have been in the pits.'

Drake muttered back, 'Now you see.' Kirby, still slightly in awe of his fellow musician, noticed that 'after *Bryter Layter* bombed, it [became] apparent that all was not well'. He even came to believe that, such was his friend's disenchantment, he 'stopped writing for a while'. Meanwhile, Drake's bright and beautiful sister, who had her own upward career trajectory to consider, couldn't see why her brother's music was not selling and determined to find out why his record company was failing him. She was in for a surprise:

> **Gabrielle Drake:** I think the crux came around the time he produced *Bryter Layter* . . . I rang up Island because we thought he was deeply depressed at that time because Island weren't supporting him, that he'd brought out a record, and they'd never give him dates and things like that . . . They said, 'We'd do anything for Nick, give him publicity, but he won't do [any of] it.' . . . I suddenly realized that . . . [here] was not where the problem lay.

The sister began to fear for her brother's state of mind but felt powerless to intervene, while Nick continued to drift downward, invisible to the world he had once hoped to impress in song.

*

Meanwhile, another cracked actor feared for the very future of his own troubled sibling; and was equally fearful of whether he, too, might succumb to the schizophrenia that threatened to consume his entire family. Like Gabrielle Drake, David Bowie had tried his best to help his (half-)brother, Terry, but by the winter of 1971 he had come to feel the familial bonds tying him to his schizoid sibling were holding him down, too. Although Terry had not been definitively diagnosed with schizophrenia until 1969, the signs had been there for some time. Indeed, to brother David's mind, he was simply living out the family curse. Some ten years older than his half-brother, Terry was thirteen when his aunt Una was interned at Park Prewett, a Victorian asylum near Basingstoke, where she was diagnosed with schizophrenia and given electro-shock treatment. By April 1957, she was dead (from cancer, though some in the family seemed convinced she took her own life). When David's cousin Kristina was temporarily housed with his family, as her mother slowly succumbed to the familial disturbance of the mind, it seemed to the young David a question not of if, but when:

> **David Bowie:** It scared me that my own sanity was in question at times, but on the other hand I found it fascinating that my family had this streak of insanity . . . [Terry] was manic depressive and schizophrenic. I often wondered at the time how near the line I was going and how far I should push myself. I thought that it would be serving my mental health better if I was aware that insanity was a real possibility in my life . . . [] . . . It had tragically afflicted particularly my mother's side of the family . . . There were far too many suicides for my liking – and that was something I was terribly fearful of. I think it really made itself some kind of weight I felt I was carrying. [1993]

That weight was something Bowie liked to turn to his advantage. Tony Zanetta, Main Man Records employee turned memoir-writer, recalled how in the Ziggy years 'the genetic madness that lurked in his family was a theme to which he turned whenever his life seemed out of control, or he made mistakes that he did not wish to acknowledge. It could be used to explain anything.' He also had a certain a tendency to place himself at the centre of a psychodrama, family or otherwise, though in real life he preferred to be ever the observer, one step removed from others' meltdowns.

Thus, by the time the BBC broadcast their exhaustive 1993 overview of his career. Bowie was vividly describing his brother in the throes of a psychotic episode on the way home from a a February 1967 Cream concert they'd attended in Bromley. As he tells it, Terry: 'collapsed on the ground and he said the ground was opening up and there was fire and stuff pouring out of the pavement, and I could almost see it for him, because he was explaining it so articulately.' It is an enticing description, were it not for its distinct similarity to the account from Terry's own lips of his first psychotic episode outside Chislehurst Caves, reproduced in the Gillmans' *Alias David Bowie* seven years before Bowie gave his version, which led to him sleeping rough for eight days before turning up at his mother's house, just as David was making one of his rare visits:

Terry Burns: I heard a voice saying to me, 'Terry, Terry,' and I looked up and there was this great light and this beautiful figure of Christ looking down at me, and he said to me, 'Terry, I've chosen you to go out into the world and do some work for me.' He said, 'I've picked you out.' And the light of his face was so intense that I fell to the ground. I was on my stomach resting on my hands looking down and when I looked around me there was this big burning, a big ring of fire all around me, and the heat was intense, it was terrible. And then it all disappeared.

In Terry's version, though, his brother was nowhere to be seen, and Bowie's version – which seems to have been accepted at face value by just about every Bowie author since its 1993 appearance, despite its belated, somewhat suspicious appearance after Terry's death – raises its own sorts of questions. Though he doubtless did hear about this and other such episodes from family members, and perhaps from Terry himself, Bowie had by the time of the episode fled his mother's coop and was ensconced at Ken Pitt's place. He was almost certainly in denial about his brother's true mental state for some time (he made no mention of it to Pitt in those early months). Indeed, if his realisation of the true state of his brother's schizophrenia coincided with its appearance as subject-matter in his songs, these only stated to appear early in 1969 with songs such as 'Janine' and 'Unwashed and Somewhat Slightly Dazed', the latter a whimsical precursor to 'All the Madmen'.

Both songs would remain in the set through February 1970, when Bowie debuted the first song he intended for *The Man Who Sold the World*, 'The Width of a Circle' (which in its complete form would include the couplet, 'He struck the ground, a cavern appeared / And I smelt the burning pit of fear', a seeming reference to the Chislehurst Cave incident or something like it). If Bowie did witness a similar episode after going to see a Cream show in London, it seems doubtful that he would have let it gestate so long before coming out in song. In fact, only the band's farewell performance at the Albert Hall on 26 November 1968 really fits this timeline.

Something certainly provided a tipping point in Bowie's songwriting. Pre-1969, allusions to his family's predisposition are non-existent; whereas Terry's breakdown became the perennial backdrop to his work in the period 1969–70, when he started to write the kind of songs that made him the iconoclast most likely to. At the same time he became (almost simultaneously) involved in relationships with two women who remember constant references to the family curse. Mary Finnegan, for much of this period both landlady and lover, believed it was 'the fact of Terry . . . which explained his refusal to take LSD, for the drug was suspected . . . of inducing . . . schizophrenia'. And then when Bowie met the refreshingly hedonistic Angie Barnett, some time around April 1969, he couldn't wait to bring up the rattling skeleton in his family's cranial closet:

> **Angie Bowie:** David told me how he worshipped Terry, and how Terry had been such a big influence on him, introducing him to music, politics and poetry – and also to a haunting fear . . . Diagnosed as a paranoid schizophrenic . . . Terry was in a mental ward, as David revealed himself to me that [first] night in Beckenham, confessing to an awful dread that he might follow his half-brother's path. It was an especially frightening prospect, he told me, because Terry was in fact one of several people in his mother's family who had become unhinged. David said that sometimes when he got drunk or stoned, he could almost feel the family madness in him.

One further clue that Bowie had consciously placed himself on that tightrope separating sanity from insanity throughout the period leading up to the writing and recording of *The Man Who Sold the World* (*TMWSTW*) – only to then disown the album for the next decade – comes from an intentionally flippant comment he made to a *Creem* interviewer in October 1971, on the verge of starting *Ziggy Stardust*: 'There was nothing ambitious about *The Man Who Sold the World*, except maybe the ambition to crawl out of a cave.' That cave, one suspects, had a name.

There was also a more immediate reason why Terry remained on David's mind throughout the six months it took to create *TMWSTW*. Bowie's now-wife Angie had taken pity on the forlorn figure, no longer welcome in his mother's home, and took her husband at his word when he said that 'he worshipped Terry'. As such, she brought Terry temporarily into the Bowie household as shelter from the storm now raging inside his head, inviting him to stay at Haddon Hall 'for up to four weeks at a time'. Hence why, when photographer Ray Stevenson called at the hall, Bowie's closest musical associate, producer/bassist Tony Visconti, told him 'not to make jokes about "loonies".' The reality of living with a schizophrenic, though, ultimately proved too wearing for the would-be *wunderkind* and his wife, who were forced to recognize that Terry's madness was real and that Cane Hill was the only place for him.

Before that decision was made, however, Terry's presence at the recently established communal headquarters of Bowie Enterprises seems to have directly inspired Bowie to write his first real song of brotherhood, 'All the Madmen'. Here he positively welcomed the possibility that he might end up among 'the madmen', being 'quite content they're all as sane as me!' And whenever the subject came up in interviews at this time – usually at *his* prompting – he painted Terry's internment at Cane Hill in glowing terms, though nothing could have been further from the truth: 'The majority of the people in my family have been in some kind of mental institution. As for my brother, he doesn't want to leave. He likes it very much . . . He'd be happy to spend the rest of his life there, mainly because most of the people are on the same wavelength as him.'

Angie was not so bowled over by the sentiment of a song in which the narrator is 'on the same wavelength' as the madmen. By now, the pair had established a routine where 'he would play me what he'd just written. If I liked it – well, even if I didn't, even if I judged it too dark or twisted or melodramatic, as I did "All the Madmen" – . . . he'd polish it up.' This time she couldn't relate, but 'All the Madmen' was set to define the latest and most convincing Bowie persona, while the rest of the songs cut for his next Mercury album would follow its lead into equally dark, twisted terrain.

Never entirely comfortable with the skeletons he now chose to confront in song, it would take Bowie thirty years to admit he had been feeding off his own fearfulness: 'I'd been seeing quite a bit of my half-brother during that period, and I think a lot of it, obviously, had been working on me . . . I think his shadow is on quite a lot of the [Man Who Sold the World] material . . . I think I was going through an awful lot of concern about what exactly my [own] mental condition was, and where it may lead.'

Of the songs contained on TMWSTW, 'After All' is perhaps the scariest. Straight out of Village of the Damned, these children really do 'sing with impertinence, shading impermanent chords'. While for all the megalomania unleashed on side two (the title track, 'Saviour Machine', 'The Supermen'), what is wholly absent from this newlywed's new album is any song of love. Its one 'love song' is the jaundiced 'She Shook Me Cold', where a maneater 'sucked my dormant will', even as he willingly offers to 'give my love in vain / to reach that peak again'. Throughout the album, wholesome emotions are put behind frosted glass; a lesson Bowie's father had taught him. As Bowie told The Times back in 1968, adopting his father's voice (and values): 'To get emotional about something, well, that's only fit for the servants' quarters – like mental illness.'

Bowie's post-'Fame' description of TMWSTW songs as 'all family problems and analogies, put into science fiction form' was meant as an oblique allusion to the album's real subject matter at a time when his true biography remained misted by myth. More disingenuous was a simultaneous assertion – at a time when cocaine was wont to do the talking for him – that the 1970 album was a case of 'holding . . . some kind of flag for hashish. As soon as I stopped using that drug, I realized it damp-ened my imagination'.

In truth, his wild imagination rarely ran riot as it did on the nine *TMWSTW* . . . songs. He had finally delivered the goods – even if he had to be given a strong nudge in the right direction by right-hand men guitarist Mick Ronson and producer Tony Visconti. (Visconti later complained: 'David was so frustrating to work with at the time. I [just] couldn't handle his poor atti-tude and complete disregard for his music.') In fact, it seems to have been Visconti and Ronson who were largely responsible for the sheer heaviness of the sound on the album; with Bowie allowing them to have their way, as he openly admitted to journo Penny Valentine on its release:

David Bowie: It was my idea initially to get heavier – just to try it another way – but [Tony Visconti] got it all together. I probably needed a heavier sound behind me, and obviously it's worked. It's not that I have a very strong feeling for heavy music – I don't. In fact I think it's fairly primitive as a musical form. [1971]

Two months before he had begun work on *TMWSTW*, Bowie had described a very different record to the same female pop journalist: 'The next album will be more solid. As the first side will be completely augmented it means specially writing a whole set of new material. The second side will just be me with a guitar.' The half-acoustic/half-electric format – which may have originated with manager Ken Pitt, publicist to Dylan when

Clinton Heylin

he had used said format to such effect on his apocalyptic 1966 tour – was adopted by Bowie in concert throughout 1970–71. But when it came time to make the album, it was primarily Ronson who imposed the sound on Bowie's songs; and as Visconti says, 'Mick's idols were Cream. [So] he coached Woody [Woodmansey] to play like Ginger Baker and me to play like Jack Bruce.'

For the first time, the intensity of the music matched Bowie's edgy new lyrics, the doom-laden message being further reinforced by the (original) album sleeve. Both Bowies had happily approved a cover they had commissioned from their Arts Lab friend Mike Weller, which placed a rugged rifle-toting cowboy in the foreground and Cane Hill in the background. Weller would later make the extraordinary claim that it was *his* 'idea to design a cover that depicted Cane Hill, [the] main impetus [having come] from visiting a friend who was a patient there'. That original *TMWSTW* cover, though, is such an exact visual representation of 'All the Madmen' – with a hint of 'Running Gun Blues' – it would be somewhat incredible to discover it was not Bowie's conception. Perhaps Weller's assertion was his way of getting back at Bowie after the singer replaced Weller's sleeve – with the infamous 'dress cover' – for the UK edition.

By the time Weller delivered his evocative sleeve at the end of 1970, the singer-songwriter was already starting to think he may have put too much autobiography into his latest creation, and began to back-pedal. The change of sleeve was probably one manifestation of this concern, though it came too late for his American label, who were preparing to 'rush-release' the album to coincide with Bowie's first US visit in February 1971[18]. Yet once he was thousands of miles away from Beckenham, he seemed happy addressing the album's more autobiographical elements. When *Creem*'s Patrick Salvo noted that 'growing up before one's time can . . . lead to any amount of various functional disorders, [and] this is found quite plainly in some of your writings', the still largely unknown Bowie did not summon his disingenuous self. He simply agreed: 'You're right. It happened to my brother . . . I mean, there's a schizoid streak within my family, so I dare say that I'm affected by that.'

Back home, though, the English album, issued the following April, was hastily housed in the ill-conceived 'dress cover', perhaps another attempt to sabotage the album's prospects; or just another ill-conceived attempt to construct an image ironic enough for a young rock audience and outrageous enough to worry their mamas and papas. After all (by jingo), he had called the band he formed back in the winter of 1970 The Hype, a name he claimed at the time he 'deliberately chose . . . because now no one can say they're being conned'. Although the glammed-up ensemble looked more like Village People than The Spiders From Mars, Bowie would later claim a direct lineage. At the July 1972 Dorchester press conference his manager organized to introduce Ziggy, he told the largely American press: 'We died a death. [But] I knew it was right . . . and I knew it was what people would want eventually.' Tony Visconti, The Hype's legendary stardust cowboy bassist, would go on to claim that The Hype's Roundhouse debut was 'the very first night of glam rock . . . [There was] Marc Bolan visibl[y] resting his head on his arms on the edge of the stage, taking it all in.'

If the BBC broadcast of The Hype's debut concert suggests they were still a long way from the finished article, it confirmed that the songs had started coming thick, fast and heavy. Almost the whole of *TMWSTW* would be written from scratch in the two months following The Hype's live debut, including at least a couple of songs – 'Black Country Rock' and 'The Width of a Circle' – for which the final lyrics were only produced when there was a backing track already recorded and a vocal track urgently required. The former track, according to Visconti's lively autobiography, 'was actually its working title, which simply described the styles of music we'd used. [But] David [then] cleverly incorporated those words into the song.' As for the Bolanesque wail, mid-song, 'David spontaneously did a Bolan vocal impression because he ran out of lyrics.' Scrabbling around for song ideas, he even nicked the refrain for 'Saviour Machine' from 1968's unreleased 'Ching-a-Ling'.

Ironically, the frenetic way the album was pulled together gave it a real unity of sound and vision. Yet at the time, *TMWSTW* made very few waves. In the UK, the hook-free non-album single 'Holy Holy' didn't help, proving that when Bowie said, 'I don't want to be one of those singers whose career depends on hit singles', he wasn't joking. In the US, not only was the album released a couple of months earlier, it was supported by the altogether more appropriate lead-single, 'All the Madmen', the perfect introduction to the darkened grotto of *The Man Who Sold the World*. Despite Bowie's refusal to champion what he (plus Ronson and Visconti) had wrought, taken as a whole *TMWSTW* was a real statement of intent. And it was one that was recognized, by *NME*'s Nick Kent at least, as a musical manifesto for the 1970s:

[The album is] a great epic work of tortured third-generation rock & roll poetry. Whether it was the 'Width of a Circle', an eight-minute odyssey where Dante and Genet meet and do battle in Bowie's own inferno of crazed puns, homosexual encounters and black magic symbolism; or 'All the Madmen', where 'the thin men walk the streets, while the saints [sic] lay underground'; or the menace of 'Running Gun Blues' and the neurotic and blaringly sexual 'She Shook Me Cold'. Bowie delivers them all in a style that can only be paralleled with such works as 'Desolation Row' and *Astral Weeks*, while his band, led by Mick Ronson, played like the Cream on a forced diet of Valium.

Even Kent's verdict, though, was not delivered until October 1972, when the world was just about catching up. By then, wife Angie and new business manager Tony Defries had begun to drill into Bowie that mystery was a necessary prerequisite for superstardom. As of March 1971 – with the UK finally succumbing to T-Rextasy with their first number one, 'Hot Love' – he also had the example of his close friend Marc Bolan to draw on. On March 10, Bowie entered Radio Luxembourg's London studio to cut some demos of songs he had been working on during his trip to the States. The first demo, 'Moonage Daydream', was a sci-fi analogy-in-song destined to form a key part of Ziggy's repertoire. Another demo, initially called 'Song for Marc', would be introduced to the rock world the following year as 'Lady Stardust'. Stardom beckoned for Bowie, as a theme if not an actuality. The megalomania of the man who sold the world was about to give way to the kind that drew on the unquestioning adulation of a rock audience.

4. 1971–72: Half In Love With Easeful Death

I had no hope of producing anything like the expansive music I had envisioned and attempted to describe in my fiction, but certain people around me believed that was my target. Whispers of 'madness' fluttered backstage like moths eating at the very fabric of my project.
– Pete Townshend, 1999 (describing the 1971 *Lifehouse* project)

I got things inside my head / that even I can't face.
– David Bowie, 1969

That whole LP [*Muswell Hillbillies*] was a story about a person who was thrown into an environment and had to come to terms with it, and went through depressions, nervous breakdowns. That was what it was all about.
– Ray Davies, 1971

By 1971, the biggest touring acts in the world, all English, were at the very zenith of their ziggurat. The Who and The Stones, the great survivors, were doing very special things at Leeds

University, and anywhere else that would have them. Led Zeppelin and Deep Purple were making English hard rock so heavy it would have made Cream curdle. And Pink Floyd seemed intent on taking their form of cerebral space-rock to the whole planet, music hall by music hall.

Each had their own way of dealing with the poppier aspects of psychosis in song. If The Stones turned the Boston Strangler into some lascivious back-door man doing the midnight ramble, and Deep Purple stretched their hit-single paean to a 'Strange Kind of Woman' to almost album-side length by year's end[19], the Floyd started dabbling with demons a lot closer to home than some notorious US serial killer or a slightly crazed groupie. Waters, who was now exercising total control of the band's lyrical direction, was particularly keen to turn the band away from space-rock. 'If', one of the better tracks on *Atom Heart Mother*, had been the first gear shift, as Waters acknowledged in hindsight: '"If" is about not presenting the caring side of oneself . . . There's lines in there like . . . "If I go insane, please don't put your wire in my brain" . . . [which has] some of what I [then] did on *Dark Side of the Moon*.'

The rest of the band also recognized it was time to stop 'blundering in the dark'. As Nick Mason told the *Live at Pompeii* director the following year: 'We [were] in danger of becoming a relic of the past. For some people, we [had come to] represent their childhood, 1967, underground London, the free concert in Hyde Park.' The breakthrough, as far as guitarist Gilmour was concerned, was the twenty-five-minute live epic debuted at another large London open-air show, Crystal Palace Bowl, in May 1971. Half-jokingly referred to in this period as 'The Return of the Son of Nothing', in the fullness of time it would become 'Echoes'. The transition in subject matter from outer- to inner-space, from Kubrick to Coleridge, was signalled by the opening line's change from 'Planets meeting face to face' in early live performances to 'Overhead the albatross' by the time it was fixed to disc. The Floyd was increasingly confident about developing such songs live prior to taking them into the studio; or even between bouts of further shaping in the studio. And the process immeasurably improved the final cut. As EMI engineer John Leckie notes: 'They'd got ["Echoes"] into shape because they'd been playing it live.'

Unfortunately, such relentless touring brought its own problems – and the scale of US tours invariably brought the biggest headaches. Boredom, frustration and loneliness fed those inner voices and spawned ever greater ennui in the air-conditioned comfort of room-service, with the latest grateful orifice there to wile away the hours till the next gig, the next buzz. (The epoch is captured in all its jaded glory in The Rolling Stones' 1972 tour documentary, *Cocksucker Blues*, which was hastily scrapped and an anodyne alternative, *Ladies and Gentlemen*, substituted. It has still never been officially released.)

If the Floyd avoided many of the more obvious temptations, the one band they seemed to enjoy crossing paths with on the road was the wholly hedonistic Who. Waters was particularly impressed by Keith Moon's artistic way of demolishing hotel rooms, calling him, 'a very sophisticated smasher', while Nick Mason considered the self-proclaimed Moon the Loon 'very good company . . . [when] a lot of [rock] people are just drunken maniacs'. The 1971 Moon was still playing court jester to the (other) stars. And both bands found themselves traversing the States in November 1971 with sets intended to advance on all previous incarnations. The Floyd had finally cast aside all Barrettian detritus, while The Who had reduced their own albatross, *Tommy*, to a five-song medley; debuting the bulk of *Who's Next* to the throbbing throngs instead.

For The Who, touring *Tommy* around the arenas of America had been a financial necessity. They had never really dug themselves out of the various holes created first by busting up their equipment nightly, then their hugely expensive decision to extract themselves from the talons of producer Shel Talmy, and finally by letting manager Kit Lambert and resident looney Keith Moon take any personal sense of inadequacy out on the nearest inanimate (or sex) object, until they ran out of objects or energy. For Townshend, though, the success of *Tommy* was stopping him and the band from moving on, and he was starting to feel a little antsy:

Pete Townshend: *Tommy* and America – the great consumer nation – took us over and said, 'There are fifty million kids that wanna see you perform; what are you gonna do about it – are you gonna stay in Twickenham and work on your next album, or get your arse over there?' So you get your arse over there and you get involved in the standing ovation and the interviews, the nineteen-page *Rolling Stone* articles, the presentations of the Gold Albums, you know . . . and that takes two years to get out of the way, and then you realize that it's gonna take another two years to work on the [next] thing. [1971]

Descriptions such as 'the most important milestone in pop since Beatlemania' – *Rolling Stone*'s verdict on *Tommy* – were dogging its creator's footsteps and doing his head in. In fact, Townshend had already started to see all the flaws in his former creation and wanted to change it, even as an American mass-audience caught on: '*Tommy* was very clumsily put together . . . [but] the American audience thought that it was completely watertight, and that . . . everything hung together.' His immediate ambition was to transcend *Tommy*'s triter elements with what came next, while insisting that '[*Tommy*] was highly overrated . . . it was rated where it shouldn't have been . . . [in that] it attempted to tell a story in rock music.'

The relentless slog around America was not doing wonders for Townshend's writing muse, either. The Oo's first single since smash-hit 'Pinball Wizard', and their first post-*Tommy* statement, came with an appropriate title, 'The Seeker'. It just didn't come out in the studio quite how Townshend had envisaged it, though it 'sounded great in the mosquito-ridden swamp I made it up in – Florida at three in the morning, drunk out of my brain . . . But that's always where the trouble starts, in the swamp. The alligator turned into an elephant and finally stampeded itself to death on stages around England.'

This subdued re-entry into singledom certainly didn't stampede into the Top Ten – suggesting The Who's days as a singles band might be numbered. Townshend would persevere, though, issuing their best run of non-album singles since 'I Can See for Miles' – 'Let's See Action', 'Join Together' and 'Relay' – in rapid succession. None of them were exactly box-office, certainly not in the US, where they wanted something more; that is, more like *Tommy*. Such failures only fed Townshend's inner doubts, reinvoking the pre-*Tommy* paranoia that he might have lost his touch, and pushing him to ever more grandiose alternatives while the rest of the band watched and wondered:

John Entwistle: All those [early Seventies singles] represent [Pete] trying to talk to the kids in general. Pete was trying to get the same feel that 'My Generation' had, but it didn't really work. You see, they weren't pointed at the latest generation – they were pointed at ours, which had already grown up. That was the time when

Townshend honestly thought that he was losing his 'feel' and that he could no longer communicate. [1976]

Ironically, the biggest single success in this confused period was a brutally truncated version of an album track ('Won't Get Fooled Again'). The true state of Townshend's psyche, however, was not to be found on that FM-friendly A-side, but rather on its nakedly honest B-side, 'I Don't Even Know Myself', a song left over from an earlier, abandoned EP. Here was a song Townshend had been working on for a while. Back in May 1970 he had informed *Rolling Stone*'s Jonathan Cott that the song was his way of 'kinda blaming the world because you're fucked up . . . I think that the Self is an enemy that's got to be kicked out the fucking way so that you can really get down to it.' In the same interview, Townshend confessed that he was now trying to avoid writing in such a personal style, and that 'The Seeker' 'started off as being very much me, and then stopped being very much me . . . The whole thing is that, as soon as you discover that songs are personal, you reject them.'

There was one wholly personal song written that autumn he was smart enough not to reject or second-guess, instead making it part of the abstract *Lifehouse* concept. 'Behind Blue Eyes', with its unmistakeable anti-drug reference, 'If I swallow anything evil / Stick a finger down my throat . . .', was the song of a smiling self-assassin bottling up a lot of angst. Not that Townshend was the only member of The Who to feel frustrated by the need to reinforce their hard-won (if fully deserved) reputation as the greatest live rock band in the world.

In a band dominated by Townshend's ever twinkling muse, John Entwistle had never really been allowed the requisite outlet for his own songwriting, and now he was starting to write more and more first-rate material, which he worried might go to waste. Unlike George Harrison, whose sudden (and ultimately fleeting) metamorphosis into a songwriter who could hold his own with Lennon and McCartney had precipitated the Fab Four's demise, Entwistle didn't want to quit The Who. But he did want to find a forum for some of the sickest pop songs this side of Tom Lehrer, even if he was unabashed about the worldview he espoused in song: 'My whole idea of the world is sick. What do you expect from ten years in The Who? I write macabre songs.'

With their own UK record label, in the form of Track Records, and an American label, MCA, desperate for any Who-related product, Entwistle duly got the green light to begin a debut solo album in November 1970. The songs, some of which were two years old, had been bubbling up inside the bassist until, as he told *Record Mirror* in May 1971: 'I had to do the album or I'd have gone out of my head. There was so much bottled up inside me that I had to let it out.'

Yet anyone expecting a soul-searching examination of the inner life of the Ox soon found out *Smash Your Head Against the Wall* was nothing of the sort. Although it had plentiful visions of 'heaven and hell' – including a reworking of the fabled The Who set-opener of the same name, and a hilarious song sung from the devil's point of view, directed at all the damned souls coming his way ('You're Mine') – Entwistle was inclined to make a joke of life, the universe and everything. If the music was heavy, the lyrics verged on the Swiftian. Even the cover contained its own secret sick joke, Entwistle's death-mask face being transposed against an X-ray of the lungs of a terminal heart patient. The album was still well received by those who got the joke(s).

Townshend, on the other hand, was finding life less of a joke. And more like a concept. He had been toying with his next concept throughout the whole eighteen-month period the band

spent turning *Tommy* into a self-contained one-hour performance piece[20]. As Townshend recalled at the end of the Seventies,
'Virtually as soon as we finished recording [*Tommy*] I was thinking of other things: *Rock is Dead, Long Live Rock* – an early
version of *Quadrophenia*; *Lifehouse*; maybe developing "Rael"
from *The Who Sell Out*; just searching for something which we
could get away with.'

By autumn 1970 he had locked on a project called *Lifehouse*
that would be a film, an album and a series of 'spontaneous'
performances. Townshend had always been a proselytizer for
the affirmative potential inherent in pop music, but with
Lifehouse he clearly decided he would deliver something that
was genuinely 'a reflection of spiritual awareness' to The Who's
audience. Not surprisingly, given his predisposition and advo-
cacy of Meher Baba, there was a touch of messianism in the
language he used. He even suggested in print that *only* The
Who could do this:

> **Pete Townshend:** We're waiting for the follow-up to
> *Tommy*, for the follow-up to 'My Generation', for the
> rock revolution. We're waiting for rock . . . to indicate a
> direction . . . We've got to shake ourselves up, musically,
> and do something new and we're the only group in a
> position, financially and idealistically, to pioneer a new
> form of performance . . . We have that high enough
> ideal. [1971]

Lifehouse's origins went back to a premise that originally under-
lay *Tommy*, but which had been barely developed during its
transition from *Amazing Journey* to artefact. He had mentioned
the idea to US critic Paul Nelson when *Tommy* was taking shape:
'The first channel of vibrations through [the kid]'s ears is the

word Tommy, which *completely* blows his mind . . . and throws him right off the course of what he was on to before, which was very basically one note.' In September 1970 he expanded on the 'one note' idea in the second of a series of monthly columns he had begun writing for *Melody Maker*:

> Here's the idea, there's a note, a musical note, that builds the basis of existence somehow. Mystics would agree, saying that of course it is OM, but I am talking about a MUSICAL note . . . This note pervades everything, it's an extremely wide note, more of a hiss than a note as we normally know them. The hiss of the air, of activity, of the wind and of the breathing of someone near. You can always hear it . . . I think everybody hears the same note or noise. It's an amazing thing to think of any common ground between all men that isn't directly a reflection of spiritual awareness. The hearing of this note is physical, very physical.

From hereon the *Melody Maker* column, which lasted until April 1971, would chart the transition of *Lifehouse* from inchoate concept to full-blown The Who project. It was a part of the process; and of Townshend's ongoing attempts to maintain a dialogue between artist and audience, the veritable crux of *Lifehouse* – even if the audience was supposed to be wiped out by 'this note [that] pervades everything'. An October 1970 interview in *Disc* saw him explaining how this note 'basically creates complete devastation. And when everything is destroyed, only the real note, the true note that they have been looking for is left. Of course, there is no one left to hear it.'

In fact, the whole original *Lifehouse* concept was circular. The new suite of songs would open with 'Pure and Easy' ('There once was a note, pure and easy . . .'), and conclude with 'The Song is Over', segueing back into 'Pure and Easy' as the forces of totali-tarianism burst in upon this 'illegal concert, which they were trying to track down and stamp out . . . [But] when they finally break in, the concert has reached such a height that the audience are about to disappear.' It was a rather apocalyptic conclusion to a story bearing a close resemblance to the part of Corinthians describing the so-called Rapture. Again he was writing songs with a sense of mission, one which would have made Peter Green proud – to make music itself the new religion:

Man must let go his control over music as art or media fodder and allow it freedom. Allow it to become the mirror of a mass rather than the tool of an individual. Natural balance is the key. I will make music that will start off this process. My compositions will not be my thoughts, however, they will be the thoughts of the young, and the thoughts of the masses. Each man will become a piece of music, he will hear it for himself, see every aspect of his life reflected in terms of those around him, in terms of the Infinite Scheme. When he becomes aware of the natural harmony that exists between himself as part of creation he will find it simple to adjust and LIVE in harmony . . . We can live in harmony only when Nature is allowed to incorporate us into her symphony. Listen hard, for your note is here. It might be a chord or a dischord. Maybe a hiss or a pulse. High or low, sharp or soft, fast or slow. One thing is certain. If it is truly your own note, your own song, it will fit into the scheme. Mine will fit yours, and yours will fit his, his will fit others . . .

For the first time, though, Townshend failed to take the rest of The Who with him on this amazing journey. Daltrey says he 'got the gist of something important – that was – if you ever found the meaning of life it would be a musical note – it's a great idea, but Pete had fifty billion others . . . And that was always the problem with Pete.' When in a less forgiving mood, Daltrey would bluntly describe 'the narrative thread of [*Lifehouse* as] about as exciting as a fucking whelk race!' Even Townshend duly admitted that the dystopian aspect of *Lifehouse*, set in a future 'when rock & roll didn't exist', was 'very derivative of *1984* and *Fahrenheit 451*, and a lot of stuff [which] has now been covered by *Clockwork Orange*'. But it was the 'one note' aspect of the story that really disturbed Daltrey. And it was not just The Who singer who thought Townshend was going off the deep end. Kit Lambert, his key supporter on the *Tommy* project, was lukewarm; Chris Stamp was simply baffled; and producer Glyn Johns was adamant – it didn't make sense:

> **Pete Townshend:** Just before Glyn programmed *Who's Next*, he took me out to a pub [and] said, 'Pete, tell me just once more about this *Lifehouse*.' I thought, Oh God! So I told him the story. And he sat there thinking. I thought he was going to say, 'Now I get it!' And instead he said, 'I don't understand a fucking word that you said.' [2000]

Having invested his whole (well-)being in the project, Townshend teetered on the very brink of a real breakdown. As he openly admitted to his close friend Richard Barnes after the fact: 'I think for a while I lost touch with reality. The self-control required to prevent my total nervous breakdown was absolutely unbelievable . . . I'd spend a week explaining something to somebody and it'd be all very clear to me, then they'd go, "Right. Okay. Now can you explain it again?" There were about fifty people involved, and I [simply] didn't have the stamina to see it through.' In November 1971, eight months after finally acceding to the abandonment of *Lifehouse* as *Tommy's* successor, he described in almost confessional terms the dispiriting outcome to a West Coast journalist:

Pete Townshend: It sort of ended up me against the world . . . In that particular case, I had one idea about what the group should be doing, and the group had another idea . . . I really felt [*Lifehouse*] was a follow up [to *Tommy*] – the film, the album, the event, the disappearing theatre. The kind of thing I want to do still: the definitive rock movie . . . Roger got incredibly irritable, 'cause he felt I was trying to commandeer the group . . . And I was progressively getting worse [and worse]. I mean, I started to hallucinate . . . And I thought I must be getting schizophrenic. So in the end, about half way through the recording with Glyn, I just phoned up Chris Stamp . . . and said, 'Look, we've got to knock it on the head. Let's just put out an album, otherwise I really will go crazy.' And I would have done; no doubt about it . . . One time, when we were recording in New York at the Record Plant, I thought I was . . . standing in the middle of the room vomiting, vomiting, vomiting all over everybody. [1971]

In the same interview he also elliptically alluded to another occasion when he was 'sitting in a room, and everybody in the room . . . suddenly turn[ed] into frogs'; though he did not expand on the incident any further. And though he would periodically refer to suffering 'the first nervous breakdown of my life' at this point, it was not until he wrote a 1995 article for the *Richmond Review* – reproduced in the 'Deluxe' 2003 *Who's Next* CD reissue – that he admitted he had been on the verge of ending it all; and that when he began seeing frogs, it was in the middle of a meeting with Lambert to discuss the film of the album of the gig, and he was having a full-on mental meltdown:

'During [a 1971] meeting [in New York about *Lifehouse*], as Kit stamped around the room pontificating and cajoling, shouting and laughing, I began to have what I now know to be a classic New York Alcoholic Anxiety Attack Grade One. Everyone in the room transmogrified into huge frogs, and I slowly moved towards the open tenth-floor window with the intention of jumping out. Anya spotted me and gently took my arm . . . She saved my life. I was by that time a kook.'

A chastened Townshend duly returned to London with a tape of six *Lifehouse* tracks the band had recorded at Record Plant in New York with Leslie West (of Mountain) on rhythm guitar. Initially, he was convinced 'they were all great, like a new Who' – and there was one instance, the firing-on-all-cylinders 'Love Ain't for Keeping', where he was right. But Glyn Johns convinced him it would be even better if he came to Olympic studios in Barnes. So, as Townshend recalls, 'We went to Olympic and we suddenly realized that it wasn't Kit or the Record Plant at all, but The Who who had discovered another facet . . . [And when] we heard the tapes we'd done in the States [we decided] they weren't really very good.' Thoroughly disillusioned with the whole *Lifehouse* saga – though continuing to write songs for a possible resurrection[21] – he let Johns do his worst with the Olympic tapes. The result was *Who's Next*, The Who's finest set of songs and most consistent-selling album:

Pete Townshend: We left Glyn to compile the album . . .
So Glyn played us the album the way he thought it

should be, and we said, 'Great, put it out.' . . . My biggest disappointment with *Who's Next* was 'Baba O'Riley'. It was a long, nine-minute instrumental, and I kept cutting it and cutting it and cutting it; until eventually I cut all the length out of it and turned it into a rock song, [after I] shoved some words on it. [1971]

The words he shoved on to 'Baba O'Riley' actually came from another *Lifehouse* song, 'Teenage Wasteland', his first song of teen-angst to be told from the vantage point of adulthood. It was a good way to bookend an album destined to end with 'Won't Get Fooled Again'. The other 'new' Townshend song added to the equation at Olympic was 'Bargain', a sarcastic swipe at those, himself included, who had agreed to the bargain of the century by which *Lifehouse* became *Who's Next* ('I got to lose me to find you / I gotta give up all I had'). That sense of self-loathing would receive yet more column-inches on Townshend's next concept album.

Meanwhile, as he informed *Zigzag* at the time, he didn't feel he had delivered the 'natural successor' to *Tommy* that *Lifehouse*, in his fevered imagination, really could have been: 'A lot of people are waiting for the next Who album, which should really be some event in and around The Who; which is a logical next step from *Tommy*, which *Who's Next* wasn't. *Who's Next* wasn't a logical step in anyone's language. *Who's Next* was a stepping stone.' The following year he called it 'a compromise album' to Penny Valentine. By then, he had started on, and abandoned, a 'part-fiction rock documentary' called *Rock is Dead: Long Live Rock*, the next stepping stone on the long road to *Quadrophenia*.

The respite gave John Entwistle the opportunity to turn his hand again to songs of twisted Englishness, and this time he really locked on an aspect of the English psyche only hinted at in the songs of his more esteemed peers: the fool for love, the cuckold, the sexual inadequate. The 1972 *Whistle Rymes* [sic] was so morbid that if Townshend had actually thrown himself out of the ten-storey window in New York, it might have merely served as another song-idea for the bassist's macabre muse.

Over the ten songs that constitute *Whistle Rymes*, Entwistle evenly divided his concerns between peeping toms ('The Window Shopper'), like-minded perverts ('Now I Was Just Being Friendly', 'Apron Strings') and suicidal chumps who have discovered their true position in life ('I Feel Better', 'Thinkin' It Over' and 'I Found Out'). With Peter Frampton lending a hand between bands, the result was Entwistle's most thoroughly realized, elegiacally twisted album; and American fans seemed to love it. The album racked up quite respectable sales Stateside (175,000). The English public were more lukewarm, perhaps because, as one *Sounds* reviewer put it, Entwistle had finally revealed himself to be 'a colourful eccentric waiting to flash'.

★

The real irony was that for all Townshend's regular championing of The Kinks, it was Entwistle who had produced an album which closely accorded with Ray Davies' own warped worldview. *Whistle Rymes* and The Kinks' *Muswell Hillbillies* – issued a year apart – were not only perfect period-pieces, they were entirely of a piece (with Richard Thompson's *Henry the Human Fly* there to do the arbitrating). They even sold similar numbers in the States, their main target audience[22]. For Davies, though, there had been excess baggage to dump in the record-company dept., a couple of 'novelty' hit singles to write, long nights spent listening to bad English country 'covers' bands and two full tours of the US experiencing the real thing, before he felt ready to make a 'whole LP . . . about a person . . . thrown into an environment . . . [that meant he] went through depressions, nervous breakdowns'.

All the Madmen

It was a song about confused sexual identity – previously more Entwistle's forte – that first showed Davies a way back to the charts. 'Lola', the single that re-established The Kinks on *Top of the Pops*, was innuendo upon innuendo about a man attracted to a very butch 'girl' he met in a Soho bar. At one point the singer drops to his knees as Lola says, 'That's the way that I want you to stay', almost daring the BBC to ban such a blatantly transsexual song. (In the end they almost did, though not because of its transvestite theme, but rather because it name-checked the brand name Coca-Cola.)

The Kinks' return to the charts, though, only inspired further bitterness, amply expressed in the sarcastic 'Top of the Pops', and this time Ray was unambiguous about the perks of success: 'I've been invited out to dinner with a prominent queen.' With the finishing line of his relationship with Pye, The Kinks' managers and the Sixties pop establishment in sight, he let loose with both barrels. The album he built around his latest hit single, *Lola Versus Powerman and the Moneygoround, Part One* – which spawned another peculiar Kinks hit, 'Apeman' – promised to point a searing searchlight at the record industry itself. As he told *Disc*'s Lon Goddard during the sessions: 'I live in a strange world to some, but I think the straight world is a lot stranger . . . My whole intention [now is] to build a complete record. The LP we're doing has a storyline and 'Lola' is part of that.'

But for all the talk of another underlying concept, the album and its title track had almost nothing in common, as Davies for the first time seemed to be more concerned with the message than the music. As it happens, the album's main message was expressed in just four words, the title of the closing track, 'Got to Be Free'. *Lola Versus . . .* was Davies' not-so-fond farewell to Pye (and Reprise) – save for a half-assed soundtrack to the nudge-nudge wink-wink film, *Percy*. Starting in the spring of 1971, he set about charming a new suitor, RCA Records, the label responsible for the birth of country.

RCA had been resting on its laurels for a long, long while, until sometime in 1971 they realized the rock revolution was passing them by. Appointing a new head of A&R, Dennis Katz, they decided to splash the cash. In which case, Davies was their man. As he told authorized biographer Jon Savage: 'RCA wanted us so bad, I just said . . . "Ask for another hundred thousand pounds." And they offered it.'

In fact, someone in A&R had been doing their homework. The three signings RCA completed in September 1971, to much fanfare, included two A-list Sixties songwriters, both entirely free of other label obligations, and an underappreciated English singer-songwriter who was set fair to deliver his second classic album of the Seventies to his latest suitor. All three were invited to New York to share in the hype. Ray Davies, as an early fan of 'Space Oddity', knew of David Bowie, but one imagines Lou Reed's work with The Velvet Underground had largely passed him by. If Reed and Bowie both had impressive sets of songs stockpiled – with Reed demoing twenty-two songs for his first solo LP the following month, while Bowie delivered *Hunky Dory* on signing with another album's worth of songs ready to record – Davies had taken twenty demos with him into the studio in August. He was soon putting the finishing touches to The Kinks' follow-up to the lacklustre *Lola Versus* . . . The result: a real return to form.

Muswell Hillbillies, issued the last week of November 1971, was an album that straddled three of Davies' perennial preoccupations (family, a fantasy inner life and the lost past), and as such represented a welcome return to the rich territory of *Village Green* . . . and *Arthur*. This time, though, he set it to those most English of themes – social dislocation and depression. The musical backdrop was a pastiche of styles largely American in origin, ones pioneered by RCA. Not that his new record label was any more understanding of his music than Pye. As Davies told pop historian Peter Doggett, 'I don't think RCA knew what they wanted or what they were actually going to get. I think they wanted the brand-name.' To RCA, *Muswell Hillbillies* was a dozen songs by The Kinks, and they seemed to think that would be enough. Davies, though, did not, and began to tell anyone who would listen that the album was not all it could have been:

Ray Davies: I wanted [*Muswell Hillbillies*] to be a double album. To start [with], it's about making people something they're not. I wanted it to be like *Arthur*, but I didn't have the time to finish it because I had a lot of things to do this year. I wanted to make little statements about England and what's happened to some of the people . . . What amazes me is there are new towns like Harlow in England, and in these towns . . . there are all these people who've been taken out of the East End of London and put into these places . . . They're trying to keep things the same as when they lived together in London, but they have to break down eventually . . . It's very disturbing to see this happen. They're knocking down all the places in Holloway and Islington and moving all the people off to housing projects in new towns . . . My Gran used to live in Islington in this really nice old house, and they moved her to a block of flats, and she hasn't got a bath now. She's got a shower . . . And she's ninety years old, she can't even get out of the chair, let alone stand in the shower . . . They took her around and showed her where she was gonna live, and [told her] she didn't have any choice . . . The government people think they're taking them into a wonderful new world, but it's just destroying people . . . People can't meet each other anymore . . . [It's just] people looking through all those little spy holes at each other. The album is a condensed version of all these ideas. The first side is trying to live in this world, the other side is concerned with the old world. I'd like to make a little film out of it. [1972]

Like Townshend, Davies had too many ideas for just one album – if not quite enough for two. One strand that never made the released artefact was a picture-postcard version of rustic back-woods America. Represented by two outtakes, 'Mountain Woman' and 'Kentucky Moon', it would be hinted at by just one song on the album, the dreamy 'Oklahoma USA'. At this early stage, according to Davies, the album was intended to be an Anglicized version of the hit American TV show, *Beverly Hillbillies*: 'In the beginning it was written as . . . a script for a film . . . about the rehousing that was going on at the time. Mum and Dad lived in Islington and they were happy there. I don't know what happened, but they had to move out of the city. Anyway, my image of it was getting on a truck like the Beverly Hillbillies and putting all the stuff on the back. That was the start of the film.'

If this premise didn't last long, it did establish a framework for the project, and he was soon up and running. Although American-centric songs fell by the wayside, the idea of basing the whole album's sound around its music did not. Davies had been spending a lot of time at the Archway Tavern in Holloway, north London – the interior of which is featured on the cover of *Muswell Hillbillies* – acquiring a taste for bitter and listening to

'bad country and western music' with the vestiges of his immediate family ('I used to go down there with a couple of my
sisters and my Dad on a Thursday night – [they were] the last
real family outings that we had, actually'). He even perversely
boasted: 'At that time the [Archway Tavern] had the worst
country and western band in the world. They were Irish, trying
to play country music. I wanted us to mimic that. Obviously it
was more rock & roll because we were doing it, but my vocals
were [deliberately] slurred.' Over the years Davies has been less
effusive about his abiding love of country music. Only in the
1990s did he really explicate its formative effect on his own early
musical leanings:

> **Ray Davies:** Before [the age of fifteen] the bounds of my
> musical world had been marked out by watching Rodgers
> and Hammerstein musicals; listening to country-and-
> western music on the radio; hearing my sister's be-bop
> records and early rock & roll; and family gatherings
> around the piano . . . [while] Hank Williams became my
> favourite combination of singing and playing. His songs
> had a crying quality to them that seemed to sum up some
> of my own darker doubts about the world. [1994]

All of these styles would now be thoroughly referenced on
Muswell Hillbillies – though in a way that was self-consciously
Anglicized. Hence, his use of Mike Cotton's band to proximate
a trad-jazz sound, which served a quite distinct purpose, one
duly noted by *NME*'s Phil McNeill in his worthy 1977 three-part
Ray Davies profile in *NME*: 'Ray takes the brass from The Mike
Cotton Sound . . . and inflicts the lugubrious cadences of The
Salvation Army and Twenties Music Hall upon them . . . The
deliberately unglamorous sound is itself conceptual: the band

assumes an overall aural image to suit the requirements of the album, a sound in sympathy with an older, greyer, even more bewildered generation. Depression music that captures the sad facelessness of the cover shot.' Indeed, throughout the album The Kinks demonstrated a degree of musical ambition that had not always been evident in the 'Quaife era', flirting with everything from New Orleans jazz to 'Sally Army' brass. As brother David pointed out, 'It's so rooted in our London backgrounds, yet it has all the emotional elements, and a lot of the instrumentation, of American blues.'

An integral element in the conceptual mix was that sense the album has of 'family gatherings around the piano'. It is particularly there on 'Oklahoma USA', a song imbued with the memory of his sister Rene's death on his thirteenth birthday. She had bought Ray a guitar, 'played the family piano for the last time and gone to the Lyceum Ballroom, where she collapsed and died while the orchestra played a song from *Oklahoma!*' Not surprisingly, as Davies told readers of *X-Ray*, '*Muswell Hillbillies* was a homage to the family that used to be. All the songs, like "Uncle Son", "Holloway Jail", "Oklahoma USA", were songs about people who actually existed in the lives of my parents.' The title track was one such tale of young promise that went unfulfilled:

Ray Davies: [Rosie was] my mother's best friend when they were about sixteen. They used to walk up the Holloway Road, and all the boys whistled at her because she was very big and well-endowed . . . She had a very sad life, and she never felt fulfilled as a person. On the original demo for the album there was a whole song called 'Rosie Rooke'. Leaving Rosie Rooke behind is like leaving everything behind. She symbolized all that for me. [1972]

That track was part of the side 'concerned with the old world'. But the album also addressed the conundrum of 'trying to live in this world'. Indeed, it was with the songs of dislocation that the scarier side of Davies' own psyche became manifest, beginning with album-opener '20th Century Man'. On the face of it, this song is a distant cousin of 'Apeman' (the narrator, given half a chance, says he would be 'taking off [his] clothes and living in the jungle'). But there is a more sinister side to him. The lyrics, printed on the inner sleeve of a Kinks album for only the second time, tell us the singer, one more 'paranoid schizoid product of the twentieth century', is struggling to 'keep a hold of my sanity'. What isn't clear from the song alone is that Davies had in mind someone who was a cross between a suicide bomber and that galactic hitchhiker, Arthur Dent:

Ray Davies: I remember writing a [film] scenario for . . . '20th Century Man'. It was just a madcap idea . . . This guy was almost like a suicide bomber at the end of a building that was going to be knocked down, and he said, 'If you're going to knock the place down, I'll just blow myself up.' . . . The '20th Century Man' is the last man on the block. [2000]

If the '20th Century Man' was a 'paranoid schizoid product of the twentieth century', the next song concerned another. Set to a funereal *Big Easy* arrangement, 'Acute Schizophrenia Paranoia Blues' was a 'genuine story, again about my Dad.' – "Even my Dad lost the best friend he ever had / Apparently his was a case of acute schizophrenia." – as indeed was 'Alcohol', the most overtly ironic song on *Muswell Hillbillies*, but one that would soon return to bite him. In his delivery, Davies even attempted to emulate his father on those family occasions when 'he would stagger over to the piano and belt out a song. He was often so drunk that he would not so much sing the words as assume the attitude of the lyrics.' Davies' extended family also served as the inspiration for the opening two tracks on the second side, 'Have a Cuppa Tea' and 'Here Come the People in Grey', both written with his grandmother in mind; the former being primarily 'concerned with the old world', the latter being about 'trying to live in this world':

> **Ray Davies:** 'Have a Cuppa Tea' is my gran. We used to go round to her with a problem. She was like a fairy godmother . . . She used to go to the pub, The Copenhagen, walk all the way herself, order a gin and Guinness, drink it and go home, every night until the day she died. You could sit with her . . . and she knew everything . . . I just wish she and her knowledge could be around now. [1984]

'Here Come the People in Grey', with its subtext that these might as well be men in white come to take her away, returns the album to its central theme: 'People being moved out of the city and moved into this new environment that they can't comprehend.' 'Complicated Life', the final song from the side that is 'trying to live in this world', summed up Davies' predicament (drawing on an old joke: guy goes to doctor, says he wants to live to be a hundred; doctor says cut out sex, gambling, booze, cigarettes; guy says, 'Will I live to be a hundred?'; Doctor says, 'No, but it'll seem like it.') As Davies explained on the album's appearance, the song wasn't 'about big business deals or having lunch with Rothschilds bankers; it's worrying about the electricity bill and petty things that are always there.'

Muswell Hillbillies is, in fact, just as angry an album as *Arthur*. On 'Here Come the People in Grey', Ray expresses anger on behalf of his grandmother, whereas on 'Complicated Life' – which had a single-word working-title, 'Suicide' – he is projecting the anger of someone more like his brother-in-law, a character he described the previous year as being 'worried about the unions, things like that . . . [So] when he's had a few pints, yeah, a few Guinnesses, then maybe he'll break down a little bit, start shouting, you know, get it out. You get a bit twisted inside, your guts get twisted up. [Whereas] I do it the other way, I go to bed all right and I wake up twisted.' Twisted was just how he felt throughout making and promoting *Muswell Hillbillies*.

Here was an album that was more than a mere 'homage to the family that used to be'; it was an attempt to reclaim something he had inadvertently lost. As Davies recently informed *Uncut*, 'I was still living in north London, and Dave was. But the empathy with our surroundings had gone. My relationships were not the same with my family. I felt that I'd lost contact with them . . . *Muswell Hillbillies* was an attempt to get back to where we were from.' And a valiant attempt, too; one that Davies was rightly proud of, though he fully admits 'it was the classic thing of not delivering what people think you're going to deliver'.

Unfortunately, 'it kind of set everything back a few years.' Back to 1968, in fact. And it didn't help that Davies seemed initially reluctant to promote an album he later classed as one of his favourites. When The Kinks landed in America in November 1971, all primed to push the brand-name on a three-week US tour, their leader was not quite ready to unveil the *Muswell Hillbillies* in person. The set-list at their Carnegie Hall show two days before the album's release included a single song from the LP, 'Acute Schizophrenia Paranoia Blues'. When they returned to the same hall four months later – with the album long gone from the chainstore racks – they were performing two-thirds of it.

Go figure. It was one thing to deliberately give the record label no obvious single (leaving them with '20th Century Man', an apposite but uncommercial follow-up to 'Apeman'). It was quite another to leave the album to fend for itself when every other English touring band based their sets on their current project. As a result, *Muswell Hillbillies* never had a fighting chance of replicating the chart position of *Lola Versus Powerman*, which peaked sixty-five places higher.

Meanwhile, it seemed that this cathartic reimmersion in the family and its communal past had not so much freed Davies' inner demons as fed them. If his new label-mates, Bowie and Reed, thought they were the new Weird and Gilly, they were absolute beginners compared with the premier Kink. When a US interviewer asked him what he thought of the RCA party that announced their joint signing, Davies told her, 'I sent my robot, an imitation robot dressed up as me. I stayed at the hotel. He taped the thing on video for me and played it for me the next morning.'

By the time the band returned to the States the following spring, Davies was talking freely about his own death: 'I hope it's a very grand day when I go – although I did write in my diary the other day, "I hope it will be soon . . . and alone." [But then,] I was very upset . . . People think that I'm strong and I'm not.' If this kind quote wasn't alarming enough, he was openly discussing whether he was going a bit bonkers: 'My world . . . is not a little world anymore. It started off as a little world but there are infiltrators in my little world . . . It makes me think that I'm mentally not all there. It would be great for me to be actually mad, [but] I've got a terrible feeling that I'm not.'

His brother, who knew the signs well enough, was not so convinced. Dispirited by yet another commercial failure for the band, Dave was seriously considering whether 'to give it up and go and live in an ashram in Tibet, but I could see that Ray was deteriorating emotionally'. As he began performing the bulk of the *Muswell Hillbillies* songs night after night, brother Ray seemed to be turning into the acute schizoid paranoid he'd previously depicted on vinyl.

The performances that March in New York – recorded for a possible live album – were almost a send-up of The Kinks' glorious past *and* the album they had just made; as if Ray realized he had inadvertently laid himself bare. As Phil McNeill smartly concluded: 'The balance [now] tilted away from desperation and into jovial resignation.' The shows only reinforced the suspicion voiced in some reviews that *Muswell Hillbillies* was essentially a satirical work – as opposed to a deadly serious one. As a result, when the next breakdown came, no one outside the band had seen the writing on the fold-out inner sleeve.

Compounding Davies' sense of disillusionment was his foundering relationship with his new record label: 'When we signed with RCA they thought they were buying Kodak films, "Don't change the name, just put the Kodak out and it'll be an instant hit." . . . But it wasn't.' When he wanted some help financing the costs of filming their two March Carnegie Hall shows, the label informed him, 'We're not in the talent business, we're in the record business.' They had bigger fish to fry.

*

It was not a phrase that ever crossed their lips when Tony Defries came a-knocking. He was most certainly in 'the talent business', and nothing was going to stop him making David Bowie the biggest star of the 1970s. Nor did he let RCA in on a little secret when he allowed them to sign Bowie to an exclusive deal covering the next three LPs for the minimal advance of $37,500 per record – *they* would be underwriting most of the costs of the outlandish campaign Defries had already mapped out in his head.

In cahoots with both Bowies, Defries was determined to fulfil the prophecy contained in 'Star', one of the many new songs Bowie had penned in the months leading up to his becoming an RCA artist on 9 September 1971 – 'just watch me now!' That song would serve almost as a blueprint for Bowie's first year as the Seventies' first important pop artist; but it was one largely superimposed on an earlier outline, that of his friend Marc Bolan, who by the time Bowie signed to RCA was proclaiming himself to be the biggest British pop star since The Beatles. Bowie agreed, even if he implicitly called his buddy a whore to a *Creem* reporter who was in New York for the RCA signing:

> **David Bowie:** The most important person in Europe and England today is Marc Bolan, not because of what he says but because he is the first person who has latched onto the energy of the young once again . . . Rock should tart itself up a bit more, you know. People are scared of prostitution. There should be some real unabashed prostitution in this business. [1971]

The notion of artist as prostitute was not new to Bowie (or Jean Genet). He had told *Rolling Stone* something similar nine months earlier, just as he was electing to portray himself as a beckoning courtesan on the British cover of *The Man Who Sold the World*. He was already gearing up to pastiche the entire rock creed while insisting to the increasingly self-important US periodical: 'What [rock] music says may be serious, but as a medium it should not be questioned, analysed, or taken so seriously. I think it should be tarted up, made into a prostitute, a parody of itself.'

And Bolan was showing him the way, harnessing all the energy of *TMWSTW* (and co-opting producer Tony Visconti into the bargain) for his definitive statement, *Electric Warrior*, issued in October 1971 and shooting straight to number one in the UK (and a respectable thirty-two in the US). Bolan's ambition burned brighter but briefer than Bowie's because to him becoming the quintessential star was an end unto itself. Bowie had always been more ambivalent about the 'curse' of fame. Hence Bolan's astute assessment, offered only a few months before his demise: 'I never got the feeling from David that he was ambitious . . . David got his drive to be successful once I'd done it with the T. Rex thing.' (By 1977, Bowie had long eclipsed Bolan's fading star.)

What seems to have changed Bowie's mind was seeing becoming a star as a project in itself, not merely a by-product. As Ken Pitt, still his manager (at least in name) in the spring of 1971, told Johnny Rogan: 'David had bouts of laziness and I would get a little sharp with him from time to time. Yet the moment he got interested in a particular scheme he outran everybody else. But he had to be turned on and fired with enthusiasm.' By now it was Tony Defries who was pulling the strings, though their relationship was not formalized until August. Defries would be the Grossman to Bowie's Dylan, the man who kept him focused on a single goal – stardom.

Defries, never one plagued by self-doubt, believed he could see through Bowie's many personae. He was also never convinced that Bowie really feared for his sanity. As one ex-Main Man employee witness to the Defries-Bowie dynamic recalled:

'Defries [once] observed that Terry's [mental] illness was one of a horde of things that obsessed David for the minute. Like a fickle child, he was always finding something new to preoccupy him. The only thing about Terry's madness that seemed to be a constant was David's ability to use it as a public-relations ploy, something he would refer to when he wanted to capture someone's attention or impress a reporter with "truths" about the pain of his existence.'

Not so coincidentally, it was at just the time when Defries was starting to make his presence felt that Bowie quietly subsumed this side of his family history, allowing the star in him to take over; until Defries really began to believe this ch-ch-change was for real. This shift was reflected in the songs Bowie now earmarked for his second album of the decade, *Hunky Dory*, on which he seemed determined to banish those demons previously summoned on *TMWSTW*. In this sense, *Hunky Dory* fits neatly with his later description of it as an album that 'got a lot out of my system, a lot of the schizophrenia'.

A poignant part of that process involved renunciating his brother not only in song but in person; something he now decided was painful but necessary. Bowie's previous claim that Terry quite liked the Cane Hill asylum was shown to be the purest poppycock when his mad brother did a John Clare, and simply walked out of the place one afternoon in late winter/early spring 1971. He spent a fortnight sleeping rough before finally turning to his aunt Pat (she found him on her Finchley doorstep, in a highly agitated state). Unable to look after him herself, and remembering how supportive the Bowies had been the previous spring, she took Terry to Haddon Hall. When Angie answered the door, Pat asked if they would mind if he stayed the night, and hopefully they could take him to the doctor's in Beckenham the following morning. As Angie hesitated, David apparently appeared and said, 'I'm sorry, we're busy.' And that was that. He did not even go out to speak to Terry, who sat in the car throughout the confrontation. It would be two decades before they spoke again. Bowie's wife could only look on in despair, tinged with a little anger.

It is not clear when exactly Bowie dispensed this crushing rebuff to the brother 'he idolized', but it was very probably after he had returned from his February promotional trip to the US, when Terry's name had been repeatedly invoked to 'impress a reporter [or two] with "truths" about the pain of his existence'. He had also spent some time with his cousin Kristina, now based in New York, where he again brought up the subject of why Terry was cursed and he himself was left untouched. Whatever the date of Terry's expulsion from Haddon Hall, the experience seems to have inspired one of Bowie's most brilliant, if misunderstood, songs, 'The Bewlay Brothers', with which he would conclude *Hunky Dory*, his final offering before putting Defries' scheme into operation.

'The Bewlay Brothers' was the antidote to 'All the Madmen', the distance between the two songs being the width of a now-closed circle. The ending even mirrored the babbling coda to the *Man Who Sold . . .* track, with its schizophrenic double-tracked vocal resembling a cackling gnome. The jointly sung nursery rhyme at song's end (an overtly Barrettian touch) may well be alluding to Terry's flight from Cane Hall: 'Leave my shoes and door unlocked / I might just slip away / Just for the day.' Other allusions to Terry herein cast him as the more Promethean figure championed in earlier songs and conversation:

> Now my brother lays upon the Rocks,
> He could be dead, he could be not, he could be You.
> He's chameleon, comedian, Corinthian and caricature.

But although Bowie had happily trailblazed 'All the Madmen' as a song inspired by his brother's predicament, he was considerably more reluctant to own up to a similar biographical component to this cryptic production. Indeed, he was guarded enough to claim to new producer, Ken Scott, at the album sessions that the song was written 'specifically for the American market'. When Scott asked him what he meant, he apparently rejoined, 'Well, the lyrics make absolutely no sense, but the Americans always like to read things into things, so let them read into it what they will.' He was equally unforthcoming in the (unused) handwritten song-notes intended for the album sleeve, depicting the track as just 'another in the series of David Bowie confessions'. In fact, it was the *last* in a series of confessions-in-song written during the extraordinarily fruitful period that preceded his starry guise.

If 'The Bewlay Brothers' was intended to serve as a reminder, it quickly became one he would rather forget. It went unperformed with The Spiders from Mars, and even in 1993, when Bowie did address some aspects of his history honestly for a BBC radio retrospective, he still asserted: 'I saw so little of [Terry] . . . I think I unconsciously exaggerated his importance. I invented this hero-worship to discharge my guilt and failure, and to set myself free from my own hangups.' It would take another seven years for him to finally address the song's subject matter *directly*: '[That was] another vaguely anecdotal piece about my feelings about myself and my brother, or my other doppelganger. I was never quite sure what real position Terry had in my life, whether Terry was a real person or whether I was actually referring to another part of me. I think "Bewlay Brothers" was really about that.'

Back in 1971 he was more worried about any possible lingering legacy from the family's fucked-up gene pool. And that concern came out in everything he wrote, even in what seemed like a whimsical 'filler' song such as 'Kooks', written for his newborn son, Zowie. What seemed, on the surface, like little more than a lighthearted exposition on life with 'a couple of kooks', voiced a greater concern, one he shared in the album notes: 'The baby was born and it looked like me and it looked like Angie and the song came out [saying something] like, If you're gonna stay with us, you're gonna grow up bananas.' The song's debut on a BBC In Concert in early June suggested the father hadn't quite got 'All the Madmen' out of his system as he offered to 'take the car downtown / And we'll watch the crazy people race around', a couplet he wisely expunged from the album version.

And there was another song Bowie specifically cited when he admitted in 1976 that 'a lot of the [*Hunky Dory*] songs do . . . deal with . . . schizophrenia'. That honour he bestowed on 'Oh! You Pretty Things', because apparently, 'according to Jung, to see "cracks in the sky" is not really quite on[23] . . . I hadn't been to an analyst – my parents went, my brothers and sisters and my aunts and uncles and cousins, they did that, they ended up in a much worse state – so I stayed away. I thought I'd write my problems out [instead].'

'Oh! You Pretty Things' – which had just become Bowie's biggest hit since 'Space Oddity', albeit with the vocal cords of ex-Herman's Hermit Peter Noone attached – also flirted with the end of the world, as did the explosive 'Bombers', which predicted, 'We're in for a big surprise / right between the eyes', after a nuclear bomb test results in 'a crack in the world'. But it was not yet time to tell the world the end was nigh, and the latter song was hastily replaced with the vastly inferior 'Fill Your Heart' (penned by 'Biff' Rose), a Deram-esque return to Anthony Newley territory.

Allowing the old self-doubts to rear up again, Bowie remained unsure what kind of album he wanted *Hunky Dory* to be. A riveting cover of Jacques Brel's 'Port of Amsterdam' was overlooked entirely (it would not appear for another two years, when it fittingly appeared as the B-side to 'Sorrow'); as was a cover of Ron Davis' 'It Ain't Easy', which was put on an eight-track pre-release promo (along with 'Bombers' and an alternative 'Eight Line Poem'), yet three months later failed to make the final cut. Instead, it became the closing track on side one of *Ziggy Stardust*, where it stuck out like a thore sumb.

Perhaps we shouldn't be surprised to find that for all its attempts to 'deal with . . . schizophrenia', *Hunky Dory* came out pretty schizophrenic itself. Half of it, in Bowie's mind, 'reflected my new-found enthusiasm for this new continent that had been opened up to me. It all came together because I'd [just] been to the States.' 'Quicksand' was one such item, an 'epic of confusion' which, according to the hastily scribbled notes of Chairman Bowie, was something 'the calamity of America produced'. With its references to 'living in a silent film . . . of dream reality'; being 'drawn between the light and dark'; and repeatedly, 'sinking in the quicksand of my thought[s]'; it suggested he hadn't quite mastered the lad insane who still resided inside.

His future direction, though, was more accurately indicated by a trio of intentionally connected songs on side two – 'Andy Warhol', 'Song for Bob Dylan' and 'Queen Bitch'. Indeed, when he debuted the three tracks in strict album order at a show in Aylesbury in late September, he broke off between songs to explain to the crowd that he had written 'a spate of people songs. I got hung up on writing about people – just kinda well-known figures and what they stood for. I believe very much in the media of the streets, street messages.' 'Queen Bitch' was his attempt to emulate The Velvet

Underground, having finally got to meet Lou Reed – thanks to Mercury's A&R man Paul Nelson on a temporary sabbatical from rock criticism. 'Song for Bob Dylan' was another song containing sentiments he wasn't quite ready to take responsibility for. Only in 1976 did he own up to the fact that the track clearly 'laid out what I wanted to do in rock. It was at that period that I said, OK, if you don't want to do it, I will.' In that sense, it was a sister-song to the already-written 'Star', which he was holding back for his own second coming.

To his mind, *Hunky Dory* was just the aperitif. Magnificent a collection as it was, – a votive offering to the RCA A&R department to prove he could write a tune, and craft a radio-friendly album – it was a mere taster. (The album was already being dangled in the label's faces when Katz was locked in contractual negotiations with Defries.) What they didn't yet know was that Bowie had already stockpiled another album's worth of songs – many of which pre-dated those on *Hunky Dory* – which had a quite different message, and targeted a wholly different audience. In fact he had already hinted at said stockpile of songs to the English music press back in March, boasting to *Melody Maker* that the just-issued *TMWSTW* 'is actually a year-and-a-half old. But I've got my next one in the can [sic], and another half completed . . . My writing was schizoid, but it's much more simple now.' Saying something similar to Penny Valentine, an early press advocate, he revealed that in the intervening 'twelve months I've already written enough stuff to do another two albums'.

Some songs didn't make it to either *Hunky Dory* or *Ziggy Stardust*. At least one suggested he was not as free of the influence of his 'alternating Id' (his expression) as he liked to claim. 'The Man', a.k.a. 'Shadow Man', was one song that survived all the way from Haddon Hall to the *Ziggy* sessions, but not to the album itself. Again, Bowie found himself fearfully tap-dancing with another doppelganger, perhaps the future self who could still fulfil the family curse: 'Look in his eyes and see your reflection . . . the Shadow Man is really you . . . Your eyes are drawn to the road ahead / And the Shadow Man is waiting round the bend.' (An atmospheric 2000 studio record-ing, for the aborted *Toy* album, suggests he may have finally gleaned the Shadow Man's identity.) Meanwhile, Bowie spent the months leading up to the *Hunky Dory* sessions demoing the likes of 'Lady Stardust (Song for Marc)', 'Hang On to Yourself', 'Ziggy Stardust', 'Star', 'Moonage Daydream', 'Right On Mother', 'How Lucky You Are' and 'Looking for a Friend' at a cheap London demo studio leased from Radio Luxembourg.

Every demo seemed to show someone more than a little starstruck. But he still wasn't sure it was for him, and through-out 1971 he anxiously farmed out a number of these demos to would-be ciphers also seeking chart success, even releasing the Luxembourg prototypes of 'Moonage Daydream' and 'Hang On to Yourself' under the pseudonym of Arnold Corns (and then shamelessly concocting a story that claimed a gay dresser of his acquaintance was the voice of Corns). But once Defries came on board, he was quickly disabused of these Warholian notions of stardom by proxy. Bowie later dated his decision to get 'down to serious writing and trying not to diversify too much' to *Hunky Dory*'s completion, admitting that previously he 'would try and get involved in anything that I felt was a useful tool for an artistic medium, from writing songs to putting on art shows and street theatre . . . [I was] trying to be a one-man revolution.'

What he didn't do, certainly not at the time, was credit either Defries or his wife Angie with key roles in the process (and even in 1976, when embroiled in a protracted dispute with his now ex-manager, he was only half-prepared to come clean, crediting Defries 'and the [other] crazies who were running around at that time', but not the wife). But then, as Angie points out in one memoir: 'My husband . . . possessed the unfortunate character defect of needing everything he did to be his own idea, even when most of his ideas really came from other people.' Another former confidant saw only too clearly that David was initially living out Angie's fantasy, not his own:

Mary Finnegan: [Angie] created this whole star myth. She used to say all the time, if you want to be a star you've got to live like a star . . . She was the worldly sophisticated one and he was just a small town boy. She put herself behind him a hundred per cent and so, gradually, they both became weirder and weirder.

Bowie still wasn't convinced he was psychologically robust enough to grasp the crown. It took the unholy alliance of Angie *and* Defries to make him believe. But when he did believe, the effect was really quite startling. Mick Ronson – sidekick, sounding board and band-leader to The Spiders from Mars – was one of those stunned by the change in him. When Defries, having put their arrangement into legalese, asked Bowie to sign his life away in a Faustian pact, the accompanying Ronson realized his friend 'just wanted to get signed up and get on the move. He didn't pinpoint things in contracts . . . He just wanted to be a star.' It would prove an expensive oversight. Photographer-journalist Mick Rock, who had not known the pre-*Ziggy* Bowie but knew the inspirational Syd Barrett better than almost anyone in rock, subsequently portrayed the Bowie he met in March 1972 as someone who was 'as ambitious as any person

I'd ever come across up to that point in my life . . . He was projecting heavily, before it actually happened – that's the fascinating part.' Even if the shadow man remained ever on his tail.

★

Another singer-songwriter haunted by the shadow man was also returning to the studio just as *Hunky Dory* was rolling off the record presses. Nick Drake even had a name for 'him' – 'Pink Moon' ('None of you stand so tall / Pink Moon gonna get you all'). But unlike Bowie, Drake lacked a plentiful supply of songs fit for purpose. He barely had a bushel of ballads, certainly not a full fruit tree. And what he did have, he seemed reluctant to share with any like-minded musos. According to *Fruit Tree* sleeve-writer Arthur Lubow – only the second writer (after Nick Kent) to research Drake's life – 'Nick would never perform any songs from *Pink Moon* for his friends.'

Perhaps he didn't consider (m)any of the new songs to be public pieces. Maybe they were too damn raw; they just needed to be gently rubbed until they shined in the dark. It was like he finally planned to make his own *Astral Weeks*. 'Cause it sure sounded like the man who made *Pink Moon* was in terrible pain, pain most of Nick Drake's previous work had only suggested. And yes, there was a redemptive element in the blackness. One just had to listen hard enough to glean this message from what were increasingly slim pickings.

By the end of 1971 something had happened to the songwriter that conspired with his copious cannabis consumption to stop him in his tracks. Whether because of the chronic depression that had enveloped him during the making of *Bryter Layter*, or an ongoing writer's block that was itself probably a contributory cause to the self-same depression, new songs were fitful visitors these days. In fact, as Peter Hogan points out in his guide to Drake's music: 'No one is too sure where and when the

[*Pink Moon*] songs were written. Robert Kirby recognized guitar phrases and fragments that Nick had been toying with back in his Cambridge days [while] . . . others have stated that many of the songs date back to 1969 or thereabouts.'

Whenever and however they came, the songs that for so long had served as a refuge for his inner feelings, weren't serving their master so well. This time the sum would need to exceed the parts. It is no coincidence that the only pair of songs on *Pink Moon* that run to more than a dozen lines – save for the two eight-line poems that make up 'Which Will' – are 'Things Behind the Sun' and 'Parasite', songs whose genesis predates *Bryter Layter*. Also from the same time (and place) was 'Place to Be', a three-verse lyric replete with the kind of natural imagery he once mined so meticulously. Here he directly addressed the muse he thought he knew so well, asking her to explain why he is 'darker than the deepest sea . . . weaker than the palest blue'.

Only with these three older joins would the new construct prove solid enough to stand tall. Even father Rodney was unsure when the other songs were penned, admitting in interview, 'Where and how and when he wrote [*Pink Moon*] is difficult to say.' The overseer of Drake's estate, Cally von Callomon, knows better. He informed Amanda Petruisch, the most recent writer to tackle *Pink Moon* in monograph: 'Nick was incapable of writing and recording whilst he was suffering from periods of depression. He was not depressed during the writing or recording of *Pink Moon* and was immensely proud of the album, as letters to his father testify. Some journalists and book writers have found this fact disappointing.'

Actually, this 'book writer' finds our indentured man's statement plain incredible. Not to say blatantly contradicted by the recipient of said 'letters', who had already stated: 'He was beginning to get very withdrawn and depressed then. He was very down when he wrote *Pink Moon*.' And if ever there's a record that sounds like the product of someone who 'was very down', it is *Pink Moon*. Maybe the gentleman with the Germanic surname saw something Byronic in Drake; for he, too, left an estate that claimed 'unpublished letters' proved the man was a saint, and what a shame no one else was allowed to see the evidence.

And *why* exactly would Drake be writing letters to his parents at this juncture? After all, he was spending most of his time at his parents' home – part of what Joe Boyd has dubbed 'the steady progress of retreat' – even though it wasn't where he really wanted to be. (He confessed to his mother Molly, 'I don't like it at home, but I can't bear it anywhere else.') 'Place to Be', that product of another time and place, was at least partly about longing to go home. One of Drake's former songwriter-muses, Robin Frederick, reckons the song 'was written by someone who wants to tell us how lost he feels, how much he yearns to go home, to find a place to be. Before he has even finished the musical introduction, we are as lost as he is. He starts on the tonic (home), plays just those couple of chords that assure us we know where we are, then starts sing-ing . . . in the middle of the progression . . . the middle of nowhere! Suddenly you have that sensation of floating, of falling . . .'

Such a remembrance of that hopeful yesteryear had become a necessary prop to a painful present. But if Drake could still communicate 'real' feelings in a song like this, he barely conversed with his parents when back home, which makes the idea of gregarious letters about how well the songwriting was going, and how proud he was of the songs, doubly unlikely. Drake, who was now monosyllabic in person and whose lyrics had become so pared down he was almost writing haikus, by autumn 1971 had retired to some place where even his friends could not find him:

> **Brian Wells:** Nick just seemed to become isolated. You'd go see him and the conversation would become uncomfortable and I would have to leave. And then he wound up going back to his parents' place, and I think he felt quite embarrassed about that, ashamed that he hadn't been able to cope in London . . . And he did wind up in hospital a couple of times, and he was treated with anti-depressant drugs . . . [But] I see it more as an existential thing, that the world was becoming a rather futile place [to be]. He wasn't like Peter Green or Syd Barrett, where the chemicals precipitated an underlying schizophrenic tendency. [But] I did get a sense of [chronic] low self-esteem – [Hence,] 'I am a parasite who clings to your skirt.'

The remaining eight songs (one an instrumental doodle) on a collection that times out at a mere twenty-eight minutes – which would be parsimonious for a mid-Sixties Beach Boys album, let alone a singer-songwriter statement of the early Seventies – were pared to the bone, lyrically, musically and spiritually. This is exactly what he had intended. Apparently every note from the two night-time *Pink Moon* sessions ended up in its well-spaced grooves, save for a forty-six-second snippet of the eighteenth-century French standard, 'Plaisir D'Amour' – which had been positioned to open side two on the original album master.

The message of that traditional song was certainly one Drake related to as much as anything by Joan Baez, whose version of the song provided him with a template (along with 'All My Trials (Will Soon Be Over)', another pertinent 'cover' he once liked to play). The refrain of 'Plaisir D'Amour' (in translation) goes, 'The pleasure of love lasts only a moment / The pain of love lasts a lifetime.' But Drake did not intend to voice the sentiment, merely alluding to it. In the end Drake decided even this little gesture might be misunderstood, and the song was cut; leaving *Pink Moon* as the era's shortest album-length statement of consequence. As producer John Wood told Arthur Lubow: 'He had no more material, and he thought that was part of the deal. And he was right. I wouldn't want to hear any more before turning it over. If something's that intense, it can't really be measured in minutes.'

Certainly, no careful listener leaves *Pink Moon* less than sated. 'Intense' could almost be a synonym for *Pink Moon*, as could 'compacted'. Even Drake sensed it, choosing to give half the songs on the album single-word titles – 'Road', 'Horn', 'Know', 'Parasite', 'Ride'[24] – that reflected his own monosyllabic divided self. The opener and title track, which would be responsible for introducing Drake to a mass audience when used in a US Volkswagen TV ad in 2000, comprises just five lines. The beguiling 'Road' runs to four; as do 'Harvest Breed' and 'Know'. In fact, 'Know' comprises just twenty words – but manages to say more about Drake's then-state of mind than twenty-hundred words from anyone else, even Nick Kent, who called the song 'a paean to schizophrenia':

> Know that I love you
> Know that I don't care
> You know that I see you
> You know I'm not there.

In less than two-dozen syllables, Drake elucidated the paranoid panorama of his own condition. As he knew only too well, his problem was precisely that no one ever really got to 'know' him, not even his current (platonic) girlfriend Sophie Ryde. And Drake was now so internalized that he wasn't even sure he could get the message through to *her*. In fact, Ryde tells a story about the day of the first *Pink Moon* session, when Nick called by at her flat and asked her if she would mind typing up the lyrics from his exercise book for the session; a slightly odd request given that he had extremely readable handwriting and the exercise book was his 'fair copy', anyway.

When she came to one of the new songs, 'Free Ride', with its obvious lyrical play on her surname, she grew mildly miffed, feeling that this was a 'none too subtle plea for her to be more understanding'. She even took the reference to 'the pictures that you hang on your wall' to be a sly dig at the post-Impressionist paintings that decorated her small flat. But such was the barrier separating him from her, and every-one else he held dear, that his only way to communicate with her was to show her these lyrics, like a repressed school-boy passing notes in class.

Significantly, each verse to 'Free Ride' asserts 'I know you . . . I see through', as if his songs gave him a one-way ticket to the outside world, which he could summon were he not so afraid he might not come back. But without external stimuli, the songs were drying up – hence, that preternatural feeling on *Pink Moon* that this is someone almost writing from memory, half-recalling how it used to be. The writer in him seems to know that this is probably his last shot. For all the references to the light of the sun on *Pink Moon*, it seems Drake set out to prove Pascal's truism that 'too much light darkens the mind'. The signs of imminent mental collapse could no longer be ignored.

The portrait of Drake in Arthur Lubow's 1978 retrospective piece for *New Times* said it all:

> Some nights Sophia [sic] would return from work and find him sitting in total darkness. After *Bryter Layter* he retreated to his parents' home, but he would [still] make occasional forays into London . . . To Brian Wells he said, 'I can't cope. All the defences are gone. All the nerves are exposed.' . . . He wasn't able to write. 'There's music running through my head all the time,' he told his father. Yet he couldn't get it down.

The album, for all its sense of skeletal unity, acts like a series of sketches for songs – hints of an unobtainable future now lying permanently in the past. Unlike Barrett's second solo LP, though, one senses throughout that Drake is fully cognisant of the effect he is going for; that, end of his tether or not, this was a conscious artist reworking the core sensibility of 'the blues' in a way firmly consistent with his own uniquely English sensibility. There is a deliberation to everything here, which dates back to the immediate aftermath of *Bryter Layter* and 'the idea of just doing something with John Wood, the engineer at Sound Techniques'.

Even after Boyd removed himself from the process by splitting for California, Drake had retained his faith in Sound Techniques engineer John Wood, the studio technician he now made complicit in the decision to strip himself bare. Yet it was only at the sessions themselves that Wood realized just how internalized the introspective singer-songwriter had allowed himself to become. As he revealed on a Dutch 1979 radio retrospective:

John Wood: Nick was determined to make a record that was very stark, that would have all the texture and cotton wool and . . . tinsel that had been on the other two pulled away. So it was only just him. And he would sit in the control room, and sorta blankly look at the wall and say, 'Well, I really don't want to hear anything else. I really think people should only just be aware of me and how I am.'

Despite Drake's quiet insistence that he didn't 'want to hear anything else', Wood thought he might at some point say, 'I want you to get hold of Robert Kirby.' And so it was that the producer turned around at the end of the second evening and said, 'Well, what do you think? What do you want me to put on?' And the singer said, 'I don't want anything on.' 'Absolutely nothing?' 'No, that's all I want.' Less was now officially more. Robert Kirby, for one, thinks that his friend was both afraid he no longer had the mental energy to sculpt the songs and consumed with the very real fear that its impact would be diluted by any embellishment. From here on, the nerve ends would be there for everyone to hear:

Robert Kirby: Each of the songs on [*Pink Moon*] contains a wealth of material that earlier he would have spent time developing. I do not mean by [necessarily] adding other instruments, but just himself. I think he [now] felt that he could trust nobody to help him, or just couldn't be arsed . . . I sometimes feel guilty listening to it . . . because he is just too exposed. It's almost like attending a public execution.

Any embellishment would also have required a degree of communication now beyond Drake. The one confirmed visitor to the sessions, Linda Thompson, remembers someone who 'was in a dreadful state, totally incommunicado. I'm surprised he didn't throw me out. He didn't [even] talk to John Wood.' He didn't talk to his record label much, either. Even when the album was completed – to, one must presume, his satisfaction – the only time he showed his face at Island was to give them the master tapes. The rest was now in the hands of the gods of commerce. David Sandison, still lending his brand of Islandic evangelism to the vestiges of the Witchseason roster, wrote about that visit in a piece that appeared in certain English music papers the following February:

> The last time I saw Nick was a week or so ago. He came in, smiling that weird smile of his and handed over his new album. He'd just gone into the studios and recorded it without telling a soul except the engineer. And we haven't seen him since . . . Nobody at Island is really sure where Nick lives these days. We're pretty sure he left his flat in Hampstead quite a while ago . . . The chances of Nick actually playing in public are more than remote. So why, when there are people prepared to do anything for a recording contract . . . are we releasing this new Nick Drake album, and the next (if he wants to do one)? Because we believe that Nick Drake is a great talent [even though] his first two albums haven't sold a shit.

Sandison's refreshingly heartfelt appeal appeared in the papers not because there was a resurgence of interest, or because he had been commissioned to write about the shy, retiring songwriter. Island had actually paid for the page Sandison used to express his feelings, in the form of an ad, it being the only way they could think of to promote *Pink Moon* when its *auteur* wouldn't do interviews, radio shows or gigs.

He wouldn't even pose for a set of publicity photos (as his sister would say of the photo of him sitting on the park bench that bedecks the inner sleeve, 'All Nick's desire to pose has gone – he's not even aware of the camera'). Photographer Keith Morris, who had already worked with Drake on the past two albums, was shocked when he saw the man who turned up for this December 1971 photo-shoot: 'By the time the last album came out, he was seriously withdrawn. It was actually quite . . . a dramatic departure from the Nick that we knew . . . You'll meet people that will tell you he was depressed at other times, but nothing was quite like that final session . . . It was like doing a still life.'

Although Sandison expressed the prophetic hope that 'maybe one day someone in authority will stop to listen to [Drake] properly . . . and maybe a lot more people will get to hear Nick Drake's incredible songs', his gambit yielded no immediate dividend. For now, *Pink Moon* didn't sell shit. Even the songwriter's few supporters in the music media were starting to feel the reclusive aura was becoming annoying. Jerry Gilbert, in his *Sounds* review, thought it was 'time Mr Drake stopped acting so mysteriously and started getting something properly organized for himself'; while *Melody Maker* journo Mark Plummer's intuitive response was that 'the more you listen to Drake . . . the more compelling his music becomes – but all the time it hides from you'.

Plummer had been steered in the album's direction by one of Drake's few musical contemporaries to believe he was one of a kind: John Martyn. Martyn, though, was in full agreement with Gilbert that Drake needed to snap out of it, stop 'acting so mysterious' and start meeting his fans halfway. In fact, it would appear that Martyn and Drake had a furious row on this very subject shortly after the *Pink Moon* album was completed. The way mutual friends heard it, Drake 'said that Martyn's music was becoming insincere in an attempt to be more commercial. When Martyn replied that he wanted his records to be heard, not to drop off an abyss as Nick's had, Nick was furious . . . He called Martyn "devious" and drove away' [in the night].'

The record that Drake and Martyn were discussing, presumably over a pint (or seven), may well have been the truly awful karaoke 'single' version of 'May You Never' that Martyn recorded with a full band in November 1971, a particularly misguided attempt on Martyn's part to generate a hit single. Significantly, when he re-recorded it for the emblematic *Solid Air* album, a whole year later, it was to an arrangement cast by the light of a pink moon; which may be as close to a *mea culpa* as the belligerent Scot ever got. By then Nick's own music had truly dropped off an abyss, prompting another, gentler form of cajoling from Martyn's pen, 'Solid Air'.

The title track to Martyn's breakthrough album was about Drake, though Martyn seemed surprisingly coy about the song's subject at the time of its release, claiming 'it was done for a friend of mine, and it was done right, with very clear motives'. He also phoned Paul Wheeler, a mutual friend, who was house-sitting for the Lennons at Tittenhurst Park, the night he wrote the song. Wheeler recalls, 'John had just visited Nick [sic] and he sang me an a capella version of "Solid Air".' The starkly expressive song was a plea for their friend to rejoin the human race, prompted by their most recent meeting:

> Don't know what's going wrong in your mind
> And I can tell you don't like what you find
> When you're moving through solid air.

By the time *Solid Air* appeared in the winter of 1973 the music of Nick Drake was on nobody's lips. He, and the album in which he had 'been painting it blue', had disappeared from the public consciousness with nary a whisper. Even his closest friends feared that there was no way back. Brian Wells, who had been abroad when *Pink Moon* appeared, picked it up on his return and, as he duly informed Nick Kent, 'marvelled at the fact that Nick, though quite lost in confusion and personal depression, could produce a work that captured him in the complete creative ascendant'. Arthur Lubow would also laud the sheer willpower it took to deliver a statement this intense:

In personal terms, the achievement is astonishing, for when he wrote and recorded [*Pink Moon*], Nick was so depressed that he could barely speak, so confused that he would stand helplessly at an intersection, unable to cross . . . It is despair without the comfort of self-indulgence. It is suffused with a bare and horrifying beauty. It is the last work of a prematurely mature artist.'

What other people made of the album in the half-decade after its release has gone largely undocumented, though Connor McKnight, writing for the counterculture's favourite music monthly, stumbled on the record in the winter of 1974 and felt compelled to tell *Zigzag*'s readership about it. And without the attendant myth that would attach to Drake after his early death, and knowing precious little detail about the man behind the records, he still concluded: 'It is impossible to avoid the seering [sic] sensibility behind [*Pink Moon*]. The album makes no concession to the theory that music should be escapist.' And nor does it. Even the iconoclastic Nick Kent couldn't help but note that he found it full of 'obliquely sinister overtones', in his 1975 *NME* overview of Drake's career.

Conceding nothing to commercial considerations, and as

spartan and ghost-ridden as the songs of Robert Johnson, Drake mustered all that he had in him in order to realize twenty-eight searing minutes of song. All that was now needed was the one grand gesture that would let the world know the suffering was real and unbearable. And perhaps if he had succeeded in his attempt to hang himself at Far Leys a few months later, as appears to have almost happened[25], then *Pink Moon* might indeed have been accepted as 'the last work of a prematurely mature artist'. But Robert Johnson he was not, and the end would not be so swift, or so poetic – even if the twenty-four-year-old knew full well that, in the end, 'Pink moon gonna get you all.'

5. 1971–72: Nowt Strange As Folk

Every exertion of my will, every attempt to put an end to the disintegration of the outer world and the dissolution of my ego, seemed to be a wasted effort . . . I was seized by the dreadful fear of going insane. I was taken to another world, another place, another time.

– Albert Hofmann, describing his first-ever LSD trip, 16 April 1943, in *LSD: My Problem Child*

I'm treading the backward path. Mostly, I just waste my time.

– Syd Barrett, to Mick Rock, 1971

Everybody was convincing me that I was a messiah . . . I got hopelessly lost in the fantasy . . . It became very dangerous. I really did have doubts about my sanity; I put myself very near the line.

– David Bowie, *Cracked Actor*, 1974

For Syd Barrett, the songs had simply ceased to come. Not that he had yet surrendered to the inevitable, even after he returned to the family home in Cambridge. Perhaps – like Nick Drake

– he was hoping against hope that such a move would reattach his musical muse to its wellspring. Already he was talking about returning to his original love, painting. Back in March 1971 he had described his day-to-day life to *Melody Maker*'s Michael Watts as 'pretty unexciting. I work in a cellar, down in a cellar . . . I think of me being a painter eventually.' But, by December, Barrett's muse seemed to be wholly becalmed. When his old photographer-pal Mick Rock popped in to see him in the guise of *Rolling Stone*'s English correspondent, Barrett's frustration with himself was evident in much of what he said. At one point he confessed to Rock: 'I may seem to get hung-up, that's because I am frustrated work-wise, terribly. The fact is I haven't done anything this year . . . I've got an idea that there must be someone [I could] play with.'

Rock interpreted their conversation as Syd's way of 'trying to figure out what he wanted to do. He talked about "treading the backward path", retracing his steps, trying to find himself in some way, finding the kid in him and going back there to sort out his identity . . . His mum brought us tea and iced sponge in the garden. Poor lady . . . she didn't know what the hell was going on.' Although Barrett seemed 'very up and bubbly', Rock also remembers how 'he would laugh in strange, strange moments. Like there was a joke, but it was only his joke.' Evidently he was still not sure, what exactly is a joke? For all the enforced jollity, there was this ineffable sense that Barrett already knew he'd penned his last. At the end of the afternoon, Barrett offered to show Rock 'a book of all my songs before you go', then cryptically adding: 'There's really nothing to say.' And one suspects there really was nothing to say.

If Syd himself was a spent force by the end of 1971, his influence on the future course of rock was once again about to be felt around this dark globe, as two of music's most enduring statements took the fate of the ex-Floyd frontman as a jump-ing-off point. Issued almost exactly a year apart, but both initially conceived in the weeks between Rock's conversation with Barrett and its 23 December appearance in *Rolling Stone*, David Bowie's *The Rise & Fall of Ziggy Stardust and the Spiders from Mars* and Pink Floyd's *Dark Side of the Moon* would become the two benchmarks for most forms of English rock from here to Punk. And each took its cue from the laughing Madcap himself.

Of Syd's former bandmates, Roger Waters was the one who had been thinking of writing about the man who showed him the way. It was a case of finding the right context. And that was not as part of *Meddle*, the Pink Floyd album EMI had just released when the band convened at Broadhurst Gardens for four days in mid-to-late December to begin preparing a new live set for a series of UK shows scheduled across the first two months of 1972. The song 'Brain Damage', a.k.a. 'The Lunatic is On the Grass', which he presented to the other three at their first December rehearsal, was something he had been playing around with at the *Meddle* sessions that summer but had not developed any further. Only at this point did he decide Syd was a subject matter worthy of his pen, warranting his time and providing a way of reinforcing his assumption of the de facto leadership of the band that was once Barrett's:

Roger Waters: There was a residue of Syd in all of this. It was pretty recent history. Syd had been the central creative force in the early days – [while] maybe I provided some of the engine room – and so his having succumbed to schizophrenia was an enormous blow . . . That was certainly expressed in 'Brain Damage'. [2004]

Originally intended as the closing theme to their new song-suite, the opening image of 'Brain Damage': 'The lunatic is on the grass, remembering games, and daisy-chains and laughs / Got to keep the loonies on the path', was a direct evocation of the Barrett of yesteryear. Indeed, as Waters said in 1998: 'The grass [in "Brain Damage"] was always the square in between the River Cam and King's College chapel . . . I don't know why, but the song still makes me think of that piece of grass. The lunatic was Syd, really. He was obviously in my mind. It was very Cambridge-based, that whole song.'

'Brain Damage' was more than just another song brought to a possible Floyd project; it was the trigger for an album dealing with how life's demands can lead people to the brink. The title of the piece when Floyd first toured with it the winter of 1972 said it all – *Eclipse: A Piece for Assorted Lunatics*. Even without the subtitle, there was no mistaking the album's ghost in the machine. As Dave Gilmour recently remarked: 'There are specific references to "Syd moments" in [the] lyrics of *Dark Side*. Syd was a constant presence in our minds and consciences.' At the same time, Waters already had a grander theme in mind, and it was one that would dominate all of his songwriting in the years when the Floyd were remorselessly moving towards becoming the biggest band on the planet. The plan was, in Waters' words, to 'do a whole thing about the pressures we personally feel that drive one over the top'. What he did not do was spring this concept on the rest of the band until rehearsals began to assume a direction of sorts:

Dave Gilmour: Sometime after we started and got quite a few pieces of music sorta formulated vaguely, Roger came up with the specific idea of going through all the things that people go through and what drives them mad;

and from that moment obviously our direction slightly changed. We started tailoring the pieces we already had to fit that concept, and Roger would tailor words in to fit the music that we had. [1977]

Floyd drummer Nick Mason believes that Waters actually hijacked a project originally conceived along broader lines: 'The concept was originally about the pressures of modern life – travel, money and so on. But then Roger turned it into a meditation on insanity.' Vestiges of that original conceit would continue to be represented, with 'On the Run' beginning life as 'The Travel Sequence', while Waters turned up with a home demo of the song 'Money' for the band to work on. But it was mortality and insanity that became the bedrock of their first album-length meditation on life.

Waters may simply have been trying to steer the others away from reworking the idea underlying their earlier performance-piece 'The Man & the Journey' (the subtitle of which clearly connects it to *Eclipse* – 'More Furious Madness from Pink Floyd'). If that suite had been a conglomeration of songs from other projects, old and new, cobbled together to form 'a day in the life', *Dark Side of the Moon* also began with the band scrabbling around looking for old bits and pieces they could reuse. Or to utilize Gilmour's chosen phrase, 'You jam, you knock stuff about, you plunder your old rubbish library.'

'Brain Damage' was by no means the oldest piece now attached to a new canvas. 'Us and Them' had originally been part of a twenty-minute instrumental called 'The Violent Sequence', which the band had intended for Michelangelo Antonioni's impenetrable piece of cinematic codswallop, *Zabriskie Point*. The sequence, composed by Richard Wright, was debuted in concert back in February 1970, even though it was fated to become one of half-a-dozen pieces Antonioni passed on. The new lyric they grafted on in December 1971 – with a title that had already served as a chapter heading in R.D. Laing's *The Politics of Experience* (1967) – Waters initially suggested he would sing himself. After all, these lyrics intentionally developed another of his favourite themes, which he now bolted on to the song-cycle – 'our failure to connect with each other':

> **Dave Gilmour:** When we started on a new album we'd always dredge through old tapes to see if there was anything left over we could make use of . . . [But] when Roger walked into Broadhurst Gardens with the idea of putting it all together as one piece with this linking theme he'd devised, *that* was a moment . . . You see, nobody back then had problems with the concept of concepts, so to speak. [1998]

English rock bands at this portentous juncture in rock history had no fear they would be lambasted for displaying such ambition. The concept album had yet to become a naughty word. The *NME* had still not devised their own send-up of *Tommy*, called *Dummy*, or begun to ridicule the pretensions of many an English prog-rocker with headlines such as, 'Is this man a prat?' If there was a heyday for the extended song-cycle or theme, it was now. While Floyd rehearsed their new concept, Jethro Tull were putting the finishing touches to a two-part, forty-five-minute rock symphony called *Thick as a Brick*, which told listeners to 'mark the precise nature of your fear'. Tull's frontman Ian Anderson later claimed it was 'a spoof of the genre', though if it was, he wisely avoided saying so at the time.

Other prog bands were just getting warmed up. Genesis, who within three years would create their own hundred-minute concept double-album, the triumphant *The Lamb Lies Down on Broadway*, were piecing together their twenty-five-minute seven-part epic, 'Supper's Ready'. Yes, too, were looking to record their first side-long track, 'Close to the Edge', for the album of the same name. Pink Floyd themselves, as pioneers of the side-long song, were already fully conversant with what was required to put 'it all together as one piece with this [one] linking theme'.

In fact, this was pretty much how 'Echoes' had been pieced together, as a compilation of smaller 'ideas'. As the band's engineer, John Leckie, later recalled: 'The tapes we took to Air [studios] were filled up with lots of little ideas . . . They were all called "Nothing" – "Nothing One", "Nothing Two" and so on . . . ["Echoes"] was conceived as one big thing, [but from] bits in various sections . . . [and] recorded that way.' Floyd coterminously developed the work over a series of live performances, until they were absolutely satisfied they had found a way to make the whole thing blend.

This modus operandi would also inform both the new work, and its successor, *Wish You Were Here*. In both cases, Floyd would work on the album while simultaneously touring the material around the world for a year or so. Even in an era when bands regularly debuted their new songs months before they recorded or released them, this was a unique way of working. For now, Floyd saw an album as the conclusion of the tour-promotion-album process, not the starting point. As Gilmour points out, 'In those days tours got booked in. And back then, they weren't promotional vehicles; they were entities in their own right.'

Floyd were certainly treating the new piece as an entity in its own right. The UK *Eclipse* tour programme even came with a lyric sheet for the new songs. But certain segues were not so seamless. *Eclipse* in its earliest guise comprised five sequences

– 'Breathe', 'Time', 'Money', 'Us and Them' and 'Brain Damage' – stitched together with a series of musical joins, some solid, others audibly coming apart at the seams; making for almost a return to the sons of nothing.

'The Mortality Sequence' linking 'Time' and 'Money' was an instrumental piece over which the band projected taped letters of St Paul, though it wasn't entirely clear whether the fiercely agnostic Waters was lampooning the solace religion could provide in death, or demonstrating that religious fervour led irredeemably to madness. As well as these tape cut-ups, a long 'Travel Sequence' gave Gilmour and Wright an opportunity to jam to their heart's content – as of now, they didn't know what they were 'On the Run' from. As such, *Eclipse* still contained echoes of its side-long predecessor, being the kind of music that in Richard Wright's view, 'we created . . . when all three of us [sic] got together and collaborated, rather than individually coming to the studio with a song'.

Nor for the time being was there any redemptive coda to *Eclipse* – the album charted the passage from birth ('Breathe') to mental breakdown. (One can't help but wonder how the album might have fared if this had continued to be the case.) As such, the final line of the work as debuted at Portsmouth Guildhall on 21 January 1972[26] was, 'I'll see you on the dark side of the moon'; the expression 'dark side of the moon', 'always [being] considered [by the band] to be a metaphor for the other side of madness', [as cover designer Aubrey Powell avers].

Even at this juncture the band thought that single phrase was the real title of the new song-suite – though they publicly called the piece *Eclipse* (Medicine Head had just used Floyd's preferred title on their own album). And Waters claims that, when he wrote this concluding line, he fully intended to suggest he personally identified with that lunatic on the grass:

'When I say, "I'll see you on the dark side of the moon", what I mean is, If you feel that you're the only one . . . that you seem crazy 'cos you think everything is crazy, you're not alone. There's a camaraderie involved in the idea of people who are prepared to walk the dark places alone. A number of us are willing to open ourselves up to all those possibilities.' In another discussion of the album's genesis, Waters suggested that fear was another very real factor in the lyrics he was now writing:

> 'For me, it was very much "There but for the grace of God go I." . . . I did feel at times close to madness myself. I can remember being in the canteen at Abbey Road [during the *Dark Side* sessions. I was] sitting at the table with everybody, and suddenly there was no pain; everything – the table, all the people at it – receded. The sound became tinny, and the room looked like I was looking at something through the wrong end of a pair of binoculars.'

Eclipse, as such, would be superseded as the album title by the time recording started in earnest. Clarity was the order of the day. Hence, the printing of the lyrics for concert-goers even when the suite was just a performance piece – a conscious attempt to strip any residue of spacey ambiguity from their current work. Gilmour remembers Waters stating that 'he wanted to write it absolutely straight, clear and direct. To say exactly what he wanted to say for the first time and get away from psychedelic patter and strange and mysterious warblings.' This lurch towards a certain lyrical articulacy was perhaps *Dark Side*'s greatest departure from Floyd's already redolent history. Even as they embarked on their latest month-long sojourn, culminating in four nights at London's Rainbow, the members of the band sensed that maybe they really had managed some kinda breakthrough:

Dave Gilmour: The process went on, the rehearsing, the writing, the performing live . . . All these things came together and it became clearer and clearer, probably gradually, that we had definitely made progress and that this was going to be a bigger, better thing than [anything] we had previously done. [2003]

The Rainbow shows – which ran from 17 to 20 February 1972 – were the first point at which the world began to sit up and take notice of the new Floyd opus (though not, as legend would have it, because of the famous *Tour '72* bootleg, which contrary to myth, was not issued at the time; nor when finally released a year later did it sell in anything like the kind of numbers that have long been attributed to it). The reviewers for the music press were out in force, and took it as read that a new Floyd stage show was something worth writing about.

These shows also brought the curious, the already converted and the general prog-rock concert-goers out in their thousands. Among the curious was one Roger 'Syd' Barrett, who had hoped to sneak in to the show incognito: only for the unfortunate lad to bump into Mike Leonard, the man responsible for all those innovative early Floyd light-shows. As Leonard recalls, 'I [had gone] to a post-Syd Pink Floyd concert in Finsbury Park, quite an important one for them, and I met Syd lurking in the hall. I don't think they'd even invited him, he'd just come on his own.' If Leonard thought 'he looked a bit . . . gaunt', it seemed 'he was still Syd'.

So Barrett was once again keeping tabs on 'his band'; and one imagines that, after hearing 'Brain Damage', he gave the

boys in the band one of those trademark quizzical looks, especially if he caught that last couplet right – the most explicit of
references to his time in the band: 'And if the band you're in
starts playing out of tune[27] / I'll see you on the dark side of the
moon.'

At the Portsmouth concert, this preceded the music coming
to a shuddering, synth-induced halt, like a sonic depiction of
the dying of the light, but at The Rainbow 'Brain Damage'
segued into a new piece, 'Eclipse', that seemed like a concession
to the kind of hippy idealism the rest of the album rejected.
Waters, ever one for the grand gesture, says he 'felt as if the
piece needed an ending . . . The ['Eclipse'] lyric points back to
what I was attempting to say at the beginning.' It was rather a
way of making the album end with a comradely call to all of
those 'people who are prepared to walk the dark places alone',
as opposed to the wholly Barrettian 'Brain Damage'.
Nonetheless, one imagines the so-called lunatic left the hall at
last impressed by a Gilmour-era Floyd show.

Syd now had something to follow, which, four days later, is
exactly what he set out to do. It could well be he was at The
Rainbow that night precisely to check out the opposition
before he debuted his new band, ironically christened Starz,
at the Cambridge Corn Exchange, sharing the bill with
Detroit's loudest rabble-rousers, the MC5, who were now
very much on their last, drug-addled legs. Having wondered
aloud to Mick Rock back in December whether there was
someone out there he could play with, Syd was in full
rehearsal mode by the beginning of February with a band
that also comprised the ever-industrious Twink of Pink
Fairies/*S.F. Sorrow* fame and bassist Jack Monck. It was an
impromptu jam session with Twink and Monck, after an
Eddie 'Guitar' Burns gig at the Kings College Cellars on 26

January, which convinced him to give it one more go. Again, though, he had placed too great a burden on his sagging shoulders, and for those – like *Melody Maker* reviewer Roy Hollingsworth – who expected some epiphany, the 24 February gig proved to be the night of the big letdown.

It all began swimmingly with a slow version of 'Octopus' – Barrett resuming at the very point he had previously left the stage – followed by competent renditions of 'Dark Globe', 'Gigolo Aunt', 'Baby Lemonade' and 'Waving My Arms in the Air', before he ignited the night with what Rob Chapman called in his *Terrapin* review, 'a remarkable version of "Lucifer Sam"'. Misguidedly, instead of segueing into 'See Emily Play', a song they had rehearsed that afternoon, and leaving the crowd wanting more, Barrett decided to try to rediscover the spirit of that initial jam session. As such, in Chapman's words, he 'concluded [the set] with a couple of shapeless ragged 12-bar instrumentals, [which] ended [only] when Syd's right index finger began bleeding rather badly'. Hollingsworth – the man who later the same year would dismiss the New York Dolls as a bad joke – concentrated on the latter part of the set in his review, reinforcing the cliché that was Madcap Syd:

He played and played and played. No tune in particular, no tune in fact. He sounded out of tune most of the time anyway. But the tune was most certainly in his head . . . I don't know how much Syd Barrett remembered, but he didn't give in. Even though he lost his bassist and even though Twink couldn't share Syd's journey, Syd played on . . . As the clock ticked into the small hours of Friday morning, Syd retreated to the back of the stage, trying to find one of those [guitar] runs. He messes chords together. There is no pattern. But if you think very hard, you can see a faint one, you can see some trailers in the sky . . .

With a single stroke of his injudicious pen, Hollingsworth signed Starz's death warrant. As Twink told Kris DiLorenzo: 'The reviews [sic] were really bad, and Syd was really hung up about it; so the band folded. He came 'round to my house and said he didn't want to play anymore.' Hollingsworth later insisted it was not his intention to press the autodestruct; but if he did not realize how fragile Syd's ego was, he was a reviewer in a million. According to one Floyd biographer[28], Barrett's own response to the Corn Exchange gig was even more dramatic and emotive. After the show he had returned to the Hills Road house, where he started smashing furniture before retreating to his bedroom in the cellar, where he commenced smashing his head repeatedly against the ceiling.

Shortly afterwards, he turned up at the door of Sheila and Mick Rock's London home. As Mick remembers it: 'For a moment he was thinking of doing something in London, but it just seemed to pass through his mind briefly . . . It wasn't like he said, "Fuck it, I'm never going to play again." . . . [but] he knew he wasn't wired for a life like David Bowie . . . He was just trying to make up his mind, really, about getting off the bus.'

★

Just as Barrett got up to get off the bus, who should he pass on the stairs but sorcerer's apprentice David Bowie. The last time he heard that man's name he was reviewing Bowie's Deram single, 'Love You Till Tuesday', for *Melody Maker*'s Blind Date column back in 1967, when still having a laugh. Back then, he called Bowie's effort 'a joke number', but not in a bad way. As he helpfully explained, 'Jokes are good. Everybody likes jokes.'

And now Bowie was namechecking him in the very weekly that was sending Roy Hollingsworth to slag off Starz. The increasingly androgynous boy from Brixton was on the front cover of England's most popular music magazine, pronouncing himself gay. In the 22 January 1972 issue of *Melody Maker* Bowie unveiled his Ziggy persona for the first time, and the only English rock star he referenced (alongside Iggy and Lou, the two Americans he was explicitly courting) was Syd Barrett. Bowie described to Michael Watts how 'it is because his music is rooted in this lack of [self]-consciousness that he admires Syd Barrett so much. He believes that Syd's freewheeling approach to lyrics opened the gate for him.'

Ever one to seize a vacant mantle, Bowie already knew that Barrett had abdicated his pop throne by the time he took *Ziggy Stardust* on the road in February 1972. He was soon spending his nights and days with the last man to see Syd standing: Mick Rock himself. When he and Angie heard that Rock was coming to see a show at Birmingham's Town Hall on 17 March, they were both secretly thrilled. For Angie, it may have been Rock's position as *Rolling Stone* correspondent that excited her, but Bowie surely knew the name from the sleeve of his copy of *The Madcap Laughs*, and maybe even the 23 December 1971 issue of *Rolling Stone*, which had just carried Syd's last interview. Rock was certainly left in no doubt about how highly Bowie regarded Barrett: 'Bowie worshipped Syd. He always saw him in the same bracket as Iggy Pop and Lou Reed.'

The Ziggy persona that Bowie formally introduced during a February 1972 TV appearance on *The Old Grey Whistle Test* had actually been given a quick spin around the block already, in a less measured guise, with the two singles by 'Arnold Korns' that first gave the world unrealized renditions of 'Hang On to Yourself' and 'Moonage Daydream'. Korns, originally conceived as a transvestite singer 'discovered' by Bowie, took his name from another famous transvestite, the one Barrett celebrated on the first Floyd A-side, 'Arnold Layne'. Indeed, if the androgyny of Ziggy had a prototype in English pop, it was from

Barrett, a debt Bowie openly acknowledged: '[He was] the first bloke I'd seen wear make-up in a rock band to great effect. Me and Marc Bolan both noted that.' The fact that Syd always had 'this strange mystical look to him, with [his] painted black fingernails and his eyes fully made up', provided Bowie with just the inspiration he needed to go the whole hog, dye his hair, put eye shadow on, and generally prostitute his art along lines he'd outlined a year earlier.

Barrett also had a profound effect on the style of songs that Ziggy sang. As Bowie duly acknowledged in the same year he recorded his own version of 'Arnold Layne' in concert[29]: 'Along with Anthony Newley, Syd was the first guy I'd heard sing pop or rock with a British accent. His impact on my thinking was enormous.' From the first line of Bowie's 1972 album, 'Pushing through the market square . . .', sung in an accent that would have made Eliza Doolittle glow, there is no mistaking the singer's proximity to the bells of Bow. In a world where a transatlantic accent, or a Jaggeresque Southern slur, were almost de rigeur, Ziggy placed himself full square in the little cul-de-sac off Regent Street, where he was snapped for the album's iconic cover. At the time, Bowie even joked that his ability to switch between 'stone the crows' cockney and BBC English was 'part of me general schizophrenics'; while Ken Pitt well recalls the way 'he would sometimes come into a room looking like a ravishingly beautiful girl then, ten minutes later, he'd be a "Gor blimey" yobbo. He would turn the cockney persona on and off.'

In constructing Ziggy, Bowie continued taking a leaf or two from the Dylan he was still nightly celebrating in song (nor should one discount the effect of Anthony Scaduto's widely read biography, published the previous autumn). Where Dylan had constructed his backwoods folkie persona from archetypes who were either dead (Hank Williams, Cisco Houston, Robert Johnson) or artistically moribund (Woody Guthrie), so Bowie carefully built his own iconic alter ego around recent casualties found at the side of the road to excess. And of those figures, Barrett and Hendrix were the ones that seemed to loom largest. This pair, rather than the colourful but essentially inconsequential Vince Taylor, would be the true templates to Bowie's new alias. (Mark Paytress exposes Bowie's likely motive for repeatedly citing Taylor in his slick monograph on the *Ziggy* album: 'Although it is easy to see in Ziggy elements of all the casualties of the counterculture – especially Hendrix, [Peter] Green and Barrett – Bowie's . . . citing of the obscure Vince Taylor as his defining model [is] typical of his desire to wrap himself, and his work, in the cloak of mystery.')

Bowie has continued to muddy the waters ever since he was first asked, whither Ziggy? In a 1992 *Life* article he brazenly claimed that his first inspiration in rock 'was John Lennon, [along with] some of the Stones and Kinks, and then it got hammered in with guys like Bryan Ferry, King Crimson, Pink Floyd . . . [before I started] applying Dada, creating those absolutely frightening, extraordinary monsters of rock that nobody could possibly love'. But portraying Ziggy as some Dada creation – more Dalí than dahling – merely provides further evidence 'of his desire to wrap . . . his work in the cloak of mystery'. In early 1972, Bowie's main points of reference were strictly musical. Art was the one with a voice in Simon & Garfunkel. As Simon Frith astutely observed in *Let It Rock* the following June, 'Ziggy Stardust is the loving creation of a genuine rock addict.'

This is not to say that Bowie hadn't self-consciously decided to bring the theatrical side back to pop music. In this he was inspired not only by the theatricality of early English glam-rock (and Alice Cooper) but by the Warholian antics of a New York acting troupe who descended on London in the summer of 1971, to perform the risqué *Pork*. When he met the American cast after opening night he even told troupe-member Tony Zanetta, who would end up working for him: 'I'm going to play a character called Ziggy Stardust. We're going to do it as a stage show. We may even do it in the West End. When I'm tired of playing Ziggy . . . someone else can take over from me.'

He had been ruminating on creating a stage caricature of the rock star for some time now, telling *Rolling Stone* back in February 1971: 'My performances have got to be theatrical experiences for me as well as for the audience. I don't want to climb out of my fantasies in order to go up onstage – I want to take them on-stage with me.' In the late 1990s he duly confirmed that 'the initial framework [back] in '71, when I first started thinking about Ziggy, was [essentially] as a musical-theatrical piece. And it kinda became something other than that.' Understatement of the year of Glam.

The theatrical idea was already some way advanced by the time Bowie began recording Ziggy's intended repertoire in November 1971. When during the sessions he met up with music journalist George Tremlett – who had interviewed him a number of times over the years – ostensibly to promote his latest album, *Hunky Dory*, Tremlett asked him whether he had finished arranging the new stage act he had mentioned to him the previous April. Bowie responded, 'That's what we're work-ing on now.' What sort of stage act would it be? 'Outrageous. Quite outrageous, but very theatrical . . . It's going to be costumed and choreographed, quite different to anything anyone else has tried to do before.'

Bowie was already professing to have little time for 'anything anyone . . . tried to do before', even as he entered the choppy waters of glam-rock a full year *after* other pop pioneers first started glitzing up pop. He gives Alice Cooper short shrift in his January 1972 interview with Michael Watts, refusing to recognize Cooper's Detroit credentials or the trailblazing nature of his early stage-act. And looking back in 1993, he was especially bitchy about British glam-rockers The Sweet, who 'were everything we loathed; they dressed themselves up as early Seventies, but there was no sense of humour there'. Actually it was Bowie who missed the joke, from a band whose tongues remained firmly in their cheeks throughout a series of gloriously camp hit singles such as 'Little Willy' and 'Wigwam Bam'. (The real source of his later enmity may be their appropriation of the 'Jean Genie' riff for their own tail-chasing chart-topper, 'Blockbuster'.)

Thankfully for Bowie, by spring 1972 he had chanced upon the fully conceptualized Roxy Music – contemporaneously championed by another *Melody Maker* journalist, Richard Williams – who were starting to make waves of their own. At the same time he began encouraging the likes of Mott the Hoople, Iggy Pop and Lou Reed to glitter up and pout their lips, hoping to create a second wave of glam that would be altogether more exclusive. As he later claimed, 'We took ourselves for avant garde explorers, the representatives of an embryonic form of postmodernism. [Whereas] the other type of glam-rock was directly borrowed from the rock tradition, the weird clothes and all that. To be quite honest, I think we were very elitist.'

Meanwhile, his friend Bolan continued holding the high ground, chart-wise, all the while camping it up with a series of five memorable back-to-back number-one singles, 'Hot Love', 'Get It On', 'Jeepster', 'Telegram Sam' and 'Metal Guru'. But as far as Bowie was concerned, all of those who glammed up before him were not really *transgressive*. Their campness was an act, and obviously an act; not so much the gesture of a social deviant as the archetypal music-hall cross-dresser.

He had far grander ambitions with *his* creation, or so he would claim twenty years later: 'From a very early age I was always fascinated by those who transgressed the norm, who defied convention, whether in painting or in music or anything. Those were my heroes – the artists Marcel Duchamp and Salvador Dalí and, in rock, Little Richard.' If, as seems to be the case, he was expressing a genuine viewpoint here, it was couched in artistic reference points he learnt to apply after he gave up on rock.

If we can believe his right-on mother, Peggy – who told a reporter in the early 1980s of one occasion when, as a little boy, she found him wearing her make-up and 'told him that he shouldn't use make-up. But he said, "You do, Mummy." I agreed, but pointed out that it wasn't for little boys' – Bowie was just as confused about his sexual identity as the young Barrett. He made an allusion to such experiences in the second of his *Ziggy*-era conversations with Michael Watts, prior to his legendary August 1972 Rainbow concert: 'I spent all those formative teenage years adopting guises and changing roles . . . just learning to be somebody . . . I've always been camp since I was about seven . . . My interests weren't centred around obvious seven-year-old interests, like cowboys and Indians. My things were far more mysterious.'

It was high time he threw off his rags and revealed himself. After all, he had been dropping hints of the direction he was heading in for a year or more, albeit in some out-of-the-way places. On a local San Francisco radio station in February 1971 he had told the DJ that *TMWSTW* was in fact 'a collection of reminiscences about his experiences as a shaven-headed transvestite'. But it was really the messianic streak he'd unleashed on *TMWSTW* that was now leading him on. In New York for the RCA signing in September, he told a reporter for the

Detroit-based *Creem*: 'As the earth has probably only another forty years of existence, this would be a fine time to have a dictatorship. I'm fed up being free.' Although no one was yet ready to take such statements seriously, he had informed *Disc*'s Dai Davies the previous January that he thought the coming youth revolution would be led by someone who was an amalgam of Adolf Hitler and Jimi Hendrix:

> **David Bowie:** The whole Nazi thing was given the image of a mission by their very effective publicity machine, and it really appealed to the youth of an entire nation. The Leader that's going to take this country over will have to be a lot more youth-orientated than [Enoch] Powell[30]. It's the youth that are feeling the boredom most; they are crying out for leadership to such an extent that they will even resort to following the words of some guitar hero. [1971]

This was the kind of conceit he could get away with in a theatre, and for now that was the extent of his (and Ziggy's) ambitions. He even had a setting for his messianic story, and it was fittingly apocalyptic. The rise of Ziggy Stardust would be set during the last five years on Earth, and 'Five Years' – recorded in November – would set the stage for the emergence of this 'guitar hero' who would herald the end of days. Was it a case of today Broadway, tomorrow . . . who knows?

Decades later, in his introduction to Mick Rock's collected photos of the Ziggy era, *Moonage Daydream* (2005), Bowie again provided a suitably pretentious way of explaining how he conceptualized rock's first self-consciously conceived rock star: 'Writers like George Steiner had nailed the sexy term post-culture and it seemed a jolly good idea to join up the dots for

Rock. Overall, there was a distinct feeling that "nothing was true" anymore and that the future was not as clear-cut as it had seemed . . . Everything was up for grabs. If we needed any truths we could construct them ourselves.'

As it happens, by the time Ziggy took to the stage he was no longer some cracked actor – he was Bowie's stage alter ego. The theatrical show had fallen by the wayside as soon as he started recording the songs and found that a cogent theatrical concept was not the same as a cohesive concept album. When Bowie revisited the making of *Ziggy Stardust* for a mid-Nineties *Mojo* special, he remembered 'there [had been] a bit of a narrative, a slight arc, and my intention was to fill it in more later – [but] I never got round to it because before I knew where I was we'd recorded the damn thing', a recollection that tallies with the facts. The bulk of the album was completed over a single week at Trident, nine songs being cut from 8–15 November 1971, including six of the eight songs that tell the story of Ziggy.

By 15 December, he had a provisional tracklisting with the first three songs already solidly in place, though at this juncture the story of Ziggy ends with 'Lady Stardust', his homage to Marc and Syd. That original album sequence (surprisingly called *Round and Round* on the tape box), which made it as far as two master-tapes, included three songs, two of them covers, that never made the final artefact: Chuck Berry's 'Round and Round', Jacques Brel's 'Amsterdam' (a leftover from *Hunky Dory*) and the glam-era curio 'Velvet Goldmine', with its hummed outro straight out of *Paint Your Wagon*.

According to comments Bowie made over the phone to an American radio DJ in January 1972, as he set about reconfiguring the artefact, 'Round and Round' 'would have been the kind of number that Ziggy would have done onstage. He jammed [on] it for old times' sake in the studio, [but] our enthusiasm for it probably waned after we heard it a few times.' Actually the Berry standard, just the kind of number that not only Ziggy but Vince Taylor 'would have done onstage', made it as far as the final test-pressing. Bowie was already looking to explain away what happened to the story of Ziggy Stardust and his band, offering this version to the US radio audience:

David Bowie: It wasn't really started as a [full-on] concept album. It got kinda broken up because I found other songs that I wanted to put in the album that wouldn't fit in with the story of Ziggy. So at the moment it's a little fractured and a little fragmented. What you have on that album when it finally comes out is a story which doesn't really take place. It's just a few little scenes from the life of a band called Ziggy Stardust and the Spiders from Mars, which could feasibly be the last band on earth, because we're living the last five years on earth . . . It depends what state you listen to it in. Once I've written an album, my interpretation of the numbers on it are totally different afterwards than when I wrote them. And I find that I learn a lot from my own albums about me. [1972]

It took until the end of January before he finally had the three songs needed to round out the album. The most important addition was a quickly penned, catchy single, 'Starman', which seems to have been prompted by something he said to Michael Watts the week he recorded it: 'We have created a new kind of person . . . a child who will be so exposed to the media that he will be lost to his parents by the time he is twelve.' Here was a man now wholly estranged from his own immediate family, looking to claim those twelve-year-olds for his very own Jean Brodie of glam. But the song was never really part of the Ziggy concept – it was always a commercial palliative as producer Ken Scott confirmed, '"Starman" was a separate inspiration that was added on later, 'cause the record company didn't hear a single.'

Initially, Bowie even clung to the idea of releasing 'Starman' as a stand-alone single, with 'Round and Round' still holding its place in a 2 February sequence. But two days later, the Chuck Berry classic had given way to a song that was a natural successor to his last hit song, 'Oh! You Pretty Things'. The two other brand-new songs recorded at the same session(s) shifted the album's axis: 'Suffragette City' and 'Rock 'n' Roll Suicide'. They would make the story of Ziggy end not with his 'rise', but with his 'fall'. 'Rock 'n' Roll Suicide' was both some kind of wish-fulfilment and a spell to keep death at bay. Its first line, 'Time takes a cigarette, puts it in your mouth', was Bowie's way of saying, 'Life is a cigarette, smoke in a hurry or savour it', a sentiment he attributed to Baudelaire, though it actually originated with Manuel Machado. Looking for the supreme gesture of the messianic rock god, he had found it in another of his little literary lifts.

On the other hand the death of Ziggy, the Dionysian rock star, drew from immediate examples rock had considerably provided for him, particularly the recent demises of Brian Jones, Jimi Hendrix and Jim Morrison. As he later confessed, 'At this point I had a passion for the idea of the rock star as meteor. And the whole idea of The Who's line: "Hope I die before I get old."' The death of so many family members, culminating in his father's just weeks before 'Space Oddity' charted, had left internal scars. But even before that life-changing event, he felt haunted by death, or so he informed Michael Watts: '[When I was young] I would pull moodies and say things like, "I think I'm dying", and sit there for hours pretending I was dying.' The idea of dying on stage was bound to be enticing one to someone who even as a child had dramatized his own death in his head; and now confided to new inner-circle entrant Mick Rock, 'I know that one day a big artist is going to get killed on stage, and I know that we're going to go very big. And I keep thinking – it's bound to be me.'

Having self-consciously created a character who 'because I never drew a template for a storyline too clearly . . . left so much room for audience interpretation', he was almost apologetic about the album in its finished form, keen to downplay any notion of conceptual unity therein. Six weeks after the album was sequenced – and three months before it chased 'Starman' into the charts – Mick Rock's notes to his first interview with Bowie, shortly after the Birmingham show, reveal the would-be star's inner doubts:

> Ziggy Stardust – rise & fall of. It started off unfortunately as a concept of the life-cycle of a rock & roll star but it ended up as fragmented songs on an album, but I've still retained the original title which really only relates to the first side now. The other side is a collection of different songs. A very mini-concept album. Very melancholic view of the star-trip.

It seems even Ziggy's *auteur* did not know which pieces of the puzzle fitted where. In the end it would be side one that would have the sensual superfluity of 'Soul Love', 'Starman' and 'It Ain't Easy', while the second side would build steadily up to the ultimate 'Rock 'n' Roll Suicide'. While Bowie wasn't quite sure what *Ziggy Stardust* was mutating into, he was adamant that his creation was not a cipher for his own deep-rooted neuroses. Laurel Canyon constituted no part of this Londoner's address. Disavowing the solipsistic universe of the singer-songwriter – before it rejected him – Bowie was insisting: 'My

songwriting is certainly not an accurate picture of how I think
at all.'

At the same time he complained about 'the half-bakedness
of myself, and everyone else in the rock business. Songs these
days are supposed to be representative of the writer's attitude
and mind, instead of just being [something] on record.' Coming
from a man who two years earlier was telling *Top Pops*,
'Everything that one writes is personal, but . . . what I do is take
something that has happened to me and put it into . . . some
kind of symbolism', such pronouncements smacked of someone blowing smoke from behind a big green screen.

Naturally he had an explanation for the change – a personal
epiphany some time between *Hunky Dory* and the *Ziggy* sessions:
'I used to come out with great drooling nine-minute epics . . .
[Then] I decided it wasn't worth singing about myself, so
instead I decided to write anything that came to mind.' [One
'drooling nine-minute epic', 'The Width of a Circle', still
remained the centrepiece of every Ziggy show from The
Rainbow to Hammersmith Odeon, marking the point in the set
when Ziggy became a lad insane.) He knew he was consciously
disavowing 'one of the principles in rock: . . . that it's the person
himself expressing what he really and truly feels . . . [whereas] I
always saw it as a theatrical experience.']

But, try as he might to deny it, Bowie's latest creation was as
much a part of his identity as his estranged family. Nor was his
solution such an original one. As Peter and Leni Gillman
astutely noted in their fiercely independent Bowiebio, *Alias
David Bowie* (1986): 'The concept at the very heart of the [1972]
album, of inhabiting the character of Ziggy, had close similarities with some schizophrenics' strategy of adopting a series of
personas as if searching for one that will allow them to function
and survive.' Bowie almost got around to embracing the

Gillmans' charge in 1993, describing his Seventies strategy thus: 'I felt that I was the lucky one because . . . as long as I could put those psychological excesses into my music and into my work I could always be throwing it off.'

The prime question, though, quickly became not how much of himself did he put into Ziggy but where exactly did the creator end and this 'absolutely frightening, extraordinary monster of rock' begin? Wife Angie saw at first-hand how the starry monster initially served its master well: 'By creating Ziggy to go out and front for him, David never had to act like himself in public if he didn't want to, which in turn meant that he could pursue art and applause without having to deal with his . . . frigid self-loathing.' Talking to one reporter on his first US tour as Ziggy, he owned up to the validity of his wife's portrait, 'I'm a pretty cold person . . . [Yet] I have a strong lyrical, emotional drive and I'm not sure where it comes from. I'm not sure if that's really me coming through in the songs.'

For most of 1972 he retained the requisite degree of control over this emotive doppelganger, even during that infamous first interview with *Melody Maker*'s Michael Watts, witnessed by Angie, when 'he was [already] speaking at least half of his lines from the persona of his hype-spawned sacrificial-alien rock star'. At the time he really did seem to know what he was doing. Six years later he was not so sure. Talking to Watts again, Bowie recalled how he 'was starting to build Ziggy . . . and I was naturally falling into the role; and . . . you sorta pick up on bits of your own life when you're putting a role together . . . I was sorta half-serious there when I said that I'd developed a school of pretension within rock & roll . . . He was Ziggy, he'd been created . . . so I had to work with him for a little while.'

For the next nine months the on–off switch would continue to work as, in Bowie's own words, he 'carried the character into interviews, newspapers, onstage, offstage – whenever there was media around . . . to keep those characters concrete'. Again, it would be some years before he would gamely admit that the whole thing had been his way of conquering 'an unbearable shyness; it was much easier for me to keep on with the Ziggy thing, off the stage as well as on the stage . . . It was so much easier for me to be Ziggy.'

Despite turning twenty-five in January 1972, Bowie was still finding himself; and psychoanalysing himself into the bargain. As he told Watts: 'My own work can be compared to talking to a psychoanalyst. My act is my couch.' And talking to musician-journalist Lenny Kaye in July 1972, he 'explained' Ziggy in terms of an ongoing internal quest: 'I'm searching all the time for an identity, and it comes through in the form of images.' However, he was subsuming himself to find himself. Becoming Ziggy onstage and off empowered him, but such was the power of his own creation that he soon failed to recognize the person staring back at him in the mirror: 'That flamboyant front was very useful to me. It gave me a platform: I talked to people as Ziggy . . . who was a cracked mirror . . . [And] David Jones was in there somewhere. But not much.'

At least Davey Jones was not alone. A relentless musical magpie, Bowie was still picking through others' ideas for a self he could call his own. Early on in the Ziggy 'experiment', he confided in Mick Rock: 'I'm more like a focal point for a lot of ideas that are going around. Sometimes I don't feel as if I'm a person at all; I'm just a collection of other people's ideas.' He had certainly co-opted a fair proportion of Ziggy's characteristics from previous models of rock stardom, hoping that before pop ate itself he would become the consummate rock star. Not all of those from whom he borrowed these jigsaw pieces were amused or appreciative. According to Tony Visconti, who throughout 1972 continued to conjoin his future to T. Rex: '[Bolan] seethed with contempt for David when he came up with *Ziggy Stardust*. When Bowie's album came out he made some very petty and nasty comments.'

As for the two American degenerates Bowie flew into London in July 1972 at Main Man's expense, one doubts that either Iggy Pop or Lou Reed thought the fey Englishman was anything more than a means to an end (a record deal for the former; a hit record for the latter). Thankfully, Iggy was not there the night in February when Bowie attempted to walk out across the audience at an Imperial College gig, à la the Stooge, only for the fans to recoil at the very idea. In fact, according to Woody Woodmansey, the Spiders from Mars' unloquacious drummer, there had been a wholesale rethink immediately after the March show in Birmingham attended by Rock: 'Initially, audiences did not like that show . . . So we stopped touring briefly. It was only when "Starman" got all over the radio that things turned.'

Bowie sensed that the audiences were still not embracing this whole Ziggy schtick: 'Ziggy was a case of small beginnings. I remember when we had no more than twenty or thirty fans at the most. They'd be down the front and the rest of the audience would be indifferent.' Rock's photos of these early shows bear out his recollection. Bowie was simply playing to the wrong audience, one he had built up with some of the best AOR (adult-oriented rock) this side of Prog. But if he was going to tap into the same constituency as his embittered old friend Bolan, he needed not only to make his music more raunchy, but also to sex-up the show they then came to see. And a teen market brought up on a soundtrack of T. Rex, The Sweet, and even the touchy-feely-creepy Gary Glitter, demanded something more like the transgressive theatre of the Weimar Republic (albeit Christopher Isherwood's take on it) and less like the mock-glam that was *Hunky Dory*. When Bolan drooled, 'I'm a vampire for your love / And I'm gonna suck ya!' he sounded like he meant it.

When UK shows resumed in late April, Bowie was determined to make Ziggy more androgynous and more sexualized. The following month at a show in Oxford he went down on Ronson's guitar for the first time, a form of fellatio emblematic of the real thing, but not graphic enough to actually get him banned. His fabled *Top of the Pops* appearance in the first week in July, when he languorously placed his arm around Ronson, turned 'Starman' into a Top Ten single, and made him the subject of a number of 'think pieces' on the Bowie phenomenon before it was one.

He was trying every trick in the book, while carefully mirroring Bolan's proven template musically. The same week he appeared on *Top of the Pops*, he headlined a show at the Royal Festival Hall, a benefit for whales, which brought yet more rhapsodic reviews from a smitten music press. And then he temporarily pulled the plug. While the band took a brief sabbatical, he set about creating a very special evening, a 19 August show at The Rainbow that would be the formal unveiling of Ziggy. Like the Floyd six months earlier, Bowie knew that The Rainbow would be the perfect place to unveil the work that would forever define him.

The Rainbow show was a spectacular triumph. The most powerful moment of all came at the start of the evening, when Bolan's visage was projected on to the back of the stage as Bowie walked to the piano and began to sing, solo, 'Lady Stardust', the song for Marc that had led him to this place. But that night was also the death of Bowie's original theatrical dream. As he later wrote:

At appropriate moments [photographic] stills of rock icons – Presley, Little Richard, Bolan, etc. – were projected to give a semblance of continuity to the Ziggy theme, as though he was already one of them . . . [Yet] ironically enough, this would be the first and last time I would ever stage the Ziggy show on such a scale. We simply couldn't afford it. For the rest of his existence . . . the Ziggy shows themselves were just great music and rather smart costume changes, the emphasis . . . being on the actor and not the plot.

By this time, Bowie was no longer acting. Ziggy was taking him over. When the American media was invited to the Dorchester in mid-July – after being taken to Friar's, in Aylesbury, to see a real Ziggy show – the Bowie they met was not entirely in control. Although he assured the reporters, 'I'm still . . . involved with Ziggy. I probably will be for a few months, getting it entirely out of my system . . . ' he inadvertently betrayed his divided self by then suggesting, ' . . . and then *we*'ll don another mask'. The mask and the man were slowly fusing into one just as he was learning the truth of Oscar Wilde's aphorism, 'Give a man a mask, and he'll tell you the truth.' Having created his first 'extraordinary monster of rock', Bowie had forgotten that Ziggy's downfall had been the result of his own messianic fantasies:

David Bowie: When I first wrote Ziggy it was just an experiment; an exercise for me and he really grew out of proportion . . . Ziggy overshadowed everything . . . His own personality [was] unable to cope with the circumstance he found himself in, which was being an almighty prophet-like superstar rocker, who found he didn't know what to do with it once he got it. It's an archetype . . . it often happens. [1974]

Now it was all happening to Bowie himself. And he wasn't sure he had the willpower to resist. As he later confessed: 'I felt very, very puny as a human. I thought, "Fuck that, I want to be a superman." I took a look at my thoughts, my appearance, my expressions, my mannerisms and idiosyncrasies, and didn't like them. So I stripped myself down, chucked things out and replaced them with a completely new personality.' That 'new' personality, entirely created in his own image, began feeding on an inner self as messianic as his brother's: 'Everybody started to treat me as they treated Ziggy: as though I were the Next Big Thing, as though I moved masses of people. I became convinced I was a messiah. Very scary.'

And just as he was becoming subsumed by his androgynous alter ego, Bowie learnt that he would at last be taking the show to America for his first US tour. However uptight the UK mass media had proven, it was as nothing to its cousins in the land founded by Puritans. Describing his 1972 arrival four years on, Bowie expressed his amazement that, in America, 'Sex was still shocking. [So] everybody wanted to see the freak . . . Unwittingly, I really brought that whole thing over [here] . . . Nobody understood the European way of dressing and adopting the asexual, androgynous everyman pose. People all went screaming, "He's got make-up on and he's wearing stuff that looks like dresses!"' (His own record label, RCA, decided not to release the non-album follow-up to 'Starman', 'John, I'm Only Dancing', because they considered it too risqué to generate radioplay.) At the time, though, he couldn't wait to introduce the glamorous Ziggy to the colonials.

And so, in September 1972 two English acts who had been flitting around the US charts for the past couple of years without ever setting them alight, brought radical new stage acts to the other side of the pond. It is highly unlikely that either Bowie or the Floyd saw the other as ploughing a furrow akin to the one dug by the now-spectral Syd (though each had a song called 'Time'). But after five years of English rock tours, with proper powerhouse P.A. systems, Americans were ripe for a little more musical repatriation, though Pink Floyd had barely begun recording the album they were now debuting, and David Bowie was still chasing his first US hit 45.

For Pink Floyd, the September tour, running from the ninth to the thirtieth without ever touching the East Coast, was their second Stateside sortie of the year. The night of their greatest triumph this time around was unquestionably the show at the Hollywood Bowl, when employees of their US label, Capitol, came out in force, and searchlights strafed the L.A. sky during the finale of the now definitively titled, ecstatically received *Dark Side of the Moon*. (Their US record company chairman enthused, 'It was like watching [a] great Verdi opera for the first time.')

A week later, on a different coast, David Bowie took Manhattan for the first time, and almost as a reminder to himself played his own mortality sequence, in the form of a song first introduced at The Rainbow, an acoustic version of Jacques Brel's 'My Death' that served as the prelude to the symbolic summoning of Ziggy that was 'The Width of a Circle'. By now – as Bowie admitted to a BBC documentary crew shortly after extracting himself from Ziggy's maws – 'I was so lost in Ziggy. It was all that schizophrenia.' Being wholly 'lost in Ziggy', Bowie was starting to believe he should give Ziggy a whole album of his own and, who knows, this time he might manage to sustain the basic concept all the way through. That was, if he didn't go crazy in the process.

6. 1972–73: The Reclaiming of America

I went through a stage of trying to analyse what I was doing
and play it by their game . . . and the music became pretentious,
and I did. Not me, but 'I' through my work – because my work
was me.

– Ray Davies, 1989

It became easier and easier for me to blur the lines between
reality and the blessed creature that I'd created – my
doppelganger. I wasn't getting rid of him at all; in fact, I was
joining forces with him. The doppelganger and myself were
starting to become one and the same person. Then you start
on this trail of psychological destruction and you become . . . a
drug casualty at the end of it.

– David Bowie, to Paul Gambaccini, 1983

Dark Side of the Moon . . . though it was largely about him . . .
was the record where they escaped from Syd.

– Peter Jenner

> The story [of *Quadrophenia*] begins with the kid sitting on a
> rock. He's gone out to this rock in a boat and he's completely out
> of his brain . . . This whole thing explains how he got there . . .
> The whole point of it [all] is that the geezer's completely mixed
> up.
> – Pete Townshend, 1973

Seven months before Bowie brought Ziggy to New York's
Carnegie Hall, The Kinks were selling out two nights at the
same esteemed enclave of the arts. It was less than four months
since these London lads had last passed through these plush
corridors, but the shows in November 1971 and March 1972
were as different as chalk and Camembert. For some time now
Ray Davies had been bleating about how he would 'like to
develop a more professional stage act – not slick, but a complete
act that's entertaining. And not just a string of our best-known
songs.' He now seized his chance.

Before the resumption of shows in the new year, Davies had
decided it was time for a wholesale overhaul of The Kinks' set.
After four concept albums they had never really toured with, he
was suggesting he'd 'like to do a presentation based around our
1969 [sic] *Village Green* album and take it around small-sized
halls . . . like a village theatre type of thing', but save for the
reintroduction of the title track in the year's set, this was
another idea destined to be put on hold. When it came time to
unveil the new set at The Rainbow (for a BBC broadcast) at the
end of January, he again hedged his bets, sandwiching a couple
of cuts each from *Arthur* and *Muswell Hillbillies* between the
usual hits of yesteryear.

But he was still determined to break the shackles of the
band's history – to draw a line beneath the Sixties and start
afresh, and Carnegie Hall seemed as good a place to start as any.

So it was that on 2 March at Carnegie, he unveiled a show the central ballast of which was the last two Kinks albums, which was as close as Davies had yet come to renouncing his prolific past. Opening the show with a burst of songs from *Lola Versus Powerman*, he played just 'Sunny Afternoon' and a crowd-pleasing encore of 'You Really Got Me' / 'All Day and All of the Night' from the band's so-called classic era[31]. The core of the night's 'entertainment' was a selection of songs from *Muswell Hillbillies*, eight of them, to the accompaniment of the Mike Cotton Brass Band, intermittently interspersed with brief, ersatz renditions of the kind of music-hall favourites the characters who peopled *Muswell Hillbillies* might have sung themselves ('Banana Boat Song', 'Mammy', 'Baby Face'). For those moments, he was back home at one of the family singalongs. The audience and critics, though, were left largely mystified.

For those who didn't get the joke, Davies proceeded to issue the bulk of the *Hillbillies* portion of the Carnegie show – and a smattering of those oddball music-hall covers – as the second volume in The Kinks' first two-disc set, *Everybody's in Showbiz*, hastily constructed over the summer and rush-released in August. As *NME*'s Phil McNeill duly observed, it was 'a curious choice of material, as the renditions were not so different from what had come out just the previous year, except with the balance tilted away from desperation and into jovial resignation. Music hall ruled OK.' Band-members were nonplussed by the thinking behind the live element of this extravagant gesture on RCA's part.

John Gosling: I don't know if Ray was trying to make a statement [on *Everybody's in Showbiz*] but he put the worst tracks on the live side; they were rubbish. Old music-hall songs, all the camp stuff at the expense of the decent hits. At the time you wonder what the hell he's doing, but in hindsight he was obviously making a statement about the band. It wasn't just about hits for him.

That Davies felt 'it wasn't just about [the] hits' had long been obvious. What he was going to do about it was less clear. While The Who cleared their own decks later that year with a definitive reminder of their days as a singles band, *Meaty, Beaty, Big and Bouncy*, The Kinks' former US label, Reprise, 'retaliated' for their defection to RCA by issuing a rarities-heavy double album, *The Kink Kronikles*, which, to Davies' immense annoyance, charted higher than *Muswell Hillbillies*. But in order to escape a glorious past, he needed songs that had an equivalent resonance with his audience – and perhaps telling them to count the blessings of an obscure existence was not the best way to reach them.

The songs on the studio part of *Everybody's in Showbiz* – which included The Kinks' last UK hit single, 'Supersonic Rocket Ship' – were largely reflections on the curse of rock stardom, but at a time when Davies was no longer England's champion songsmith and maybe not even a contender. Thankfully, two songs put him in with a chance of reclaiming his crown. 'Celluloid Heroes', which gave the album its title, turned the mirror around on 'Oklahoma USA', showing the reality underlying that twinkling image up on the screen: 'People who worked and suffered and struggled for fame.' Meanwhile, the heart-rending 'Sitting in My Hotel' updated the concerns of 'All of My Friends Were There', that song about his 1966 breakdown, as the evidence suggested he was heading that way again:

> If my friends could see me now . . .
> They would tell me that I'm just being used
> They would ask me what I'm trying to prove.

They would see me in my hotel . . .
Writing songs for old-time vaudeville revues,
All my friends would ask me what it's all leading to.

If Davies' response offstage was to write more songs of self-doubt, onstage he made the *Muswell Hillbillies* songs ever more indicative of a man on the brink. The introduction to the live 'Acute Schizophrenia Paranoia Blues' – 'Now I warn you it's a really, really heavy number; if you can't take it, leave the building' – made it clear *he* didn't think the pastiche of musical styles was serving to obscure its underlying sensibility.

The highlight of those 1972 shows was, in fact, a full-blown brass-band version of 'Alcohol', which by allowing Ray to act as the souse in the song was becoming an excuse for him to imbibe enough to find release from being himself. The song was always a cautionary tale, but now it was one he did not always choose to heed: 'I've got this drink in my hand, and again I've got a character . . . and I have to become that character, so I start drinking. One night I nearly finished a bottle of tequila during that song.' Sure enough, the inevitable occurred: 'All of a sudden you become what you're pretending to be. You play the role you've written for yourself, and a bit of it rubs off . . . And if you play that show night after night, you start to think, "Hang on, how much of me is there in this?"'

Once again it was brother David who was the first to express real concern, knowing he would bear the brunt of any encroaching breakdown. Having been around a crazed Ray for such a long time, he was of the opinion that, for his brother, any schizophrenia was an intrinsic part of his creativity: 'The whole [creative] process is schizophrenic. Look at . . . the imaginary characters [he creates].' Perhaps David had been around his brother a little too long (he would later claim:

'Schizophrenia is quite normal, I think . . . I feel that it's a necessary part of the mind').

For those outside the Davies family circle, proof that Ray was spiralling downwards came when he began to talk about, and in the voice of, his alter ego. It would not be 'his' first or last appearance. Early on in *X-Ray*, his 1994 autobiography, Davies wrote (in the third person!) about this constant 'war with some alter ego whom he felt was trying to suppress him all his life . . . This mysterious dark figure . . . was always looming in his subconscious, looking for an opportunity to knock him from his pedestal.' By then, this alter ego (who at some point acquired the moniker 'Max') had become a familiar figure in Ray Davies interviews.

Alluding to 'him' in an interview three months after his July 1973 White City collapse, Davies claimed: 'He's gone now and maybe I can [finally] come out.' But the voice had only been temporarily stilled. Throughout the summer of 1973, Davies continued feeling decidedly boxed in. Describing his then-mindset some time later, the litany of why he had come to feel like such a loser was a lengthy one: 'I felt bad about playing my hits, I felt bad about writing new stuff; people felt it wasn't as good. I didn't really want to hang on to anything. I just wanted to get out. I felt trapped by the job I was doing.'

He had become his very own '20th Century Man', who no longer wanted to be here. On 15 July he found his band booked beneath the equally troubled Sly and the Family Stone at an all-day bash at White City Stadium, playing to a crowd of around 30,000, most of whom knew The Kinks only by their hit singles. Davies decided if he couldn't blow himself up, he could at least make a very public proclamation that he 'wanted out'. It was just after a four-song *Muswell Hillbillies* suite ended with a particularly besozzled 'Alcohol' and just as the band segued into the ubiquitous medley of earlier hits that still served as a Kinks finale, Davies placed a can of beer on his head and announced, 'I quit':

John Gosling: Nobody knew that he was going to announce his retirement onstage; certainly nobody knew he was going to do it with a can of beer balanced on his head! He used to put across this persona of being a bit of a lad and a drinker but he wasn't really that. But at White City I think he was really out of it for once, and shortly after that he tried to commit suicide.

There was a good reason why Ray was so out of it. He had been mixing up his medicine, self-medicating himself into oblivion. His wife had just told him their marriage was over, and with a future stretching out ahead which that to comprise writing and performing 'songs for old-time vaudeville revues', he reached for the bottle of pills his doctor had given him, telling him, 'Take one of those when you feel a bit down, it'll make you feel better.' As Davies says, 'I felt down every ten seconds, so I just kept taking them. The next thing I knew I was in a hospital.' Only when he collapsed backstage at White City, and was rushed to Whittington Hospital, did the medics realize how close the singer had come to concocting a lethal combination of booze 'n' pills:

Ray Davies: I did try to kill myself that day. I took what must have been uppers, the whole bottle. I went to Whittington Hospital and I said, 'My name is Ray Davies and I am dying.' And they laughed. I had my stage make-up on and a clown's outfit, and they said, 'Oh, we believe you. Why don't you write down the names of

two people who are next of kin?' I wrote the first one.
The second one I couldn't see. I fell over and they knew
they had a real case. They dragged me into the ward, got
the stomach pump and made me throw up. I remember
[feeling] such terrible guilt . . . [and] sending Dave out for
some records . . . I put one on – it was Mahler's ninth,
his last symphony, his version of the end of civilization.
I could relate to that. I decided I was going to leave the
music business completely. [1984]

It was 1966 all over again. And just as in 1966, The Kinks'
management was on the phone to journalists the following day,
trying to make light of Ray's 'retirement'. Meanwhile, Ray took
two weeks off, staying at his brother's house in Southgate, and
listening to anything other than the kind of music that still
provided the brothers with their bread and butter. By the start
of August, the band were back recording again, though, as John
Gosling recalls: 'We all had to pretend like nothing had
happened, so there was this strange atmosphere in the studio all
the time. Ray was doing weird things like walking around with
glasses with no lenses in and nobody was supposed to say
anything. No one did until one of our roadies went up to Ray
and said, "What are those glasses for – reading or long distance?"
and we fell about.'

Pretending White City had never taken place, Davies
resumed working on a new version of an old concept:
Preservation Act 1, a reworking of 1968's *Village Green
Preservation Act* that had grown out of some new material he
had written for a Drury Lane concert in January. It was here
that he finally got to perform the show he had been talking
about for a year or more, combining the songs of 1968–69
with ones that shared a similar mindset from the here and

now, beginning with 'The Village Green Overture' and ending with 'Celluloid Heroes'[32]. He also, for the first time, used movie footage and photo stills as a backdrop to what was very much a one-off performance. The visual backdrops included pre-war family photos (to accompany *VGPS*'s 'Picture Book'), and images of Mary Quant, the Rolling Stones and the Krays (to go with 'Where Are They Now?').

But again, Ray felt he should meet the audience halfway. As he admitted to one music journalist, 'I had to decide whether to present a Kinks show or a theatrical performance. I didn't want to disappoint people who already had tickets for a Kinks show. So in the end, I made it a combination of the two.' Not surprisingly, Drury Lane failed to abate those conflicted feelings 'about playing my hits . . . [and] about writing new stuff [that] people felt . . . wasn't as good'. Nonetheless, he persevered with this new version of *VGPS*, and by the end of August he had all but completed the first instalment of this Seventies re-creation of that Sixties idyll. Under duress from label and management, he even penned a *mea culpa* for his behaviour at White City:

> Several weeks ago I wrote a letter to the world; it turned out to be a letter to me. But I do feel I made a decision, whether emotionally motivated or not, to change the format of the band. The White City was not a good place to say goodbye. The sun wasn't shining, and anyway rock festivals have never held many happy memories for me personally. The Kinks are close enough now to be able to work as a team in whatever they do, and anyone who thinks they are only my backup band is very mistaken. There are still things to extract from The Kinks on an artistic level – whether or not it turns out to be commercial remains to be seen.

★

Like many a celluloid hero before him, Davies discovered the hard way that it was not so easy to get off the merry-go-round or to disown one's past. The month before *Preservation Act 1* appeared – to almost universal indifference – he heard about a nice little royalty cheque he would be receiving from a 'cover' version of the first important song he wrote voicing his disaffection with the painful present, 1965's 'Where Have All the Good Times Gone?' It now constituted the closing track on *Pin Ups*, David Bowie's album of Beat-era covers, which hit the number one spot the week before *Preservation Act*'s release. Ostensibly, it was intended to serve as Bowie's fond farewell to the rock-star persona he killed off at Hammersmith Odeon in July.

Twelve days before Ray Davies attempted a genuine rock & roll suicide, Bowie had successfully, if metaphorically, killed off his own alter ego at the end of an exhausting fifteen months of unrelenting touring, recording and projecting. Unlike Davies' White City epiphany, Bowie's goodbye to Ziggy from the Hammersmith stage had made the world sit up and take notice. The symbolic death of Ziggy Stardust was front-page news in the British music press, while the near death of the authentic Ray Davies warranted a single column on page three. Such was the power of Bowie's all-consuming conceit. And the genius of manager Tony Defries' strategy.

Unlike Davies, Bowie (and his mentor turned protégé, Lou) had now delivered to RCA a series of albums that were all commercial and critical successes (Mr Reed had even taken a leaf out of Ziggy's book, creating the concept album *Berlin* out of half-a-dozen Velvet Underground outtakes and then concocting a storyline to disguise his own creative torpor). In Bowie's case, RCA had even managed to turn his two Mercury albums, (the rechristened) *Space Oddity* and *TMWSTW*, into bestsellers.

This boy from the 'wrong' side of the Thames had not

only consumed all the A&R energies of the record label to whom Davies had also tied his fortunes, but in the year since his own Carnegie Hall debut had become the UK's first bona fide rock star of the 1970s. And in the land of celluloid heroes, he had already started insisting on living like one. In the year leading up to *Pin Ups*, every little trick seemed to work; every gesture assumed a significance, not necessarily the one intended. That the great strategy was a rickety edifice, built on RCA advances and the inexorable necessity of cracking the American market, was a secret Bowie and Defries preferred to keep to themselves.

Not that RCA's ongoing incomprehension always worked in Bowie's favour – as evidenced by their decision to reissue the anachronistic 'Space Oddity' in December 1972. But as long as they didn't enquire how long was this piece of string, Defries the puppetmaster remained content. It was one of his inspired ideas to purchase Bowie's two albums from Mercury for the giveaway price of $20,000 each, paid for by RCA, who now *leased* the albums from Main Man for seven years for an advance of $37,500 each. By the end of 1972, *Space Oddity* was selling 15,000 copies a month Stateside, *TMWSTW* half that (probably because Mercury promptly dumped truckloads of 'cut-outs' on the second-hand market). In the last week of November both albums entered the UK album charts, where they would resolutely remain for the next six months. Coming hard on the heels of the belated chart-entry of *Hunky Dory* in September, it gave Bowie four albums in the Top Thirty – every one of them judiciously represented in the live set he was now touting around America.

The Fall 1972 US tour stands as perhaps the most leisurely in rock history. Bowie played just twenty-one shows in sixteen cities across two-and-a-half months, allowing him to settle into his Ziggy persona as he travelled by train between cities. Reporters were now granted very limited access to him and his doppelganger, relying on hearsay to learn that he had popped up again at a Mott the Hoople show, or at a Rodney Bingenheimer-organized private party. With the hype yet to hit hyperdrive Stateside, by the end of the tour RCA were looking at losses of over a quarter of a million dollars. On the coasts, and in traditional rock & roll enclaves such as Cleveland, they rose to acclaim the rise of Ziggy; but in the hinterlands Bowie felt increasingly like an alien who had landed without his copy of *The Hitchhiker's Guide to the Galaxy*. Thankfully, this was the ideal frame of mind in which to start writing songs for the album that would introduce Aladdin Sane to his acolytes.

For the next leap into the unknown, Bowie decided to go yet further into the cracked world of his alter-creation. It was, as he later observed, a necessary 'process of transforming [oneself] into the thing you admire, becoming it, finding out what makes it tick'. But it was also proving 'quite easy to become obsessed night and day with the character. [And as] I became Ziggy Stardust, David Bowie went totally out of the window.' Already, he was leaving certain collaborators behind. Mick Ronson, his nightly foil onstage and mainstay of the Main Man sound, would later inform Tony Parsons, 'Ziggy definitely affected him . . . He had to become what Ziggy was; he had to believe in him . . . They lived off each other.' As Bowie began to believe he was a star by right, his trusty record producer, Ken Scott, remembers a much changed David turning up to begin work on *Aladdin Sane* at the end of 1972:

Ken Scott: He was becoming a different person, and if he had the same people around him they always . . . acted with him the same way as he used to be. But he wasn't that person any more, so he couldn't have anything to remind him . . . Bowie began believing that all the trappings of success which Defries provided, the limos and that kind of thing, had to be there. In fact, they weren't trappings any more, but necessities.

The songs Bowie brought to these sessions had little of the ironic distance evident in the *Ziggy* songs. Composed almost entirely on his travels through the vast vistas of the new world, the album, like the alter ego, had taken on a life of its own. At least he was seizing the days. Barely was the ink dry on two of his latest crash-courses for ravers than he was in the studio, catching the moment. 'Jean Genie' and 'Drive-In Saturday', recorded in the States at opposite ends of the Stateside trip, were already prepped to become the next two singles. He also now revisited the classic song he had donated to a moribund Mott the Hoople, 'All the Young Dudes', a failsafe in case he came up short with the right stuff just as the pop world was at his feet.

'Jean Genie', cut in New York before the landmark show at Carnegie Hall, was the intended signature tune to his latest chameleon change. And even if his US record label didn't feel like issuing Ziggy's second signpost, 'John, I'm Only Dancing', they still wanted a single for the pre-Christmas market, preferably one in the American vernacular. Bowie duly obliged ('Jean Genie snuck off to the city . . .'). Having test-run another testosterone-fuelled classic on his bedazzled audiences he already knew he had a hit on his hands.

At a handful of shows in November he also gave 'My Death' a respite, and instead played an acoustic version of his latest dystopian disquisition, 'Drive-In Saturday'. Set in a society where people have forgotten how to make love, and have to re-learn the art from watching old movies, it was another disturbing view of the future from someone who had transferred his lovemaking technique to the stage, but had lost his own mojo in the process. Another contemporary song made this transference doubly explicit. 'Cracked Actor', appropriately written in Hollywood, was perhaps his most Bolanesque production to date. A *Star is Born* parable at the expense of a jaded has-been ('he's stiff on his legend, the films that he made'), Bowie again seemed content to project a possible future self-portrait.

Despite the huge physical and psychological demands now being placed on the still-starstruck Mr Jones, the above tracks proved that he was still writing strong songs. They just didn't represent a seismic shift in his interior worldview. If 'Watch That Man' crossed 'Queen Bitch' with 'Star', 'Panic in Detroit' – set to a pitch-perfect pastiche of a Motor City riff – vamped on portents of revolution previously test-run on 'Five Years'. In truth, he had been mining the same vein now for the past four albums. But this time he felt less in control of the process than ever.

Initially, for all his work ethic, he felt he was shy of an album's worth of singles. His solution was simple: recut three songs already foisted on the UK singles-market: 1970's 'Prettiest Star' (now as relevant to his own persona as his wife's), 'John, I'm Only Dancing' (beefed up with the sax sound found throughout *Aladdin Sane*) and 'All the Young Dudes'. In the end he omitted the latter two, after writing 'Lady Grinning Soul' and cutting his raciest cover to date {though 'John, I'm Only Dancing' was originally down as a superior album-closer).

Fortunately, whatever his attendant conceit, the songs still retained a certain life of their own. As he duly admitted: 'I have concepts. I have storylines for the albums, but . . . the actual inspiration comes suddenly, and is written as it comes.' In fact, the whole album was as raunchy as the recent Ziggy shows. First, there was his almost pornographic retake on The Stones' 1967 single, 'Let's Spend the Night Together', banned in the US back then; then there was that unnuanced portrait of a faker whose only contact with the opposite sex was his daily blowjob ('Cracked Actor'); and finally, the one song that directly addressed his nightly stage ritual, 'Time', which 'flexes like a whore, falls wanking to the floor'.

The hook on which to hang the collection, though, came after he fled America. Only at the last minute did 'A Lad Insane' become 'Aladdin Sane', Bowie writing the off-key title track on the boat back from America while pondering how many puns his audience could take. The (change in) persona, immortalized by the painted lightning flash that splits his face on *Aladdin Sane*'s iconic cover, was finally relayed to the media during a conversation between Bowie and *NME*'s Charles Shaar Murray in mid-January 1973, as he put the finishing touches to the hastily assembled album in the brief respite Defries allowed him before renewing their assault on the new world. When Murray asked who was going to take Ziggy's place, his unabashed reply was: 'A person called Aladdin Sane. "Aladdin" is really just a title track. The album was written in America. The numbers were not supposed to form a concept album, but looking back on them, there seems to be a definite linkage from number to number. There's a general feeling on the album that I can't put my finger on.'

The unabashed insanity at the heart of his marginally modified creation was supposedly just another case of Bowie as detached observer, using his work as his personal psychiatric couch. In the 1974 BBC documentary, *Cracked Actor* – made when he really had lost himself in his creation(s) (and cocaine)

– he tried to make light of the lad's schizoid nature: 'Aladdin Sane was schizophrenic, which accounted for why there were so many costume changes – because he had so many personalities.' Others realized that the feted star's split nature was hardly now confined to the clothes he wore onstage. Mick Rock, still snapping away at Bowie's behest, writing of *Aladdin Sane* at the time, inadvertently spilled the truth: 'The grinnin' madman is Mr B himself, and to him you're just a pale reflection of some other world, because his look goes so far beyond you, even tho' he's looking straight into your eyes.'

That 'general feeling' imbuing *Aladdin Sane* and the shows reflected an outsider's view of the new world's vast landscapes seen from the other side of tinted glass in his private carriage/cabin to nowhere, presaging the role he would make his own in *The Man Who Fell to Earth*. Hence, presumably, why Bowie himself has never been quite sure what to make of the result.

In conversation, he has often been dismissive of *Ziggy*'s sequel, describing it in the mid-Seventies as, '*Ziggy Stardust* meets *Fame* . . . *Aladdin Sane* was himself talking about being a star, and hitting America . . . So it was a subjective [version of] Ziggy.' He also suggested he had been trying to move on, but failed to remove the mental straitjacket that was Ziggy: 'I didn't want to be trapped in this Ziggy character all my life. And I guess what I was doing on *Aladdin Sane*, I was trying to move into the next area – but using a rather pale imitation of Ziggy as a secondary device. In my mind it was *Ziggy Goes to Washington*.' And yet, by the time it turned twenty-five, he had come around to seeing what had seemed 'almost like a treading-water album [as] . . . the more successful album – because it's more informed about rock 'n' roll'.

In part, this is because he had created the ultimate well-oiled rock machine in The Spiders, while Ken Scott was ideally suited to produce the perfect fusion of 'born to boogie' pop. And while the songsmith of *Hunky Dory* is almost lost from view, such is the strength of his creation's icy grip that one can't help but share the man's strange fascination with his latest guise. What was not so apparent to English fans at the time was how much Bowie was distancing himself from the verities that had informed his work to date. *Aladdin Sane* was not just a 'souped-up Ziggy', he was a Ziggy who had found 'this alternative world that . . . had all the violence, and all the strangeness and bizarreness, and it was really happening. It was real life and it wasn't just in my songs. Suddenly my songs didn't seem so out of place.' All too soon he would call this place home.

Aladdin Sane was Bowie's idea of a land grab – and the territory in question was America. By June 1973 *Ziggy Stardust*, even after the year of The Hype, had sold a mere 320,000 copies in the States – perfectly respectable sales figures for an English cult artist, but hardly The Beatles. So the tougher sound and salient subject matter of *Aladdin Sane* was designed to engage with more Americans. He had even toned down his luv-a-duck accent. And when, on 14 February 1973, he opened his second US tour with the first of two shows at New York's 6,000-seater Radio City Hall, booked more on faith than sales figures, the whole second half of the show was given over to the live debut of *Aladdin Sane* (with just 'Lady Grinning Soul' being absent). He was evidently determined to get the message across.

But he was also tiring fast. By the end of the month-long tour, the set was down to seventy-five minutes and it was the songs from the new album that suffered. Meanwhile, the re-issued 'Space Oddity' was still garnering more airplay than 'Jean Genie'. Shows on the coasts continued to generate Ziggy zealots, but large tracts of the subcontinent seemed determined to remain immune to his camp charms.

Returning to Britain by the start of May – via Japan, where a ten-day April tour was greeted as the return of the rising son – Bowie took another gamble on his mass appeal, opening his two-month UK tour show at the cavernous Earls Court. Although he sold out the 17,000-capacity venue, the show was a disaster, with many fans unable to see the stage or hear the band, such were the dreadful sightlines and even worse acoustics at this sorry excuse for a concert hall. If the reviews the following week were damning, by now he just wanted his life back. As he would later write in *Moonage Daydream*, 'After Earls Court, I really did want it all to come to an end. I was now writing for a different kind of project and, exhausted and completely bored with the whole Ziggy concept, couldn't keep my attention on the performances . . . Strangely enough, the rest of the tour was an astounding success.'

If anything, this is an understatement. Even when he played two shows a night – as he did on no less than eighteen occasions in May and June 1973 – the energy levels were astonishingly high, buoyed by still-ecstatic fans at every venue. He knew the end was in sight, and immediately after the last show of the tour he informed critical confidant Charles Shaar Murray: 'Those were the final gigs. That's it. Period . . . From now on, I'll be concentrating on various activities that have very little to do with rock and pop.' What he needed most was time to recharge his batteries, and weed himself off the drugs that had become a necessary crutch when he felt all crippled inside. For all his earlier protestations, the pace of his helter-skelter existence and the need to inure himself from a hostile world had inexorably led him – like Syd, Lou and Iggy before him – to artificial uppers. And it was fast becoming a problem:

David Bowie: [By then] my drug addiction [had] really started . . . You could pin it down to the very last months of the Ziggy Stardust period . . . [It was] enough to have probably worried some of the people around me. And after that . . . we got into *Diamond Dogs*, that's when it was out of control. From that period onwards I was a real casualty. [1999]

It would take Bowie a good while to see the trap he had sprung for himself. By 1978, when he had again reverted to the persona of the detached observer (and was, as such, generally unengaging), he finally felt ready to admit that constructing such personae 'mixed me up quite a lot. I began to think I was Ziggy. And then, of course, Ziggy began to merge with the others, and I wasn't quite sure whether I'd completely dropped the last one or not. Bits and pieces would keep creeping through.'

Even the metaphorical killing of an alter ego requires a steady hand and an iron will. And Bowie was still not quite ready to debrief his audience about this future that would 'have very little to do with rock and pop', appealing as the whole idea sounded in the immediate aftermath of his Hammersmith farewell. The final Ziggy show merely meant the end of The Spiders from Mars, who back in April had been cruelly but prophetically described by *NME*'s Nick Kent as 'just a useful appendage to the current fantasy'.

By October, Bowie had been persuaded to make one 'final commitment to Ziggy as a performance character', an American TV show called *The Midnight Special*. The producer, Burt Sugarman, approached Bowie 'about doing something which personified my theatre shows but . . . I had "retired" Ziggy earlier that year'. *The 1980 Floor Show*, as it was billed, was a curious melange of *Aladdin Sane*, the more narcissistic parts of

Pin Ups, and one song from the concept album he now planned to do around George Orwell's *1984*, 'Dodo (You Didn't Hear It from Me)'. Only ever broadcast in the States, the hour-long special left this US TV audience mystified, converted and/or appalled in roughly equal measures. But it seemed like he was having fun, displaying that abiding penchant for deviant visual imagery by dressing up Marianne Faithfull as a nun as they dueted on 'I Got You, Babe', while a series of fake hands clasped the naughty bits of his own outlandish stage outfit. Despite this primetime push, though, year's end brought no sign of either *Pin Ups* nor *Aladdin Sane* replicating Ziggy's moderately solid sales Stateside, let alone their UK position, where both comfortably topped the album charts.

And still Bowie refused to close the circle on Ziggy. As his English fans mourned Ziggy's demise, and American fans wondered what came next in the masterplan for world domination, he began work on the conceptual successor to *Aladdin Sane*, *Diamond Dogs*. Once again, he had in mind 'a quasi-Orwellian concept album about a future world where the clockwork orang-utans skulk like dogs in the streets while the politicians etc, and blah blah blah', to quote Lester Bangs' sarcastic swipe at the album as released. But even as Bowie was hard at work turning his 'quasi-Orwellian' remake of *1984* into something original, if only rock & roll, he still found that 'every time I got close to defining [Ziggy] more, he seemed to become less than what he was before'.

At the turn of the year, in conversation with William Burroughs – the arch-exponent of the 'cut-up' technique to which Bowie disingenuously attributed much of his lyric writing – he again resumed talking about plans to turn *Ziggy Stardust* into a theatrical production. Determined to impress a sceptical Burroughs, the story he now built around the 'Ziggy' songs confirmed that the further he got away from his original self-conscious aspirations, and gave in to paranoia, the more eccentric his ideas became:

The [proposed] production of Ziggy will have to exceed people's expectations of what they thought Ziggy was . . . The time is five years to go before the end of the earth. It has been announced that the world will end because of lack of natural resources. Ziggy is in a position where all the kids have access to things that they thought they wanted. The older people have lost all touch with reality and the kids are left on their own to plunder anything. Ziggy was in a rock & roll band and the kids no longer want rock & roll. There's no electricity to play it. Ziggy's adviser tells him to collect news and sing it, 'cause there is no news. So Ziggy does this and there is terrible news. 'All the Young Dudes' is a song about the news. It is no hymn to the youth as people thought. It is completely the opposite . . . [So] Ziggy is advised in a dream by 'The Infinites' . . . who are black-hole jumpers . . . to write the coming of a starman, so he writes 'Starman', which is the first news of hope that the people have heard. So they latch on to it immediately . . . Ziggy has been talking about this amazing spaceman who will be coming down to save the earth . . . Now Ziggy starts to believe in all this himself and thinks himself a prophet of the future starman. He takes himself up to incredible spiritual heights and is kept alive by his disciples. When the Infinites arrive, they take bits of Ziggy to make themselves real because in their original state they are anti-matter and cannot exist in our world. And they tear him to pieces on stage during the song 'Rock & Roll Suicide'. As soon as Ziggy dies on stage the Infinites take his elements and make themselves visible.

Before he completely cracked, Bowie took elements of this still-born fantasy and fused them with the 'quasi-Orwellian' to form *Diamond Dogs,* while simultaneously putting the finishing touches to a new stage show which, to use his own grandiose description, would be '*Metropolis* meets *Caligari,* but on stage, in colour and [with] a rock 'n' roll soundtrack'. So much for introducing a series of 'activities that have very little to do with rock and pop'. The album he finally finished by February 1974 he was almost apologetic about, describing it as another from the 'usual basket of apocalyptic visions, isolation, being terribly miserable . . . I'm saying the same thing a lot, which is about this sense of self-destruction . . . There's a real nagging anxiety in there somewhere.'

Only when he was halfway through another hugely expensive attempt to wow the colonials with the stage show to end all stage shows, did Bowie realize that Ziggy, starved of attention, had finally died of his own accord. It was time to replace soul love with plastic soul. Even as he continued to wonder what he could do to win over the American mainstream, *Ziggy Stardust* was selling steadily and relentlessly. For all his graft, all it took was time for the rest of America to catch up with their cousins on the coasts, who had got Ziggy straight away. By the end of 1974 *Ziggy Stardust* had sold close to half a million copies, well in excess of its three Xeroxed successors. And by the time he returned to the US stage again, in 1976, it had become the benchmark for all future Bowie incarnations.

Part of the explanation is that the Ziggy shows themselves quickly became the stuff of legend, a fact well attested by the fortunate few with a local bootleg outlet from whence they could obtain either or both of the professional-sounding audio documents that those nice men at TMQ and TAKRL had considerately released without obtaining RCA's okay. *Live at*

Santa Monica, a double album of an October 1972 KSAN broadcast from Bowie's first-ever LA show, and/or *Ziggy's Last Stand*, a single disc of the final Hammersmith show, taken from Pennebaker's one-hour *cinéma vérité* version of this historic gig, targeted those very fans on each coast who caught the wave just in time. They were soon essential additions to any self-respecting rock fan's record collection.

★

Equally collectible, and desirable, were the steady trickle of Pink Floyd bootlegs that at the same time served to whet the appetite of fans who had caught the US *Dark Side of the Moon* shows, and wanted to know – and hear – more. If the English *Tour '72* album took its time making its way over the pond, there was no shortage of live FM 'in concerts' of the band from 1970–71 ripe for unofficial release. Meanwhile, the band continued to take its own sweet time coming up with an official version of the show they had been playing now for over a year, still blithely unconcerned at the prospect of being, in Gilmour's words, 'bootlegged out of existence'.

Indeed, such was their belief that the world, or at least their target audience, would still be waiting patiently by the check-out till when they got around to putting out the 'real' album, that they recorded another of their 'soundtrack' albums in the interim. The surprisingly cogent *Obscured by Clouds* – composed for the French film, *La Vallée* – was recorded between the English and Japanese legs of the *Dark Side* tour. It included at least one Waters lyric, which really should have been holding hands with the lunatic on the grass, 'Childhood's End': 'You set sail across the sea of long past thoughts and memories / Childhood's end, your fantasies merge with harsh realities.'

Yet the ongoing delays to *Dark Side* only furthered its momentum both within the record label, and out in the racks.

Bhaskar Menon, the US Capitol chairman, thinks 'the fact that they had played this music in concert was very important [because] I, and a lot of the people who worked at Capitol, knew about it long before the record came out'. Even the fact that Floyd had already informed Capitol they were leaving the label after *Dark Side of the Moon* didn't forestall the label's lavish plans for the album when it was finally ready in the winter of 1973.

Quite why the band spent so long putting the album together – it was recorded in just thirty-eight days, but the sessions were spread across seven months and did not start until late May 1972 – has never been adequately explained. Certainly by the time Floyd played the Hollywood Bowl in September the album was a fully realized piece. If, as Dave Gilmour told Capital Radio's Tommy Vance, 'When we first got [*Dark Side*] together, took it out and did it in shows, it changed all the time', by the time they reached the West Coast they had 'cemented it into being'.

Fittingly, 'Speak to Me' had made its first live appearance at the 28 June show at the Brighton Dome, hastily scheduled to make amends for the 'abandoned' performance back in January, when *Eclipse* was supposed to have been debuted in all its then-glory before the backing tapes broke down. And 'The Great Gig in the Sky', musically recognizable, though missing the orgasmic wailing of Clare Torry, had replaced 'The Mortality Sequence' by the time of the Hollywood Bowl performance.

But still the album was not finished, and wouldn't be until 19 February 1973, a mere two weeks before the Floyd began their third US tour in a year, and just four weeks before they followed Bowie into Radio City Music Hall, willing New Yorkers to pass judgement on their own testament to the capacity of English rock musicians for internalizing some of their more dysfunctional traits. Only at the end of March did EMI (and Capitol) 'rush-release' the album, ahead of Bowie's near-certain chart-topper (to no avail – though *Dark Side of the Moon* went on to spend a record-breaking 292 weeks in the UK album charts, it never made number one!).

The show at Radio City really marks the end of *Dark Side*'s journey – not only was there now a spectacular light show, but the two songs that did not find their berth until they were cut in the studio, 'The Great Gig in the Sky' and 'Time', at last received form and structure, courtesy of two external partners in the recording process, engineer Alan Parsons and singer Clare Torry; the latter having been brought in at Parsons' suggestion to improvise vocal sounds that would fit Floyd's concept for the new 'mortality sequence'. Neither would receive a share of the great riches that the album would bring, at least not until 2005, when Torry's threats to bring suit forced a settlement from the band.

As Torry recalls: 'They [just] explained the album was about birth, and all the shit you go through in your life and then death. I did think it was rather pretentious [but] of course, I didn't tell them that.' Instead, she just let herself go, and although in Gilmour's opinion, 'she wasn't too quick at finessing what we wanted, . . . out came that orgasmic sound we know and love'. No one hearing the album (or indeed the live performances where three girl-singers attempted, and patently failed, to emulate the passion in Torry's original vocal) can doubt her entitlement to a share of the credit (or cash) her great gig generated.

Parsons' own contribution came from a more prosaic place, but it gave 'Time' that explosive opening it had lacked to date. As the former EMI engineer himself says, 'I had recorded [the clocks] previously in a watchmaker's shop for a quadraphonic sound demonstration record. I went in with a mobile and recorded each one separately, ticking, then chiming.' Already, Floyd's new album had been earmarked as a likely candidate for a quadraphonic release, and the band quickly realized that getting the clocks to go around the speakers fit perfectly with the kind of 360-degree sound they had been using in their live set-up for years, until a crescendo of chimes exploded from every corner of the room. Parsons, as an EMI employee, had no recourse to reimbursement for this creative contribution, so contented himself with mentioning his 'major' input at every opportunity.

'On the Run' had also been given an altogether punchier ending. So, rather than drifting into 'Time', it ended with 'some kind of crash', to co-opt Roger Waters' chosen phrase. Inevitably, it was the bullish Waters who pushed Gilmour to come up with something more than just another noodling guitar-link. (As Gilmour has openly admitted, '[At the time] we were all very, very happy to have a driving force like Roger who wanted to push for these concepts . . . Jointly and severally, we wanted each piece of music to have its own magic.') The beguiling end result – and its almost universal acceptance – still took everyone aback:

> **Dave Gilmour:** Until the very last day we'd never heard them as the continuous piece we'd been imagining for more than a year. We had to literally snip bits of tape, cut in the linking passages and stick the ends back together. Finally, you sit back and listen all the way through at enormous volume. [1998]

> **Richard Wright:** [*Dark Side of the Moon*] was not a deliberate attempt to make a commercial album. It just happened that way. [But] we knew we had a lot more

melody than previous Floyd albums and there was a concept that ran all the way through it. The music was [that much] easier to absorb. [1996]

Thankfully, throughout the tortuous recording process the band's unity had remained fully intact. As Nick Mason recalled: 'The recording [of *Dark Side . . .*] was lengthy, but not fraught, not agonised over at all. We were working really well as a band.' Gilmour, too, remembers 'massive rows about the way it should be – but they were about passionate beliefs in what we were doing'. However, the shift in direction after the consummation of massive commercial success would ensure that from now on it would be Waters' way or the highway.

And Waters liked his song-cycles. As *Let It Rock*'s John Hoyland highlighted a few months after the album's appearance: 'Roger Waters seems to need to apply himself to themes in order to produce really good songs . . . [Although Pink Floyd] have achieved the sombre intensity of feeling that pervades this record before, here it is linked up with an examination of the social causes of madness.' As it was in this new beginning, so it would be for ever more. For all of Waters' fears about going insane during the making of *Dark Side of the Moon*, it would be the album's epoch-defining success that would actually send him teetering into a form of musical megalomania that would define Floyd's future direction for the foreseeable.

*

Another Sixties pop figure would also have the 'M' word thrown at him by his long-standing musical collaborators long before he had completed the project that would occupy him for the last half of 1972 and the whole of 1973. In Pete Townshend's case, the madness would pass soon enough, though not before he had been rendered unconscious by a well-timed punch from

Roger Daltrey, or trashed most of The Who's stage equipment when the same thing that happened to Pink Floyd when first performing *Eclipse* laid The Who low, early on in a brief UK tour presenting their rock opera, *Quadrophenia*.

For the Floyd, it was a mere hiccup; for The Who, it proved a presentiment to the mounting problems a live production of *Quadrophenia* presented. But then, Townshend's determination to deliver a rock opera that would knock *Tommy* into a cocked hat had been fuelling his workaholic ways for three years now. And *Quadrophenia* was the third rock opera the band had set out to record in that time, albeit the first to make it to the shops.

If the autumn 1971 release of *Who's Next* proved that Townshend's songwriting skills remained undiminished, the ideas underlying *Lifehouse* lingered well into 1972. When The Who assembled at Olympic studios to start work on its successor, the songs Townshend brought to the sessions – tracks such as 'Put the Money Down', 'Relay', 'Join Together' and 'Long Live Rock' – did rather seem like vestiges of either *Lifehouse* or *Rock is Dead*, two conceits mentioned to the press the previous year (the inclusion of the first three as demos on the 2000 *Lifehouse* boxed-set confirms such a suspicion).

At the time, Townshend insisted the intention was 'to have one side of the [next] album just good tracks, and the other side a mini-opera', presumably the already trailered *Rock is Dead: Long Live Rock*. But these weren't the only tracks he had in a form The Who could record. Aside from the likes of 'Riot in a Female Jail' and 'Can't You See I'm Easy', which would stay as demos, there were two songs of a quite different hue, the self-doubting 'Is It In My Head?' and the life-affirming 'Love, Reign O'er Me'. As the band worked with *Who's Next* producer Glyn Johns on these two tracks in June 1972, Townshend turned to

Johns and said, 'Look Glyn, I don't think I can stand this another moment longer – I've got to write another opera.' And this time he would not be dissuaded by Johns' usual scepticism:

Pete Townshend: So I went off and started working on that, and [having] got really excited about an idea I had, put about fourteen or fifteen songs together, and went rushing back [to the band] and said, 'Listen, I'm not gonna play this stuff, but I can tell you . . . [it] knocks shit out of what we have already done, so let's . . . put a couple [of tracks] out as singles, and I'll incorporate some [of the] others and do a new opera.' . . . You know, we couldn't keep treading water and I [had] had this idea for a project for a long time. It really came out of The Who [having] been going for ten years, and lots of backward looking, and I thought it would be nice to have an album that encapsulated everything The Who had ever done. [1972]

By September he already had a whole double album sketched out in his head; telling *Rolling Stone* he had these 'fourteen or fifteen songs' written and, by mid-November, mostly demoed. The starting point was not, as one might expect, 'Love, Reign O'er Me' – though, as 'Pete's Theme', it would serve as the climactic point of the eventual album – but rather 'Is It In My Head?', a song about a man who wonders if feelings of existential fear and self-loathing – articulated by couplets like, 'I try to number those who love me / And find out exactly what the trouble is' – are real.

Quadrophenia would be narrated from 'in[side] my head' by Jimmy the Mod who, as the story unfolds, begins to separate into four distinct personalities as his estrangement from the world grows (or, as he says in the album liner-notes, 'Schizophrenic? I'm bleeding Quadrophenic'). The original premise, as Townshend later recalled, was a simple one: 'A day or two in the life of a mod boy who comes apart and . . . realizes he needs to start again.' Interestingly, his initial point of reference, as he told Penny Valentine in early August 1972, came from one of Ray Davies' earlier works. Calling the piece a 'song cycle', not a rock opera, he suggested it would be 'much more like The Kinks' *Arthur* than *Tommy*.' How far advanced his ideas were became clear as the interview progressed, and he laid out for Valentine (and her *Sounds* readers) much of the architecture for The Who's latest artefact, fifteen months before its appearance:

> **Pete Townshend:** At the moment I'm pretty excited about [the idea]. It'll be a decade of The Who in January . . . [and I wondered,] What's happened to the individual members of the group, how they've changed? So I thought a nice way of doing it was to have a hero who, instead of being schizophrenic, has got a split personality four ways and each side of this is represented by a particular theme and a particular song. I'm the good part of the character needless to say – the choir boy who doesn't make good, the [boy] scout who gets assaulted by the scout master. Then there's the bad part, which is Roger, breaking the windows in coloured people's houses, turning over Ford Populars and things of that nature. Then there's the romantic part which is John Entwistle falling in love with the girl next door, everything going really well until her mother catches them one day in a compromising situation and flings him out and he goes off frustrated, despairing. Then there's Keith – totally irresponsible, insane. Playing jokes on his girlfriends, telling terrible lies, blowing up the place where he works. [1972]

Few of these particulars would survive the recording process, though the multiple-personality premise held firm. The queer scoutmaster, the smashing of 'windows in the houses of black people' and falling deeply in love while all his mates 'want tit and little else', all ideas dating from a July 1972 sketch, would also fall by the wayside. As would seven songs demoed in the early stages after Townshend decided 'Jimmy is better left without a child-hood, without any immature dreams and fantasies. It's better we meet him already full of anger.' Of this 'clutch of songs' – 'Get Out and Stay Out', 'Four Faces', 'We Close Tonight', 'You Came Back', 'Get Inside', 'Joker James' and 'Ambition' – just three would be worked on at the sessions themselves.

Of these, 'We Close Tonight' was intended to show 'Jimmy as a budding, but failed musician.' 'Joker James', which in notes to his 2011 'Director's Cut' version Townshend thinks may well 'contain the genesis of *Quadrophenia*', he talked about back in 1972 as a song that provides 'the basis for the image of the kid – the way he saw himself – as this kind of reasonable joker whose life doesn't come off but . . . on the outside he didn't appear that way at all, and he was very far from being a joker.'

But the most unfortunate loss was a track originally called 'Quadrophenia', which was only definitively dropped from the project at the end of July 1973, eventually being released on the 1979 film soundtrack, as 'Four Faces'. The song was, as Townshend now says, 'almost a pre-psychiatrist view: Jimmy is explaining one of his problems; he is mixed up and confused, and torn in four directions.' (In Jimmy's liner-notes he explains how he is then sent to a decidedly Laingian 'psychiatrist every week [who] never really knew what was wrong with me. He said I wasn't mad or anything . . . [that] there's no such thing as madness.') Here then was the album's original theme in its most distilled form:

'I got four heads inside my mind
Four rooms I'd like to lie in
Four selves I want to find
And I don't know which one is me . . .

There are four records I want to buy
Four highs I'd like to try
Every letter I get I send four replies
And I don't know which one's from me.'

Unlike with *Tommy*, Townshend was virtually writing *Quadrophenia* from scratch. The only songs predating the spring of '72 were 'Drowned', a 1970 Meher Baba paean, and the 1968 lyrics to 'Joker James'. As he told Valentine, "I've written a lot of stuff about this period, [but] it all comes out sounding like old Who material – quite unconsciously. And it gave me the idea to consciously do that. To start off with early Who sound and come through – more and more synthesizer, more and more snazzy recording until you get to the point where he finds himself coming together, fitting together like a jigsaw. Going from that period of sorta fucked up amazing spiritual and social desperation, despair with politics and everything – to come together as one piece of music.'

He was already minded to make 'Love, Reign O'er Me' the 'one piece of music' that would resolve the story. However, there was a problem. The storyline in his head did not naturally lead towards such a resolution. Rather, as Townshend duly acknowledged, the point at which Jimmy 'gets very desperate and tries to look around for an answer in the shape of religion, job, woman, family . . . I realized . . . was just like the end of *Tommy*'. At the same time, 'Love, Reign O'er Me' had been offered to Lou Reisner as a possible addition to the London

Symphony Orchestra production of *Tommy*, recorded in October 1972 (it went unused). For all its sense of epiphany, it would remain the piece tacked on to Jimmy's story to turn his mental collapse into an affirmation, not a final disintegration. Rock journalist Gary Herman, who talked to Townshend early in the writing process, was the first to note how the song 'bears a minimal relationship to the story of Jimmy, but is absolutely vital to Townshend's conception of the religious experience . . . It's the ultimate joining together, the final programme: Pete's theme, but not Jimmy's. You see, there really isn't any Jimmy.'

Herman, the band's first biographer, fully knew that Townshend was transplanting an awful lot of his inner self into his quadrophenic creation, just as he had invested a lot of himself in the songs he penned during the mods' mid-Sixties heyday. Even Townshend's choice of pop historian Nik Cohn to write the script for the now-abandoned *Rock is Dead: Long Live Rock* – 'about how rock had developed, but then how it had been co-opted by various factions not entirely artistic' – undoubtedly reflected Cohn's lauding of the mod lifestyle in his seminal *Awopbopaloobop* (1969). In fact, the guitarist had been idealizing that period since before the birth of *Tommy*, when he had made his first concerted attempt to explain its cultural impact to an American audience (in this instance, via *Rolling Stone*'s Jann Wenner):

Pete Townshend: One of the things which has impressed me most in life was the mod movement in England, which was an incredible youthful thing. It was a movement of young people, much bigger than the hippie thing, the underground and all these things . . . We used to make sure that if there was a riot, a mod-rocker riot, we would be playing in the area. [There] was a place called Brighton.

That's where they used to assemble. We'd always be playing there. And we got associated with the whole thing and we got into the spirit of the whole thing . . . You see, as individuals these people were nothing. They were the lowest, they were England's lowest common denominators. Not only were they young, they were also lower-class young. They had to submit to the middle class's way of dressing and way of speaking and way of acting in order to get the very jobs which kept them alive. They had to do everything in terms of what existed already. [1968]

So as far back as September 1968 Townshend had already described the hero of *Quadrophenia*, even down to the 'dirty jobs' he took to keep himself alive and in zoot suits. Five years later, he was explaining Jimmy to *Rolling Stone* again, but now 'he's a failed mod, because he's made the ultimate mod mistake: bad timing. This is 1965 and the mod scene is already falling apart – and what does he do but go to Brighton, just to remember . . . Already he's living on his past. And he meets an old ace-face who's now a bellhop at the very hotel the mods tore up. And he looks on Jimmy with a mixture of pity and contempt, really, and tells him, in effect, "Look, my job is shit and my life is a tragedy. But you – look at you, you're dead."'

If Townshend didn't realize the scale of his ambition at the time – for Pete's sake, he was writing about the death of the Sixties – he had certainly come to terms with it by 2009, when he was involved with staging the first theatrical presentation of the album as a musical play (appropriately performed in Brighton), and looking back with wiser eyes:

Pete Townshend: In a sense my mission [was] to bring back some of the greyness, the bleakness of those years, and demonstrate . . . that what happened simply had to happen, otherwise we would all have gone nuts. It wasn't a game, it wasn't an optional outing of boys playing on scooters, it was a vital rebellion. You have to understand that after the Ban the Bomb movement and the failure of Anti-Apartheid, and then the Cuban Crisis, young people felt their input was pointless. Fashion, music and daily life was elevated to a form of aloof poetry, and was very much a secret society . . . *Quadrophenia* isn't even about battles in the street, it's a musical journey inside a young man's man during a drug-fuelled psychotic episode. This is a day or two in the life of a young man who really can't do what his peers are doing, and survive. [2009]

In his own way, Townshend was unwittingly anticipating the punk revolution, itself a reaction to the death of the 1960s beat scene and its spirit of political dissent. It was a connection he would in time willingly embrace, writing in 1977 of how there was 'mixed up in *Quadrophenia* . . . a study of the divine desperation that is at the root of every punk's scream for blood and vengeance'.

What soon fell away from the 1973 song cycle, though, was any sense that by breaking their ties with their mod past, the band would succeed in moving forward. Richard Barnes, invited to Townshend's house to hear the idea fresh, remembers the guitarist telling him that he felt The Who 'were too involved in their own legend and their mod connections, and he wanted to cut this connection so they could search for new directions'. But by the time the album was completed, Townshend was ridiculing the very notion that a rock band could instigate change, inwardly or outwardly, informing *NME*: 'This album is more of a winding up of all our individual axes to grind, and of the group's ten-year-old image, [but] also of the complete absurdity of a group like The Who pretending that they have their finger on the pulse of any generation.'

The thumbnail sketches Townshend gave Valentine of the other band-members' psychological quirks, intended to form the building blocks for Jimmy's quadrophenic breakdown, became the one aspect toned down on the finished work. (In 2009 he still felt a need to clarify that original creative goal: 'It was not my intention that the personalities of each band-member were meant to be part of Jimmy. Each band-member was supposed to perform an aspect of each of Jimmy's four personality extremes . . . a crucial difference.')

Each band member also got their own theme-song although Entwistle's theme, 'Is It Me?, which was a song in its own right when Townshend demoed the material, was never recorded by The Who, but was instead placed inside the song written to capture Jimmy's inevitable breakdown. Refining the original song-idea 'where the kid is really fucked up with drugs and chicks and his family', the resultant 'Doctor Jimmy' even subtly alludes to two earlier Entwistle compositions ('Whisky Man' and 'Dr Jekyll and Mr Hyde'), as he directly addresses his disintegrating self: 'Dr Jimmy and Mr Jim / When I'm pilled, you don't notice him / He only comes out when I drink my gin.'

Describing the song's composition in *The Decade of The Who* songbook, Townshend explained how 'all of the songs from *Quadrophenia* are meant to fit together, or at least all reflect the personality of one person – as a result they are all structured similarly. But "Dr Jimmy" is the archetype, more so, in fact, than "Quadrophenia" itself . . . From a lyrical point of view it is much narrower, though; we just see the bragging lout, none of the self doubt or remoteness.' The song also reflected the hero's desire to end it all, much as Townshend almost had back in 1971:

Pete Townshend: 'Dr Jimmy' was meant to be a song which somehow gets across the explosive, abandoned wildness side of his character. Like a bull run amok in a china shop. He's damaging himself so badly so that he can get to the point where he's so desperate that he'll take a closer look at himself. All he knows is that things aren't right in the world and he blames everything else. And it's getting in a boat, going out to sea and sitting on a rock waiting for the waves to knock him off that makes him review himself. He ends up with the sum total of frustrated toughness, romanticism, religion, daredevil-desperation, but a starting point for anybody. He goes through a suicide crisis. [1973]

In keeping with an innate, abiding faith in man, Townshend was always looking to make Jimmy's story one of redemption. Even when stuck on this rock out at sea, snorting the words, 'It must be alright to be plain ordinary mad', Jimmy remains the hero, not the anti-hero. As such, in the end we must believe he will be saved. As the songwriter told Charles Shaar Murray: 'Our album clarifies who the real hero is in this thing – it's the kid on the front. He's the hero. That's why he is on the front cover. That's why he is sung about. It's his fuckin' album. Rock 'n' roll's his music . . . This isn't a direct nostalgic thing, it's more a search for the essence of what makes everything tick.'

Ill-fitting or not, the final song was always going to be 'Love, Reign O'er Me'; not that it was the only song on the second part of *Quadrophenia* to reflect Townshend's own pantheistic view of religion: 'When the tragic hero of [the album] sings ["Drowned"], it is desperate and nihilistic. In fact, it's a love song, God's love being the Ocean, and our "selves" being the drops of water that make it up.' By album's end, Jimmy has returned to the 'starting point', the blank slate, longing 'to get back home / to cool, cool rain', and Townshend – in his determination to find something 'to replace *Tommy* as the new centre of the . . . show' – had surpassed himself. He may also have signed the band's death warrant:

> **Pete Townshend:** I felt that The Who ought to make, if you like, a last album . . . It's very peculiar that this album has come out at the same time as something like Bowie's *Pin Ups* because . . . the [underlying] ideas are fairly similar. What I've really tried to do . . . is to try and illustrate that . . . the reason that rock is still around is that it's not youth's music, it's the music of the frustrated and the dissatisfied . . . If someone like Bowie, who's only been a big star for eighteen months or so, feels the need to start talking about his past influences, then obviously the roots are getting lost. [1973]

Maybe Pete was reading a tad too much into Bowie's stopgap contract filler, and not enough into his unique sign-off to the Sixties' own schizophrenia. But then, divorcing enduring import from immediacy of impact was not always within the powers of the most self-conscious rock star on the planet. And having spent months honing a whole that was so much more than its parts, he knew he would have to start all over again when The Who convened at Ramport studios in May 1973 to begin work on the album of the demos of the concept.

This time the demos would serve as more than just the guide they provided on *Tommy* and *Who's Next*. In the interim, Pete had put some of his increasingly professional-sounding demos on his first commercial solo album, *Who Came First* (1972). Now, as studio engineer Ron Nevison told Richard Barnes: 'Pete's [*Quadrophenia*] demos had him playing pianos, synthesizers, all guitars and drums plus some sound effects. It was silly to try and redo it, so the demos were used to work to, and as they overdubbed parts they wiped Pete's originals.'

This was just the beginning of the surprisingly tortuous process, however. Townshend insisted on reserving at least one-third of the sixteen tracks on the multitracks for more string and synthesizer parts. Entwistle, meanwhile, spent hours and hours arranging and multitracking the many horn parts Townshend demanded. Looking back in 1976, the bassist remembered the recording being 'so complex it took four months to put together. I was there most of the time. Moon was in the studio for about three weeks, and Daltrey took a week to do his work. But for most of the time it was just Townshend and I.'

Townshend, understandably, continued to insist on the final say; still haunted by recent failures. Of one thing he remained convinced: 'I needed to guide *Quadrophenia* alone. It was a new kind of song-cycle, a development on the system I'd invented for *Tommy*, and my previous attempt at a dramatic work (*Lifehouse*) had fallen almost at the first post. Roger had some problems with me having so much control, but that was only because he wanted to find some way into the story and I'm afraid I wasn't very helpful.' As far as the intoxicated work-aholic Townshend was concerned, for Daltrey the album was a week's work; for him it was a year's.

Where he found the energy, not even he can say. Writing

about these months, in 2009, Townshend tried to convey the sheer scale of the task: 'In [Ramport] studio, I used old-fashioned methods, big studio drums sounds, layered violins (that I played myself), John Entwistle's powerful brass choirs, banjos, backing voices, bells, and of course sound effects. All that and electric guitars. I gathered all those strands . . . Why do you think most . . . rock artists, find it so hard ever to create art as successfully as their younger selves? [Because] making good art in the rock business . . . requires tremendous energy and youthful persistence.' It also required that rare 'combination of unbelievable grandiosity and shaky self-esteem' that would be Townshend's personal analysis of his psychological make-up in 1972–73. Torn between these dualities, and feeding on 'tremendous resentments' as the process dragged on for months, Townshend again began to fear for his own sanity. In the end it all came together, though, allowing him to then make light of the experience:

> **Pete Townshend:** The problem with The Who is that if I try to draw more out of their image and their history and out of rock than rock can sustain, you end up with a situation where there's nothing left that hasn't been milked or soiled; any emotion that hasn't been buggered about with; any mountain that hasn't been climbed by some plastic, made-up geezer who climbs up to the top and says, 'I've seen God, and He's a pig.' [1973]

Naturally, the other members of The Who were determined to impose themselves on the process. As Townshend later wrote: 'As soon as the band started laying down backing tracks at Battersea, it didn't feel like the *Quadrophenia* that I thought was going to come out. It was much heavier, much more brutal.'

One of the early casualties at the sessions was 'Joker James', which was left unfinished for six years, as was 'Four Faces'. Yet still Townshend worried that the ablum lacked the spontaneity of earlier Lambert-produced Who sessions. That still-lingering sense of failure began to consume him even as he put the finishing touches to his most fully realized work:

Pete Townshend: The thing about *Quadrophenia* was that it was far too self-conscious . . . It was as if I'd given myself a brief and said 'Now come up to that', and attempted to write spontaneously within it. There are only a few spontaneous songs there, and I think they stand out like jewels in coal – stuff like 'Cut My Hair' and 'Love, Reign O'er Me'; you get the odd ones. But take a number like 'Punk and the Godfather', which is technically very good and very crisp, and '5.15' is another one – they're deliberately oblique. [1974]

That frisson of frustration soon spilled over into open conflict with his fiercest critic – Daltrey. Recalling the increasingly fraught process in 2009, Townshend described how 'towards the end of recording, Roger lost patience with me. I had kept all the cards to my chest, and he wanted to see the release of a Who album not a Pete Townshend indulgence. He insisted the faces of each band-member should be on the front cover.'

The drama did not end there. Matters came to a head during rehearsals for the two tours – UK and US – they'd already booked for November/December, without being entirely sure the album would be in the shops. Townshend, who was still self-medicating with Courvoisier, was not about to let his vision of the piece be distorted by Daltrey's sniping. And he was still thinking in terms of making it into a film one of these days. As

Daltrey remembers it, he turned up to one rehearsal to find Townshend had hired a film crew, though they never actually managed to shoot anything:

Roger Daltrey: We'd just finished 'Dr Jimmy', and I was really giving it something. I was like, 'Are you gonna sit on your fucking equipment? When you gonna start fucking filming?' Pete by this time had already drunk at least one bottle of brandy, if not two, and he came over and said, 'Shut the fuck up, they'll film when I tell them to.' [1996]

Daltrey decked him with one punch. When Townshend came round, he 'saw Roger looking at me, really, really, frightened. He was afraid that he'd killed me.' But if Daltrey's fist wasn't about to kill the man, Townshend's insane work-rate just might. That workload was so overwhelming that, in his own words, 'I not only wrote and recorded [*Quadrophenia*] in 1973, I also built two quadraphonic recording studios, did a huge tour, helped Eric Clapton and his girlfriend Alice get off heroin, began to set up the *Tommy* movie contacts for the following year and wrote a number of songs for the next Who album.' And throughout it all, he was a raging drunk.

For him, the madness was becoming as real as the search for redemption. That moment when the work would stand revealed couldn't come soon enough. Rather than waiting for the album to make the record racks and receive its plaudits (actually, initial reviews would be decidedly mixed), the first shows, in the north of England, took place a full week before the album appeared in all its lavish but delayed splendour (the insertion of a forty-page photo essay by Ethan Russell, of snapshots depicting Jimmy's monotonous existence, held up its release).

At the third show in Manchester, Townshend prefaced the

performance of an already-abbreviated *Quadrophenia* by saying: 'Now we'd like to do something from the forthcoming album. We're still finding our way with it. We were expecting the album to be out and in your possession by now, but of course it isn't. This album doesn't need too much explanation 'cause it's about everybody here, I'm sure . . . It's about a young screwed-up, frustrated, idiotic teenager.' Daltrey was not convinced – and nor were sections of the audience. As the band began touring the piece, their singing mouthpiece felt that the story-line needed explication. Townshend did not:

> **Pete Townshend:** Roger and I have different ideas about *Quadrophenia* . . . we get different things out of it. I think the story-line isn't so complicated it bears much explaining. A kid sits on a rock and remembers the things that have happened in the last few days . . . The story, after all, is just a peg to hang ideas on. When Roger gets too literal about the story, I have to cut in. [1973]

The Who singer was still complaining about the experience some two years later: 'It's hopeless trying to play people unfamiliar material. It's like the worst thing any band can do. Even if it's vaguely familiar.' Townshend, on the other hand, was not so convinced that this was the real problem, at least not in the States, where they arrived to find that their extravagant double-album was already number two in the charts. The real problem was not onstage, where the taped parts usually worked and Daltrey's attempts at a between-song narrative were soon judiciously trimmed, but out in the cavernous cattle-barns that passed for US arenas (and still do). The audience out front had changed. And Townshend knew it, noting as much at tour's end:

Pete Townshend: *Quadrophenia* has been getting blamed for our troubles this tour, but I don't think that anymore. I think the audience has changed. We've been so self-involved the last two years we've missed . . . the changed experience of the audience. It wasn't till we got here to the US that we found out such acts as Alice Cooper have not only come, but gone . . . There was a time when an audience would come to a concert and be satisfied with the myth of The Who. [1973]

It was precisely 'the myth of The Who', and of rock itself, that was starting to get in the way. The days when bands could debut unreleased, or barely released, works was fast passing, even as that supreme example, *Dark Side of the Moon*, was storming every chart in the whole wide world. Nostalgia was becoming the order of the day. And it wasn't only in those acoustical graveyards that Americans called arenas where concert-goers were starting to voice their displeasure at the conceit, nay cheek, of some rock performers for whom hubris was a Greek starter.

The night after The Who departed Manchester, after the third and fourth performances of the as-yet-unreleased *Quadrophenia*, many of the same souls trundled down to the Palace Theatre for the first night of Neil Young's UK tour, expecting to see the man who produced the previous year's rich *Harvest*[33]. Instead, they got to see the truculent troubadour debut – in its entirety – his unreleased, never-really-realized *Tonight's the Night*. Most attendees left impressed, but only by the support-act that night, the largely unknown Eagles. Townshend himself, for all his concerns about a shifting demographic among concert-goers, soon came to believe he had been wrong to take the band down the same path:

Pete Townshend: With *Quadrophenia* we did tour too soon. *Quadrophenia* was an extremely slow album . . . [And] we [simply] weren't prepared to work to gain our audiences' reactions. We wanted it instant and pat, and the way to do that is to go on and play something that they recognize . . . Roger thought that *Quadrophenia* wouldn't stand up unless you explained the story [on stage] . . . It was done sincerely, but I found it embarrassing . . . The whole thing was a disaster. Roger ended up hating *Quadrophenia* – probably 'cause it had bitten back. [1978]

Their three-week US tour did not start any more auspiciously than the UK tour. On opening night, 20 November at the Cow Palace in San Francisco, Keith Moon collapsed onstage during 'Magic Bus', and a young fan from the audience took over on drums for the encore. The official story, that one of his drinks had been spiked with an animal tranquilizer, merely masked Moon's ongoing penchant for excess, which was already starting to take its toll, and would kill him within five years. An oft-bootlegged radio broadcast from a December show in Largo was disappointingly undynamic, and remains unreleased.

They did, however, manage to give *Quadrophenia* a fitting swansong, performing a steaming one-hour version at their last gig of the year, at the Edmonton Sundown on 23 December, with Townshend tilting at windmill after windmill as the band gave Jimmy one glorious send-off. But by 18 May 1974, barely six months after the album's release, The Who's one-off stadium-show at Charlton FC featured just four songs from *Quadrophenia* ('5.15', 'Drowned', 'Bell Boy' and 'Doctor Jimmy'). Already Townshend, peering at 60,000 hometown fans from the bottom of a whisky glass, had convinced himself *Quadrophenia* was another brave, grand failure – even as its reputation grew and grew in those dorm rooms where *Ziggy Stardust* was first introduced to *Muswell Hillbillies*, and the more well-versed musos drew a straight line between *Piper at the Gates of Dawn* and *Dark Side of the Moon* (a process made a great deal easier by the December 1973 release of the first two Floyd albums as the cheap-o double, *A Nice Pair*).

Pete's friend and band biographer Richard Barnes believes that 'the fact *Quadrophenia* didn't have the success he would have liked really affected Townshend. I saw him a few months later, when he was working on [the film of] *Tommy*, and he was in a pretty depressed state. It was years until he ever attempted anything else so musically ambitious.' So much for moving forward. The next few Who albums – and the terrific Townshend-Lane long-player, *Rough Mix* (1976) – would be strictly collections of songs, good, bad and indifferent, by the oldest angry young man on the street.

In this, too, Townshend was anticipating the coming punk revolution. Like the increasingly influential English music press, he had decided it was time to put away grand conceits. Although there was still a vanguard of determined English prog-rockers – Jethro Tull, ELP, Yes and Genesis, to name (and shame) the chief culprits – who believed they could yet pull off the great English concept album – and in Genesis's case, almost did – the fall of 1973 saw the curtain coming down on the heyday of English album-length song-cycles as a reliable barometer of the mental health of its rock artists. Now, it was just a case of counting up the casualties.

7. 1974-75: The Act Of (Self-)Preservation

I got a message on acid that you should destroy your ego, and I did, you know. I was reading that stupid book of Leary's [*The Psychedelic Experience*] . . . and I destroyed myself . . . I destroyed my ego and I didn't believe I could do anything.
– John Lennon to Jann Wenner, 1970

Q: 'Why do rock stars tend to have premonitions of doom?' David Bowie: ''Cause they're pretty nutty to be doing it in the first place. We've got pretty tangled minds. Very messed up people.'
– David Bowie on *The Dick Cavett Show*, 5 December 1974

I've always thought of going back to a place where you can drink tea and sit on the carpet. I've been fortunate enough to do that.
– Syd Barrett to Michael Watts, 1971

Q: Did you have an unhappy childhood?

Ray Davies: That's a novel.

Q: Could we have the first chapter?

Ray Davies: You know, I'm still only five years old. I'm trying to convince this person at the weekends that I'm still five and that's all I want to be. I don't want to be any more because as things are I'm able to communicate on a very basic level. I know what food I like to eat. I've got two pairs of shoes – one for on and one for off stage and when they wear out I buy another pair. I'm reasonably all right. I've got enough tea bags and maybe I can start writing again, which would be a good thing.

– interview in *NME*, 20 October 1973

At the end of 1973, those in English rock's upper echelons who had survived the 1960s' psychedelic onslaught with their marbles intact – and these could loosely be said to include Ray Davies, Pete Townshend, David Bowie and Roger Waters – had lucrative careers to cushion the realization, voiced by the primal-scream Lennon on *The Plastic Ono Band*, that the dream was over. But if the concept album was on life-support, there was still at least one hardy soul from the beat boom-years who wished to pump oxygen into its ravaged body.

Unfortunately for Ray Davies, as for so many from his generation of English songwriters, 'nothing was ever the same after 1973' – the conclusion he came to at the end of his 1994 autobiography. Yet there was never any question he would keep writing and producing, come what may. For, as he also confessed partway through *X-Ray*, 'Anyone who says that creativity comes from divine inspiration is certainly wrong, particularly in my case. I wasn't writing songs for my wife, my unborn child, God or country, I was writing to stay sane.'

By the mid-Seventies, though, it had become a case of never mind the quality, fulfil the contract. The years 1973 through 1976, during which The Kinks ran down the options on that RCA deal, fleetingly promised new vistas for the band, but they all ran aground on Davies' obsession with making the songs fit the concept, not the other way round, as had been the case – and the benchmark of his achievement – in the years 1968 through 1971. Meanwhile the themes had become oh so familiar – the fear of failure, the spectre of the past, the worry that the rest of humanity would realize he was just as fucked-up as them:

Ray Davies: You can get the most sophisticated man in the world, and if he's hung up about his feet, nothing will change it. He'll go to university, he'll become a nuclear scientist, he'll fly to the moon, land on the moon – and the moonman will say, 'Hey, you've got big feet!' And he'll be back at school, because that's what they said to him at school. [1977]

Of all those ideas for an ongoing series of concept albums, it was *Preservation Act*, spread over three albums and released in two parts across 1973 and 1974, which consumed Davies in the immediate aftermath of White City. But eighteen months later, when he finished the increasingly ill-conceived concept-piece, it was clear that his heart was no longer in it. When he thought about it, he decided that he had 'spent . . . five years – storing up ideas for *Preservation [Act]*, and *The Village Green Preservation Society* was like a rough sketch'. What he failed to realize was that, despite having worked himself into (and out of) another breakdown, in this particular instance the rough sketch was a rich tapestry and the full-blown version a rank xerox. Although he would return to the songs on *VGPS* repeatedly, those from

Preservation Act would rarely be preserved in the memories and/or collections of rock fans.

But still he would not be dissuaded. Before 1975 was out, he had another song-cycle to peddle – and this one cracked the US Top Fifty. The theme of *Soap Opera* was again a familiar one: 'It is about mental illness.' When he found it hard to come up with anything new to say, he excused his mindset in somewhat familiar terms: 'It's very difficult if you've been brought up to be factory fodder to then find that people are interested in what you have to say. Always [this], what am I? Who am I?' When that album also failed to find favour at home, he decided to return to his school days for the vaguely embarrassing *Schoolboys in Disgrace* (1976). Something deep inside continued sending him back to those days when life was simple – and sweet:

> **Ray Davies:** I'll tell you when it was good. When I was walking down the road with Michelle Gross, whose dad owned the sweetshop. She was about a foot taller than I was and she had her arm around me and I said, 'God, if I can stay with this girl forever I can have all the sweets I ever want.' That was when it was good. [1989]

Hence, Pete Townshend's mid-Seventies swipe at his songwriting mentor: 'He writes like an old man who is forever looking back on his life.' And still more Kinks records kept trundling off the presses. Even a switch of label, to Clive Davis's Arista, did not seem to slow Ray Davies down. But try as he might, he could not shake the sense that he was not like everybody else, that he would never *belong*. He was set apart, kept apart from those he was trying to reach. And even as he hurtled towards his next breakdown, he knew that no matter how many therapists they sent him along to – and the first words of the doctor who treated him after White City were, 'Tomorrow you will have some analysis' – only the songs could ever unlock the boy inside:

Ray Davies: I'm trying to picture somebody's head – all the open thoughts and the thoughts they've got locked in. Everybody has that little safe, which nobody is going to look into . . . I want to be like everybody else. I want my mind to click into place and say, 'Yeah, that's right, there's nothing unusual about doing what everybody else is.' . . . [I mean,] I can get on with people. I can make anybody laugh, but I just can't *think* like them. [1974]

★

At least Davies had cut down on the self-medicating slugs of booze, unlike his songwriting shadow, Pete Townshend, who was also having trouble reconciling his overwhelming desire to communicate with the realization that most of those with whom he communicated didn't relate to his songs on anything more than a superficial level. Talking to *Melody Maker* the year after *Quadrophenia*, he even seemed to be suggesting he had done wrong in attempting to say something more meaningful than 'I hope I die before I get old':

Pete Townshend: The unique thing about me as a writer is that I've done that sorta rock opera thing, and I did it solely and purely to try to expand the outward possibilities of rock . . . It happened to be very successful communicatively into the bargain. But it didn't do anything for rock & roll; and it didn't do anything for me as a rock writer. I still think that rock works most effectively on a song-by-song basis. [1974]

This sense that it had all been in vain increasingly wore away at Townshend's veering self-belief. In 1974 he saw the realization of his long-cherished dream to have *Tommy* made into a film. Not only that, but the meandering Ken Russell-directed film was a huge commercial success, bringing yet more converts to the very concept album that had sparked this entire psychoanalysis-by-song-cycle genre in rock. And yet, when he arrived at the London Leicester Square film premiere on 26 March 1975, he was appalled. As he told *NME* shortly afterwards, his first thought was, 'Who the hell were all those people at the *Tommy* premiere? Whoever they were: I'm certainly not in their gang.'

The perceived failure of *Quadrophenia*, the relentless grind of the road, and the onset of his first serious writer's block in six years now conspired to place Townshend on his own solitary rock, and on this promontory he was slowly drowning in an ocean of booze. In the long interview he gave for the book of the movie of the album he admitted: 'I got dragged very low by the amount that I was drinking, and by the fact that . . . [touring] was a very low level of existence . . . There was really no magic in the [shows] for me.' Ironically, the 1974 shows were held in generally high regard by The Who's hardcore fans, perhaps because it was the first time The Who really delivered the 'greatest hits' show they had always wanted; prompting Townshend to remark, 'The Who have become a golden-oldies band and that's the bloody problem.'[34]

Unfortunately, try as he might to convince himself that 'rock works most effectively on a song-by-song basis', he had not recorded a single song with The Who that was not part of a larger conceit in such a long time that he'd forgotten how to do it. As he openly admitted in 1978, when the clouds had partly lifted, 'I didn't have any songs or any subject matter apart from the same old stuff that had brought forth all the dreary *Who by Numbers* material – alcoholic degradation.' Indeed, almost the first song he demoed for that underrated 1975 album pretty much drunk that particular subject dry. It had the working title 'No Way Out', but ultimately appeared on album as 'However Much I Booze'. Either way, he was drinking himself into an early grave, while the band's other spokesman was telling anyone who would listen that their songwriter was bang out of order. And Townshend knew it:

Pete Townshend: When Roger said I was drunk . . . he was right. Drunk? Was I drunk?!! . . . I was falling to bits. At the same time I was going slightly barmy. I was hallucinating. I was forgetting big chunks of time . . . At that particular period I felt the band was finished and I was finished and the music was dying. [1975]

Such is the solipsistic nature of addiction that Townshend even convinced himself he had formed a pact with drummer Keith Moon to stop drinking. Moon – who had returned from a lost weekend in L.A. that lasted almost a year, definitively cost him his already-failing marriage and almost bankrupted him – was on a drug designed to make it impossible for him to drink: Antabuse – the clue's in the name. Townshend decided to join him at the Teetotallers Inn. Unfortunately, as he wrote in a long confessional piece the *NME* would run in 1977 under the heading, 'Pete Townshend's Back Pages':

When . . . recording *Who by Numbers*, Keith's courageous attempts to head off his alcoholism moved me to stop drinking too. I stopped overnight. The results were quite interesting. My hair started to fall out. Another remarkable side effect was that I carried on drinking without my knowledge . . . Apparently, at the end of one session which I had gotten through by pulling incessantly at a total of about twenty cans of Coke, I wished everyone good night, walked up to the makeshift bar set up on an amplifier flight case at the back of the studio and drank down a bottle of vodka. I just don't remember doing that . . . The shock that hit me as the pieces fell into place was even more frightening than the black holes in my head.

Such were these feelings of 'alcoholic degradation' that when producer Glyn Johns attempted to introduce some light and shade into an album of excoriating self-loathing by including the Formby-esque 'Blue, Red and Grey', Townshend responded by exclaiming, 'What?! That fucking thing. Here's me wanting to commit suicide, and you're going to put that thing on the record.' The fact that for the first time in a while he had written a song that celebrated the simple things in life did not change things a jot.

The May 1975 *Who by Numbers* sessions were close to rock-bottom for Townshend, who would begin to climb out of his empty glass by the time his old mucker and ex-Face Ronnie Lane suggested they make an album together at the end of 1976. It had been eight years since Pete had first expressed an interest in joining Lane's then-band, Small Faces, and finally they were making a joint LP, *Rough Mix*. By 1976, it was Lane who had fallen on hard times, and Townshend who had the gold albums on the wall. The years since Lane left The Faces in 1973 had turned what slim chance he had of ongoing chart action into no chance at all.

★

Certain other English figures from the same milieu who once dreamed of climbing the rocky mountaintop were no longer so keen to continue driving on to the pop summit. Whether they had ever enjoyed the intoxicating view from this peak – as Peter Green and Syd Barrett had – or stayed in the commercial foot-hills (Nick Drake, Vincent Crane), by the end of 1973 each of these troubled souls had seemingly abandoned their art and scuttled on home. For all of them, it was the last refuge from their inner scoundrel.

Vincent Crane had managed to keep an increasingly dis-solute version of Atomic Rooster together until the end of 1973, when *Nice 'n' Greasy* became their final ragbag offering. Flat broke and still crazy (at one point, he bricked up his front door to stop the bailiffs from serving him with any writs), he spent the rest of the 1970s working in theatre production, writ-ing for radio dramas and teaching music at a school in Battersea – anything that would not serve as a reminder of his days as chief bantam in a band of half-cocked crazies.

For Peter Green, the decision to walk away from the curse of fame had proven relatively simple. In a sense, he had never really gone out in the big wide world. Throughout the whole Fleetwood Mac circus he had continued to live at home with his parents, and as his friend, guitar-shop owner Paul Morrison, told his biographer: 'I think the reason is that he felt very vulner-able out in the big wide world. He was never able to cope with being a star.' But even at home, he couldn't quite live down his past; and on occasions he would take off without warning, leav-ing his bemused parents (and girlfriend) to fend for themselves, as he did one morning in 1973, when he woke his girlfriend to tell her 'he had to go to Israel and be with his people'.

But when he sent her a postcard from the land of Zion a few weeks later, it was to announce that he was thinking of joining the PLO. One confidant throughout these years, Mich Reynolds, recalls: 'It wasn't a nervous breakdown; it was a slow decline . . . A lot of the time I [just] thought he was taking the piss out of people. It was difficult to know when he was doing it for effect and when he couldn't actually help it.' By 1974 Green's parents had concluded 'he couldn't actually help it', and he was finally committed to the kind of mental hospital to which Crane had periodically retreated. This one, recommended by a doctor for whom his mother used to work, was at West Park in Epsom. According to Green, his spell in this place, far from making him better, prolonged his time in the wilderness:

> **Peter Green:** They tricked me into agreeing to go to a nice place where Jewish boys and girls would be and then they took me to the hospital in Epsom, the madhouse . . . Next thing I knew I was stuck there and eventually they gave me ECT [electro-convulsive therapy] . . . injections and tranquilisers.

His desire to bypass the problems thrown up by that brief, hugely creative period of self-discovery, had led him to a life spent in a semi-permanent drone-like state. Far from curing him of any earlier psychosis, the experience merely convinced him he had been on the right path all along: 'I [still] wanted the wisdom of LSD, but I couldn't quite get back again . . . It took me somewhere where I wasn't Peter Green and I had no cares at all; it was great.' Shortly after he was finally sprung from this dreadful place by his then-girlfriend he wrote her a note, which he handed her one day while she was working at the booking agency where they first met. It read:

All the Madmen

The depression you try to escape from
Is your lonely soul's broken heart
Realizing its mistake, and crying
You are torn between the tragic truth of a lost soul
And the falseness you have been led to believe is your
   way of life
I choose the first to be my *self*
If you look hard and deep you will see it in all Man
If you don't see it – you will see madness.

The pair made plans to marry in September 1975, but two days before the supposedly happy day the lady realized that Green was still not a well man and decided to return home herself. When she asked if he would mind taking her there, he replied, 'Not at all.' Even he had come to realize he must travel the road to recovery alone. That road had a few more potholes along the way – including a short spell in prison in 1977 for pulling a pump-action shotgun on his long-time manager, Clifford Davis – before he picked up the guitar again late in 1977, and began re-learning those Robert Johnson riffs that once served as a shamanistic incantation.

*

Green was not the only hugely gifted guitarist who at some point in 1972 took a sabbatical from the unholy instrument to concentrate on expelling those inner demons, while the professionals of health care tried every faddish trick in the mental manual. Nick Drake also apparently spent a couple of months in full-time treatment for his chronic depression some time that year, but the medication merely dulled the senses and stilled his muse. By the time he returned to his parents' home in Henley-in-Arden, he was in full retreat. As his mother Molly later remembered, 'I think he felt it was a kind of refuge. He had to come back here. He tried many times to go away . . . I think he had rejected the world. Nothing much made him happy.'

The one thing that had once brought Drake relief – and release – had been taken away from him, and he didn't know why. When he finally picked up the guitar again, he just felt he was going through the motions. Previously, as sidekick Robert Kirby fondly recalls, 'he would spend days developing a particular phrase or chord sequence. He was always writing. He would also play the blues – but as a study exercise, getting ever more complex.' Now, though, he would sit at his parents' home 'strumming the same chords over and over again on his Gibson acoustic guitar', as if trying to grasp how such a rare gift could have passed so out of reach. Perhaps the devil had stopped him at the crossroads, one night when out driving his parents' car, and reclaimed his largesse.

At least Drake could still hear the spirit of Robert Johnson coming through his phonograph, even as he confessed to long-time friend Ben Lacock that he believed he could sense the same 'hellhound on my trail'. That hellhound finally got a name when Drake wrote his first documented song since *Pink Moon* got to him. 'Black Eyed Dog', written towards the end of 1973, was unlike anything in the Drake canon to date and the first of five tracks he would record at sessions in 1974, having again asked John Wood to act as his mediator.[35]

The first session in February was quite unlike anything Wood had experienced to date: first, Drake no longer felt he could do justice to the songs unless he recorded the guitar part first, and then overdubbed a vocal; second, the process of paring down the lyrics – first apparent on *Pink Moon* – had reached such a point that they made the twelve-bar blues of Robert Johnson seem like epic ballads. 'Black Eyed Dog', five unsparing lines long, centred on a single premonitive couplet, 'I'm growing old and I wanna go home / I'm growing old and I don't wanna know.' It was Drake's 'Me and the Devil Blues'. This black-eyed dog already knew his name when he came a-knockin' to tell him it was time to go. Producer Wood did not know what to make of the pared-down lyrics or the scratchy staccato accompaniment, and wondered aloud if Drake might be 'having a problem with words'. Drake's response was a scary insight into the interior life of someone prematurely weary of the world: 'I can't think of words. I feel no emotion about anything . . . I'm numb – dead inside.'

It seems Drake also began work on one or two other songs at this session – probably 'Voice from the Mountain' and 'Tow the Line', each of which seemed to inhabit the world of Hampstead and Cambridge. There was a reason why. He had been performing them in prototype as far back as 1969. They reflected a more garrulous world of possibilities, the former track in particular ticking all the usual boxes when it came to Drake's pastoral lexicon of imagery: 'voice from the mountain', 'voice from the sea', 'a tune from the hillside', 'a chime in the night' – only to end on an ominous note, 'Tell me, my friend . . . where can it end?'

Meanwhile, in the case of the tonally upbeat but verbally ambiguous 'Tow the Line', there would be another ham-fisted attempt on the part of the Drake estate to rewrite history when the track was finally released on *Made to Love Magic* in 2004. In the sleevenotes 'Cally' set about asserting that: 'Nick left us with a song full of assurance and a contemplative calm that adds another dimension to the notion that he was at the end of any tether at that time.' No mention of its compositional status as a relic of the past, or its scratch vocal. 'Cally' also claimed that the track was unmarked on the reel, and only 'made itself known [when] the tape was allowed to run on . . . never having been mixed or, indeed, heard since 1974'. But 'Tow the Line' was not so much a lost track, as a lost vocal. The song had been circulating on bootleg for years as a backing track, so the story about the tape running on to reveal this 'unknown' track was just another myth for the funereal pyre.

In keeping with the other 1974 tracks, 'Tow the Line' was cut instrumentally and then overdubbed with a vocal, which means it must have been marked on the multitrack. The final nail in the coffin of Cally's arch-revisionism was applied when Joe Boyd, the producer of the July 1974 sessions, told one Drake biographer he had no recollection of working on the track. It may well have received a guide vocal in February, but Drake had probably already rejected it as a candidate for the fourth album by the time he resumed his association with Boyd in July.

The resumption of their collaboration had been in the works for a few months, Boyd having already been warned by Wood, 'Nick had said that he had some tunes but no words.' When Boyd himself pressed Drake to explain what he had meant, at a meeting that spring on a trip to London, the songwriter informed Boyd: 'I haven't got any tunes anymore.' Boyd told him to go away and find some.

By the July sessions, Drake had indeed penned two seem-ingly new songs, 'Rider on the Wheel' and 'Hanging on a Star', the latter of which ran to six whole lines, each and every one directed at Boyd for leaving him in the lurch at the end of 1970 after promising him the pop world. The song seems to have been directly inspired by what David Sandison called 'a good talking-to' and the protagonist himself called 'a pep talk', given by Joe to Nick at that spring meeting. According to Sandison, 'What he did was to tell Nick that he was wasting and abusing a real and valuable talent and that he ought to stop pissing about and knuckle down to work.'

If Boyd had initially hoped the 'pep-talk' might work, hearing the self-pitying 'Hanging on a Star' made him realize just how fragile his favourite songwriter had become, and that 'the failure of his music to be successful in his lifetime was . . . the [real] source of his unhappiness'. In those final months that acute sense of failure would begin to consume Drake. The sessions in July merely brought home to him that a whole album of new material was beyond him. (The four songs they finished to Drake's satisfaction took longer to record than the entire *Pink Moon*.) And without the prospect of any more music, why even go on? One evening that summer, he turned to his mother and said, 'I have failed in everything I have tried to do.' Molly vainly attempted to elaborate on 'all the things that he had so patently done. It didn't make a difference. He felt that he'd failed to get through to the people that he wanted to talk to.'

Ironically, just as Drake was about to give up the ghost, there came the first sign that the world was catching up: in the pages of perhaps the most influential rockzine of the Seventies, *Zigzag*. In its June issue, Connor McKnight wrote a heartfelt first piece on the elusive work of the man, under the prophetic title, 'In Search of Nick Drake'. Drake himself even showed it to his parents, and according to one American who interviewed them after their son's death, 'In the weeks after [it appeared, he] began to work on songs again' – presumably a reference to 'Rider on the Wheel' and 'Hanging on a Star'.

Those looking for some presentiment in these last lyrics of what was to come could probably seize on the last verse of 'Rider on the Wheel': 'I don't feel the same / But I ain't gonna blame / The rider on the wheel'. But then, they could just as easily lock on to a song like 'Outside', written in 1967–68, the concluding couplet of which read, 'If the world is all wrong / I won't be staying long.'

None of this may matter a great deal *if* Drake's death, in the early hours of 25 November 1974, was the result of an accidental overdose, and not the suicide that the official coroner concluded it was. But there are too many people close to Drake who had seen it coming for this to be a credible conclusion. A few weeks earlier, Drake had asked his mother(!) to invite the Martyns to their home. Although Beverley was too pregnant to make the journey, John came and they made their peace.

But, as Beverley wrote in her recent autobiography, *Sweet Honesty*, her husband's account of their reconciliation filled her with an ominous feeling: 'He had wanted to make up his friendship with us and apologized for that last evening. With hindsight, it was as if he was tying up the loose ends in his life. I was glad we were all friends again but I felt that he was going to do something bad. I told John I thought we were going to lose him, but it still came as a shock when the phone rang.' John Martyn later told his own biographer: 'It seemed so obvious at the time that it would come. It was inevitable. He was surrounded by a loving family, they adored him. [But] he was just too distant.'

Suicide had been on Drake's mind throughout those last few months (returning from a brief trip to France, he handed his mother a copy of Camus' *The Myth of Sisyphus*, a philosophical discourse on whether suicide is morally justifiable), and maybe for some time before that. His friend Paul Wheeler remembers one occasion when he had been playing Stephen Stills' 'Four & Twenty', from *Déjà Vu*, and a visiting Drake became extremely agitated. At the time of the incident, Drake was approximately the same age as the narrator in Stills' song, who is contemplating taking his own life:

Morning comes the sunrise, and I'm driven to my bed
I see that it is empty, and there's devils in my head.
I embrace the many-colored beast.
I grow weary of the torment. Can there be no peace?
I find myself wishin' that my life would simply cease.

Drakes long-term girlfriend, Sophie Ryde, had also finally broken off their on–off relationship, prompting Drake to write her one last letter the night before his death. What he didn't pen that night was a suicide note, which at the time convinced *NME*'s Nick Kent – who would write the most influential profile of the singer-songwriter just three months after his self-induced death – that it was probably an accidental overdose of the all-too-lethal anti-depressant Tryptizol, not the last act of a desperately depressed individual. Kent later recanted his view: 'At the time I made great play of the fact that no suicide note, no grand flourish, had accompanied the act – yet this in all honesty is probably exactly the way Drake would have ended it all.'

In fact, the twenty-six-year-old did leave behind everything he wanted to say. An exercise book of his lyrics was at his bedside when his mother found him the following morning, slumped across his bed. Nor did Molly find the absence of a suicide note so curious. As she later said: 'He never wrote anything down, never kept a diary, hardly even wrote his name in his own books . . . It was as if he didn't want anything of himself to remain *except his songs*.'[my italics] The exercise book of his songs, bought when he was at Cambridge University and the songs still flowed effortlessly from his sloping pen, would remain Molly's solitary reminder – his recordings excepted – of her son's remarkable gifts.

Meanwhile, the songs from those final sessions would take their own sweet time appearing. Richard Williams, head of

A&R at Island in the mid-Seventies, even put about a story that they had been destroyed. But finally in 1979, with Island preparing the release of a three-album boxed-set of Drake's recorded work, *Fruit Tree*, it was decided to place the four finished 1974 tracks at the end of *Pink Moon* (finally making it a forty-minute album). Seven years later these same tracks got their own album, *Time of No Reply*, a collection of assorted studio outtakes and home demos that climaxed with the same quartet of songs. And that seemed to be that, until 2004, when history was again up for grabs, thanks to Drake's estate. This time, the now-five tracks were scattered around a new thirteen-track set, and 'Tow the Line' became his final word. (Wood himself participated in the myth-making, describing it in his notes as 'the last song Nick ever recorded'.) Not so.

*

In the summer of 1974 Drake was not the only burn-out victim who had returned to his inner child's home base with an exercise book of old lyrics to hand. Nor was he alone in discovering that his old record label was prepared to fund further recordings on the back of a revival of interest from an influential rock writer, pushing for proof that the flame still burned. In April 1974 Nick Kent, still ten months away from turning his attention to the permanently-stilled Drake, published perhaps his most famous piece: a five-page *NME* cover-story on the enigma that was Syd Barrett, the front-cover caption of which read: 'Whatever happened to the cosmic dream?'

With *Dark Side of the Moon* still in the charts a full year after its release, and with no news of Syd Barrett in more than two years, Kent felt that now would be a good time to remind *NME* readers of Syd's central role in the band's early career (on the back of *Piper*'s re-release as the first part of *A Nice Pair*). He even hoped to remind Barrett himself that he still had an audience, claiming 'demand for more Syd Barrett material is remarkably high at the moment and EMI are all ready to swoop the lad into the studio, producer in tow, at any given moment'. (The previous month, Capitol US had issued a double album of the two solo Syd LPs to a positive reception.)

The real problem, according to Peter Jenner, was finding out whether in fact 'Syd Barrett is [now] unable to write songs . . . or [if] he writes songs and won't show them to anyone'. There was only one way to know for certain: book a studio. So it was that on 12 August 1974, Jenner and Barrett resumed where they left off some six years earlier – recording whatever Barrett had in his locker, even if it was just meandering bluesy improvs. The hope was that the results could sit alongside a couple of lost tracks from the Floyd era and a smattering of tracks that could, and maybe should, have made the two solo LPs. Engineer John Leckie says the thinking behind these sessions was simple: 'There were things that [eventually] came out on *Opel* like 'Dolly Rocker' . . . [as well as] 'Scream Thy Last Scream', 'Vegetable Man' [but] there wasn't enough to make an LP up, and [so we] were at least hoping to get at least a couple of new tracks from Syd, so that we could mix it all together.'[36]

Jenner recalls that 'there was some indication that he wanted to do it'. But who did Jenner think would turn up: Roger K. Barrett or his creative alter ego Syd? Did he even still think of himself as 'Syd'? According to the contracts he had recently signed with EMI – for the two reissues released in the past nine months – he did. He had signed both, 'Syd Barrett', which would be all well and good had he not previously always signed his official contracts with his real name, 'R. K. Barrett'. Only after his muse was permanently stilled did he start signing himself 'Syd', suggesting this was still one crazy diamond.

Jenner's attitude was suitably philosophical: 'Give Syd all the tools and then see what he comes up with.' Thinking ahead, Jenner had even booked a whole week of studio time, in case the first day or two proved a bust. But the Barrett who dutifully turned up for the first four days was a shell of the former shell. When Jenner's gentle cajoling failed to produce anything, agent Bryan Morrison gave Syd one of *his* pep-talks, 'Come on, Syd, come on, Syd, get it together.' Barrett just kept noodling away at guitar-parts for songs he knew he would never finish and after four days of this torture walked out of the studio, never to return. One imagines the experience was at least as painful for him as it was for a disabused Jenner. Not one note was usable (though this hasn't stopped bootleggers from releasing several meandering snippets searching forlornly for a musical berth), and the idea of an album of outtakes was quietly put to bed. It would be 1988 before the project saw the light of day, as *Opel*, and even then the Floyd exercised their veto when it came to the two unreleased 1967 masterpieces that would have made the album a chart prospect.

And that was that. Barrett stopped kidding himself he was still Syd, gave up his latest flat in London and returned to Cambridge. By now, this had become a pattern of sorts. As Hester Page told Rob Chapman: 'Like a homing pigeon, if he started to feel a bit out of it he went back to where it was familiar and he was safe . . . In the end it was safer to go back to Cambridge and not be pestered by this world he felt he couldn't fit into anymore.' In his mind, he never really had left home. As Mick Rock observed at the time of his friend's 2006 death: 'Syd never really left Cambridge, never really left England particularly. He returned to the house he grew up in, living like this mad uncle upstairs, occasionally floating down.'

And yet, just like Drake and Green, it seems Barrett didn't really like it at home; he just couldn't bear it anywhere else for very long. He had told Steve Turner as much, back in March 1971, as he was preparing to fade from view: 'Cambridge is very much a place to get adjusted to. I've found it difficult . . . [but] it's the home place where I used to live . . . It's a nice place to live really – under the ground.' Much like the Mole in Kenneth Grahame's *The Wind in the Willows*.

At least he retained that unique sense of humour. And he would need it now, as the ill-assorted set of individuals that had once constituted 'his band' became one of the two or three biggest concert attractions in the world. In the four months that separated Nick Kent's eulogistic piece on Syd from those final, frustrating sessions with Jenner, Floyd fans heard the first whispers that the band was finally getting down to work on a successor to the record-breaking *Dark Side of the Moon*. In June, they played a short set of shows in France, where they unveiled two new compositions, both lengthy, the ten-minute 'Raving and Drooling' and the epic, nine-part 'Shine On You Crazy Diamond' – and there was no doubting which mad gem they meant. Waters talked about the initial inspiration for the latter song in a 1975 interview with *Rock et Folk*, while continuing his boycott of the British music press:

Roger Waters: We didn't start out with the idea of making a record based on the theme of absence . . . We began to put the music for 'Shine On You Crazy Diamond' together, and from that we got a very strong feeling of melancholy . . . When I wrote the words, I don't know why, but I began to write about Syd's [creative] demise. And then a few other sections got written . . . I wanted to force myself into what I felt at the time and to write something about it all . . . projecting my feelings about what was going on inside me. [1975]

But there was a lot more to Waters' decision to write about Barrett that spring than mere happenstance, or rank sentiment. He was clearly responding to Nick Kent's article, which implied that the band stopped being interesting the day he gave Syd his marching orders. Not that an affronted Waters was about to acknowledge Kent. No, no, no, he was responding to *all* the recent articles about Barrett in those impertinent English music papers – sum total as of May 1974, one:

Roger Waters: For my part I've never read an intelligent piece on Syd Barrett in any magazine. Never. No one knows what they're talking about. Only us, the people who knew him, who still know him a bit, only we know the facts, how he lived, what happened to him, why he was doing certain things . . . They make me laugh, these journalists with their rubbish. In actual fact, I wrote that song . . . above all to see the reactions of people who reckon they know and understand Syd Barrett . . . Because he's left, withdrawn so far away that, as far as we're concerned, he's no longer there. [1975]

Waters' own song to Syd – indeed, all three of the new songs he had now written for *Dark Side*'s successor – soon became a battleground for the spat to end all spats between Waters, as self-appointed spokesman for the pretentious wing of English prog-rock, and the king rat of rock critics, Mr Kent ('You Gotta Be Crazy', the title of the other track debuted at autumn UK concerts was, according to Waters, 'a reply to the English press'). When Kent was dispatched by *NME* editor Nick Logan to review the first of three sold-out Floyd shows at Wembley's dilapidated Empire Pool Arena on 15 November 1974, he was given the opportunity to expand further on his former treatise and did not stint:

Incisiveness has never been something the post-Syd Floyd have prided themselves on, and so one has to wade through laboured sections of indolent musical driftwood before, lo, the plot is resumed and one is sent careering back to our Roger's bloated denunciation . . . [which] ends with a mildly potent 'j'accuse' blast of postured psychological cause-and-effect ranting.

Waters was furious. Yet he wasn't about to respond directly to Kent's critique of the band's current failings. As he would tell *Rock et Folk*, 'I don't think it's really essential to institute a dialogue with the rock critics . . . there are more interesting minorities . . . Rock critics . . . are not an explanatory medium between us and the public.' It was simply a coincidence that they formed such an insistent backdrop to his recent output (including a song he never finished but mentioned in passing, 'Flight from Reality'). The following year he would ratchet up the personal paranoia to heights even Barrett never scaled, telling Capital Radio that 'because we're very successful, we're very vulnerable to attack and Syd is the weapon that is used to attack us'.

As of December 1974 – with Floyd's follow-up to *Dark Side* . . . still seven months away – it was left to Gilmour, who had previously tracked down Kent in order to ensure some personal input in his Barrett article, to now denigrate the man's critical faculties. Gilmour duly informed *NME*'s Pete Erskine that his fellow scribe 'goes on about Syd too much and yet, as far as I can see, there's no relevance in talking about Syd in reviewing one of our [current] concerts'. In fact, the words 'Syd Barrett' were mentioned exactly once in Kent's 3,000-word review of the Wembley show; and anyway, to suggest that the subject had 'no relevance' when the centre-piece of the new set was a twenty-five-minute 'tribute' in song to their former leader, and the second half of the show was a live re-creation of an entire album haunted by Syd's spectre, was disingenuous at best.

Actually, Kent had done the band a big favour. The result of his attack – and it was certainly that – was ultimately a positive one. As Kent later revealed: 'I saw Rick Wright after that piece came out and he actually thanked me for it. He said he didn't like what I'd written, but at the same time it stimulated some kind of intra-group discussion, because as a group they had [started to] become so detached from each other.' Some unity was now needed because, as of January 1975, when Erskine's counter-piece appeared in *NME*, the Floyd had not even started recording the most eagerly awaited rock album of 1975, *Wish You Were Here*.

And still, any fears about bootlegging – and this time the Floyd really were the target of those shady preservers of musical history, with *Tour '74* capturing all three new songs live from Stoke in startlingly good audience stereo, housed in a laminated sleeve with lyrics – remained secondary to the band's belief that the songs were immeasurably strengthened by being forged in the furnace of live performance. In the case of 'Shine On You Crazy Diamond', they were right. But the longer they worked on the new songs, the more convinced they became that they should change the dynamic. By early June 1975, when they were finally putting the finishing touches to *Dark Side*'s superior successor, they had put aside Waters' latest songs of madness – 'You Gotta Be Crazy' and 'Raving and Drooling' – to make the twenty-minute 'Shine On You Crazy Diamond' not only the album's centrepiece, but its bookends. All it needed now was a few judicious overdubs.

And so it was that the band convened at Abbey Road on 5 June 1975, to celebrate Dave Gilmour's wedding to his long-term girlfriend, and to apply those last dabs of the audio brush to a song they had now been working on for a solid year. Because the wedding reception was being held in the Abbey Road canteen, there were a lot of people from the band's wacky past milling around that day, most of them at Gilmour's behest. They included Jerry Shirley, who had made such a contribution to those Gilmour-Barrett sessions. And there was a large, bald man with no eyebrows, who was sitting next to Shirley in the canteen, wearing a slightly dazed look, and a huge grin. It was Syd.

Waters seems to have been more fazed by Barrett's appearance that day than the others, or perhaps than he really should have been. He later commented, 'For him to pick the very day we start putting vocals on a song about him – very strange.' And yet it was hardly the only occasion Barrett had kept tabs on 'his band' since his 1968 departure, or the first time he had decided to visit them in the studio. As for his timing, the press had been talking about this track for the past nine months. Who, in such a situation, wouldn't be the least bit curious to hear what the fuss was about?

Of course, he did look a bit odd with those shaved eyebrows and ill-fitting white suit.[37] But then, he had always enjoyed yanking the chain of these former architecture students. And, as Duggie Fields once observed, 'You weren't always sure with Syd whether he was winding you up . . . He liked challenging people.' So was this impromptu appearance a case of the madcap having one last laugh? According to his sister Rosemary, it was. In a rare interview, published in Luca Ferrari's *A Fish Out of Water*, she suggested: 'Syd was actually joking, and . . . everything from the white outfit to the shaved head and eyebrows was meant in jest.'

If so, he must have left that evening chortling to himself

about how Waters was still the same po-faced, uptight control freak he had been back in the day. There are enough clues in Barrett's few reported words that he was having a rare old time. At one point – according to the other Roger's version of events – Barrett actually stood up and said, 'Right, when do I put my guitar on?' Waters broke it to him gently, 'Sorry Syd, the guitar's all done.' Now what sort of myopic muso can't see the validation even a scratchy guitar riff from the man himself would have brought such a track? After all, the side-long song had no shortage of Barrettian touches, of which that little four-note guitar riff that introduces part one was the most blatant, self-consciously evoking Syd Barrett's lead-in guitar phrase on 'Astronomy Domine'. It seems Waters couldn't even bring himself to humour Syd by pressing record, then wiping the result from the final master – *if* it was anything like those recordings made the previous August.

Further proof that the wise fool still knew how to laugh at himself, and the world of rock, came when Waters played Syd the finished track and wondered aloud, 'Well, Syd, what do you think of that?' His response was a peach: 'Sounds a bit old.' Been there, done that; try to follow me if you can. By June 1975 Barrett may have lost that understanding for good, but he still had the jump on the leery Waters. He, at least, knew what French symbolist Arthur Rimbaud meant when he had written, a century earlier, high on absinthe: 'A poet makes himself a visionary through a long, boundless and systematic disorganization of the senses . . . and if, demented, he finally loses the understanding of his visions, he will at least have seen them!'

By now Waters had genuinely come to believe he could 'aspire to Syd's crazed insights and perceptions', a claim he was to finally make in print in 1987 as part of a one-man campaign to denigrate the very notion of the Floyd carrying on without *him.* At least Barrett probably left Abbey Road knowing they were no longer 'his band'. They were the answer to every rock promoter's prayer.

In 1975 Rock itself was unrecognizable from what it had been in 1968. And although it had travelled a long way, it had also lost a fair few of the brightest and the best, and not just those who had taken too much for granted. Of those who had always been enticed by the bright lights, big cities across the pond, some willingly allowed themselves to be whisked away into California's air-conditioned nirvana where they could indeed be comfortably numb.

★

In the period 1974–78, Keith Moon, David Bowie, Marc Bolan, Peter Green and John Lennon would all temporarily relocate to la-la-land. For Moon the Loon, the life of the rock star was just too enticing a substitute for real life, and he had soon returned to his manic ways. A protracted spell in Los Angeles in 1974 convinced him – and not only him – that this was the life. But as the band's manager recalled to Moon's biographer, if there was one place Keith Moon shouldn't be allowed, it was the headquarters of hedonism that was L.A., *c.* 1974–75:

> **Chris Stamp:** L.A. was a fucking nightmare. [Keith] was living in one of these expensive, cold Beverly Hills houses. Ringo and Harry Nilsson came around a lot and . . . they were *fucked up.* And they were good people. Surrounding them were the roadies and the drivers and the dealers . . . [and] they were even more fucked up. So it was madness. The wrong place for him to be – because L.A. is just L.A.

Moon was hardly alone in finding this Babylon of the West to his jaundiced taste. In the city where it was never winter, they had their own special snow and it got up people's noses. Moon was delighted to find a rock-solid ex-pat community of would-be hedonists with not a party-poopin' wife in sight. He had already experienced the tail-end of L.A. rock's most infamous lost weekend, the 1973 booze-fuelled bender that culminated in the infamous John Lennon-produced Harry Nilsson album, *Pussycats* – ostensibly contributing drums to two of the more ramshackle tracks ('Loop de Loop' and 'Rock Around the Clock').

Inspired, if that is the right word, by an album that pretty much killed Nilsson's career stone-dead and sent Lennon hurtling back to the missus, Moon returned to L.A. the following summer, after a few large-scale Who shows replenished the coffers, to begin his own solo album, *Two Sides of the Moon*. These sessions would make the *Pussycats* sessions sound like *Please Please Me*. Becoming the stuff of legend, they proved once and for all that cocaine, willing chicks and creativity do not mix. The resultant platter would make MCA choke on the bill for an event with hardly any paying diners.

Into this modern Sodom arrived in early September 1974 a certain David Bowie, halfway through a six-month on–off US tour designed to promote his latest fab waxing, *Diamond Dogs*, and to put to bed once and for all the alienating androgyny of Aladdin and Ziggy. Along for the ride was a BBC documentary crew, and an English director, in Alan Yentob, who wanted to know, what gives? Bowie, caught between rock and a more soulless place, decided in a rare moment of articulacy to come clean to Yentob about all those earlier creations of his:

David Bowie: One half of me is putting a concept forward, and the other half is trying to sort out my own emotions, and a lot of my 'space' creations are, in fact, facets of me ... [though] I wouldn't even admit that to myself at the time ... Ziggy would relate to something ... [in] me. Major Tom, Aladdin Sane, they're all facets of me, and I got lost at one point. I couldn't decide whether I was writing characters, or whether the characters were writing me. [1974]

In his coke-fogged mind, Bowie thought he was being mighty clever, owning up to a glorious past he was disowning nightly onstage. Already, he had managed to convince himself he had wriggled free of those all-consuming creations. Backstage at his 'triumphant' return to Radio City Music Hall, a month later, he told Alice Cooper: 'It's easy to get trapped by your stage presentation; the secret is to find a way to move on.' Yet it was Cooper who had moved on. He had just disbanded the bestselling band of the same name, and begun work on his very own welcoming *Nightmare*. Whereas Bowie had simply abandoned everything he had ever believed in, even as he sought to present his *volte-face* as another artistic act of (re)creation:

David Bowie: About two years ago, I realized I had become a total product of my concept character Ziggy Stardust. So I set out on a very successful crusade to re-establish my own identity. I stripped myself down and took myself down and took myself apart, layer by layer. [1976]

Once again, Bowie was informing anyone who would listen that he would be 'concentrating on various activities that have very little to do with rock and pop'. And this time he wasn't joking. What he didn't admit was that the change had been forced on him by the economics of touring the States with his lamest collection since he was a denizen at Deram. Two punchy preview 45s culled from Ziggy's reject locker – 'Rebel Rebel' and 'Diamond Dogs' itself – did not an album make. And he was being called to account. Lester Bang's August 1974 *Creem* review of *Diamond Dogs* – surely assiduously assimilated by an avid rock-press reader like Bowie – did not sugar-coat the facts:

> *Diamond Dogs* reaffirms what an incredible producer Bowie is even if most of the songs are downright mediocre . . . He was always weary, and pretentiously likes to think of himself as the prescient chronicler of a planet falling to pieces . . . [but] this is the sloppiest Bowie album yet . . . He really doesn't seem to care as much as he used to.

The man was losing even the elements of the American rock constituency he had previously thought he could rely on. As such it was doubly important to his commercial well-being Stateside that he told everyone he had been kidding all along and that, although it had been a helluva ride, it was over:

> **David Bowie:** At the time that I did *Ziggy Stardust*, all I had was a small cult audience in England from *Hunky Dory*. I think it was out of curiosity that I began wondering what it would be like to be a rock & roll star. So basically, I wrote a script and played it out as Ziggy Stardust onstage and on record. I mean it when I say I didn't like all those albums – *Aladdin Sane, Pin Ups, Diamond Dogs, David Live*. It wasn't a matter of liking them, it was, 'Did they work or not?' Yes, they worked. They kept the trip going. [But] now I'm all through with rock & roll. Finished. I've rocked my roll. It was great fun while it lasted, but I won't do it again. [1975]

All the Madmen

What he wasn't inclined to admit was that his latest gambit, the *Diamond Dogs* tour – running initially from June through July 1974 – had lost a fair few old fans, while barely winning over an equivalent number of new fans. On the tape of the third show, Toronto (16 June), fans can be heard shouting, 'Where is Ziggy? We want Ziggy!' Yet even before the arrangements had found their feet he was recording shows in Philadelphia for a live album, at the insistence of Defries. What Defries didn't spell out was the sheer necessity of the ruse, in order to recoup some of the huge losses brought on by the grandiose stage show and the ten-piece live band, out of all proportion to Bowie's pulling power. Bowie, a reluctant participant in the process, later suggested that *David Live* should have been called *David Bowie is Alive and Well and Living Only in Theory*. But it had finally been spelt out to him – by his long-suffering record label – that record advances had been subsidizing all three US tours, and the buck stopped here, and now.

On 2 September, when Bowie resumed touring at L.A.'s open-air Universal Amphitheater, gone were the hydraulic lifts and post-industrial scaffolding that passed for the *Diamond Dogs* set. They were replaced by a five-piece group of backing singers and Bowie's idea of sweet soul music. His explanation, proffered to Tony Zanetta after the first L.A. show, was that he wanted 'the focus of the tour to be on the music and not on theatre'.

Key members of the band, already soured by a financial dispute over payment for the *David Live* recordings, began to make their feelings known in private. Michael Kamen, effectively the musical director, was unhappy to find that 'the stage was [suddenly] full of large black people going "Halleluiah" and shaking tambourines, and poor David was very thin and very white and completely out of his element'. Guitarist Earl Slick was equally unimpressed: 'David had gone completely in a direction I didn't like, not to mention it wasn't the way I play.'

Nor did the audience hecklers let up. At Radio City in November, one reportedly shouted, 'We want our money back. We want Ziggy Stardust.' They, at least, remembered what Bowie had told the US press the day he introduced Ziggy to them at the Dorchester Hotel in July 1972: 'I'm never gonna try and play black music 'cause I'm white. Singularly white!' And English. For the diehards, the version of 'John, I'm Only Dancing' that he recut at Philadelphia's Sigma Sound in a new, supposedly soulful guise – which reinvented the song so successfully that it really was only about dancing – was a form of sacrilege.

By now the set-list was being nightly overhauled, with Bowie introducing new songs such as 'Footstompin'', 'Can You Hear Me?' and 'It's Gonna Be Me'[38], soundalike soul songs that fell largely on deaf ears. Perhaps things would have been clearer if he had introduced into the set another song he'd just cut at Philadelphia's Sigma Sound studio, 'Who Can I Be Now?'. Yet he still wanted it both ways – all ironic distance as far as his rock fans were concerned, but Mr Sincerity when finally booked to appear on *Soul Train*, America's one concession to black music on mainstream TV. When he threatened to call his new 'white soul' album *Shilling the Rubes*, though, bosses at his US label put their foot down and said, no way, Ishmael.

Well, this Ishmael had a whopper to tell. Barely had Bowie unveiled his new sound to the she-creatures of Hollywood than he was telling their daily bible, the *L.A. Times*, 'I was [always] trying to put forward concepts, ideas and theories, but this [new] album doesn't have anything to do with that. It's just emotional drive . . . There's not a concept in sight.' Nor were there any decent riffs in sight. Or at least not any which came from the once-febrile mind of Davey Jones. 'Footstompin'' was not a bad riff, but it was one that guitarist Carlos Alomar had come up with, only for Bowie to decide he could cut up a guitar part just as easily as he could a line of lyrics – or coke:

> **Carlos Alomar:** David had recorded my chord changes and riff, and he hated it. He took out the lyrics and ended up with the music, and cut it up on the master so that it would have classic r&b form. He . . . experiment[ed] with the original tape, running it backwards, cutting it up . . . [The resultant] 'Fame' was totally [a] cut up. When he had the form of the song he wanted, he left.

Having generated the song-form he wanted, Bowie set about writing a new set of lyrics that put the boot in. As he later recalled, what he came out with was 'quite a nasty, angry little song'. He had recently experienced some 'very upsetting management problems, and a lot of that was built into the song'. Having finally got around to reading the contract he had signed with Defries back in August 1971, he had no dilemma deciding what he wanted to get off his chest:

> Fame, lets him loose, hard to swallow
> Fame, puts you there where things are hollow . . .
> Fame, it's not your brain, it's just the flame
> That burns your change to keep you insane . . .
> Fame, what you need you have to borrow.

He had already been warned about Defries by, of all people, John Lennon, former client of Allen Klein and drinking buddy of Morris Levy. Lennon's presence at the 'Fame' session, and his suggestion that Bowie add 'all . . . the high-pitched singing', would be enough to garner him a co-credit on the track. In the meantime, irony of ironies, the song Bowie wrote as a retort to the one man who believed in him way back when, and had hocked his own (and RCA's) future to give him that one shot, soared to number one on the American charts in the summer of 1975, turning around his fortunes in the land of the free lunch. It also turned him into a know-it-all, who had all the answers when down-on-his-luck friend Marc Bolan wondered why he couldn't crack the charts Stateside with the same formula that worked back home:

Tony Visconti: During the *Young Americans* days, David told me that he had recently talked to Marc . . . David was already quite successful in America then, which is something Marc wasn't. Marc's way was to slag other people off to make himself look bigger, and he tried to have a go at David that night, telling him that he was doing things wrong; and David just put him very straight about where he was at, that he wasn't going to break America with his present attitude, that he should bend a little and listen more to American taste.

What Bowie did not tell Bolan directly was that he had achieved his own success by changing his whole vocal style into something as transatlantic – and homogenized – as Half and Half. He had tried and failed to sell the States on a form of English rock as glam as 'Get It On', and as camp as 'Blockbuster', so it was time to come clean: he didn't have the patience (or the money) necessary to wait for Middle America's mall-children to catch up. Meanwhile, a disconsolate Bolan, who back in 1971 had fleetingly had America in the palm of his hand, stuck to his template, even as Bowie was happily boasting that his success, long fought for and hard won as it was, really was a case of 'shilling the rubes':

All the Madmen

David Bowie: 'Fame' was an incredible bluff that worked. Very flattering. I'll do anything until I fail. And when I succeed, I quit, too. I'm really knocked out that people actually dance to my records, though. But let's be honest; my rhythm and blues are thoroughly plastic. *Young Americans*, the album 'Fame' is from, is, I would say, the definitive plastic soul record. It's the squashed remains of ethnic music as it survives in the age of Muzak rock, written and sung by a white limey. [1976]

Not everyone fell for *Young Americans'* charms. Dylan, who knew a rube when he saw one, reportedly told Bowie he thought the album was terrible. And when Bowie insisted on playing the whole thing to Paul McCartney and wife Linda – twice! – the ex-Beatle snapped, 'Can we hear another album?' However, Bowie no longer craved the validation of peers – or mentors. Fame had indeed taken him over. Actually, it had swallowed him whole. As Mick Rock notes: 'Externally he handled it well . . . [but] internally he was having problems.' Symptomatic of his slide into the swimming pool of his very own rock & roll fantasy was his decision at the end of the Soul Tour to relocate to Los Angeles His wife Angie was soon fearing for his very soul:

Angie Bowie: [By 1974] David's whole life [had] changed . . . He started living largely in the dark, in the company of other coke freaks. He visited home only when he needed to, or could be assured that his nearest and dearest, or other non-cocaine people, wouldn't bother him. I saw less and less of him, and I just hated that. I couldn't stand watching the David I knew vanishing from his own life . . . [So I found] a beautiful Art Deco house [in L.A.] on six acres, an exquisite property and terrific value at just $300,000. But he took one look at a detail I hadn't noticed, a hexagram painted on the floor of a circular room by the previous owner . . . and got hysterical. [1993]

If cocaine had taken over as the drug of choice by the time he played the Universal in September 1974, Bowie quickly discovered that when it came to the Peruvian marching powder, southern California was the land of plenty. One day during the Universal residency, Fran Pillersdorf, production co-ordinator on the tour, was obliged to go past his bedroom door on the way to the bathroom: it was, she recalled, 'dark in the middle of a bright California day. There were bottles and cocaine from the night before, and there was David lying in the dark room with the door ajar. He was bone tired and freaked out.'

He stayed in pretty much the same state of mind and body throughout the whole Californian mini-tour that month, and it was here that the cameras of Yentob's *Arena* crew caught the ex-Spider, still weaving his web of self-deceit. But if the live clips from the L.A. shows were meant to convince his fans back home he still had something to say, while the fey cockney accent he adopted offstage would hopefully convince them he remained 'one of us', then the strategy was flawed from the very start. Broadcast at prime-time on a February evening in 1975, with the UK release of *Young Americans* just around the corner, the programme was very much an exercise in *cinéma vérité* – save that Bowie was not the orchestrator this time, he was Yentob's victim. Charles Shaar Murray, who had acted as Bowie's trustworthy conduit to the impressionable readers of *NME* for the past two years or more, was unsparing in his assessment of the former Emperor of Pop, who now had to stand naked:

Bowie's all nerves, like some strange insect trapped in a jar. His conversation runs around in circles like a rat on a treadmill, he radiates cocaine paranoia and his eyes squirm in their sockets. He says that he's glad to be rid of Ziggy and to start being himself, but that seems to be proving his undoing. Ziggy was a stronger and more fascinating creature than David Bowie; Ziggy sucked him dry. What Yentob got in his viewfinder were the dregs.

Americans had already been given their own insight into what happens when a star is sucked dry by his own ego, having witnessed Bowie's first national prime-time interview on *The Dick Cavett Show*, broadcast on 5 December 1974. The live performance of three songs, including the unmodified 'Footstompin'' and an earnest 'Young Americans', still seemed to suggest he might have something to say. But the ensuing interview was painful to watch, as Cavett tried every trick in the book to get more than a mumbled platitude out of the man. What the hell had happened to rock's most articulate self-promoter? The most revealing remark in the whole sorry saga came when Cavett ventured into David's background, asking about his parents, specifically his mother. Bowie briefly stopped playing with his cane like some autistic child to half-jokingly suggest: 'She pretends I'm not hers. She doesn't talk much [to me]. We were never that close.' In fact, it was him who was doing the disowning, from six thousand miles away, even as he continued playing the 'mad family' card to the American media:

David Bowie: My brother Terry's in an asylum right now. I'd like to believe that the insanity is because our family is all genius, but I'm afraid that's not true . . . I'm quite fond of the insanity, actually. It's a nice thing to throw out at parties, don't you think? Everybody finds empathy in a nutty family. Everybody says, 'Oh, yes, my family is quite mad.' Mine really is. No fucking about, boy . . . [But] I haven't spoken to any of them in years. My Father is dead. I think I talked to my mother a couple of years ago. I don't understand any of them. [1976]

To escape the family curse, he had turned his back on everyone he once held dear, and flown halfway around the world – only to find that all his psychological baggage had again arrived first. When self-denial didn't work, he shut off his emotions – and the work suffered. Estranged wife Angie learnt the hard way that his 'real psychological problem in the years I knew him was his emotional frigidity, the cure in his case being worse than the family disease. The real crazy stuff, the mania, delusions, and paranoia he exhibited during the second half of the decade . . . coincided precisely with his ingestion of enormous amounts of cocaine, alcohol and whatever other drugs he had on hand; his "madness" simply didn't happen unless he was stoned out of his mind.'

His next creation would be a freeze-dried coke fiend with a streak of megalomania hardwired in. The Thin White Duke was another artistically successful alter ego, but it was a case in point of placing someone 'there, where things are hollow'. By now, he really thought he had found some unique way to control those inner demons. Interviewed for *Playboy* by Cameron Crowe as he prepared to take the Thin White Duke around the world – with the shortest of pit-stops in London – he was asked if he thought he was schizophrenic: 'One side of me probably is, but the other side is right down the middle, solid as a rock . . . My thought forms are fragmented a lot, that much is obvious . . . [But] being famous helps put off the problems of discovering myself. I mean that.'

It took until the fag-end of 1976, and a protracted trip to East

Berlin intended to cleanse him and his symbiotic sidekick, Iggy, of the new world and old habits, for the boy from Brixton to realize that there was a reason he was always crashing in the same car. When he did realize he had been living in the land of hollow men, he snuck on back to the city of New York, to which his new friend, Lennon, had already retreated. For the pair of them, this island of insanity off the East Coast of America was quite close enough to the childhood homes they alluded to repeatedly in their early-Seventies songs, but spent the second half of the decade disavowing. Lennon even explained his reasoning on the dangers of returning home: 'That's one time when you can't hide from yourself. The records, the fame – none of it shields you. You remember exactly who you are deep inside.'

Bowie's old friend, Bolan, had also eventually tired of his own season in the L.A. sun. By the beginning of 1975 he was ready to board the trans-Euro express. Stopping off in France for a detox and a musical rethink, he re-emerged in 1976 a slimmer, leaner Marc. Like Keith Moon, he had found his time in L.A. to have been desperately unproductive, merely fuelling a sense of dislocation bordering on homesickness. For both these party animals, London would prove to be their final resting place – literally. Both would be dead by the end of 1978, the former killed by the worst-placed tree in west London, the latter by an overdose of the same anti-depressant that killed Drake.

If Bowie finally split the L.A. scene because he had started to see pentagrams on floors and demons at the windows, it took one of Ziggy's surrogate fathers, ex-asylum inmate Peter Green, to class the people around him in the city of angels as in league with Lucifer. It was 1978 before Green made it back to L.A., but when he did, it was to indulge in an ill-fated marriage to one of L.A. witchy women, which ended in a matter of months because, as Mick Fleetwood says: 'He felt that she had made a covenant with the Devil.' A bemused Green had already found that his former band had reinvented itself as the quintessential radio-friendly AOR band, coming up with their own FM-freeway phenomenon, *Rumours*, the previous year. For their new audience, though, the period with Green was essentially an irrelevance and 'Black Magic Woman' was a Santana song.

Indeed, by this time much of English rock was an irrelevance Stateside. And the change had come about in 1974–75, while all these English rockers were cavorting in the pools of Hollywood and Burbank. For at the very same time, up in Laurel Canyon, the likes of Joni Mitchell and Neil Young were laying down their own response to these difficult times – and in 1974, that meant *Court and Spark* and *On the Beach*, two pure-bred pedigree examples of California's own new wave of singer-songwriters, a little burnt out but beautifully self-absorbed. Meanwhile, in Malibu, the granddaddy of them all, Bobby D., was sleeping on the floor of his empty new mansion with Bay Area girlfriend Ellen Bernstein, and writing the album that best expressed the time when 'revolution was in the air', *Blood on the Tracks*. Fittingly, it was he who closed the book on the Sixties' socio-musical legacy. And on the timeless 'Tangled Up in Blue', he could have just as easily been describing the madcap Barrett as rather consciously evoking his own Rimbaudian muse:

> There was music in the cafés at night,
> And revolution in the air.
> Till he started into dealing with slaves,
> And something inside of him died.

Well, in Syd's case, something or someone inside *had* died. As of 1975, *I* really was *another*. After his little 5 June stunt at Abbey Road, Roger would not let Syd come out to play. The following year, when Capital Radio DJ Nicky Horne called on Barrett at his home to ask if he would co-operate in a radio retrospective on the Floyd, 'this huge fat man answered wearing only pyjama trousers. He looked down at me, and said, "Syd can't talk." When I told Dave Gilmour [what happened], he said the man had been Syd, and he'd been telling the truth. He really couldn't talk any more.'

Meanwhile, the Pink Floyd of Gilmour and Waters remained one of the few English rock acts to retain and expand a US audience through the second half of the Seventies. The Who maintained their live audience by pandering to them, while The Kinks just stopped trying. And Bowie took regular two-year breaks from the stage to stoke up demand. The English wave of musical madness that had so spectacularly crashed on foreign shores was just about done, with Punk just around the corner, ready to impose the last rites on the kind of musical indulgences that the Sixties mindset had given licence to.

But although it still had plenty to say about this English malady itself – and in the form of Ian Curtis, its own Drakean poster-boy for the new depression – English rock had lost its grip on that international mass audience. It had also developed an ideological aversion to albums on which the sum was more than the parts. Art was again supposed to be consumed in three-minute sound bites cut for seven-inch vinyl.

The term 'conceptual unity' was banned by the Ministry of Punk Propaganda at King's Tower. The idea of creating order from inner disorder, and calling it a piece of art, was a no-no – even after Siouxsie & The Banshees managed to slip their own concept album about suburban madness between the covers of their own long-playing debut, *The Scream* (1978). The Fall's first EP, *Bingo Master's Break Out*, was another 1978 mini-masterpiece wholly inspired by Mark E. Smith and girlfriend Una Baines's experiences working at the local asylum. Who knew?

But for the likes of Poly Styrene, who formed X-Ray Spex at the mid-point between two nervous breakdowns, a Bowie-esque flight from childhood remained the order of the day – even as her song 'Identity' ripped the lid off this barely maintained pretence. If many Sixties rock artists had burned, burned, burned until they just burned themselves out, it would be as nothing to Punk's headlong rush into self-ignition. X-Ray Spex would be just one of a number of punk bands that had the lifespan of a plate-juggler's act. But then, even the punk drug of choice foreshortened the arc of creativity: 'A lot of speed / is all I need', to quote a particularly Rotten phrase.

And still the English continued sacrificing the brightest and the best at the altar of its very own rapacious art-form, rock music. And if the drugs didn't help, perhaps it was never that simple. As Syd Barrett's replacement in the Floyd once said: 'Acid and stuff . . . acted as catalysts . . . [but] it's more that he couldn't handle success on that level . . . And [something] to do with his past life, his father dying and all that stuff.' In fact, as Barrett knew only too well from his own reading, his complaint was hardly his alone. It was, in fact, symptomatic of a very English malady.

'We really all were very happy for a while, sitting around not toiling but just bullshitting and playing, but it was for such a terribly brief time, and then the punishment was beyond belief: even when we could see it, we could not believe it.'
– Philip K. Dick, *A Scanner Darkly* (1977)

Afterword: '. . . They First Make Mad'

Wherever the intellect is most excited . . . there is an increase of insanity. This malady prevails most widely, and illustrates its presence most commonly in mania, in those countries whose citizens possess the largest civil and religious liberty . . . whose free, civil and religious institutions create constantly various and multiplying sources of mental excitement.
– *Praying a Grant of Land for the Relief and Support of the Indigent and Incurable Insane* . . . , Dorothea Dix, 1848

It seems to me that in England all feelings, selfish and liberal, religious and moral, low and high, are extremely active. Not only the feelings, but also the intellectual faculties, have no restraint but that of their own power. If genius be not always encouraged, its activity at least is not suppressed . . . Thus, the powerful activity of the mind seems to me a great cause why insanity is so frequent in England.
– *Observations on the deranged manifestations of the mind, or, Insanity* by J.G. Spurzheim, 1833

Throughout the eighteenth and nineteenth centuries, continental intellectuals were convinced that the unusual civil liberties enjoyed by the English – and its English-speaking ex-colony across the way – at least partly accounted for its tendency to produce a disproportionate number of lunatics. Although J.G. Spurzheim also mentioned the English proclivity for liking a drink, and connected this to 'deranged manifestations of the mind', he made no mention of the role of drugs in such an endemic *dérèglement*. John Jones' *The Mysteries of Opium Reveal'd* (1700), though, had already commented on how opium, freely available by then, 'in excessive dose, do[th] cause, at first, Mirth, and afterwards a kind of Drunken Sopor in some, in others Fury, or Madness', while, 'long and lavish use . . . causes a dull and moapish disposition'.

Likewise, the idea that a particular genus of mental disease was quintessentially English precedes Spurzheim by at least a century. It was one subscribed to by George Cheyne, who in 1733 published an entire book on *The English Malady, or, A Treatise of Nervous Diseases of all Kinds*. And in his introduction, Cheyne observed: 'The Title I have chosen for this Treatise, is a Reproach universally thrown on this Island by Foreigners . . . by whom nervous Distempers, Spleen, Vapours and Lowness of Spirits, are in Derision, called the English Malady. And I wish there were not so good Grounds for this Reflection.' Cheyne's own explanation – it was 'the Variableness of our Weather' and 'the Richness and Heaviness of our Food' – may even now have its advocates. It may also partly explain why there was a network of private asylums around England – along lines established by the medieval hospital at Beth'lem (or Bedlam) in Southwark – long before any similar network grew up elsewhere in Europe.

However, any intellectual consensus conceiving of a relationship between freedom of expression and madness had long lapsed by the time the 1960s decided to test such a thesis once and for all. And this time freedom of expression came with a desire for experimentation wholly alien to the staid

Victorians, ever concerned with social order and public decorum. If, in the period 1965–75, English rock produced an extraordinary body of work – I would suggest unparalleled in its popular culture since the heyday of Jacobethan drama – it was not only a case of the postwar traumas of a sundered society finding release in the popular arts, but also that intoxicatingly heady feeling this newly permissive attitude to life, liberty and the pursuit of happiness fleetingly inspired. Such a spirit of optimism and experimentation inevitably fed into all forms of populist art.

This dewy-eyed optimism – which would-be hedonists did not merely apply to the traditional recourses of the aspiring aesthete, sex and drugs, but crucially extended to the pre-eminent form of contemporary artistic expression, rock music – died well before the concomitant spirit of experimentation did. Even in a recording studio – where the sums of money at stake could run to the millions a bestseller would bring – freedom of expression and a widespread encouragement of experimentation were the twin pillars of rock's late Sixties/early Seventies heyday.

For that is what it truly was. Bands were free to choose their producers (a relatively recent innovation), or even produce themselves; they were generally free to run up as much studio time as the demands of their artistic vision required (in the case of Pink Floyd, they had even had the wit to insist on an 'open studio time' clause in their original 1967 contract with EMI); they could and usually did employ independent designers to produce the packaging that formed such an integral part of The Album as Artefact (Floyd insisted on using their old friends at Hipgnosis, while artist Roger Dean provided bands such as Yes with their own 'house style'); and when they delivered the finished sequence, the record company was expected to issue it exactly as it was given to them. Gone were the days when American labels could dictate the content, even in opposition to any UK release, creating a generation of American consumers who thought there was a Rolling Stones album called *12x5* and a Beatles collection named *Yesterday and Today*.

Even in the case of Nick Drake – after two albums, neither of which had sold more than a couple of thousand copies – Chris Blackwell's Island not only released the twenty-eight minute *Pink Moon* exactly as they received it, but also gave the album a fold-out sleeve, and the budget to commission an artist friend of the family, Michael Trevithick, to design the cover after Drake informed them 'he wanted a pink moon'. Indeed, the only one of the half-a-dozen albums at the heart of this microcosm of madness not lovingly wrapped in a fold-out sleeve was *Ziggy Stardust*, and even that came housed in an inner sleeve with a full set of lyrics. Meanwhile, the ostentatious packaging for *Quadrophenia* would run Jethro Tull's *Thick as a Brick* and Elton John's *Captain Fantastic* close in any contest for the most O.T.T. album-sleeve in rock history.

This free spirit in English rock was also reflected in the labels themselves, which were fronted by free-thinking overseers, independent in spirit and deed; witness Immediate (Andrew Loog Oldham), Island (Chris Blackwell), Charisma (Tony Stratton-Smith), Chrysalis (Chris Ellis), Virgin (Richard Branson) and Track (Chris Stamp). To compete with these independents, the mighty EMI were obliged to set up their own 'prog' label, Harvest (to whom Floyd, Barrett and Roy Harper all absconded), while Decca came up with Deram, and Pye brought in Dawn. Between them, these 'indie' labels would release most of the groundbreaking English rock music of the late Sixties and early Seventies.

As for touring to promote the album after the fact, the record label just had to hope the artist felt like playing their newly released songs – rather than any they'd written in the interim. But, irrespective of touring activities or chart action, the record labels were expected to keep their albums in print until the world caught up – even if that was never. Meanwhile, a British concert circuit still built around many subsidised colleges and universities, town halls and larger theatres was able to sustain a veritable jamboree of pop acts who only ever teetered on the edge of chart-action.

But perhaps the greatest innovation in pop-culture, as of 1966, was the fact that no subject matter – even going ga-ga – was taboo. Once Dylan forever sundered the shackles at Newport, 'nothing is forbidden, everything is permissible' became the whole of rock lore. And although not many expected to export English rock's ever-tenuous hold on sanity as a sensibility, for a while there it proved surprisingly easy to sell to the States. (Even Monty Python, as eccentrically English as jellied eels, would find a mass audience across the pond.) Only when the English got angry at the status quo – with Punk – did the Americans recoil. By then, they had more than enough English rock music to keep them going for the next decade.

However, Punk's unnerving presence also brought a necessary stock take as the labels – many of which had now given their accountant a set of keys – realized they had been subsidizing some fine cult acts for nigh on a decade and, forgetting the virtues of classic catalogue, instituted a cull that did for the likes of Richard & Linda Thompson, John Martyn, Roy Harper, Vincent Crane and Peter Green. For those who had always preferred the nooks and crannies of cultdom, the days of wine and poppies were numbered. Gone went the ostentatious fold-out sleeves, unlimited studio time and a *carte blanche* approach to session-musician costs, along with the once-assured interest of a voracious weekly music press. In Britain this still numbered four major papers: *NME, Melody Maker, Sounds* and *Record Mirror*, but with the notable exception of *Melody Maker*, they all embraced punk with such Year Zero fever that the chances of a Roy Harper feature by 1977 were about as great as a Margaret Thatcher interview.

It was into this ocean of indifference that some of the more challenging English artists of the earlier era were hurled, and it was a case of sink or swim. Two of its leading lights threw their talented wives overboard in the process. By 1980 Martyn had chosen to swim in his own pool of booze and recrimination, captured on his last Island album, *Grace & Danger,* leaving Beverley to experience her own nervous breakdown in the aftermath of their marriage, culminating in a spell in a mental ward in 1984. Meanwhile, Richard & Linda Thompson got their more successful friend Gerry Rafferty to subsidize an album they never released (the original *Shoot Out the Lights*[39]), and then re-recorded it when Linda was heavily pregnant and suffering from an intermittently chronic case of dysphonia. Not surprisingly, the resultant record was their last together, and it would be 1984 before Richard Thompson was back on a label that could actually provide tour support and promotion – Polydor.

Both Martyn and Thompson were among the fortunate few survivors from the maelstrom of madness that had maintained such a grip on English rock, and had produced such a remarkable outpouring of bittersweet inspiration, through the first half of the 1970s. Although neither of these shipwrecked survivors ended up deranged by their trips into the unknown, each was a little damaged (in Thompson's case, his flight into a Sufi community in the mid-Seventies has clear parallels to Peter Green's earlier soul-searching). For others less blessed, the road to recovery was still awaiting the next delivery of rocks and gravel.

*

Indeed, throughout the early Eighties, strange things were happening in the land of rock, none stranger than the record Vincent Crane and Peter Green decided to make together in 1982. In a gesture of communal musical therapy, they agreed to make a blues album under the name *Katmandu*. It was in that autumn the musically gifted but perennially troubled pair found themselves jamming at ex-Mungo Jerry frontman Ray Dorset's studio when an affluent Swiss entrepreneur turned up and made them an offer they couldn't refuse: 'I'll buy anything you guys do.'

Both of them had been easing themselves back into the fray since the end of 1979, neither with any marked degree of success (at least outside of Germany, where Green's 1979 album, *In the Skies*, was a sensation of sorts). In Crane's case, a 1982 Atomic Rooster reunion album (*Headline News*) that even featured Dave Gilmour on four tracks still proved something of a commercial turkey, and he soon returned to life as a self-medicating slum landlord. Green himself had played with a succession of increasingly unsympathetic combos, searching for that Munich vibe. But already the business aspects of showbiz were once again giving him the blues.

Unexpectedly, the resultant album was something of a return to form for both parties, even though it started with the most ramshackle version of 'Dust My Broom' this side of shantytown. 'Crane's Train Boogie' showed Vincent in his element, suffusing a trainwreck of blues with some Southern soul, while 'Who's That Knockin'' almost suggested Green had dusted off his broom and was ready to reclaim the room. But what the album lacked was any new lyrical insights from Crane or Green. Those they left to the author of 'In the Summertime' and 'Baby Jump'.

And, predictably, once the jam sessions became something more real, the pressure proved too much for Green. His mood swings and day-long silences delayed everything, until the others wondered if an album would ever be completed. When the record was finally finished, at the end of January 1983, it then took a year to see the light of day as Mr Mungo Jerry tried to wheel and deal it into a Dorset-plus-band release, by which time Green had disappeared under the covers, not picking up the guitar again for twelve long years. He still wasn't ready – perhaps because, as he candidly admitted during a rare visit from his old friend Mick Fleetwood, 'I sort of overdid it, you know.'

Meanwhile, the classically trained Crane became a pianist for hire on one of the longest series of sessions in rock history, intended to produce the third album by one of the most successful acts of the early 1980s, Dexys Midnight Runners. The resultant album, *Don't Stand Me Down*, took even longer than *Katmandu* (or *Tusk*, for that matter) as bandleader Kevin Rowland insisted on recording everything live in the studio, refusing to overdub the slightest mistake, and narrating seemingly extemporized (but actually scripted) chunks of dialogue over the tracks, one of which revamped the riff to Warren Zevon's 'Werewolves of London'. The album took eighteen months to complete, and it was not until September 1985 – a full three years since a very different Dexys topped the charts with 'Come On Eileen' – that it appeared. But when it did, the combination of musical styles and off-mike rapping put an end to Rowland's own lucky streak.

For Crane, it was a last reminder of how things had changed, and not in a good way. He began to sink into another whirlpool of fear and self-loathing. And this time it claimed him for good. By 1988, as his good friend Paul Green ruefully recalls, 'He was living from one moment of delusion to another.' On Valentine's Day 1989, he took 400 aspirin, convinced that he had let everyone down, especially his ex-wife Jean, and they would be better off without this irrepressible firebrand. He was just forty-six.

The other Vince to intersect our tale was also by this time waist-high in dark waters. Vince Taylor, the king of failed comebacks, had made the last of half-a-dozen attempted resurrections in 1979, before moving to Switzerland in the early Eighties, hoping to deal head-on with his depression and chronic alcoholism. By then, he had published a fanciful autobiography, appropriately called *Alias Vince Taylor* (1976), and received a nice-size royalty cheque for The Clash's 1979 cover of 'Brand New Cadillac'. But a protracted spell in a Montreux rehab clinic in 1987 failed to chase those rhythmic blues away, and by now his health was fast deteriorating. He died in August 1991, ostensibly of cancer, but essentially just worn out from too much living in too short a time.

★

Coincidentally – or not – it was only after Taylor disappeared from people's radar that a certain David Bowie began to talk of him as the prototype for Ziggy Stardust. At the same time, Bowie began performing Ziggy's signature song in concert for the first time in twelve years. Twenty years after his breakthrough LP, *The Man Who Sold the World*, the ex-pat rock star was promoting his past again, as he announced his first 'golden oldies' tour on the back of a three-CD boxed-set retrospective called *Sound + Vision*, pending the reissue of all his RCA albums on Rykodisc/EMI. The set-list of the 1990 shows – partly compiled from the feedback of fans – confirmed what observers had long suspected: the years 1970–73 still held the strongest fascination for his worldwide audience. Nigh on half of each night's show would be devoted to songs he once performed through Ziggy's eyes.

It seemed there really was no escaping the shadow of Ziggy. Determined to debunk the notion that he had turned into an oldies act, Bowie told reporters that the tour would be his way of saying goodbye to the past, to 'do these songs for the last time – just do them on this tour and never do them again'. But a disastrous second Tin Machine tour, and an even worse-selling album the following year, put paid to any idea that a large live audience would pay to see his latest metallic manifestation. They wanted Ziggy.

As such, by 1997 Bowie was again reconciled to serving him up in bite-size pieces on his largest-scale tour in a decade. As a preview of sorts for another reclamation of the past, he even arranged a fiftieth birthday pay-per-view TV bash at Madison Square Gardens on 9 January, with a number of musical guests from the trendier parts of the big country invited, none save Lou Reed with any obvious connection to his own illustrious history. The set-list took the cream of a choice crop ('The Man Who Sold the World', 'Quicksand', 'Moonage Daydream', 'Queen Bitch', 'All the Young Dudes', 'Jean Genie'), but blended in with much that was of a recent vintage and which no amount of laying down could salvage.

The most unexpected guests were the mighty Sonic Youth, New York's finest, who were asked to back Bowie on a song from his latest release, 'I'm Afraid of Americans', even though they had all pretty much stopped listening to his records by the time the band was formed in 1980. If the reasoning behind their employment as backing band was lost on the four youthful members, they were even more nonplussed when during rehearsals Bowie called out, 'Schizophrenia'. It was a request – one of their cherished own, from their seminal *Sister* album – and an appropriate one, at that. The decade-old lyric had evidently struck a chord with the still-attentive Englishman:

> I went away to see an old friend of mine
> His sister came over, she was out of her mind
> She said Jesus had a twin, who knew nothing about sin,
> She was laughing like crazy at the trouble I'm in.

Slowly but surely Bowie was readying himself to slay some old ghosts. The day before his cable TV birthday bash, the BBC broadcast a nine-song studio session he had recorded during the Garden rehearsals, and six of the songs were from those golden years: 'The Man Who Sold the World', 'Supermen', 'Andy Warhol', 'Lady Stardust', 'White Light / White Heat', 'Quicksand' and 'Aladdin Sane'. He was playing mind games with his fans again, just as he had on his previous tour, in 1995, when a giant mobile hung over the stage, which read 'Ouvrez le chien', the repeated refrain at the end of 'All the Madmen' – though the song stayed wholly absent from the shows.

He may have been willing to belatedly acknowledge the importance of Ziggy and his crazed cousin Aladdin Sane, but he remained more ambivalent about those paeans to his real brother, Terry. Perhaps he was still recoiling from the family feud he had reignited back in 1993, when he released 'Jump They Say' as the first single from his first 'comeback' album of the 1990s, *Black Tie / White Noise*. The song, which by his own admission was 'semi-based on my impression of my stepbrother' [sic], was another case of him playing the 'mad brother' card. This time, though, Terry was no longer around to hear the result – he had killed himself in January 1985, throwing himself under a train after absconding from Cane Hill for the second time in a month with the clear intention of taking his own life. He was one year older than Vincent Crane.

Terry's aunt Pat, who had already painted an unsparing portrait of Bowie's treatment of his *half*-brother in the Gilmans' 1986 biography, was still around, however, and had evidently not mellowed with age. She was of the publicly expressed opinion that 'he is using [Terry's] tragic death to put his record in the charts and I find that not only macabre but pathetic. The picture of David [on the sleeve] upset me terribly. There is a real resemblance. David looks just like Terry did when he became schizophrenic.'

The controversy, splashed across the *Sun*, reopened wounds Bowie had done his level best to cover over, eight years earlier, when the Gilmans' own serialized articles was splashed across the *Sunday Times*. Appearing just three months after Terry's death, they described in detail the two brothers' growing estrangement. The Gilmans were duly informed that Bowie 'objected strenuously to the suggestion that there was any link between the content of his work and the traumas that have afflicted his family and, especially, his half-brother, Terry', before setting his record company on to the Gilmans, claiming copyright infringement for daring to quote song lyrics in context – always the last refuge of the artist exposed. But the Gilmans' book, published the following year, provided more compelling testimony of how Bowie had continued to pay lip-service to his guilt right up to the early Eighties, telling one reporter during the time he was acting in *Merry Christmas, Mr Lawrence*: 'I have a step-brother [sic] I don't see any more. It was my fault we grew apart . . . but somehow there's no going back.' It was a long way from Manhattan to Cane Hill, after all.

At the time of this interview Terry had recently been re-committed to Cane Hill, his condition having worsened after his own marriage breakdown, and he became prone to bouts of violence which merely brought heavier medication to dull the raging inside. Finally, in the summer of 1982, a near fatal cry for help brought Bowie to visit him in Mayday Hospital, where Terry lay recuperating from his first serious suicide attempt. Four weeks earlier he had thrown himself from a second-storey window (the ostensible inspiration for 1993's 'Jump They Say'). After this visit, Terry became convinced that his brother would finally orchestrate the means necessary to get him out of Cane Hill. He did not, and, in fact, from then on all contact ceased. Even Terry's next cry for help in December 1984 – when he test-ran throwing himself in front of a train, but pulled back at the last second – did not bring his brother running. It just brought him five more days in a locked ward and a further dose of deadening drugs.

At his wits' end, Terry finally ended it all three weeks later, this time seeing through his premeditated act. But even this did not prompt his brother to come and say one last goodbye. Bowie avoided the funeral. Instead, he sent a basket of flowers, with a strangely impersonal note that read: 'You've seen more things than we [sic] could imagine but all these moments will be lost, like tears washed away by the rain. God bless you – David.' Wisely, he said no more until that ill-advised 1993 track, though it is surely no coincidence that throughout the 1987 *Glass Spiders* tour he regularly included, for the first and last time, 'All the Madmen'.

*

Not that Bowie was the only London-born brother still at war with his elder sibling after years of internecine strife. Ray

Davies' relationship with his brother David had always been fraught, but the 1980s had been a particularly difficult decade as The Kinks made album after album that proved the good times really had gone. Ray's decision to disband The Kinks in 1995 (one he kept from his brother for quite some time) proved the last straw for the ever-supportive Dave, who had already begun to sketch out his own personal account of the band's history, *Kink*. Published in February 1996, *Kink* was a rollicking read that suggested Ray was not the only brother with 'issues'. According to its editor, the publisher had been obliged to heavily prune the finished text, removing a great deal of stuff about alien angels at David's side. But he couldn't stop the former Kink from telling interviewers of how, on the road in 1982, he 'began hearing these strange voices [in my head] . . . two of them said they had always been my spiritual guides and two others were entities that were not of this earth'.

If Ray, in his own autobiography *X-Ray*, published eighteen months earlier, had paid minimal lip-service to the vital role David had played in keeping The Kinks together in the years before angels came to his aid, at least he had learned to recognize the value of what he himself had wrought in the cultural inferno of the Sixties and early Seventies. (The 400-page 'unauthorized autobiography' ended in 1973.) For the first time, this most difficult of interviewees wrote in his own words about his mental problems, albeit using two distinct voices.

Creating another of his alter egos – a young novice social historian who is sent by dystopian powers-that-be to interview a retired rock star called R. D. – *X-Ray* is told partially in the first person, and partly through the eyes of this ingénue – proof, were it needed, that Ray still had yet to resolve the source of these inner monologues – Max or him. He also re-analysed his recorded work with a surprisingly judicious ear for what still stood up. Although he devoted just two pages to his 1971 cult classic – making no mention of the *Muswell Hillbillies* play he claimed in 1979 he had been working on – the fact that twelve of *X-Ray*'s twenty chapters took their titles from lines on the album spoke volumes.

And as if to reaffirm the continuing relevance of all those songs castigating urban renewal, the loss of traditions and the scrapping of all things old, he took his autobiography on the road – spending eighteen months in 1995–96 performing for the first time as Ray Davies – *The Storyteller* – not as frontman to The Kinks. The shows, which would invariably include '20th Century Man', 'Days', 'Victoria' and 'Village Green', drew almost exclusively from the 1967–71 heyday of the band, reminding enthralled attendees of the sheer quantity of great songs the man had penned in that half-a-decade of inspiration, attendant upon the realization, 'I'm Not Like Everybody Else'.

By the time *The Storyteller* shows ran their course, brother David had realized the prospects of The Kinks continuing as a viable outfit were slim to negligible. He therefore decided he, too, would take his own version of The Kinks' recorded history on the road. And so, in 1997, Dave Davies, bolstered by a band from the nearest garage, gave a version of The Kinks' kanon that also included 'I'm Not Like Everybody Else', but precious little from post-1968. It was a battle royal for the right to define where the real Kinks legacy lay. And it was one David was bound to lose.

The whole issue of who got to define a band's legacy as an ongoing, viable touring entity had just been fought out over the far more lucrative battleground that was Pink Floyd, culminating in a 1994 world tour by the Waters-less Floyd that broke a number of records for tour grosses (which only served to piss off Waters a little bit more). The tour provided the English Rock Album of the early Seventies with a new kind of validation. Hundreds of thousands of young fans scrambled for tickets when it was announced that a band calling itself Pink Floyd (minus its main songwriter/s) would be performing *Dark Side of the Moon* in its entirety. A European tour, including a record-breaking fifteen nights at the still-soulless Earls Court arena, resulted in the inevitable CD/DVD, *Pulse*.

Although Roger Waters had not been in Pink Floyd for thirteen years now – and had even initially pursued an expensive legal case to stop the others using the group's name, proof positive he really thought it was 'his band' – this was the second world tour the residue trio had successfully undertaken. And this time they were determined to celebrate every aspect of the band's history, from the preferred nightly opener, Barrett's 'Astronomy Domine', to the latest song that concerned itself with 'the state of Syd', Dave Gilmour's 'Poles Apart' ('I thought of you and the years . . . I never thought that you'd lose that light in your eyes').

Gone but not forgotten – at least not by the ever-generous Gilmour – Barrett's recorded solo legacy had in the interim been given its own boxed-set validation. In 1993 EMI issued a three-CD set that expanded the two solo albums and 1988's welcome archival trawl, *Opel*, with alternative takes and bonus cuts. And if that remembrance of things past didn't fully reaffirm his fleeting genius, there was also a thirtieth anniversary edition of the Floyd's still-astonishing debut long-player, the timeless *Piper at the Gates of Dawn*, in its correct mono form, complete with a 'bonus disc' of all three official singles – 'Arnold Layne', 'See Emily Play' and 'Apples and Oranges' – from the Syd era. It was a much-needed reminder that the world was still catching up with Syd's space-age imagination.

Syd himself, though, was now long lost in the woods, and when the band was inducted into the Rock & Roll Hall of Fame on 17 January 1996 – along with David Bowie and The Velvet Underground (the latter having been turned down in 1992 so that Sam and Dave, I kid thee not, could be inducted) – he was as absent from the occasion as the band's latterday frontman, Roger Waters. Thus did Barrett, Bowie and Reed join the likes of The Beatles, The Rolling Stones and The Kinks in this shrine to the notion that *Rolling Stone* could define this thing called Rock 3,000 miles away from its epicentre.

Already successfully inducted were The Who, who in 1996 returned to the stage themselves, just not at the Waldorf Astoria at a thousand bucks a head. Instead, they prepared to perform the album that through most of the 1970s had been viewed as their albatross – *Quadrophenia* – determined to prove how much it had grown in stature in the intervening years. And no longer was Townshend an apologist for it. He was now its proud father. After debuting it to a huge London crowd at a Prince's Trust concert in Hyde Park in June, he finally took the album to New York – the one obvious pit-stop they bypassed on the original 1973 tour – for five triumphant nights at Madison Square Gardens. Townshend himself had no doubts as to why the fans came out:

Pete Townshend: One of the reasons I wanted to do this . . . [was] to draw attention to this great, great record, probably the best record that The Who made. Really, I think it's almost perfect. I could write more material, I could edit it, but what we've actually done is tried to be very faithful to what is there . . . I've written a script around the album and that's what people will see. [1996]

He had indeed worked on the presentation, making for a tightly scripted performance of the entire double-album with brief narration at appropriate junctures, and with special guests playing some of the key roles (and hitting some of the notes Daltrey could no longer scale), including a surprisingly convincing Gary Glitter, pre-disgrace, as the Godfather, and Billy Idol as Ace Face. Finally, Townshend had successfully reclaimed the album from Franc Roddam's 1979 film, which made some bogus love story out of Jimmy/Pete's existential angst, and which even an enthused Pete admitted at the time 'doesn't have much to do with the musical journey I mapped out'. Such was the demand for this slice of Seventies nostalgia that the reconstituted Who proceeded to tour the album around the States for five weeks in the fall of 1996, and around Europe in the spring of 1997, culminating in a final show at Wembley Arena at the end of May.[40] Throughout it all, the work continued to stand proud.

*

It seemed at times like almost any album from this rich period was now ripe for re-evaluation, as this most populist of centuries wound down to a musically 'retro' conclusion. There was even a place to be for Nick Drake, the songwriter who, back in 1968, had sung of how 'men of fame can never find a way / 'Till time has flown far from their dying day'.

For the longest time it had seemed like Drake – of all those English artists who shattered their psyches in the cause of pop-as-art back then – was destined to remain known only to the *cognoscenti*, while his searing sensibility had been seen as a near insurmountable obstacle to widespread recognition Stateside. As far back as 1978 Neil Powell had pointed out, in the incongruous setting of *The London Magazine*, the fact that Drake 'delineates more tellingly than any other contemporary songwriter the hinterland between despair and fragile happiness which is the territory of a peculiarly English melancholia'. (John Martyn always felt that 'the thing that set him apart . . . [was] his implicit, innate Britishness'.) Even a tragically early death, usually the smartest of all career moves, had failed to produce more than a slowburn of cultish interest in keeping with the deeply personal, introspective nature of his music. The expanded, four-disc edition of the boxed-set *Fruit Tree* (1986) seemed like the final word, even as the demand for more – scratch that, any – information was imperceptibly achieving critical mass.

Then in 1994, a sixteen-track introduction specifically for the CD age, *Way to Blue*, compiled and sequenced by Joe Boyd, proved that the cult was in full swing critically, if not commercially. It prompted both a two-page overview in *Q* by Stuart Maconie – who at the end of his article pulled to pieces those who 'make romantic noises about his being "not of this world" . . . while ignoring the fact that he was mentally ill' – and a ruminative think-piece in the *Independent* by Ben Thompson.

Lucinda Williams had already made 'Which Will' (penned by Nick Drake), a cathartic coda to her magnificent 1992 album, *Sweet Old World*, when Mark Eitzel gamely attempted to get inside his fellow songwriter's head, writing a brief verbal riff about 'Pink Moon' for *NME*. Eitzel, the main songwriter in those critical darlings American Music Club, considered 'Pink Moon' quite an 'inarticulate song, which is where it gets its power . . . Even though you don't know what the catastrophe is, you know there is no pretence to him [Drake]. The only hook is the descending chorus [when] you get the feeling that you're descending with him.' So, no romantic noise emanating from this direction, even as the album and title track almost imperceptibly continued to make its disturbed presence felt across that lonesome ocean. A year later, an alt-grunge rendition of 'Pink Moon' by Sebadoh, on their album, *Sebadoh Vs Helmet*, proved beyond a shadow of doubt that Drake's songs could survive even the most head-banging of arrangements.

Finally, in February 1997, the diffident Drake graced his first major magazine cover, as *Mojo* ran a lengthy profile by respected pop journalist Patrick Humphries – hard at work on his long-threatened biography of the songwriter. And despite all the usual obstacles that a first biographer of an obscure dead artist must surmount, Humphries' 280-page study, published at year's end, finally filled in a fair few blanks. Three years later, *Mojo* gave Ian MacDonald thirteen more of its internationally distributed pages for a think-piece on Drake that attacked 'the aura of romantic doom which accompanies [his work] like some unwanted orchestra dubbed on by sentimental hindsight'. MacDonald even decided to challenge the view that Drake was cripplingly depressed by the time he recorded his 1972 album:

> *Pink Moon* is spoken of as bleak, skeletal, nihilistic, ghoulish, a suicidal plea for help. This grim view is unfair, the crowning misconception created by viewing Nick Drake as a troubadour of tragedy . . . This uncanny, magical record, far from bleak and ghoulish, is a stark, sparingly beautiful meditation on redemption through spiritual trial. *Pink Moon* isn't about death, but about resurrection.

This eloquent case for the defence was clearly written from the heart, being a view that the chronically depressed MacDonald was himself desperate to believe. Indeed, shortly before taking his own life in 2003, he would place the unedited version of this article as the final, telling piece in an anthology of his collected writings, *The People's Music*. It certainly opened up the debate on what drove Drake, as well as how much drugs had played a part in both his music-making and decline into silence. But even MacDonald's angle on this touchy subject smacked of the unregenerate hippy idealist: 'Drake's interest in drugs is well documented but less well understood. Nowadays associated with pure pleasure, drugs meant something different in the Sixties, being often linked with the . . . quest for "enlightenment" . . . His drug use . . . involve[d] a fascination with perception and reality.'

What MacDonald refused to acknowledge was that this 'aura of romantic doom' was commented on by every reviewer who wrote of Drake's work in his short lifetime. Indeed, according to John Martyn – and he should know – it was something Drake himself assiduously cultivated. Shortly after his friend's death, Martyn depicted Drake as someone who 'was quite conscious of the image portrayed in his songs. He was not [just some] manic depressive who picked up a guitar; he was a singer-songwriter in every sense.' Brian Wells, not only an intermittently persistent presence throughout Drake's decline into despair but an eminent addiction counsellor in his own right, also came to the view that, although 'the most obvious diagnosis to make . . . was one of depression, it was more of an existential state that he'd gotten himself into, rather than . . . the kind of depressive illness that medical students learn about'.

By 2000, though, there were forces at work determined to shape the narrative of Drake's short life and intricately woven canon in a more benign, less contradictory direction. Gabrielle Drake, Nick's surviving sibling and executor, had refused to help Humphries fill in the gaps as only she could, concerned that she would not be allowed the final say on any portrait poor Patrick might produce. At the same time, she began assuming a pro-active role in her brother's legacy. In that year she finally approved the use of one of Nick's songs in a TV ad, albeit for a car he wouldn't have been caught dead in.

As a result, at the end of November 2000, America was blasted with repeat broadcasts of the title track of his third album, *Pink Moon*, on prime-time TV, the soundtrack to a one-minute advertisement for the Volkswagen Cabrio convertible. People who then watched the ad on the VW website were invited to click on one of two buttons: to learn about the car, or purchase the music. As a result, annual US sales of Drake's most resolutely downbeat album jumped from 6,000 to 74,000, and America at large was finally introduced en masse to this most English of singer-songwriters. Here was 'Pink Moon', on the face of it the least accessible of introductions, setting off any number of inner fires.

Nick Drake – who, in his lifetime, had lived continually in the shadow of Island contemporaries such as Thompson, Denny and Martyn – had by the simple act of biding his time beneath the fruit tree, now superseded them all as a cultural reference point. Denny's own premature death in 1978, killed by her mother's sense of propriety (I refer interested parties to my Sandy biography, *No More Sad Refrains*, for the full story), had generated no such groundswell of misty romanticism. Martyn had just made ever more mediocre demonstration discs for his beloved Echoplex effect pedal. Even Thompson, whose Seventies canon remains a full fathoms five deeper, and who slowly built his own American audience by annual touring from 1982 on, had produced a body of work just too damn eclectic and erratic to reach this constituency.

Drake's three-album career, on the other hand, seemed to provide a remarkably straight trajectory. The moonstruck car manufacturer even went as far as to claim, in their initial press release, that the track 'Pink Moon' 'is actually a very good introduction to Nick Drake, if you're not familiar with him'. In truth, it was only ever a good introduction to *Pink Moon*, the album. Those who plumped instead for Boyd's 1994 anthology, still on catalogue, would have found the same sensibility elsewhere, but hardly in the same undiluted, unadorned form.

There was now a demand for Drake's work that could only be fuelled by a new product – which, in this case, meant doing away with some old product. *Time of No Reply*, the well-conceived single LP of outtakes and lost songs, which ended with the four recordings from 1974, was quietly deleted. In its place came a new 2004 compilation, *Made to Love Magic*. This time the 1974 tracks – bolstered by the addition of the 'unheard' demo version of 'Tow the Line'[41] – were scattered across a set that forsook the intimacy of those home versions of 'Fly', 'Strange Meeting II' and 'Been Smoking Too Long' for newly orchestrated versions of 'Time of No Reply' and 'Magic'.

If the latter would always be mere juvenilia, whether it was Richard Hewson or Robert Kirby scoring the strings, the former needed no (such) embellishment. Indeed, alongside the unreleased, unstrung 'River Man', it only proved what attentive listeners had long suspected – the strings on *Five Leaves Left* and *Bryter Layter* were a mistake Drake rectified on *Pink Moon*. *Way to Blue* was meanwhile superseded by another inferior anthology, *A Treasury*, an estate-approved compilation that lacked the skilful sequencing seasoned producer Boyd had brought to the earlier set. Stuck on the end of this otherwise ill-conceived CD was all forty-six seconds of 'Plaisir D'Amour', wholly decontextualized.

The rewriting of history continued through 2007, when the *Fruit Tree* box was reissued in an inferior, remastered form, minus *Time of No Reply*. A DVD version of the fifty-minute 2002

Dutch TV documentary, *A Skin Too Few* – a skilled exercise in selective storytelling made with Gabrielle Drake's approval – took its place. In tandem with this reconfiguration of the canon came another Drake archival release, *Family Tree*, a selective cherry-pick of the oft-bootlegged home demos put together under Gabrielle's eagle eye, bookended with a couple of tracks by Nick's mother, Molly, designed to illustrate the similarity in their vocal style, but largely demonstrating that his accomplished mother lacked her son's divine spark.

Try as she might, Drake's sister still could not control the now-public discourse on Nick's worth as a songwriter, the deep-rooted causes of his depression and the role drugs might have played in his downward spiral and (possible) eventual suicide. Even before 2007's concerted exercise in rebranding, another biographer, Trevor Dann, had thrown his hat into the ring. And though his *Darker Than the Deepest Sea* (2006) would inevitably tread much the same ground as Humphries' study, Dann seemed less inclined to tow the party line, and more willing to mention the elephant in this well-to-do living room:

> Still smoking what his friend and collaborator Robert Kirby describes as 'unbelievable amounts of cannabis', [by 1971 Drake] was beginning to exhibit the first signs of psychosis . . . Not until many years later did scientists begin to prove a link between cannabis and schizophrenia, [but] schizophrenia doesn't only mean split personality. Among its other symptoms are lack of emotion . . . low energy . . . lack of interest in life . . . affective flattening (a blank, blunted facial expression) . . . alogia (difficulty in speaking or inability to speak); lack of interest or ability to socialise with other people . . . By 1972 he was exhibiting all the signs . . . Nick's behaviour over a long period is highly suggestive of a cannabis-fuelled psychosis, a

mild schizophrenia, which a combination of prescribed and illicit drugs did nothing to cure and most probably worsened.

The very fact that Drake expressed so consistently and cogently that 'peculiarly English melancholia' convinced Ian MacDonald and others – but not Dann or I – that he was merely exercising an artistic conceit in his songs. In truth, a predisposition to melancholia was one thing Drake shared with a number of other, equally talented English contemporaries. But so was his penchant for imbibing the kind of psychotropic drugs that might act as a creative trigger, even if – like any trigger – it might end up blowing one's brains out. It was a fateful combination. Unfortunately for him, and those others, once the doors of perception were opened by that mighty wind blowing, it took the strength of generational experience to close them again.

*

It proved a difficult lesson for some to learn. Many a badly singed survivor became an apostate from acid, but only in the fullness of time. It took until the 1980s for the teachings of Laing and Leary to really be discredited in countercultural eyes. In Allen Ginsberg's case, it took him some three decades to fully acknowledge the truth in Edith Sitwell's observation, made directly to him at her Oxford lodgings in 1958: 'No poet should need a drug to produce extreme sensibility, which must be, if he is any good, a part of his equipment.' But even this fierce advocate of LSD's potential beneficence duly admitted to Steve Silberman in 1987: 'I've changed my mind about the relationship between acid and neurosis – it seems to me that acid *can* lead to some kind of breakdowns . . . I think in the Sixties I wasn't prepared to deal with acid casualties from the point of view of a reliable technique for avoiding those casualties.'

Ginsberg was lucky, in one sense anyway. His was a surprisingly unintrusive kind of fame (as anyone who ever walked down a New York street with the man can confirm) – for his was the benign face of free-thinking – even if his fraught relationship with an increasingly disturbed Peter Orlovsky, troubled family relations and prodigious drug-taking suggested someone who never overcame the traumas he suffered as a child. For others, fame itself became the drug and the disease. And such a fate was not reserved solely for rock stars.

By 1968, 'anti-psychiatrist' R. D. Laing was one such troubled soul, perhaps because he already lamented what the generally sympathetic Daniel Burston called 'the decline in creative power that seemed to follow on his increasing infatuation with fame'. No matter how much Laing changed the angle of attack, he was forever fixed in mass-media eyes as this psychedelically charged, highly politicized psychiatrist who refused to call anyone plain mad. In fact, much like Ginsberg – and undoubtedly influenced by the man he shared a rostrum with at the Dialectics of Liberation – Laing consciously attempted to remove himself from the limelight, travelling to India in 1970 to spend eighteen months studying Buddhist meditation and Shiviite yoga. When he returned, he was a changed man, proclaiming that 'a kind of gentle, Buddhist austerity [was] the best path to liberation'.

But by that time Laing's cherished Philadelphia Association, the umbrella organization he hoped would set up Kingsley Hall-type establishments around the world, had been hijacked by people who had little time for his endlessly shifting theories. Burston has described how Laing returned to find that 'many former colleagues [had] left the organization, like David Cooper, Aaron Esterson, Morton Schatzman and Joseph Berke, ha[ving] published books and acquired followings of their own. Moreover, many old allies on the left who were wounded or puzzled by his retreat to Asian mysticism now turned on him. [While] in the mental health field . . . [the likes of] Peter Sedgwick, Joel Kovel, Giles Deleuze and Felix Guattari vigorously denounced him.'

By the late 1970s Laing was largely an irrelevance in psychiatric circles, while remaining fixed in the wider public's eyes to ideas he never really held (or at least not in the simplified terms that were increasingly assigned to him). As Burston, Laing's most vociferous modern advocate, has written: 'Mention Laing nowadays and most people can dimly conjure up a flamboyant rebel of the psychedelic era, a chum of Tim Leary, Ram Dass, and Allen Ginsberg . . . But press them to describe what he stood for, what he actually thought or said, and you'll only elicit a trickle of platitudinous sound bites.'

Being misunderstood was something else that was hardly the sole preserve of pop stars. For Laing, as for those whose world he ineluctably shaped, the 1980s proved to be hard work. Those cherished Buddhist beliefs seemed to have gone the way of some of his earlier, more controversial theories. In September 1984 he was arrested after throwing a bottle through the window of a Buddhist centre in London, and when searched was found with cannabis on him, the possession of which he was obliged to plead guilty to. The following year, in a radio interview with Anthony Clare, he admitted to bouts of severe depression and 'occasional' abuse of alcohol. In fact, he was now an alcoholic in all but name.

Finally, in May 1987, as accusations of appearing drunk before patients hovered in the wings, he reluctantly agreed to let the General Medical Council remove his licence to practise medicine, in order to avoid what would have been a very public defrocking. He had published a self-justifying autobiography the previous year, appositely called *Wisdom, Madness & Folly*, in which he baldly asserts: 'I have never idealized mental suffering, or romanticized despair, dissolution, torture or terror. I have never said that parents or families or society "cause" mental illness.' Even as he grew increasingly selective about the parts of his very public past he would own up to, he gradually allowed the booze to take hold, and his mind to fritter itself away on labyrinthine schemes destined to come to naught. He died in 1989 – at the same age (sixty-one) as his most famous non-client, Syd Barrett.

Whether the death of Laing registered with the reclusive Roger K. Barrett is never likely to be known. But his death completed some kind of circle, even as Barrett remained the one that got away. Drake was dead. Green's sporadic re-emergences merely proved that he no longer had fire in his fingertips[42]. But while Barrett's old friends from the Floyd had long ago removed themselves from Syd's closed circle, he simply refused to articulate who he was, or whom he had been, only furthering an abiding sense of mystery. If Peter Green could still maintain a hands-length relationship with those who had witnessed him at the height of his acidic madness, Barrett couldn't even manage that. And there was a reason. As his nephew Ian Barrett wrote in a 1996 internet posting, hoping to dissuade his uncle's acolytes from confronting the poor man: 'Without going into details, I [really] don't think people are prepared to understand the true extent of Roger's breakdown, or the pressures he was put under.'

Whatever the cause of the man's debilitating depression, that 5 June 1975 studio sighting proved to be the madcap's last, anywhere other than his own doorstep. From then until his death in 2006 of pancreatic cancer, Roger Barrett remained Syd's silent spokesman. If he ever wondered what really happened to that former self, he never said. Instead, in later days he scribbled notes in his copy of *The Oxford Textbook of Psychiatry* and drew up a shortlist of other psychology books he maybe should get around to reading, including Charles Rycroft's *The Innocence of Dreams* and Jonathan Glover's anthology, *The Philosophy of Mind*. What was altogether absent was the slightest reference to the works of R. D. Laing. Those he had cut up a long time ago.

NOTES

[1] – Dave Gilmour joined Pink Floyd in January 1968, and for five gigs they were a five-piece. A photo does exist of this line-up, before Barrett was ousted by the others.

[2] – Fellow writers such as Ernest Hemingway and Archibald MacLeish rushed to validate the court's decision, to save the poet from a long jail term or even execution. Hemingway memorably concluded: 'He ought to go to the loony bin, which he rates and you can pick out the parts in his *Cantos* at which he starts to rate it', while MacLeish pithily agreed 'that poor old Ezra is quite, quite barmy'. Pound, as a result, spent the next twelve years at St Elizabeth Federal Hospital for the Insane in Washington.

[3] – 'Thin Men' is a reference to Dylan's 'Ballad of a Thin Man', which divides the world into ultra-straight Mr Joneses and outlaws.

[4] – Neither song was ever attempted at the sessions for Syd Barrett's solo album(s); although 'Vegetable Man' was listed as a possible track for the initial 1968 sessions, this was only after Pink Floyd had decided against using the track themselves.

[5] – *Flat Baroque* should, of course, be pronounced 'flat broke', a little joke by Harper at his home town Manchester's expense. Locals pronounce 'broke' with such a heavy emphasis on the 'r' that it really does sound like 'baroque'.

[6] – ' The Laughing Gnome' was reissued as a single in September 1973, at the height of Ziggy mania, and astonishingly, peaked at number six in the charts.

[7] – The inner-sleeve to the 2003 *Tommy* 'Deluxe' CD reissue includes an early, handwritten tracklisting for the album, which runs as follows: 'It's a Boy', 'Amazing Journey', 'Pinball Wizard', 'How Can He Be Saved?', 'Eyesight to the Blind', 'The Acid Queen', 'Dream Sequence Short', 'D'ya Think it's Alright?', 'Fiddle About', 'Model Child', 'Cousin Song', 'Dream Sequence Long', 'Young Man Blues', 'Doctor Song', 'Tommy Can You Hear Me?', 'Smash the Mirror', 'Sensation', 'Sally Simpson', 'I'm Free', 'Tommy's Holiday Camp', 'Welcome', 'We're Not Gonna Take It'.

[8] – The unreleased 2001 Bowie album *Toy* has recently emerged in its fourteen-track entirety, and includes 21st-century re-recordings of a number of important 'lost' songs from the 1968–70 period, i.e. 'Conversation Piece', 'Let Me Sleep Beside You', 'In the Heat of the

Morning' and 'Shadow Man'. The first and last of these appear as bonus tracks on the two-CD reissue of *Heathen*.

[9] – The sad story of Jackson Frank has now been told a number of times, most recently in *Mojo* #186. The sleevenotes to the 2003 Sanctuary edition of Frank's recorded works, demos *et al.*, *Blues Run the Game*, also provide a good deal of background.

[10] – Trevor Dann dates the meeting of Hutchings and Drake to a show at the Roundhouse on 20 December, though he does not explain his reasoning (he just asserts it) – in fact, Fairport did not play on that night, nor is Drake billed on any night of that festival. The Brunel 'benefit' was on 20 January, which makes a lot more sense in terms of the timescale between Hutchings collecting his details and Drake's first meeting with Boyd in the spring.

[11] – The five songs Drake performed at that concert were as follows: 'Time of No Reply', 'I Was Made to Love Magic', 'The Thoughts of Mary Jane', 'Day is Done', 'My Love Left With the Rain'.

[12] – Clifford Davis, Fleetwood Mac's manager, recorded his own single in mid-July 1969, comprising two Peter Green songs, 'Before the Beginning' and 'Man of the World', both of which Green plays on. The single was released on Reprise in October, to general disinterest.

[13] – Bown told *Mojo* that on one occasion he not only had to take Barrett to the toilet, but had also had to unzip the man's fly. I find it hard to believe that anyone that catatonic could have been making music.

[14] – According to Barrett's most reliable biographer, he and Fields moved into the flat they shared towards the end of 1969.

[15] – The tracklisting for this session, a tape of which has recently emerged and been purchased by the Drake estate, confirms that there were, in fact, five songs, not the previously reported four.

[16] – Ralph McTell says he recalls a show at Ewell Technical College, Surrey, in June 1970, during which Drake walked off halfway through 'Fruit Tree', never to return.

[17] – Drake's use of the expression 'blow your horn on high' shows that he had immersed himself in some arcane aspects of folk song, perhaps from the English-literature angle. The line appears in 'The Elfin Knight', a medieval Child Ballad as an incantation from the lovelorn lass, summoning the outlandish knight of her romantic imagination.

[18] – The release dates of the UK and US versions of *The Man Who Sold the World* were approximately three months apart. The reproduction of the 'American sleeve' in a January 1970 *Disc* interview rather suggests that at this juncture it was still the intended UK sleeve.

[19] – The 45 version of 'Strange Kind of Woman' clocks in at four minutes. Live versions in the band's 1971–72 heyday sometimes almost hit the quarter-of-an-hour mark.

[20] – The live performances of *Tommy* were significantly shorter than the album, usually averaging between fifty and fifty-five minutes. All three of the officially available versions, all 1970 shows at Leeds, Hull and the Isle of Wight, are around fifty-four minutes.

[21] – If the *Lifehouse Chronicles* boxed-set can be taken at face value, the following latterday The Who songs all began life as vestiges of the project: 'Put the Money Down', 'Relay', 'Join Together', 'Slip Kid', 'Who Are You?', 'Music Must Change'.

[22] – According to legend, Richard Thompson's masterful *Henry the Human Fly* still remains the worst-selling album of all time for Warners in the US, which the scarcity of 'stock' copies (as opposed to promos) rather seems to confirm. At least one copy was sold in Cleveland, though, because as early as 1973, Pere Ubu co-founder Peter Laughner was performing 'The Angels Took My Racehorse Away'.

[23] – The line Bowie is referencing in 'Oh! You Pretty Things' is as follows: 'I look out my window and what do I see? / A crack in the sky and a hand reaching down to me'. His visual reference-point was more likely William Blake, not Carl Jung.

[24] – 'Ride' and 'Free Ride' appear to be interchangeable titles. The former is used on *Pink Moon* itself, but on the 1986 *Fruit Tree* set it is listed as 'Free Ride'.

[25] – The 'attempted suicide' is first mentioned in Trevor Dann's biography, though he dates it to 1973. However, other sources date it to the period immediately after *Pink Moon*'s release.

[26] – The first night of the tour was the Brighton Dome (20 January), the night before Portsmouth, but the performance of *Eclipse* was famously abandoned that night during 'Money', when the backing-tapes broke down. Therefore, the first live performance of 'Brain Damage' was at the Guildhall. A bootleg CD of both Brighton and Portsmouth performances of *Eclipse*, called *Eclipse of the Dark Side*, is drawn from first-generation copies of the audience tapes of both shows made by the same taper.

[27] – The line is later changed from 'out of tune' to 'different tune'.

[28] – According to Mark Blake, in *Comfortably Numb: The Inside Story of Pink Floyd* (2008), 'Barrett contained his anger until he was back at Hills Road . . . [but] once down there, he began smashing his head repeatedly against the ceiling.' He cites no source, but given its clear similarity to an incident cited in Nick Kent's 1974 article, dated to later in 1972 and unconnected to the Starz show, he may have just transposed the story for 'maximum effect'.

[29] – A commemorative CD EP in Syd Barrett's memory by Dave Gilmour, issued shortly after Syd's death in 2006, features a live version of

'Arnold Layne' sung by Bowie, from Gilmour's May 2006 Royal Albert Hall residency.

[30] – Enoch Powell's infamous 'rivers of blood' speech in April 1968 led many to think he saw himself as a right-wing leader, though he was nothing of the sort. Bowie was evidently guilty of just such a misunderstanding.

[31] – A live version of 'Tired of Waiting for You' appears on the 1998 remaster of *Everybody's in Showbiz*, though it is not listed in Doug Hinman's generally reliable tracklisting for these shows.

[32] – The set-list for the Drury Lane concert, discounting the half-a-dozen obvious crowd-pleasers with which Davies opened the show, was as follows: 'Have a Cuppa Tea', 'Acute Schizophrenia Paranoia Blues', 'Cricket', 'Mr Wonderful', 'Alcohol', 'Village Green' (instr.), 'Where Are They Now?', 'You Really Got Me'/'All Day and All of the Night', 'Picture Book', 'People Take Pictures of Each Other', 'Time Song', 'Salvation Road', 'Village Green Preservation Society', 'Celluloid Heroes', 'Here Comes Yet Another Day'.

[33] – Neil Young attended one of The Who's Manchester 1973 shows, and there is video footage of him sitting with the band backstage.

[34] – The 1975–76 shows would only reinforce this sense of nostalgia, with the band generally performing just two songs from their latest LP, *The Who by Numbers*, and never more than three. This marks quite a change from the shows from 1969 through 1973, which concentrated heavily on 'new' material.

[35] – The information about the February and July 1974 sessions given on the 1986 *Time of No Reply* CD and the 2004 *Made to Love Magic* CD remain contradictory. According to the former, all four 1974 songs were recorded in February. The latter attributes only 'Black Eyed Dog' to February, and the other four tracks to the July sessions, plural. The circulating backing-tracks for 'Black Eyed Dog', 'Tow the Line', 'Hanging on a Star' and 'Rider on a Wheel' rather suggests that only guitar-tracks, probably of just the first two songs, were cut in February, although the 'Black Eyed Dog' vocal may well date from July, when Boyd was back at the helm.

[36] – According to David Parker's inestimable *Random Precision*, a tape compilation made on 13 August 1974 had the following tracks: 'Milky Way', 'Wouldn't You Miss Me?', 'Silas Lang' (2 mixes), 'Opel', 'Word Song', 'Birdy Hop', 'Scream Thy Last Scream', 'Vegetable Man'. Here are all the key tracks that will eventually appear on 1988's *Opel* plus the two fabled Floyd rarities; but at just eight tracks, it clearly needs at least two or three 'new' tracks more to make up an album – hence presumably the scrapping of the project after the 1974 sessions proved a bust.

[37] – A Polaroid snap of Barrett at the June 1975 EMI session included on page 211 of Nick Mason's Inside Out confirms the various descriptions of his outlandish appearance to be wholly accurate.'

[38] – The Sigma Sound versions of 'Can Your Hear Me?', 'It's Gonna Be Me' and 'John, I'm Only Dancing' are all available on the 2007 remaster of *Young Americans*, as well as the 1991 Rykodisc CD (though they're absent from the 1999 EMI remaster!).

[39] – The original *Shoot Out the Lights* comprised ten tracks – six of which were re-recorded for the Hannibal version released in 1982. The other four cuts were 'The Wrong Heartbeat', 'For Shame of Doing Wrong', 'I'm a Dreamer' and 'Modern Woman', the first three of which feature Linda on lead vocals. The album has been widely bootlegged.

[40] – A DVD of one of the Wembley concerts is commercially available, and shows how carefully Townshend explicated the original storyline at the 1996 shows.

[41] – He's at it again. In a recent internet posting our friend Cally was claiming, 'Nick's notes show that [the 1974 material] was side one of his next album. He had ticked five songs off and there was another side of songs that weren't ticked.' I don't believe you.

[42] – Since 1996, there has been a plethora of new Peter Green releases, most with Splinter Group, but there has been a dispiriting absence of new, original songs. Blues covers, instead, are the order of the day.

APPENDIX: 'A FAST REWIND THROUGH 400 YEARS OF THE ENGLISH MALADY'

> It is worth attention that the English have more songs and ballads on the subject of madness than any of their neighbours. Whether it is that we are more liable to this calamity than other nations, or whether our native gloominess hath peculiarly recommended subjects of this cast to our writers, the fact is incontestable.
>
> – Bishop Percy, *Reliques of Ancient English Poetry* (1765)

This book seeks to provide a context – aesthetic and narrative – for a remarkable series of albums, and for something of a golden age in English rock. As such, I feel compelled to demonstrate that the 'sudden' fascination for insanity from the English rock fraternity was nothing of the sort. Although the new minstrels of the Swinging Sixties remained largely unaware of the venerable tradition they were perpetuating, this very English obsession with the oddball point of view ran deep through English society's seams – and its songs. Hence, Bishop Percy's famous observation (above), offered in the most important song collection of the eighteenth century.

Percy's *Reliques of Ancient English Poetry* (1765) sought to cover every element of song made popular over a quarter of a millennia, and he evidently thought he should provide a fair cross-sample of 'songs and ballads on the subject of madness'. In fact, Percy published a mere six-song sample from England's plentiful canon of craziness, even omitting the oldest and finest example of the form, the Jacobethan 'Tom o' Bedlam', a.k.a. 'From the Hagg and Hungry Goblin', as well as the superior broadside, 'Through Moorfields and to Bedlam I went' ('Your cruel base actions cause me to complain / for the loss of my dear has distracted my brain').

Back in Jacobethan times, there were no 'shrinks', just physicians; hence why, for Shakespeare's English audiences, his portrayal of mortal guilt driving someone mad in *Macbeth* would have seemed entirely plausible; *Hamlet*'s Ophelia succumbing to the madness of love was almost a cliché. The Jacobethans' world picture still held on to the idea that man had his humours, of which melancholy was the commonest (the most comprehensive anthology of English songs from this period was itself called *Pills to Purge Melancholy*).

In such a world do we find Tom o' Bedlam, the central figure in an English song-tradition dating back four centuries. That tradition is all the more remarkable because, even in the early seventeenth century, 'Mad Tom' songs were invariably written and sung in the first person, as if 'fashioned out of [his] own brain'. That original 'Mad Tom' song, 'Tom o' Bedlam' – already in wide circulation when first put down in Giks Earle's 1615 commonplace book – presents a fascinating insight into the olde English view of the madman. Using the first person, Loving Mad Tom casts himself as a poet who displays knowledge and powers well beyond the man of Reason:

> I know more than Apollo,
> For oft, when he lies sleeping
> I see the stars at bloody wars
> In the wounded welkin weeping.

Such was the appeal of 'Loving Mad Tom' in the Jacobethan age that any number of literary figures felt inspired to make themselves Mad Tom for a day, crafting literary *rifacimentos* based around his lore. Leaving aside Robert Graves' unproven attribution of 'Tom o' Bedlam' to Shakespeare (the article in question appears in *The Common Asphodel*), one or more other variants were also attributed to Francis Thompson and William Basse, while Bishop Corbet ('The Distracted Puritan', 1634) and Sir Francis Wortley ('Mad Tom a Bedlam's desire of peace', 1648) wrote satirical songs about Puritans and Parliamentarians respectively from the vantage point of 'Tom o' Bedlam', as the madman witnessing a world turned upside down. The tradition was so strong that it prompted comment as late as 1824, with Isaac D'Israeli, father of Benjamin, including the following anecdote in his enduringly popular *Curiosities of Literature*:

> An itinerant lunatic, chanting wild ditties, fancifully attired, gay with the simplicity of childhood, yet often moaning with the sorrows of a troubled man, a mixture of character at once grotesque and plaintive, became an interesting object to poetical minds . . . Poems composed in the character of a Tom o' Bedlam appear to have formed a fashionable class of poetry among the wits; they seem to have held together their poetical contests, and some of these writers became celebrated for their successful efforts.

Of all the doleful ditties on ditzy dames and the cunningly crazed beggar, it was the songs of Tom o' Bedlam and his equally cracked paramour, Mad Maudlin, that throughout the seventeenth and eighteenth centuries were most prone to collection and imitation. In an age when the third-person narrative ballad dominated the broadside charts, these 'Tom and Maud' songs stand apart, both in their general excellence and the blustering way that Tom boasts of his powers. Whether he is 'play[ing] at bowls with the sun and moon / And win[ning] them in the eclipses', or 'pluck[ing] the rainbow from the skies / And splic[ing] both ends together', as he is in 'Mad Tom' – or claiming, 'I'll bark against the Dog-star / And crow away the Morning; / I'll chase the Moon, 'till it be Noon / And I'll make her leave her Horning', as he does in 'Loving Mad Tom' – he always presents himself as the archetypal Holy Fool, the seer-madman writ large.

And in these bragging ballads, reference is invariably made to Tom's equally crazed companion, 'Merry Mad Maud'. 'Loving Mad Tom's chorus describes how the pair are bound together in their mutual madness: 'I will find Bonny Maud, Merry Mad Maud / And seek what e'er betides here / Yet I will love, beneath or above / That dirty Earth that hides her.' By the middle of the seventeenth century, Merry Mad Maud had developed her own repertoire, including 'Mad Maudlin is Come', where she searches high and low 'for my hungrie mad Tom', while the subject matter of the better-known 'To find my Tom of Bedlam' is equally questing: 'To find my Tom of Bedlam, Ten thousand Years I'll Travel; / Mad Maudlin goes with dirty Toes to save her Shoes from Gravel.' This song also carries a burden that celebrates the inmates of England's most famous asylum, known to most folk as Bedlam: 'Yet will I sing Bonny Boys, bonny Mad Boys, Bedlam Boys are Bonny / They still go bare and live by the Air, and want no Drink, nor Money.'

Mad Tom would retain a powerful hold on the English across the centuries. He is that paradigmatic figure, the wise fool, whose presence can even be felt – unconsciously, for sure – in a number of 1960s songs revelling in English eccentricity, whether it is John Entwistle's 'Whisky Man' (on The Who's *A Quick One*), Paul McCartney's 'A Fool on the Hill', Roy Wood's 'I Can Hear the Grass Grow', Jeff Lynne's 'The Lady Who Said She

All the Madmen

Could Fly' (on Idle Race's *The Birthday Party*), Syd Barrett's own 'Arnold Layne', or the character 'Mad John', who crops up twice on 1968 collections: one, as the seer who knows all on Small Faces' *Ogdens' Nut Gone Flake*; the other, Donovan's 'Mad Tom's Escape', based on the true story of a friend who escaped from an asylum, and his subsequent adventures. All are beholden to the original Bedlamite fool.

Sadly, with the Restoration, much of the colour went out of English popular song; and though there would be a number of latterday Bedlamite ballads, such as 'Bess of Bedlam' and 'Bedlam City, or The Maiden's Lamentation', in the popular imagination the link between madness and reason had been sundered. For the next two centuries, the dialogue would be conducted from the asylum, sometimes by the doctors, but often as not by its more poetic patients. Michel Foucault, in his radical history, *Madness and Civilization*, would even go on to suggest a causal link with the expansion of the asylums themselves:

'The constitution of madness as a mental illness, at the end of the eighteenth century, affords the evidence of a broken dialogue . . . between madness and reason.' In the same influential volume, Foucault reiterates Spurzheim's nineteenth-century view that 'madness, "more frequent in England than anywhere else", is merely the penalty of the liberty that reigns there . . . Freedom of conscience entails more dangers than authority and despotism.'

Nor was the stigma of a spell in Bedlam any great handicap to social advancement. In fact, from at least the middle part of the seventeenth century, the English seemed particularly keen to lock up its more artistic brethren, the better that they may pursue their mad muse. For the medical profession, at least, the line between the artist and the certifiable had always been a thin one, a point of view gloriously satirized as early as 1671 by James Carkesse, perhaps the first notable English poet to find a way to trade on his spell in 'Bedlam', publishing a collection of poems on his release in 1678, under the title, *Lucida intervalla: containing divers miscellaneous poems, written at Finsbury and Bethlem by the doctors patient extraordinary*:

> Doctor, this Puzzling Riddle pray explain;
> Others your Physick cures, but I complain
> It works with me the clean contrary way,
> And makes me Poet, who are Mad they say.

The hospital of Bethlem – along with a network of other private asylums – continued to be a popular stopping-off point for many of England's finest wordsmiths over the next two centuries. Carkesse's contemporary, Nathaniel Lee, was another poet who found himself incarcerated by those who questioned his sanity, as he challenged theirs. Unfortunately, as he pithily observed: 'They called me mad, and I called them mad, and damn them, they outvoted me.' Lee, who would be dead by 1692 of a drunken fit after five years spent in Bedlam, and not yet forty, seems to have learnt a little too much about dissipation and excess from time in the company of the Earl of Rochester. It is questionable whether he was ever genuinely unhinged.

'Kit' Smart, a favourite poet of Samuel Johnson (and later Allen Ginsberg), spent the years 1757–63 at St Luke's Hospital for the insane, during which he composed perhaps his two most famous works, 'Jubilate Agno' and 'A Song to David'. And just as St Luke's was letting Smart go, Nathaniel Cotton's equally infamous asylum in St Alban's was committing another devout poet, William Cowper, after a third suicide attempt. Here he wrote the memorably unhinged 'Hatred and vengeance, my eternal portions', before securing his release, though he later confessed a secret longing to William Blake: 'O that I were insane always. I will never rest. Can you not make me truly insane? I will never rest till I am so.'

Blake himself was viewed by a number of contemporaries as being quite mad, in a harmless kind of way; and though most would dispute such a view now, R.D. Laing in *The Divided Self* suggested that 'the Prophetic Books of William Blake' should be studied by psychologists 'not to elucidate Blake's psycho-pathology, but in order to learn from him what, somehow, he knew about in a most intimate fashion, while remaining sane'.

By an accident of history, Blake was just the wrong side of the Romantic divide. For after the Romantic poets, the roman-tic ideal of the madman-seer again took hold of the popular imagination. The Romantics themselves were convinced that such a fate awaited some, if not all of them. As Wordsworth wrote in 1802: 'We Poets in our youth begin in gladness; / But thereof come in the end despondency and madness.' And, though it was the besotted Lady Caroline Lamb who penned the actual line, Byron fully lived up to the epithet, 'Mad, bad and dangerous to know.' Unfortunately, Byron's wife soon became convinced that this was literally true and began to keep a detailed record of his moods and speech, even inviting a phys-ician to their home to assess her husband's state of mind.

Although Byron never actually lived long enough to sink into 'despondency and madness' (unlike his wife), one poet who followed in his footsteps did, and in doing so, at times became convinced that he was none other than Byron himself. English poetry's pre-eminent post-Romantic casualty was the self-taught 'Peasant Poet' John Clare (1793–1864), who first came to prominence in 1820 with two well-received collections, *Poems Descriptive of Rural Life* and *The Village Minstrel*. He would eventually enter Epping Forest's High Beach Asylum in 1837, suffering from delusions; coincidentally, this was at the same time that Alfred Lord Tennyson was a brief guest of Matthew Allen, the doctor who was treating Clare. Grieving for his recently deceased friend, Arthur Hallam, Tennyson was never committed to High Beach, but his brother, Edward, had been committed to an asylum in 1833, never to emerge.

Clare had voluntarily committed himself to Dr Allen's care, staying at High Beach from 1837 through 1841, suffering from the delusion that he was (interchangeably) Robert Burns, Lord Byron or the less poetic Lord Nelson. He eventually discharged himself, walking all the way from Epping to Northborough – recalling the experience in his fractured glass self-portrait, 'Journey Out of Essex, or John Clare's Escape from the Madhouse', with its instantly memorable opening couplet: 'I am lying with my head / Over the edge of the world.'

He was soon committed again, this time to Northampton General Lunatic Asylum, though he was generally free to roam the town and write his poems, which continued to usher forth right up to his death in 1864. Although he had long ago been forgotten by most subscribers to the early 'rural' collections that afforded him the public stamp of poet, the 'post-madness' poems were finally given their due in James Reeves' influential *Selected Poems of John Clare* (1954). By the 1960s, not only was Clare's reputation in the ascendant but his asylum years were generating real academic interest, while Reeves' collection soon found its way into Syd Barrett's library.

The Victorians were nothing if not broad-minded about the kind of artist they felt could benefit from the care and attention that a well-kept asylum could offer. Another Victorian defined in terms of the madman-seer was Richard Dadd. A painter of quite extraordinary intricacy and breathtaking detail, Dadd had barely begun to develop an original reputation when, in 1842, he experienced a catastrophic mental breakdown. By the following August, believing that he was being pursued by the devil, he stabbed his father to death, convinced he was the devil in disguise. Committed to Bethlem Asylum, Dadd continued to paint works that exhibited, in the words of one visitor, 'all the power, fancy and judgement for which his works were eminent previous to his insanity'. His masterpiece, self-consciously entitled *The Fairy Feller's Master-Stroke*, took him nine years to complete, and was accompanied by an impenetrable twenty-four-page guide to its meaning, in Dadd's jagged handwriting. These notes were appropriately entitled 'Elimination of a Picture & Its Subject'.

The fairy spirit also lived in John Ruskin, not a painter himself, but a social commentator and art critic of some standing, who in his 1884 lecture, 'Fairy Land', would pen the first important definition of the goals of fantasy literature. By then, he had been subject to delusions and a serious nervous breakdown after the love of his life, Rose la Touche, died in 1875, aged just twenty-seven. Ruskin, a friend of Lewis Carroll's, had been enamoured of Rose since they met when she was just ten, and in later life proposed to her continuously (in an 1886 letter to his physician, John Simon, Ruskin candidly admitted, 'I like my girls from ten to sixteen – allowing of seventeen or eighteen as long as they're not in love with anybody but me'). During his prolonged derangement, he wrote a letter in which he claimed that Rose's spirit had instructed him to marry a girl who was visiting at the time. His mania passed, though not before writing to Thomas Carlyle claiming: 'It was utterly wonderful to . . . go so heartily and headily mad . . . [after] priding myself on my peculiar sanity.'

Meanwhile, another late Victorian painter, Louis Wain, who had enjoyed a long and lucrative vogue as 'the man who drew cats', due to his series of illustrations of anthropomorphized moggies, developed a persecution complex in his early sixties. It fully manifested itself in 1924, when he claimed the flickering of the cinema screen had robbed the electricity from his sisters' brains. He wandered the streets at night, and would sporadically rearrange furniture within the family house, while spending long periods locked in his room writing gibberish. Initially committed to a pauper ward of Springfield Mental Hospital in Tooting in June 1924, Wain was finally transferred to the Bethlem Asylum the following year, where he had his own room and was supplied with art materials, resulting in a number of serious exhibitions of his work. The many drawings and watercolours he produced in his last years were widely regarded as manifestations of schizophrenia – a view now strongly challenged.

By the time of Wain's committal, the network of private asylums was starting to be replaced by institutions funded by the public purse, partly as a consequence of the number of shell-shocked ex-soldiers returning from the war. But there was still time for a young Virginia Woolf to spend time in one (and for her half-sister Laura to live and die in one). After the death of her father in 1904, and elder brother Thoby in 1906, Woolf started to hear the voices of the dead urging her to do the impossible, and in 1910 spent six weeks in a sanatorium in Burley, to which she also returned in 1913. The experience only drove her to attempt suicide. For the remainder of her life she made 'the lava of madness' her muse, writing in 1930 of how 'it shoots out of one everything shaped, final, not in mere driblets, as sanity does'.

But it also drove her to fits of despair so intense she contemplated ending her life – which, in the end, she did. Her unbearably poignant final note to her husband in March 1941 perfectly articulates the chronic depressive's sense of power-lessness when facing inner demons: 'I feel certain that I am going mad again. I feel we can't go through another of those terrible times. And I shan't recover this time. I begin to hear voices, and I can't concentrate. So I am doing what seems the best thing to do . . . Everything has gone from me but the certainty of your goodness.'

BIBLIOGRAPHY & SELECTED DISCOGRAPHY

1. General Reference Material

(i) The music scene:

Altham, Keith – *No More Mr Nice Guy* (Blake Publishing, 1999)

Badman, Keith & Rawlings, Terry – *Quite Naturally: The Small Faces Day-By-Day* (Complete Music, 1997)

Boyd, Jenny – *Musicians in Tune* (Fireside, 1992)

Boyd, Joe – *White Bicycles: Making Music in the Sixties* (Serpent's Tail, 2005)

Brown, Tony – *Jimi Hendrix Concert Files* (Omnibus Press, 1999)

Brown, Tony (ed.) – *The Complete Book of the British Charts* (Omnibus Press, 2000)

Chiesa, Guido – *Sonic Life: Inside Sonic Youth* (Italy, 1992)

Clayson, Alan – interview with Ace Kefford, *Record Collector* #179

Clifford, Mike – 'Pretty Things: Evolution Rather Than Revolution', *Beat Instrumental*, December 1968

Cohn, Nik – *Pop from the Beginning* (Weidenfeld & Nicolson, 1969)

Cohn, Nik – *Ball the Wall: In the Age of Rock* (Picador, 1989)

Davies, Mike – interview with Roy Wood, *Trouser Press*, November 1981

Floyd, Jerry – 'Roy Harper Ruminates & Reflects', *ZigZag* #11

Gilmore, Mikal – *Stories Done: Writings on the 1960s and Its Discontents* (Free Press, 2008)

Green, Jonathon – *Days in the Life: Voices from the English Underground 1961–1971* (Heinemann, 1988)

Heylin, Clinton – *The Act You've Known for All These Years: A Year in the Life of Sgt. Pepper* (Canongate, 2007)

Hjort, Christopher – *Strange Brew: The British Blues Boom 1965–70* (Jawbone, 2007)

Kent, Nick – *Apathy for the Devil: A Seventies Memoir* (Faber & Faber, 2010)

Lakey, Alan – *The Pretty Things: Growing Old Disgracefully* (Firefly Publishing, 2002)

MacDonald, Ian – *The People's Music* (Pimlico, 2003)

Marcus, Greil (ed.) – *Stranded: Rock & Roll for a Desert Island* (Knopf, 1979)

Martyn, Beverley – *Sweet Honesty: The Beverley Martyn Story* (Grosvenor House, 2011)

Paytress, Mark – *Bolan: The Rise & Fall of a 20th Century Superstar* (Omnibus, 2002)

Rolling Stone (ed.) – *The Rolling Stone Interviews Vol. 2* (Straight Arrow, 1973)

Russell, Ethan A. – *Dear Mr Fantasy* (Houghton Mifflin, 1985)

Scott, Jack (ed.) – *New Musical Express Greatest Hits* (IPC, 1975)

Tyler, Kieron – 'The Leper Messiah: The Real Ziggy Stardust', *Mojo* #84

Unterberger, Richie – *Unknown Legends of Rock 'n' Roll* (Miller Freeman, 1998)

Young, Rob – *Electric Eden: Unearthing Britain's Visionary Music* (Faber & Faber, 2010)

General background:

Boyers, Robert & Orrill, Robert – *Laing and Anti-Psychiatry* (Penguin, 1972)

Conners, Peter – *White Hand Society: The Psychedelic Partnership of Timothy Leary & Allen Ginsberg* (City Lights, 2010)

Constantin, Philippe – Inverview with Roger Waters, *Street Life* 241 / 1–6/2/76 (interview originally *Rocket Folk*)

Cooper, David (ed.) – *The Dialectics of Liberation* (Pelican Books, 1969)

Cooper, David – *Psychiatry and Anti-Psychiatry* (Paladin, 1970)

Diski, Jenny – *The Sixties* (Profile, 2009)

Fricke, David – Interview with Roger Waters, Rolling Stone, 19/11/87

Ginsberg, Allen – *The Book of Martyrdom and Artifice: First Journals & Poems 1937–1952* (Da Capo, 2006)

Laing, R.D. – *The Divided Self* (Penguin, 1965)

Laing, R.D. – *Wisdom, Madness & Folly: The Making of a Psychiatrist* (Macmillan, 1985)

Miles, Barry – *Ginsberg: A Biography* (Viking, 1990)

Porter, Roy – *The Faber Book of Madness* (Faber & Faber, 1991)

Sontag, Susan (ed.) – *Antonin Artaud: Selected Writings* (University of California Press, 1988)

(ii) Syd Barrett & Pink Floyd:

Constantine, Philippe – Interview with Roger Waters, *Street Life*, 24/1–6/2/76 [interview originally in *Rock et Folk*]

Fricke, David – Interview with Roger Waters, *Rolling Stone*, 19/11/87

Anon. – *Syd Barrett: The Press Cuttings* (pp, 1990)

Barrett, Syd – 'Blind Date', *Melody Maker*, 22/7/69

Barrett, Syd – reply to letter, *Melody Maker*, 7/6/69

Black, Johnny – 'The Long March', *Mojo* #96

Blake, Mark – *Comfortably Numb: The Inside Story of Pink Floyd* (Thunder's Mouth, 2008)

Cavanagh, David – 'Wouldn't You Miss Me At All?', *Uncut* #112

Chapman, Rob – 'The Last Gig: A Personal Report', Terrapin [in *Syd Barrett: The Press Cuttings*]

Chapman, Rob – 'Seer, Painter, Piper, Prisoner', *Mojo* #154

Chapman, Rob – *Syd Barrett: A Very Irregular Head* (Faber & Faber, 2010)

Charlesworth, Chris – interview with Richard Wright, *Melody Maker*, 16/11/74

Clerk, Carol – 'Lost in Space: Dark Side of the Moon', *Uncut* #73

Clerk, Carol – 'The Last Days of Pink Floyd', *Uncut* #85

Dadomo, Giovanni – interview with Syd Barrett, March 1970 [in *Syd Barrett: The Press Cuttings*]

DiLorenzo, Kris – 'Syd Barrett: Careening Through Life', *Trouser Press*, February 1978

Erskine, Pete – 'Dirty Hair Denied', *NME*, 11/1/75

Hamilton, Mick – 'Acid Drove Pink Floyd Star Up the Wall!', *News of the World*, 30/10/88

Harris, John – *Dark Side of the Moon: The Making of the Pink Floyd Masterpiece* (Da Capo, 2005)

Hodges, Nick & Priston, Ian – *Embryo: A Pink Floyd Chronology 1966–71* (Cherry Red Books, 1999)

Hollingsworth, Roy – 'The Madcap Returns', *Melody Maker*, 4/3/72

Horne, Nicky – 'The Floyd Tapes', *Sounds*, 6/3/76

Hoyland, John – 'Cecil B. De Mille Would Be Proud of You', *Let It Rock*, January 1974

Jones, Cliff – [Piece on Syd], *Mojo* #34

Jones, Malcolm – *The Making of The Madcap Laughs* (pp, 1982)

Kent, Nick – 'Syd: Whatever Happened To The Cosmic Dream?', *NME*, 13/4/74

Kent, Nick – 'Floyd Juggernaut . . . the road to 1984?', *NME*, 23/11/74

McKnight, Conner – 'Notes Towards the Illumination of The Floyd', *Zigzag* #32

MacDonald, Bruno (ed.) – *Pink Floyd: Through the Eyes of . . .* (Da Capo, 1997)

Miles, Barry – 'Games For May', *NME*, 15/5/76

Miles, Barry – *Pink Floyd: A Visual Documentary* (Omnibus Press, 1980)

Miles, Barry – *Pink Floyd: The Early Years* (Omnibus Press, 2006)

Palacios, Julian – *Lost in the Woods: Syd Barrett & The Pink Floyd* (Boxtree, 1998)

Parker, David – *Random Precision: Recording The Music of Syd Barrett 1965–74* (Cherry Red Books, 2001)

Paytress, Mark – interview with Dave Gilmour, *Mojo Collections* #2 (Spring 2001)

Povey, Glenn & Russell, Ian – *Pink Floyd: In the Flesh* (Bloomsbury, 1997)

Rock, Mick – 'The Madcap Who Named Pink Floyd', *Rolling Stone*, 23/12/71

Rock, Mick (with Sylvie Simmons) – 'Back to the Garden', *Mojo* #96

Rock, Mick – 'We Were Children of the Future', *Uncut* #112

Schaffner, Nicholas – *Saucerful of Secrets: The Pink Floyd Odyssey* (Harmony Books, 1991)

Sturdy, Mark – 'Twilight's Last Gleaming', *Mojo* #149

Sutcliffe, Phil – 'The Thirty Year Technicolour Dream', *Mojo* #20

Sutcliffe, Phil – interview with Dave Gilmour, *Mojo* #149

Sutcliffe, Phil & Henderson, Peter – 'The First Men on the Moon', *Mojo* #52

Turner, Steve – interview with Syd Barrett, *Beat Instrumental*, April 1971

Turner, Steve – 'Syd Barrett: A Psychedelic Veteran', *Beat Instrumental*, June 1971

Watkinson, Mike & Anderson, Pete – *Crazy Diamond: Syd Barrett & the Dawn of Pink Floyd* (Omnibus Press, 1991)

Watts, Michael – interview with Syd Barrett, *Melody Maker*, 27/3/71

Welch, Chris – 'Confusion and Mr Barrett', *Melody Maker*, 31/1/70

Whitlock, Kevin – 'Dark Side: Floyd's Finest Hour', *Record Collector* #204

Willis, Tim – *Madcap: The Half-Life of Syd Barrett* (Short Books, 2002)

(iii) David Bowie:

Bowie, Angela with Patrick Carr – *Backstage Passes: Life on the Wild Side with David Bowie* (Orion Books, 1993)

Bowie, David – '*David Bowie* Track by Track', *Disc & Music Echo*, 25/10/69

Bowie, David – '*Hunky Dory* Track by Track' [1971 press release]

Bowie, David & Rock, Mick – *Moonage Daydream: The Life & Times of Ziggy Stardust* (Cassell, 2005)

Buckley, David – *Strange Fascination: The David Bowie Story* (Virgin Books, 1999)

Cavanagh, David – 'ChangesFiftyBowie', *Q* #125 (February 1997)

Crowe, Cameron – 'Ground Control to Davy Jones', *Rolling Stone*, 12/2/76

Currie, David – *David Bowie: The Starzone Interviews* (Omnibus Press, 1985)

Dalton, Stephen & Hughes, Rob – 'Trans-Europe Excess', *Uncut* #47 (April 2001)

Davies, Dai – 'The Coming of the Tyrant', *Disc*, 30/1/71

Deevoy, Adrian – interview with David Bowie, *Q* #80 (May 1993)

Du Noyer, Paul – interview with David Bowie, *Q* #43 (April 1990)

Du Noyer, Paul – 'Contact', *Mojo* #104

Finnigan, Mary – 'An Interview with David Bowie', *International Times*, 15–21/8/69

Fisher, Ben – 'But Boy Could He Play Guitar', *Mojo* #47

Fletcher, David Jeffrey – *David Robert Jones Bowie: The Discography of a Generalist 1962–79* (pp, 1979)

Foulstone, Pete & Alexander, Alex – *David Bowie 1969–1971* (pp, 2001)

Gillman, Peter & Leni – *Alias David Bowie* (Hodder & Stoughton, 1986)

Gutman, David & Thomson, Elizabeth – *The Bowie Companion* (Da Capo, 1996)

Hoare, Ian – 'You're Wonderful, Gimme Your Hands', *Let It Rock*, October 1972

Hollingsworth, Roy – 'A Journey with Aladdin', *Melody Maker*, 12/5/73

Holloway, Danny – interview with David Bowie, *NME*, 29/1/72

'Jackie' – 'The Secret of My Lost Year', *Jackie*, 30/1/70

Johnson, James – 'The Space Oddity Comes Down to Earth', *NME*, 14/8/71

Kaye, Lenny – 'Smiling & waving & looking so fine', *Changes*, October 1972

Kent, Nick – 'Not Just a Pretty Face?', *NME*, 7/10/72

Kent, Nick – 'Show Business in the Twilight Zone', *NME*, 21/4/73

Mendelsohn, John – 'Pantomime Rock?', *Rolling Stone*, 1/4/71

Mendelsohn, John [?] – 'David Bowie: A Rock Oddity', *Creem*, November 1971

Murray, Charles Shaar – 'David at the Dorchester', *NME*, 22/7/72

Murray, Charles Shaar – 'Goodbye Ziggy & A Big Hello to Aladdin Sane', *NME*, 27/1/73

Murray, Charles Shaar – 'Thankyou and Goodnight, Masked Man', *NME*, 22/2/75

Murray, Charles Shaar & Carr, Roy – The *NME*'s Consumer Guide to David Bowie, *NME*, 2, 9+16/9/78

O'Grady, Anthony – 'Dictatorship the Next Step?', *NME*, 23/8/75

Parra, Pimm Jal de la – *David Bowie: The Concert Tapes* (P.J. Publishing, 1986)

Paytress, Mark – *Classic Rock Albums: Ziggy Stardust* (Schirmer Books, 1998)

Paytress, Mark – 'The Man Who Sold the World', *Record Collector* #185

Peacock, Steve – 'A Disillusioned Old Rocker', *Sounds*, 14/8/71

Pegg, Nicholas – *The Complete David Bowie* (Reynolds & Hearn, 2006)

'Robbie, Sandie' – 'A Real Pop Oddity', *Mirabelle*, January 1970

'Robbie, Sandie' [?] – 'David Bowie: A Super Cool Guy', *Mirabelle*, 7/3/70

Roberts, Chris – 'Gimme Your Hands', *Uncut* #70

Robinson, Lisa – 'The First Synthetic Rock Star', *NME*, 6/3/78

Rock, Mick – 'David Bowie is Just Not Serious', *Rolling Stone*, 8/6/72

Rudis, Al – 'The Man with the Stuffed Monkey', *Sounds*, 10/4/76

Salvo, Patrick – 'David Bowie: Man for McLuhan', *Circus*, May 1971

Salvo, Patrick – 'The Changing Faces of David Bowie', *Sounds*, 2/12/72 [interview from 1971]

Simpson, Kate – interview with David Bowie, *Music Now*, December 1969

Tremlett, George – *The David Bowie Story* (Futura, 1974)

Valentine, Penny – 'The Human Oddity', *Disc & Music Echo*, 11/10/69

Valentine, Penny – 'Bowie, Music & Life', *Sounds*, 6/2/71

Watts, Michael – 'Oh You Pretty Things', *Melody Maker*, 22/1/72

Watts, Michael – 'The Rise & Rise of Ziggy Stardust', *Melody Maker*, 19/8/72

Watts, Michael – interview with David Bowie, *Melody Maker*, 18/2/78

Welch, Chris – 'A Mixture of Dali, 2001 & The Bee Gees', *Melody Maker*, 11/10/69

Welch, Chris – interview with David Bowie, *Melody Maker*, 17/4/71

Zanetta, Tony & Edwards, Henry – *Stardust: The Life & Times of David Bowie* (Michael Joseph, 1986)

All the Madmen

(iv) Ray Davies & The Kinks:

Black, Johnny – 'The Hellfire Club', *Mojo* #82

Boltwood, Derek – 'Wonderboy Ray Returns', *Record Mirror*, 1969

Boltwood, Derek – 'Kinks Bum & the BBC', *Record Mirror*, 10/5/69

Burgess, Ian [?] – 'Kinks Currency Revalued', *Zigzag* #6

Charone, Barbara – 'Kinky Kapers', *Sounds*, 28/2/76

Davies, Ray – *X-Ray: The Unauthorized Autobiography* (Viking, 1994)

Doggett, Peter – interview with Ray Davies, *Record Collector* #169

Doggett, Peter – 'Sterling Albion', *Mojo* #111

Goddard, Lon – interview with Ray Davies, *Record Mirror*, 3/8/68

Goddard, Lon – interview with Ray Davies, *Record Mirror*, 25/7/70

Green, Jim – 'The Missing Kink', *Trouser Press*, June 1978

Green, Richard – interview with Ray Davies, *NME*, [6+] 13/2/71

'P.G.' – interview with Ray Davies, *Beat Instrumental*, May 1969

Hasted, Nick – 'The Kinks', *Uncut* #88

Harvey, John – 'Everybody's in Showbiz', *Let It Rock*, May 1974

Hinman, Doug – *You Really Got Me: An Illustrated World Discography of The Kinks 1964–1993* (pp, 1994)

Hinman, Doug – *The Kinks: All Day & All of the Night* (Backbeat Books, 2004)

Holloway, Danny – interview with Ray Davies, *Sounds*, January 1973

Hughes, Karen – interview with Ray Davies, *Melody Maker*, 4/5/74

Johnson, James – interview with Ray Davies, *NME*, 11/5/74

Larkin, Colin – interview with Ray Davies, *Dark Star* #21

McKnight, Connor – interview with Ray Davies, *Zigzag* #27

McNeill, Phil – 'Straightening Out The Kinks', *NME*, 16+23/4/77

Mann, Ian – 'Kinks Currency Revalued', *Zigzag* #6

Marten, Neville & Hudson, Jeffrey – *The Kinks: Well Respected Men* (Castle Communications, 1996)

Micklo, Anne Marie – interview with Ray Davies, *Rock*, 1970

Miller, Andy – *The Kinks are The Village Green Preservation Society: 33 1/3* (Continuum, 2003)

Murray, Charles Shaar – 'The Rise & Decline of The Kinks', *NME*, 6/10/79

Murray, Charles Shaar – 'Tales of Drunkeness & Cruelty', *Q* #36, September 1989

Paytress, Mark – 'Tales of Ordinary Madness', *Mojo* #148

Robinson, Richard – interview with Ray Davies, *Hit Parader*, 1970

Rogan, Johnny – *The Kinks: The Sound & The Fury* (Elm Tree Books, 1984)

Savage, Jon – *The Kinks: The Official Biography* (Faber & Faber, 1984)

Schact, Janis – 'Ray Davies Unravels the Muswell Puzzle', *Circus*, February 1972

Schulps, Dave – interview with Dave Davies, *Trouser Press*, October 1978

Tyler, Andrew – interview with Ray Davies, *NME*, 20/10/73

(v) Nick Drake:

Anon. – *A Nick Drake Compendium* (pp, 1995[?])

Brown, Mick – 'The Sad Ballad of Nick Drake', *Sunday Telegraph*, 12/7/97

Burgess, Steve – 'Nick Drake', *Dark Star* (1979/1980[?])

Creed, Jason – *The Pink Moon Files* (Omnibus, 2011)

Dann, Trevor – *Darker Than the Deepest Sea: The Search for Nick Drake* (Portrait, 2006)

Frederick, Robin – 'Truly Madly Deeply', *Mojo* #63

Hogan, Peter – *Nick Drake: The Complete Guide to His Music* (Omnibus Press, 2009)

Humphries, Patrick – 'Brief Encounter', *Mojo* #39

Humphries, Patrick – *Nick Drake: The Biography* (Bloomsbury, 1997)

Kent, Nick – 'Requiem for a Solitary Man', *NME*, 8/2/75

Kent, Nick – 'Songs of Waving, Drowning and a Sort of Sadness', *Loops* #2

Kornelussen, Frank – 'Nick Drake', *Trouser Press*, January 1978

Kornelussen, Frank – *Time of No Reply* sleevenotes, 1985

Lubow, Arthur – 'Remember Nick Drake', *New Times*, 5/1/78

McKnight, Connor – 'In Search of Nick Drake', *Zigzag* #42

Petrusich, Amanda – *Pink Moon: 33 1/3* (Continuum, 2007)

Sandison, David – 'The Final Retreat', *Zigzag* #49

Snow, Mat – 'Autumn's Child', *Mojo* #187

Thompson, Ben – 'Still in a Class of His Own', *Independent on Sunday*, 29/5/94

(vi) Peter Green & Fleetwood Mac:

Black, Johnny & Celmins, Martin – 'The Shape I'm In', *Mojo* #34

'M.C.' – interview with Peter Green, *Beat Instrumental*, April 1969

Celmins, Martin – *Peter Green: The Authorised Biography* (Sanctuary Publishing, 2003)

Ellen, Mark – interview with Peter Green, *Mojo* #6

Green, Peter – 'The Peter Green Column', *Beat Instrumental*, September 1968

Green, Peter – 'The Peter Green Column', *Beat Instrumental*, December 1968

Green, Peter – 'The Peter Green Column', *Beat Instrumental*, February 1969

Hjort, Christopher – *Strange Brew: Eric Clapton & The British Blues Boom* (Jawbone, 2007)

Thomas, Bruce – 'One Step Beyond', *Mojo* #6

(vii) Pete Townshend & The Who:

Ashley, Brian & Monnery, Steve – *Whose Who?: A Who Retrospective* (New English Library, 1978)

Barnes, Richard – *The Who: Maximum R&B* (St. Martin's Press, 1982)

Barnes, Richard & Townshend, Pete – *The Story of Tommy* (Eel Pie Publishing, 1977)

Charlesworth, Chris – *The Who: The Illustrated Biography* (Omnibus Press, 1982)

Charone, Barbara – 'Maximum R&B: The Story of The Who', *Sounds*, 18/10/75

Cott, Jonathan – interview with Pete Townshend, *Rolling Stone* (UK ed.), 14/6/69

Cott, Jonathan – interview with Pete Townshend, *Rolling Stone*, 14/5/70

Doggett, Peter – interview with Dave Davies, *Record Collector* #200

Entwistle, John – 'The Who by Numbers: The March of the Mods Revisited', *NME*, 17/7/76

Fletcher, Tony – *Dear Boy: The Life of Keith Moon* (Omnibus Press, 1998)

Gilbert, Pat – interview with Pete Townshend, *Mojo* #147

Goddard, Simon – 'The Kids Are Alright', *Uncut* #68

Goddard, Simon – 'See Me, Feel Me: The Story of Tommy', *Uncut* #83

Hanel, Ed & Carlson, Jon – interview with John Entwistle, *Trouser Press*, February/March 1977

Harris, John – interview with Pete Townshend, *Q* #117, June 1996

Herman, Gary – *The Who* (November Books, 1971)

Herman, Gary – Who's Where in the Seventies?, *Let It Rock*, February 1975

Hibbert, Tom – 'Who the Hell Does Pete Townshend Think He Is?', *Q* #34, July 1989

McKnight, Connor – 'Chatting with Pete Townshend', *Zigzag* #23, 43, 44

McMichael, Joe & Lyons, Jack – *The Who Concert File* (Omnibus Press, 1997)

Marsh, Dave – Betrayed by Rock & Roll?, *Mojo* #32

Murray, Charles Shaar – 'Conversations with Pete', *NME*, 19/4/80

Neill, Andy – *A Fortnight of Furore: The Who & The Small Faces Down Under* (The Mutley Press, 1998)

Neill, Andy & Kent, Matt – *Anyway Anyhow Anywhere: The Complete Chronicle of The Who 1958–78* (Barnes & Noble Books, 2002)

Nelson, Paul – interview with Pete Townshend, *Hullabaloo*, March 1968– March 1969 (12 issues)

Nelson, Paul – interview with Pete Townshend, *Circus*, May 1969

Peacock, Steve – interview with Pete Townshend, *Sounds*, 5+12/4/75

Perry, Charles & Bailey, Andrew – 'Spooky Tour: Quadrophobia', *Rolling Stone*, 3/1/74

Perry, John – *Classic Rock Albums: Meaty Beaty Big & Bouncy* (Schirmer Books, 1998)

Rolling Stone Editors, The – *The Who: Ten Great Years* (Straight Arrow, 1975)

Salewicz, Chris – 'John Entwistle & the Bloody English', *Let It Rock*, March 1973

Sanders, Rick – interview with Pete Townshend, *Beat Instrumental*, February 1969

Sanders, Rick – interview with Pete Townshend, *Beat Instrumental*, September 1969

Sanders, Rick & Dalton, David – interview with Pete Townshend, *Rolling Stone*, 12/7/69

Schulps, Dave – interview with Pete Townshend, *Trouser Press*, April and May 1978

Sharp, Ken – interview with Roger Daltrey, *Record Collector* #181

Sharp, Ken – interview with John Entwistle, *Record Collector* #192

Stewart, Tony – interview with Roger Daltrey, *NME*, 9/8/75

Stewart, Tony – interview with Pete Townshend, *NME*, 12/8/78

Sutherland, Steve (ed.) – *NME Originals: The Who* (*Uncut* special, 2002)

Swenson, John – 'After Ten Years of Madness the Next Stage Is . . .', *Crawdaddy*, January 1974

Townshend, Pete – 'The Pete Townshend Page', *Melody Maker*, 22/8/70; 19/9/70; 17/10/70; 14/11/70; 12/12/70; 16/1/71; 13/2/71; 13/3/71; 17/4/71

Townshend, Pete – 'Meaty, Beaty, Big & Bouncy', *Rolling Stone*, 9/12/71

Townshend, Pete – Pete Townshend's Back Pages, *NME*, 5/11/77

Townshend, Pete – E-interview regarding *Quadrophenia*, 2009

Townshend, Pete – *The Decade of The Who: A History in Music & Photographs* (Omnibus, 1984)

Tremlett, George – *The Who* (Futura, 1975)

Uncut (eds.) – The Ultimate Music Guide: The Who (*Uncut*, 2011)

Valentine, Penny – 'Townshend Talk-In', *Sounds*, 12/8/72

Van Ness, Chris – An interview with Pete Townshend, *L.A. Free Press*, 10,17+24/12/71

Watts, Michael – interview with Pete Townshend, *Melody Maker*, 12/4/75

Welch, Chris – interview with Pete Townshend, *Melody Maker*, 4/5/68

Welch, Chris – interview with Pete Townshend & Ronnie Lane, *Melody Maker*, 17/9/77

Welch, Chris – interview with Pete Townshend, *Melody Maker*, 27/1/79

Wenner, Jann – 'The *Rolling Stone* Interview: Pete Townshend, *Rolling Stone*, 14+28/9/68

SELECTED DISCOGRAPHY

Chapter One (1965–68):

The Kinks: *Face to Face* (1966); *Something Else* (1967); . . . *Are the Village Green Preservation Society* (1968).
Other important tracks from the era: 'Where Have All the Good Times Gone' (*The Kink Kontroversy*); 'I'm Not Like Everybody Else' (45 B-side); 'Dead End Street' b/w 'Big Black Smoke' (45); 'Autumn Almanac' b/w 'Mister Pleasant' (45); 'Wonderboy' b/w 'Pretty Polly' (45); 'Days' b/w 'She's Got Everything' (45); 'Mr Reporter' (*Face to Face* 1998 remaster); 'Did You See His Name', 'Where Did My Spring Go?' (*VGPS* 2004 remaster).
DVD: *All Aboard: Kinks on DVD 1964–1972* (boot).

The Move: *Move* (1968).
Other important tracks/CDs from the era: *Singles A's And B's* (2000) [contains all The Move 45s, including the unreleased 'Cherry Blossom Clinic' b/w 'Vote for Me' single].
DVD: *Video Anthology* (boot).

Pink Floyd: *Piper at the Gates of Dawn* (1967); *Saucerful of Secrets* (1968).
Other important tracks from the era: 'Arnold Layne', 'Candy & A Currant Bun', 'See Emily Play', 'Apples & Oranges' (*The First Three Singles*); 'Scream Thy Last Scream', 'Vegetable Man' (*Psychedelic Freak Out* boot CD); 'See Emily Play' – acetate version (*Artefacts from the Psychedelic Dungeon* boot CD).
DVD: *The Pink Floyd & Syd Barrett Story* (Direct Video); *Psych Fest* (boot); *Let's Roll Another One* (boot).

Roy Harper: *Flat Baroque & Berserk* (1969).
Other important tracks from the era: 'Committed' (Sophisticated Beggar).

David Bowie: *David Bowie* (1967).
Other important tracks from the era: 'Let Me Sleep Beside You', 'Karma Man', 'London Bye Ta-Ta', 'In the Heat of The Morning', 'Ching a Ling' (*David Bowie* 2010 remaster); 'Little Toy Soldier', 'Waiting for the Man' – 1967 demos (*The Forgotten Songs of David Robert Jones* boot CD).

The Small Faces: *Ogdens' Nut Gone Flake* (1968).
Other important tracks from the era: 'Here Comes the Nice', 'The Universal', 'Tin Soldier', 'Itchycoo Park', 'Wham Bam Thank You Mam' (*The Autumn Stone*).
DVD: *All Or Nothing 1965–1968* (Voyage, 2009).

Idle Race: *The Birthday Party* (1968).
Other important tracks from the era: '(Here We Go Round) The Lemon Tree', 'My Father's Son', 'Imposters of Life's Magazine', 'Knocking Nails Into My House' (*Back to the Story*); 'Imposters of Life's Magazine', 'The Lady Who Said She Could Fly' – BBC versions (*Artefacts from the Psychedelic Dungeon* boot CD).

The Who: *Sell Out* (1967).
Other important tracks from the era: 'Pictures of Lily' b/w 'Doctor Doctor'; 'The Last Time' b/w 'Under My Thumb'; 'I Can See for Miles' b/w 'Someone's Coming'; 'Dogs' b/w 'Call Me Lightning'; 'Magic Bus' b/w 'Dr Jekyll & Mr Hyde' (all 45s); 'Glittering Girl', 'Melancholia', 'Jaguar', 'Glow Girl' (*The Who Sell Out* 1995 remaster).
DVD: *Purple Hearts and Power Chords* (boot).

Chapter Two (1969):

The Pretty Things: *S.F. Sorrow* (1968).
Other important tracks from the era: 'Defecting Grey' b/w 'Mr Evasion' (45); 'Talkin' About the Good Times' b/w 'Walking Through My Dreams' (45); 'Turn My Head', 'Defecting Grey' – BBC versions (*Artefacts from the Psychedelic Dungeon* boot CD); 'Defecting Grey' – acetate version (*S.F. Sorrow* 2003 remaster).

The Who: *Tommy* (1969).
Other important tracks/CDs from the era: *Tommy Demos* (boot CD); 'Cousin Kevin Model Child' (*Tommy* 2003 remaster).
Important released live performances of the era: *Live at Leeds* ('Deluxe' 2001 remaster, with complete *Tommy*); *Live at The Isle of Wight 1970* (1996) [also available as DVD].
DVDs: *Isle of Wight / Woodstock 1969* (boot); *Live at Kilburn* (Spitfire) [includes crude 16mm footage of 1969 London Coliseum performance of *Tommy* &c.].

The Kinks: *Arthur* (1969).
Other important tracks from the era: 'Plastic Man' b/w 'King Kong' (45); 'Drivin'' b/w 'Mindless Child of Motherhood' (45); 'Easy Come, There You Went' (*The Great Lost Kinks Album* boot CD).

David Bowie: *Space Oddity* (1969).
Other important tracks/CDs from the era: 'Space Oddity' (demo), 'Wild Eyed Boy From Freecloud' (45 version); 'London Bye Ta-Ta' (1970 version); 'The Prettiest Star' b/w 'Conversation Piece' (45); 'Memory of a Free Festival Pts. 1 & 2' (45); 'Janine', 'Unwashed & Somewhat Slightly Dazed', 'Let Me Sleep Beside You' [all tracks on 2009 *Space Oddity* 'Deluxe' remaster]; 'Life is a Circus', 'Lover to the Dawn' – '68 demos (*Rare & Well Done* boot CD).

Syd Barrett: *The Madcap Laughs* (1969). [1993 remaster includes alternatives of 'Octopus', 'It's No Good Trying', 'Love You', 'She Took a Long Cold Look At Me' and 'Golden Hair']
Other important tracks/CDs from the era: *Opel* (1988) [expanded edition 1993]; 'Dark Globe' – choral version, 'Clowns & Jugglers – 3 May 1969 tk. 2 (*Psychedelic Freak Out* boot CD).

Jackson Frank: *Jackson Frank* (1965).

Van Morrison: *Astral Weeks* (1969).

Nick Drake: *Five Leaves Left* (1969).
Other important tracks from the era: *Fruit Tree* (2007); *Tanworth-in-Arden Complete* (boot).

Chapter Three (1970–71):

Atomic Rooster: *Atomic Rooster* (1970).
Other important tracks from the era: 'Seven Lonely Streets' – BBC version (*Atomic Rooster* 2004 remaster); 'Tomorrow Night' – BBC session, 'The Devil's Answer' – 1970 demo (*Death Walks Behind You* 2004 remaster).

Fleetwood Mac: *The Complete Blue Horizon Sessions 1967–1969* (1999) [six-CD set including expanded versions of the following: *Fleetwood Mac* (1968), *Mr Wonderful* (1968), *The Pious Bird of Good Omen* (1969)]; *Then Play On* (1970).
Other important tracks/CDs from the era: 'Man of the World' and 'The Green Manalishi' (*The Best of Peter Green's Fleetwood Mac*); *Peter Green's Fleetwood Mac Live at the BBC* (1995); *The Vaudeville Years 1968–70 Volume 1.* (1998); 'Intergalactic Magicians Walking Through Pools of Velvet Darkness' – BBC session 27/5/68; 'Before the Beginning' b/w 'Man of the World' (Clifford Davis 45); 'Beasts of Burden' (1972 Peter Green 45).
Important released live performances of the era: *Shrine '69* (1999); *Live at the Boston Tea Party Vols. 1–3* (1998); *Show-Biz Blues 1968–70 Volume 2.* (2001)

[includes April 1970 *BBC in Concert*]; *Dead Bust Blues* – New Orleans 30/1–1/2/70 (boot two-CD).

Syd Barrett: *Barrett* (1970). [1993 remaster includes alternates of 'Baby Lemonade', 'Waving My Arms in the Air', 'I Never Lied to You', 'Love Song', 'Dominoes', 'It is Obvious']
Other important tracks/CDs from the era: *Opel* (1988) [expanded edition 1993]; *Peel Session* CD EP (1988); 'Bob Dylan Blues' (*Wouldn't You Miss Me: The Best of Syd Barrett*); 'Baby Lemonade', 'Dominoes', 'Love Song' – BBC session 16/2/71 (*The Final Countdown* boot CD); 'Terrapin', 'Gigolo Aunt', 'Effervescing Elephant', 'Octopus' – Olympia 6/70 (*Magnesium Proverbs* boot CD).

Nick Drake: *Bryter Layter* (1970).
Other important tracks/CDs from the era: 'Parasite', 'Place to Be' on *Tanworth-in-Arden Complete* (boot).

David Bowie: *The Man Who Sold the World* (1971).
Other important tracks/CDs from the era: *Bowie at the Beeb: The Best of the BBC Radio Sessions 68–72* (2000); Lightning Frightening (*TMWSTW* o/t), 'Moonage Daydream', 'Hang On to Yourself' (Arnold Korns 45s) (all on *TMWSTW* 1990 remaster); 'Tired of My Life', 'Holy Holy' (45), 'How Lucky You Are' (*MissingLinksOneZiggy* boot CD); 'Lady Stardust', 'Right On Mother' – Radio Luxembourg demos 3/71 (*Freddi & The Dreamer* boot CD).
Important released live performances of the era: 'Amsterdam', 'God Knows I'm Good', 'The Width of a Circle', 'Unwashed & Somewhat Slightly Dazed', 'Cygnet Committee', 'Memory of a Free Festival' – The Sunday Show 2/70 (*Bowie at the Beeb*) [the full thirteen-song performance is on the boot CD, *A Semi-Acoustic Love Affair*, but in significantly inferior quality].

Chapter Four (1971–72):

The Who: *Who's Next* (1971).
Other important tracks/CDs from the era: *From Lifehouse to Leeds* (boot); *The Lifehouse Chronicles* (2000); 'Heaven and Hell', 'Join Together', 'Let's See Action', 'I Don't Even Know Myself', 'Relay' on *Rarities* (1991).
Important released live performances of the era: Young Vic, London, April 1971 [disc two on *Who's Next* 'Deluxe' Ed. (2003)].

John Entwistle: *Smash Your Head Against the Wall* (1971); *Whistle Rymes* (1972).

The Kinks: *Lola Versus Powerman and the Moneygoround* (1970); *Muswell Hillbillies* (1971).

Other important tracks from the era: 'Mountain Woman', 'Kentucky Woman' (1998 *Muswell Hillbillies* remaster).

David Bowie: *Hunky Dory* (1971).
Other important tracks from the era: 'Bombers' (*Hunky Dory* 1990 remaster), 'Amsterdam' (*Pin Ups* 1990 remaster).
Important released live performances of the era: Friars, Aylesbury, 24 September 1971 (assorted boots); *A Crash Course for the Ravers, BBC in Concert*, 20 June 1971 (boot).

John Martyn: *Solid Air* (1973).
Other important tracks from the era: 'May You Never' 45 (*Bless the Weather* 2005 remaster).

Nick Drake: *Pink Moon* (1972).
Other important tracks from the era: 'Plaisir D'Amour' (*Nick Drake: A Treasury*).

Chapter Five (1971–72):

Pink Floyd: *Meddle* (1971); *Obscured by Clouds* (1972).
Other important tracks from the era: 'The Violent Sequence' (*A Journey Through Time & Space* – boot). [Now released on 6-CD 2011 boxed-set *Dark Side of the Moon*.]
Important released live performances of the era: *Eclipse of the Dark Side* (boot); *Tour '72* (boot); *At the End of the Rainbow* (boot). Important released live performance of the era: Three tracks from the June 1972 one-off Brighton concert have been included on the sixth disc of the 2011 6-CD *Dark Side of the Moon* boxed-set: 'The Travel Sequence', 'The Morality Sequence' and 'Any Colour you Like'

David Bowie: *Ziggy Stardust* (1972).
Other important tracks from the era: 'Sweet Head', 'Velvet Goldmine', 'John, I'm Only Dancing' (*Ziggy Stardust* 1990 remaster); 'Round and Round' (*Sound and Vision*); *Bowie at the Beeb* (2000); *The Year of the Spiders* (boot).
Important released live performances of the era: *Santa Monica '72* (1994); *Ziggy's Invasion of America* (boot); 'I Feel Free', 'My Death' on *RarestOneBowie* (1995); 'John, I'm Only Dancing', 'Changes', 'The Supermen' – Boston '72 (*Sound and Vision* – 1989 ed.); 'Oh! You Pretty Things', 'Queen Bitch', 'Five Years' – OGWT 72; 'Starman' – TOTP 72 [all on *Best of Bowie* DVD, 2002].

Jethro Tull: *Thick as a Brick* (1972).

Yes: *Close to the Edge* (1972).

Genesis: *Foxtrot* (1972); *Selling England By the Pound* (1973).

Chapter Six (1972–73):

The Kinks: *Everybody's in Showbiz* (1973).
Important released live performances of the era: *Kinks on Holiday* [1972 *BBC in Concert* recordings] (boot). Other important tracks/CDs from the era: An earlier, prototype version of the *Dark Side of the Moon* ???? is included on the sixth disc of the 2011 6-CD *Dark Side of the Moon* boxed-set.

David Bowie: *Aladdin Sane* (1973); *Pin Ups* (1973).
Other important tracks from the era: 'John, I'm Only Dancing' [sax version]; 'All the Young Dudes' [*Aladdin Sane* outtake] – both on 2003 'Deluxe' two-CD remaster of *Aladdin Sane*.
Important released live performances of the era: *Ziggy Stardust and the Spiders from Mars: The Motion Picture Soundtrack* [Hammersmith '73] (2005) [DVD/ two-CD]; *The 1980 Floor Show* (boot); 'Drive-In Saturday' on *Russell Harty Show – Best of Bowie* DVD (2002).

Pink Floyd: *Dark Side of the Moon* (1973).
Other important tracks/CDs from the era: *The Alternate Dark Side of the Moon* (boot). An earlier, prototype version of the *Dark Side of the Moon* album is included on the sixth disc of the 2011 6-CD *Dark Side of the Moon* boxed-set.
Important released live performances of the era: *Dark Side of Radio City* (two-CD boot).

The Who: *Quadrophenia* (1973).
Other important tracks from the era: 'Four Faces', 'Joker James' – *Quadrophenia: Soundtrack* (1979); 'Put the Money Down', 'Long Live Rock' – *Odds & Sods* (1974); 'We Close Tonight' – *Odds & Sods* 1998 remaster; *Quadrophenia Demos* (boot); *Demos for Quadrophenia* (boot). No less than twenty-five Townshend *Quadrophenia* demos are featured over two discs on the five-CD *Quadrophenia* boxed-set, released November 2011, including the previously undocumented 'You Came Back', 'Get Inside', 'Any More' and 'Wizardry'.
Important released live performances of the era: *Tales from The Who* (boot); *The Cow Palace* (boot DVD); *Live at Charlton 1974* (two-CD boot).

Chapter Seven (1974–75):

The Kinks: *Preservation Act 1* (1973); *Preservation Act 2* (1974); *Soap Opera* (1975).

The Who: *The Who by Numbers* (1975).
Other important tracks from the era: 'No Way Out' [demo of 'However Much I Booze'] – *Scoop 3* (2001).

David Bowie: *Diamond Dogs* (1974); *Young Americans* (1975).
Other important tracks from the era: 'Candidate' on 1990 CD remaster of *Diamond Dogs*; 'Rebel Rebel' (45 mix) on *Sound and Vision* (1989); 'Can You Hear Me?', 'It's Gonna Be Me', 'John, I'm Only Dancing' on 1991 *Young Americans* remaster.
Important released live performances of the era: *David Live* (1974); *Strange Fascination* [LA 9/74] (two-CD boot); *1974* [Madison 10/74] (two-CD boot); *The Dick Cavett Show Rock Icons* three-DVD set (2005) [contains complete 12/74 appearance inc. interview].

Nick Drake: *Time of No Reply* (1986).
Other important tracks from the era: 'Tow the Line', 'Hanging on a Star' [alternate take] – *Made to Love Magic* (2004); 'Black Eyed Dog', 'Tow the Line' – [backing tracks] *Tanworth-in-Arden Complete* (two-CD boot).

Pink Floyd: *Wish You Were Here* (1975).
Other important tracks from the era: *The Final Countdown* (two-CD boot) [includes half a dozen 'tracks' from August 1974 Syd Barrett sessions].
Important released live performances of the era: *British Winter Tour 1974* (three-CD boot); *Knebworth Park* (three-CD boot). In November 2011, Pink Floyd finally released the Wembley 1974 performances of 'Shine On You Crazy Diamond', 'Raving and Drooling' and 'You Gotta Be Crazy' on a 2-CD Deluxe version of *Wish You Were Here*.

Genesis: *The Lamb Lies Down on Broadway* (1974).

Acknowledgements

Thanks first and foremost to my editor, Leo Hollis, for believing in the idea and seeing it through to publication. Thanks also to those who have read and commented on various drafts of the mighty tome as it went its way from draft to draft, notably Andy Miller and Mick Gold.

Thanks, as ever, to my beavering muso-friends who have dug through their paper and audio archives to hunt out the obscure and the esoteric on my badgering behalf: Scott Curran, Peter Doggett (despite being engaged on his own related tome), Colin Harper, Brian Hinton, Andy Neil, Steve Shepherd and Mr Miller (again).

And finally, thanks to those who shared their memories of the period to me, whenever and whatever the pretext, especially Joe Boyd, Peter Jenner and Miles.

Clinton Heylin, October 2011

INDEX